Pistols at Dawn

RICHARD HOPTON

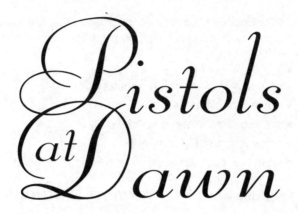

A HISTORY OF DUELLING

PORTRAIT

Visit the Portrait website!

Portrait publishes a wide range of non-fiction, including biography, history, science, music, popular culture and sport.

Visit our website to:
- read descriptions of our popular titles
- buy our books over the internet
- take advantage of our special offers
- enter our monthly competition
- learn more about your favourite Portrait authors

VISIT OUR WEBSITE AT: www.portraitbooks.com

First published in 2007 by **Portrait**
an imprint of Piatkus Books Ltd
5 Windmill Street
London W1T 2JA
e-mail: info@piatkus.co.uk

The moral right of the author has been asserted

A catalogue record for this book is available from the British Library

ISBN 0 7499 5102 8

This book has been printed on paper manufactured
with respect for the environment using wood from
managed sustainable resources

Edited by Andrew John
Text design by Paul Saunders

Data manipulation by Phoenix Photosetting, Chatham, Kent
www.phoenixphotosetting.co.uk
Printed and bound in Great Britain by
William Clowes Ltd, Beccles, Suffolk

For my father

Acknowledgements

I have been helped in the writing of this book by numerous people, but I would like particularly to thank Denis Cross, Richard Davenport-Hines, Lord Falkland, Alastair Forsyth, David Luard, Ann Nevill, Isabel Nevill, Andrew Newell, Adam Poynter and Marcus Scriven. My father, as always, provided a steady flow of historical references, some less obscure than others. I would like to thank the staff at the London Library and the British Library. Professor Collier, Chief Librarian of Catholic University at Leuven, and his staff made me most welcome during my visit and helped me trawl through the riches of the A.H. Corble Collection. Archivists at County Record Offices across the kingdom have answered efficiently all my requests for information. I thank them all. Alan Brooke has been encouraging throughout and was admirably patient when disaster struck within sight of the finishing line. Lastly, but by no means least, I should like to thank Caroline and Clementina who have, in their very different ways, helped ease this book into the world.

Richard Hopton
August 2006

NOTE TO THE READER

The names of numerous French duellists and other key players appearing throughout this book may not always display typical French accenting. This is because many of these names were drawn from English sources which, in publications of the time, omitted all accents from names of French origin.

CONTENTS

PROLOGUE
London, March 1804

EARLY IN THE MORNING of Wednesday, 7 March 1804, two men rode out from London, past Hyde Park Corner, towards Kensington. Following behind them was a post chaise, in which sat two other men, and behind them were some other figures on horseback. This little cavalcade trotted along the road towards Kensington and, a couple of hundred yards past the milestone marking the two miles from Hyde Park Corner – modern Kensington High Street – it pulled up on the north side of the road at the Horse and Groom inn. Behind the inn were the water meadows that stretched up to the large and well-tended gardens of Holland House.

This was an area known as the Moats, at this time still a series of fishponds, although they were later converted into an ornamental lake. The meadows were low-lying wetland, and, since it was the early spring, noticeably swampy. The nearest house was Little Holland House, where a Mr Ottey lived. The two men and their seconds moved from the inn into the meadows and took up their positions at a distance of 30 paces – exactly 29 yards – from each other, the distance being clearly discernible from the combatants' footprints in the waterlogged ground.[1]

At a quarter to eight in the morning, George Robinson, the head gardener at Holland House, noticed four gentlemen 'at the top of the fields', 300–400 yards away. Robinson then heard the report of one pistol followed, two or three seconds later, by another and a puff of smoke. One of the men fell to the ground. As Robinson was making his way towards the scene, two of the men he had seen a few moments earlier ran up to him, imploring him to help the wounded man, before disappearing. One of the undergardeners, James Sheers, had already reached the wounded man and was propping him up on the ground, which was so wet that 'the water had run into his half-boots'. Then, with the help of the remainder of Lord Holland's gardeners, the wounded man was lifted into a chair and carried to nearby Little Holland House, a distance of perhaps 200 or 300 yards. Once there, he was carried upstairs and put on a bed, where, in due course, he was examined by Simon Nicholson, a surgeon.

The wounded man was 29-year-old Thomas Pitt, the second Lord Camelford, a cousin of William Pitt the Younger, who had been Prime Minister for most of the previous 20 years. His opponent, who, together with his second, had fled the scene, was Captain Best, a naval officer. The two men had been boon drinking companions whose carousing had got them into many an enjoyable scrape together. They had fallen out over some remarks that Best had made at the opera about Camelford to a woman, known only as 'Mrs S.', whose favours Camelford was at the time enjoying but who had previously been Best's mistress.

Camelford, having been told by Mrs S. about Best's remarks, went to the Prince of Wales's coffeehouse, where they usually dined, in order to take up the matter with him. 'I find, Sir,' said Camelford, 'that you have spoken of me in the most unwarrantable terms.' Captain Best denied the accusation, whereupon Camelford called him a 'scoundrel, a liar and a ruffian'. In the circles in which Camelford and Best moved, that kind of intemperate language could mean only one thing: a duel. Accordingly, both men nominated a second, who, in due course, fixed the time and place of the duel.

Captain Best left the coffeehouse 'much agitated' and shortly afterwards a note was delivered to Camelford. The staff of the coffeehouse, sensing that there was a duel in the offing, with 'a truly laudable anxiety' alerted the police in the hope that the duellists might be intercepted before they could do each other any harm. The police, despite keeping watch throughout the night on both men's lodgings, failed to apprehend them. The following morning, Camelford and Best met once more in a coffeehouse, as arranged by their seconds. Here Best attempted to get Camelford to retract his insults.

'Camelford,' began Best, 'we have been friends, and I know the unsuspecting generosity of your nature. Upon my honour you have been imposed upon by a strumpet. Do not insist on conditions under which one of us must fall.' But Camelford answered, 'Best, this is child's play, the thing must go on.' It seems likely that Camelford had refused to withdraw his accusations because of Captain Best's reputation as one of the most proficient pistol shots in England. Camelford feared, of course, that to compromise with such a man would expose him to accusations of cowardice.

Camelford was a bundle of contradictions. He, like Best, had served in the navy, where he had earned for himself 'a well-founded opinion of his gallantry and bravery'. He was notably eccentric in matters of dress and appearance. He was irascible and loved fighting; boxing, which was at the time highly fashionable, was a passion of his. He involved himself in a variety of disputes.

Part of the ritual of duelling was the agonised whiling away of time the night before the encounter. Men often used the long hours to settle their affairs, compose their wills or write to their loved ones. The night before his duel, Camelford wrote and inserted into his will a paragraph containing the following.

> … I am fully and entirely the aggressor, as well in the spirit as in the letter of the word. Should I therefore lose my life in a contest of my own seeking, I most solemnly forbid any of my friends or relations, let them be of whatsoever description they may be, from instituting any vexatious proceedings against my antagonist, and should, notwithstanding the above declaration on my part, the laws of the land be put in force against him; I desire that this part of my will may be made known to the King, in order that his royal heart may be moved to extend his mercy towards him.

Camelford's wish was granted, as neither Best nor either of the seconds was prosecuted.

Nicholson, the surgeon who was summoned to attend the wounded Camelford, did not entertain much hope that his patient might recover. Best's bullet had entered Camelford's chest at the fifth rib and, passing through the right lobe of the lungs, had lodged in his spine, at the sixth vertebra. His lower body was paralysed and his chest cavity filled with blood. Camelford lingered in agony for three days until Saturday evening, when he died.

His will revealed a final eccentricity in specifying that his body was to be taken to Berne in Switzerland, to be buried at the foot of a particular tree on the Isle of St Pierre, in the Lac de Bienne. Camelford had studied in Switzerland as a young man and had a nostalgic fondness for this spot. For this purpose, Camelford left £1,000 to the city of Berne, a gesture that was to one acquaintance 'a proof of his madness'.[2]

Lord Holland, on whose estate the duel took place, erected a monument to Camelford in the form of an 'antique Roman altar', at the spot where he fell.[3]

*　*　*

The duel between Lord Camelford and Captain Best stands as a paradigm of all duels everywhere – a universal duel. There are aspects to it that are wholly characteristic of the duel, whether it took place in Henry IV's France, George III's England or Kaiser Wilhelm's Germany. Camelford and Best, the young aristocrat and the naval officer, were typical duellists. It was fought between friends – a common and distressing feature of all too many duels – as a result of a trifling argument, which ended with one man giving the other 'the lie', that is, accusing him of lying. Thereafter pride and the weight of custom ensured that the ritual would run its course to its bloody conclusion. Camelford's exculpation of Captain Best before the event was in the best traditions of the duel. Typical, too, was the fact that it was fought in the early morning, at a place that was both convenient and (relatively) discreet. Duelling was usually illegal – if often unofficially condoned – and duellists had to be careful not to advertise their intentions. That it ended in the death of one of the principals probably makes it unusual – fatal duels, happily, were relatively uncommon –

but not outlandishly so. That Captain Best and the seconds escaped punishment, despite the fact that a man had been killed, was also wholly typical of duels everywhere, in every age.

It is also typical that the account of the duel between Camelford and Best should be so sparsely detailed. Duels were mostly secretive affairs, conducted in private and then hushed up. Occasionally, a duel caused a public sensation – one thinks of the Duke of Wellington and Lord Winchelsea or Alexander Hamilton and Aaron Burr – whereupon the ins and outs of the story became public property. But it was far more common to find the details of a duel to be as insubstantial and wispy as the morning mist in which they were often fought. The only eyewitness accounts we have of the encounter are those given by Lord Holland's gardeners to the coroner's court. By the time the coroner examined the case, one of the protagonists was dead and the other gone to ground, along with the seconds. The main actors had left the stage; it was the chorus who told the story.

INTRODUCTION
The Origins of the Duel

CHARLES MOORE, a late eighteenth-century campaigner against duelling, wrote that the origins of duelling lie in 'the ages of ignorance, superstition, and Gothic barbarism'.[1] He was not alone in his belief that duelling owed its existence to the uncivilised practices of the barbarian centuries; many writers, both before and since, have discerned the origins of the duel in the various forms of single combat that men have used to settle their differences since time immemorial.

Man has always fought man, for reasons good or ill. Dr John Cockburn, an Augustan divine who wrote a history of duelling, commented severely,

> It cannot be denied, but that the Passions of Pride, Envy, Malice, Revenge and Resentment, have always had the Ascendant over the Minds of Men, and from the beginning have been the great Springs of their Actions, which have produc'd very often both open Violence and Oppression, and also secret Murders.[2]

However, some of the earliest examples of single combat, deeply embedded in our literature and culture, are of the heroic champion, the protector of the weak, the saviour of his people. Many of these powerful, enduring literary allusions straddle the divide between myth and history: St Michael and Satan (saving the world, no less) and Beowulf (humbler in ambition, perhaps, but no less a hero for it) belong firmly in the realms of mythology. Milton gives us in *Paradise Lost* a magnificent description of the single combat between St Michael and Satan. The unknown author of *Beowulf*, too, gives us an equally stirring tale of a hero from across the seas. If Milton's angelic battle is evidently rooted firmly in the Christian tradition, Beowulf belongs to the pagan Norse mythology.

Trial by combat as a judicial method of settling differences between men began in Europe in the Dark Ages. It is thought that Gundobald, King of Burgundy, was the first ruling prince to introduce it, in about 501 AD.[3] Edward Gibbon explained the trial by combat thus:

> Both in civil and in criminal proceedings, the plaintiff, or accuser, the defendant, or even the witness, were exposed to mortal challenge from the antagonist who was destitute of legal proofs; and it was incumbent on them either to desert their cause or publicly to maintain their honour in the lists of battle.

According to Gibbon, Gundobald justified the introduction of the trial by combat with the question, 'Is it not true that the event of national wars and private combats is directed by the judgment of God: and that his providence awards victory to the juster cause?' The belief that trial by combat will reveal a just settlement between the contending parties by the operation of God's will underpins the medieval faith in the practice. Force of arms would provide an answer, unclouded by false witnesses or fabricated evidence. Gibbon continues, caustically,

> By such prevailing arguments, the absurd and cruel practice of judicial duels, which had been peculiar to some tribes of Germany, was propagated and established in all the monarchies of Europe, from Sicily to the Baltic.[4]

Gundobald's law allowed for a duel if the accused persisted in denying his offence under oath and the accuser insisted on proof by force of arms. This remained the essence of the trial by combat wherever in Europe it formed part of the judicial process. The first recorded judicial duel fought in Italy took place at Pavia in the early seventh century AD. It was fought to settle an accusation against the Lombard Queen Gundiperga. When the Lombard laws were codified in 643 by King Rothari, the judicial duel formed part of the code. The judicial duel outlasted the Lombard dynasty, which was overthrown by Charlemagne in 774; indeed, its operation was extended by various rulers into new areas of the law. In 982, for example, the Emperor Otto II decreed that trial by combat should be used in cases of perjury. In the course of its evolution the Lombard law of judicial combat could be applied in about 20 different types of case.[5]

Elsewhere in Europe the judicial duel flourished throughout the Middle Ages. At first, it even enjoyed the support of the Church as Pope Nicholas II had sanctioned the practice in 858. Established, as we have seen, in Burgundy, trial by combat soon spread to the rest of France, taking root in the Frankish kingdom and elsewhere.

In the wake of the Norman Conquest the judicial duel reached England, although there is a legend that in the year 1016 Canute and Edmund Ironside fought in single combat at the Isle of Alney, near Gloucester; the prize was England herself. During the reign of William II, William, Count d'Eu, was accused by another baron, Godefroy Baynard, of conspiring against the King. The two men were compelled to settle their differences in a judicial combat. They met at Salisbury, where they fought before the King and his court; the Count d'Eu lost. As a result he was castrated and blinded; his squire, for good measure, was whipped and hanged.

Another celebrated example of the trial by combat in England was the contest between Baron Henry de Essex and Robert de Montfort during the reign of Henry II (1154–1189). Essex, the hereditary standard bearer of England, was accused by de Montfort of dereliction of duty during Henry II's Welsh campaign of 1157. De Montfort alleged that Essex had, in the face of the enemy, abandoned the royal standard and fled the field. This was not an allegation that could be allowed to go unchallenged, so the two men met on an island in the Thames at Reading to settle their differences. Essex lost the combat and was left for dead. Luckily for him, the monks, having removed his body to their abbey for burial, discovered that he was still alive. Nursed back to health, Essex spent the rest of his life in the abbey.[6]

In France in 1386 there was a spectacular instance of judicial combat, fought between Jean de Carrouges and Jacques le Gris. The whole episode has been evocatively recreated by Eric Jager in – the slightly misleadingly named – *The Last Duel*. Jager tells the story of the slowly fomenting rivalry between the two knights culminating in the rape of de Carrouges's beautiful and considerably younger wife by Le Gris and of the judicial combat that the King of France, Charles VI, ordered to be fought to resolve the matter. Jager's account brings the elaborate pageantry and feudal protocol of the judicial combat vividly to life. The two knights faced each other across a piece of open ground in a Parisian monastery just after Christmas 1386. The King and his court as well as hundreds of spectators were looking on; it was to be a contest to the death. After a fight whose brutality belied the grand formality of the setting and the occasion, Le Gris, helpless on the ground in his heavy armour, was stabbed through the throat by his adversary.[7]

The judicial combat, whether in France, Italy or England, was, in essence, the same. It was a public event, sanctioned by the King, openly contested in front of officials, spectators and the monarch on a ground and under conditions that conferred no advantage to either side. The result of the contest was agreed by the parties to be binding. As such it could scarcely be more different from the private, illegal and secret encounter that was the modern duel. Shakespeare, as so often, captured the spirit of the trial by combat in *Richard II*. In this play the opening three scenes tell the story of the contretemps between Thomas Mowbray, Duke of Norfolk, and Henry Bolingbroke, Lord Hereford.

The King, the fount of all justice, calls the two quarrelsome barons together in order to resolve their dispute. Richard, having heard the allegations that each makes against the other, decides to attempt a reconciliation between the parties, but he fails, so orders a judicial combat to settle the matter. Shakespeare was fully *au fait* with the nature of the judicial combat. When the King, having failed to reconcile the parties, orders a trial by combat, he is acting in his judicial capacity. This is reiterated by the fact that, when the parties arrive at Coventry, prepared for battle in front of the King and his court, Richard calls off the fight and imposes terms of banishment on the two barons. It is, Shakespeare is saying, for the King, and the King alone, to dispense justice.

From the very earliest days the Church was opposed to the trial by combat. It was considered to be a usurpation of God's authority, despite the fact that the secular powers, who sanctioned the trials and the combatants themselves, believed implicitly that the combats were a sure method of invoking God's judgement in a dispute. St Avitus, the Archbishop of Vienne and primate of Burgundy, protested to King Gundobald about his legalisation of the trial by combat in 501. The Church's more active opposition to the practice began with the Council of Valence in 855. The papacy itself, at least at first, adopted a more equivocal line, opposing combats in individual cases but not attacking the institution until the twelfth century. Indeed, in 858 Nicholas I gave trial by ordeal (of which trial by combat was a subset) official papal sanction.

In Italy, after a period of popularity that lasted from perhaps the ninth to the twelfth centuries, trial by combat began to decline. One historian of the period speculates that perhaps this process began as a result of the Diet of Verona in 983. At this gathering the temporal lords of Italy decided to assert their authority over the conduct of trials by combat. Gradually, control of judicial combats passed to the secular authorities; by the mid-eleventh or early twelfth century the free cities of Italy had began proscribing the judicial combat. Genoa in 1056 or Bari in 1132 was the earliest to take this step.[8]

Elsewhere in Europe the opposition to judicial combat also came from the Church; papal pronouncements had, in theory at any rate, to be noticed and adhered to throughout the Roman world. In France, the decline of the judicial duel can be dated to the reign of St Louis (1226–1270), who promulgated decrees outlawing the practice. Some historians consider that this was an important moment in the development of the modern duel, in that St Louis's decrees, by depriving the trial by combat of official sanction, passed control of it into private hands. Thus the monarch lost, or began to lose, the power to regulate trial by combat. Philip the Fair, in 1303, enacted further restrictions on the practice. Once the institution had lost its official sanction it started to develop from the open, public method of settling disputes, conducted with full feudal pageantry, into the modern duel, the secret dawn ritual in the hidden glade.

In England the judicial duel, having crossed the Channel with the Normans, enjoyed a shorter efflorescence. The introduction by Henry II in England of jury trials began the decline of trial by combat. Men now had an alternative method of settling their disputes that seemed fairer and not so open to interest and corruption as the verdict of a single judge.

The age of chivalry is known for its devotion to the tournament. These events, part pageant, part war game, were magnificent celebrations of the ideals of the chivalrous knight and the rituals of knighthood. Embedded in the elaborate ceremonies that governed these events were the precepts of feudal loyalty that bound a knight to his liege and the King to his subjects. They also provided knights with the opportunity to perform deeds of valour before the eyes of their lady, one of the most important requirements in the tradition of medieval courtly love.

Medieval tournaments were magnificent, set-piece occasions, where knights jousted with each other in full armour on splendidly caparisoned horses, in front of the King and his court. But behind the silks and brocades, the sumptuously ornamented tents and richly woven trappings of feudalism lay a serious purpose: the chance for knights to hone the fighting skills that would enable them to perform effectively their obligation of military service. The heavily armoured, mounted knight was the strike force of any European medieval army. Fighting in full armour with lance and sword on horseback required a high degree of skill and fitness. It was essential, therefore, that knights had every opportunity to hone their skills and their fitness to a peak. Tournaments were one, possibly the best, way in which this could be achieved.

The connection between the judicial combat and the medieval tournament, with its competitive tilting, is obvious. Both can in turn be regarded as forerunners of the modern duel, although I would argue that the judicial duel is the less distant cousin. Trial by combat was avowedly an institution for the resolution of disputes between two parties; the tournament, while it pitted man against man in single combat, was, beneath all the glitter and ceremony, essentially a war game. Arguably, the medieval tournament is better regarded as a fore-bear of modern competitive sport than of the duel.

A third medieval institution, closely related to the tournament and trial by combat – indeed, it might best be regarded as an amalgam of the two – was the duel of chivalry. Its origins are obscure but we do know that it was, like trial by combat, always officially sanctioned and that, as a result, it was fought on a *'champs clos'*. It also seems to have had a notably strict set of rules about who could take part. It was, most definitely, not for the common man. Rule XII stated, 'Whoso-ever cannot prove his nobility for four generations at least by both father and mother, shall not have the honour of being admitted into the tournament.'[9]

As is the case with trial by combat and medieval jousting, the duel of chivalry has obvious claims to be regarded as a precursor of the modern duel. In particular, it existed for the settling of questions touching upon the honour of a knight or a noble. In this respect it is the direct antecedent of the modern duel. However, as with trial by combat, it is distinguished from the modern duel by the fact that it was fight conducted in public with the authority and blessing of the monarch.[10]

As trial by combat developed, so the custom of the parties' employing a champion emerged. A champion was a hired man who fought the trial on his principal's behalf. Although it enabled the prin-cipal to avoid the tiresome and dangerous obligation to fight his opponent in the lists, it did not absolve him from the consequences of the result. As one historian puts it, 'As for the principals in a capital fight by proxy, they were kept out of sight of the duel, with a rope round their necks, and the one who was beaten by proxy was imme-diately hanged in person.'[11]

Choosing a champion was, literally, a matter of life and death. The role of the champion was an aspect of the medieval trial by combat that far outlasted the institution itself, surviving in vestigial form into more modern times. The King's champion continued to enjoy a role, albeit purely ceremonial, at coronations in England. George IV was attended by his champion at the banquet in Westminster Hall following his coronation in 1821. The King's champion, in full armour complete with plumed helmet, mounted on a white charger, rode into the hall and, in front of the assembled guests, threw down his gauntlet three times, challenging anyone who disputed the King's right to the throne to single combat. There were no takers.[12]

Despite clerical opposition and the growth of the rule of law, trial by combat survived into the Renaissance, defying the receding tide of medievalism. As late as 1583 – fully halfway through the reign of Elizabeth I – two Irishmen, Conor O'Connor and Teige O'Connor, were ordered by the Lords Justices and Privy Council of Ireland to resolve their differences by force of arms. The dispute concerned allegations of treason and the trial by combat was fought in the inner courtyard of Dublin Castle. Conor was killed in the combat and his corpse beheaded.[13]

In 1547 there took place what is generally considered the last formal trial by combat or duel of chivalry in France. The celebrated contest between the Baron de Jarnac and the Seigneur de La Châtaigneraie was fought with the consent of the young King Henry II. The two nobles fought on a formally delineated duelling ground, surrounded by the full panoply of tented pavilions and elaborate stands, watched by the King himself, courtiers, heralds and numerous other spectators. It was a relic of the Middle Ages, an old-fashioned trial by combat, not a modern duel. It will be discussed in greater detail in Chapter 6.

A generation later, in 1571, a court in London ordered a trial by combat to resolve a dispute that had arisen over some land in the Isle of Harty, Kent. The defendant, one Paramour, elected for trial 'by Battel', a request that, perhaps not surprisingly, took the Court of the Common Pleas unawares. But, as the claimants were happy to accede to a trial by combat, the court could not refuse the application, however outdated it considered it to be. An area of Tothill Fields (near the modern Houses of Parliament) was set aside for the contest. Both the parties had chosen to fight by proxy, that is to engage a champion to fight for them. The claimant in the action, one Chavin, chose Henry Nailer, a fencing master, as his champion; Paramour chose a George Thorn to champion his cause.

... the Champion of the Demandant [Chavin], who came to the place apparalled with red Sandells upon his black Armour, Bare Legged from the Knee downward, Bare Headed, and Bare Arms to the Elbows, being brought in by the hand of a Kt., Sir Jerome Bowes, who carried a red Baston of an Ell long tipped with Horn, and a Yeoman, the Target made of double Leather ...[14]

Paramour's champion was accompanied onto the field by Sir Henry Cherry. Rumours of the impending contest and of the elaborate preparations would have raced around London, prompting as many as 4,000 people to make their way to Tothill Fields to enjoy this rare spectacle. Unfortunately for the thousands of eager and curious spectators, the Queen, having got wind of the intended combat, not wishing to preside over bloodshed, however indirectly, ordered that the action be settled in favour of the defendant.[15] So there was no trial by combat, no gore, no excitement; the 4,000 spectators had to make their way quietly home.

The right to elect trial 'by Battel' lingered on in English law until the nineteenth century. In 1817 one Abraham Thornton was charged with the murder of Mary Ashford. His defence counsel, evidently well versed in the more arcane areas of the criminal law, not wishing his client to risk the verdict of a jury, suggested that he elect trial 'by Battel'. Accordingly, Thornton threw down his glove in court, challenging his accuser to combat.[16] The court was taken aback by this appeal to a legal remedy that had lain dormant for many decades, if not centuries, but gave judgment for Thornton. In 1819, however, Parliament abolished trial 'by Battel'. It was said to be the only reform of the law of which Lord Eldon, the reactionary and long-serving Lord Chancellor, approved during his long tenure of office. Even the 'hard, dour and rigid' Eldon could agree to the abolition of a measure which traced its origins back to the Dark Ages.[17]

* * *

These various medieval forms of single combat were long considered to be the direct antecedents of the modern duel. Early historians of duelling traced the origins of the modern duel to the 'fierce yet gloomy

superstition of the northern tribes'.[18] It was equally generally agreed by
the same writers that the first important modern duel was the challenge issued to Francis I, King of France, by the Emperor Charles V in
1528. The facts may be obscure, the stories hazy and contradictory but
the episode did succeed in seizing the imagination of duelling historians. Indeed, it is not difficult to see why: here were the two greatest
secular rulers in Europe, two mighty princes, challenging one another
to a duel. From this moment on, so the theory ran, the modern duel
became common; 'the example was contagious' one wrote.[19]

In fact the perception that the abortive encounter between French
king and Holy Roman Emperor was the first modern duel has much
to commend it. For all the compelling similarities (ignoring for a
moment the differences) between the medieval forms of single
combat and the modern duel, the latter is essentially a creation of the
Renaissance. Italy was the cradle of the Renaissance; she gave us Bot-
ticelli, Brunelleschi and Michelangelo but she also spawned the
modern concept of the duel. As one recent scholar has written: 'during
the first half of the sixteenth century the medieval forms of single
combat were refashioned in Italy into a duel of honour which
replaced the vendetta'.[20] Charles V and Francis I were Renaissance
princes *par excellence*, so it is wholly logical that they should espouse
the new concept of the duel and the notions of honour that formed
its foundations.

If Italy in the first half of the sixteenth century was the birthplace
of the modern duel, it was the printing press that ensured the widest
possible dissemination of the new ideas. A flood of manuals and
books offering gentlemen instruction in the new precepts of honour
and more practical advice in the essential art of swordplay came off
the presses.

This stage in the modern duel's incubation coincided with a prolonged period of intermittent war in Italy, which both encouraged
men to fight and swelled the ranks of those who subscribed to the new
etiquettes. In September 1494 Charles VIII of France and his army
crossed the Alps into Italy, to assert his claim to the throne of Naples.
In doing so, he started the Italian Wars, a series of increasingly bloody,
expensive and widespread conflicts that lasted until 1559.

The Italian Wars are an important milestone in the history of duelling because they ensured the presence in Italy for long periods of large numbers of French soldiers. Consequently, substantial numbers of Frenchmen were exposed to the new notions of personal honour and to the etiquettes of duelling. They had every opportunity to put into practice what they had learned. War and times of unrest are fertile breeding grounds for the enmities between men that spawn duels and the Italy of the early sixteenth century was no exception.

The Italian Wars undoubtedly exposed the invading French soldiers to the new style of duelling; the histories are full of accounts of duels fought at this time and many of them involved Frenchmen. Bayard, Sainte-Croix, Cobios, Bourdeille, Pourvillan and La Motte are just a few of the French knights who fought duels in Italy during this period. Gaston de Foix and De Chaumont, two important French commanders, both oversaw duels fought by their fellow countrymen.[21] It was these men, and numerous others unknown, who took the new fashion back across the Alps to France.

Part I

THE ANATOMY OF A DUEL

Chapter One

HONOUR, ROGUES AND GENTLEMEN

Duel, *n*. A formal ceremony preliminary to the reconciliation of two enemies. Great skill is necessary to its satisfactory observance; if awkwardly performed the most unexpected and deplorable consequences sometimes ensue. A long time ago a man lost his life in a duel.

AMBROSE BIERCE, *The Devil's Dictionary*[1]

In consequence of a trifling quarrel, a duel took place at Barbadoes, on the 15th of January, between Captain Broadman of the 60th regiment, and Ensign de Betton, of the Royal West Indian Rangers, in which at the first fire, the former was shot through the heart, and instantly expired. The survivor immediately escaped from the island.

Annual Register, 4 March 1811

THE CONTRAST BETWEEN the glib cynicism of *The Devil's Dictionary* and the clipped formality of the notice in the *Annual Register* is arresting. *The Devil's Dictionary* ridicules the etiquette of the duel as a sham, an archaic formality that has no place in the modern world (it was composed in the 1880s), while overlooking the fact that, at least on the wilder fringes of the American West, lethal encounters akin to duels were still regular occurrences. The notice from the *Annual Register* has by contrast the tone of an announcement of the

Court and Social columns of the modern *Times* or *Daily Telegraph*, informing readers of a forthcoming marriage or royal visit. Its bald account of the fatal duel leaves the reader to imagine the terror of the encounter itself, the fear and guilt of the survivor and the grief of Captain Boardman's family and dependants. What the notice does not omit to impart is a sense of the futility of the affair: 'In consequence of a trifling quarrel …'

These two quotations offer different views of the duel; in their way both are misleading, yet both offer a grain of truth about the institution they describe. *The Devil's Dictionary* asserts that a duel was an act, a quadrille to be performed, in order to satisfy social convention. This is both right and wrong: in its heyday – the *Annual Register* gobbet makes this plain – the duel was far from a mere formality, as Lord Camelford would certainly have recognised. Yet it was, among gentlemen, a convention, rigidly adhered to and strictly regulated. The *Annual Register* notice gives the impression by its very formality that duelling was both commonplace and acceptable, like a royal visit to open a factory. This was not the case, even in 1811. There was considerable opposition, as we will see, among reform-minded layman, while the Church was staunchly opposed to the practice. While duels were, at that time, relatively common (it was, after all, only 18 months since two Cabinet ministers had seen fit to fight a duel), they nevertheless aroused disgust and shock, particularly when, as here, a participant was killed.

The modern duel lasted from the mid-sixteenth into the twentieth century. It was (as we have seen) both a development of and a departure from medieval customs. There were, of course, marked differences in its longevity from country to country. In Italy, the birthplace of the modern duel, Mussolini's fascists were happily fighting one another with sabres in the 1920s. In Britain, which espoused the practice in the late sixteenth and early seventeenth centuries, duelling had died out by 1860. In France, where by the time of the *belle époque* duelling was no longer the lethal activity it had once been, politicians and journalists were flocking to the Bois de Boulogne to settle their differences at the point of a sword until 1914. Thereafter it was less common; the slaughter in the trenches cast duelling in a different, much less acceptable light. In places as far apart as Poland and Argentina, duelling persisted well into the 1930s, yet in India and other British colonies, the practice had died out by the second half of the nineteenth century. In Germany, particularly in military circles, duelling was widespread and frequently lethal right up until the outbreak of World War One.

Duelling enjoyed a widespread efflorescence, leaving its mark in the cultures of many different countries. The next three chapters point out the similarities of the ways in which the duel was fought in all these different countries over the three or so centuries of its life. The duel had several immutable characteristics, which, despite variations from age to age and country to country, continued to define the institution. These characteristics were essentially the same in, for example, Henrician France, Georgian England, colonial India, republican America and Wilhelmine Germany. The most important of these were the challenge, the presence of seconds and the etiquette of the fight itself.

It is important to note that the duel was, throughout its existence in all countries, open only to the gentleman. Naturally, what constituted a gentleman varied: the *sieurs* of Henry IV's day would no doubt have been horrified by some of the bourgeois who claimed the right to defend their honour on the duelling grounds of *fin de siècle* France; in the same way Junkers in the Kaiser's Prussia preferred to thrash a man for an insult rather than do him the honour of killing him in a duel.

Sweaty butchers' boys settled their differences with meaty fists outside taverns; gentlemen followed the refined, civilised etiquettes of duelling. Newspapers occasionally published satirical accounts of so-called 'tradesmen's duels', that is fights between men whom the paper's editor (and, presumably, his readership) did not consider to be entitled to defend their honour in this way. This example appeared in the *Cheltenham Chronicle* in 1828:

> a respectable though very young tradesman, and an equally young driver of the quill, repaired to an excellent 'auberge' in the High-street, Cheltenham, for the purpose of spending a social hour, when ... high words

arose between them; and as the argument was probably inflamed by the influence of sun-dry libations offered to the jolly god, the young men … left the inn: but instead of proceeding peaceably to their homes, the frol-icsome Bacchus introduced them to his brother Mars, who, notwith-standing their hitherto pacific occupations, and their being mere 'bourgeois', persuaded them to settle the difference according to the laws of his court of honour …[2]

There was then some discussion as to whether a duel was the correct way to resolve the dispute but, 'Mars quickly brought the dispute to an issue by granting them (as a personal favour) a particular dispensa-tion to act as gentlemen on this occasion.' Neither of the participants was injured in the duel; the 'Knight of the Quill' fired first but missed, and his opponent's gun misfired (or 'flashed in the pan', as the con-temporary phrase went).

The conventions were always strictly interpreted: a gentleman was under no obligation to take up a challenge from someone whom he did not consider to be his social equal. In July 1925 a Pomeranian landowner, Boguslav von Somnitz, following challenges, agreed to fight three friends of his in succession as a result of a political argu-ment that had arisen during a shooting weekend. The four men all owned land in the region and regarded each other as equals as well as friends. A fourth man, one Lieutenant Kohl, who had also been present at the shooting party, considered himself sufficiently slighted to challenge von Somnitz to a duel. Von Somnitz, who perhaps had enough on his plate already, declined to fight Kohl, saying that he con-sidered the lieutenant beneath him.

Before dawn on 3 July 1925 the four men gathered in a clearing in the forest near Stolp, where von Somnitz, doggedly honourable, lined up against his three friends in succession. The report of the duels con-tinues,

At that hour it was too dark, and the 'One, two, three' was counted so rapidly that it was impossible to take any real aim, but in so far as he [von Somnitz] did, he fired at his opponents' legs. He considered it his duty to disable them if possible, being himself the father of a family.

So far as we can tell no one was injured in any of these three encounters. At this point Kohl arrived in the clearing, demanding to be allowed to redeem his honour in a duel with von Somnitz. Von Somnitz, remarkably in view of the fact that he had just fought three duels, decided that he could no longer refuse Kohl's challenge, for fear of being thought a coward, so a fourth duel was rapidly arranged. Perhaps the light had by now improved, perhaps von Somnitz had become more practised with his pistol, but poor Kohl was hit in the abdomen and died almost at once.[3]

Another example that illustrates the point concerns the so-called 'Fighting Parson', the Revd. Sir Henry Bate Dudley (1745–1824). Bate Dudley was an enthusiastic amateur pugilist as well as renowned duellist. He had been challenged to a duel by a Captain Crofts, which the parties managed to settle but not before a crony of Crofts, a Mr Fitz-Gerall [*sic*], intervened alleging that a friend of his, a Captain Miles, had been insulted by the clergyman. Bate Dudley, who described Fitz-Gerall as 'a little effeminate being', was convinced that he would never dare face him in a duel and suspected that Miles was a hired man, paid to fight him. So he agreed to meet Miles but, as he was fully entitled to do by the conventions that governed duelling, refused to contemplate a pistol duel with a man whom he considered to be a substitute. Instead Bate Dudley offered to fight him with bare knuckles. The two men fought outside the Spread Eagle Tavern and Miles received a fearful beating. As Bate Dudley wrote afterwards with understandable glee: '[T]he Captain received in about fifteen minutes the satisfaction he required, not being able to discern a single ray of light, by which to find his way home.'[4]

More recently the late Lord Moynihan demonstrated that aristocratic punctiliousness in matters of honour had survived intact into the mid-twentieth century. In 1957 an Italian monarchist challenged the British peer Lord Altrincham to a duel 'to defend the honour of monarchy the world over' after the latter had apparently made some disparaging remarks about the Queen. Moynihan, who happened to be in Italy at the time, offered to take on the presumptuous Italian, saying, 'I'll fight this Renato. He cannot be allowed to get away with this blow to British prestige.' Moynihan then added, 'Let me emphasise that it is only my extremely democratic nature that allows me to cross swords with a commoner.' A more acceptable opponent for Moynihan was suggested, an Italian count of ancient lineage, but he, it transpired, was an expert swordsman. Before the duel could be fought the Italian police intervened to prevent the encounter, a great loss to posterity.[5]

At the root of duelling lay the question of honour. When one man challenged another to a duel, he was seeking to expunge a slur, real or imagined, on his reputation, in other words, his honour. Casanova, who knew a thing or two about the importance of reputation, explained it thus in his *Memoirs*: 'The man of honour ought always to be ready to use the sword to defend himself from insult, or to give satisfaction for an insult he has offered.'[6] An Irish opponent of duelling, speaking in the 1830s, put it differently: 'No man loves to fight for fighting [*sic*] sake; he fights because he fears he cannot honourably decline the combat.'[7]

While that may be a negative view of the concept of honour, it was certainly one with which many men would have agreed. There were numerous ways in which men could, and did, consider their honour to be impugned, but one of the chief reasons for fighting a duel, as challenger or challenged, was the desire to avoid the obloquy of their peers. No gentleman could fail to take steps to expunge a stain on his honour. This requirement transcended even the grossest insults that one man could offer another. For example, Daniel O'Connell, Irish nationalist politician and not a man noted for restraint in his speech, called Lord Alvanley a 'bloated buffoon, a liar, a disgrace to his species, and heir-at-law to the thief who died upon the cross'.[8] It was the fact that Alvanley had been traduced in public that obliged him to challenge O'Connell to a duel, rather than necessarily the insults themselves, wittily offensive as they were. He could not be seen failing to take action to clear his name.

In military circles the rule was yet more absolute: failure to uphold one's own or one's regiment's honour was an offence warranting the removal of an officer's commission. This sanction applied, in general, to officers in all countries, across the entire period. For example, in Napoleon's armies officers who declined to redress slights to their honour by challenging the offender to a duel were punished. Consider, too, the case of Ensign Cowell, a Guards officer who in 1814 was found guilty by a court martial of 'making a concession' to one Commissory Hurley, who had publicly insulted him in a theatre in Bordeaux. Cowell was cashiered and dismissed from the service for, in effect, failing to fight a duel to uphold his honour and that of his regiment. In Germany, where it was by the late nineteenth century very pervasive, this type of 'caste honour' was known as *Standesehre*.

The notion of honour on which the duelling ethic was founded evolved in Renaissance Italy. It was intimately connected with questions of status and the resulting capacity to give and receive satisfaction to another gentleman in a duel. The German language has coined a hybrid word for this capacity: *satisfaktionsfahig*. It was a virtuous – or vicious, depending on how one looked at it – circle: only a gentleman could give satisfaction but only a gentleman could decide whether his potential opponent qualified as a man of honour.

The ideas behind the code of honour were explained in countless pamphlets and manuals. The earliest of these appeared in Italy in the sixteenth century and they were still being produced in the twentieth. Scipione Ferretto published his *Codigo del Honor* in Buenos Aires in 1905. It sets out in great detail the rules of behaviour in affairs of honour and gives the procedure, step by step, for conducting any subsequent duel. It was printed in a convenient, easily portable format, presumably so that Argentinian duellists and their seconds could carry the book with them to the duelling ground for reference purposes.

Those who defended the practice of duelling, and there were many, tended to lean heavily, although not exclusively, on the question of honour. There were circumstances, they maintained, when a man had no alternative but to fight. To do anything less would be eternally dishonourable. Lord Chesterfield, belletrist and wit, writing in 1737, offered this, somewhat uncharitable, definition of the man of honour: 'A man of honor is one, who peremptorily affirms himself to be so, and will cut anybody's throat that questions it …'[9]

It was this, the duellists' notion of honour, that attracted the most criticism from the reformers. Duelling's many critics, both clerical and lay, took exception to the fact that, by invoking their sense of honour, duellists were placing themselves above the law, both of God and of the land. A cleric, preaching at Cambridge University in the late eighteenth century and seething with righteous indignation, denounced the duellists' perverted sense of honour to his congregation: 'Strip this phantom of honour of the false glare with which fashion and folly hide its deformity: detest this monstrous relic of gothic barbarity, this horrible compound of suicide and assassination.'[10]

Richard Steele, journalist, Joseph Addison's collaborator and sometime soldier, suggested in 1720 that Englishmen should look to France for a solution to the madness of duelling. Here, Louis XIV had 'taught his Subjects another Way of aspiring to Honour, than by killing one another for Punctilios and Trifles; having by the Laws ... totally reduced the Kingdom of France to submissive obedience.'[11]

History suggests that Steele was mistaken in supposing that the French government was more successful in the long term in suppressing duels but he was a well-intentioned and eloquent opponent of duelling.

It was the controlled formality of the etiquette that defined the duel. In times rougher and more lawless than our own this was important, because it differentiated the duel from assault and common murder. Similarly, and the two were intimately connected, the rules ensured that, by and large, provided a duellist adhered to the conventions of duelling, he would escape the worst penalties of the criminal law in the event he killed his man.

In early modern Europe, at the time that duelling was becoming more widespread, lawlessness was rife, assault and murder commonplace; men were quick to anger and quick to draw their swords. Furthermore, the law itself, cumbersome and corrupt, was inadequate to deal with many of the quarrels that arose between men. The temptation was to take the law into one's own hands, and many did. John Aubrey, seventeenth-century man of letters and author of *Brief Lives*, reckoned that his life was in peril three times, two of them at the hand of a stranger. On one occasion he reported, 'I was in great danger of being killed by a drunkard in the street opposite Grayes-Inn gate – a gentleman whom I never saw before, but (Deo Gratis) one of his companions hindred his thrust.'

Aubrey, a founding member of the Royal Society, was no hard-living ruffian, yet was randomly confronted with the consequences of lawlessness and the private feud. He noted, for example, with apparent insouciance, that 'Capt. Yarrington dyed at London about March last. The cause of his death was a Beating and throwne into a Tub of Water.'[12]

John Evelyn, polymath and diarist, who was a contemporary of Aubrey's, recalled in his diary an incident that took place while he was travelling through France in 1650. His travelling companion, Lord Ossory, wandered through an open gate into a garden.

> There step'd a rude fellow to it, and thrust my Lord, with uncivil language from entering in: uponn this out young Gallants struck the fellow over the pate, & bid him aske pardon; which to our thinking he did with much submission, & so we parted: but we were not gon far, but we heare a noise behind us, & saw people coming with gunns, swords, staves & forks, following, & flinging stones; upon which we turn'd and were forc'd to engage, & with out Swords, stones & the help of our servants, (one of which had a pistol), make our retreate for neere a quarter of a mile, when an house receiv'd us.

Having retreated, they succeeded in beating off the attack at the cost of some minor injuries. While it is stretching the point to claim that the attack on Evelyn and his party was wholly unprovoked, the episode illustrates well the general state of lawlessness which prevailed at the time and the willingness with which people resorted to arms.[13]

Nor at this time was random violence confined to the streets of London or the byways of France: it could erupt spontaneously even in the best circles, as this account of a dinner party given by the Earl of Pembroke in 1676 makes abundantly clear. Pembroke was Lord Lieutenant of Wiltshire and a great favourite of Charles II. An argument had broken out at dinner between Pembroke and Sir Francis Vincent, when my Lord [Pembroke] began a small health of 2 bottles, which Sir Francis refusinge to pledge, dashed with a bottle at his head, & as it is said broke it, they beinge parted Sir Francis was gettinge into a coach & alarm arisinge that my Lord was cominge with his sworde drawne, Sir Francis refused to enter, sayinge he was never afraid of a naked sword in his life, & come he did, & at a passe my Lord brake his sword, att which Sir Francis Cryed he scorned to take ye advantage, & then threw away his owne sword & flew att him furiously, beate him, threw him downe in ye kennell, nubbled him, & dawb'd him daintly & soe were parted.[14]

In a society where violence was part of everyday life and the law an inadequate remedy, duelling was not the barbaric, archaic anomaly it might appear to us. To some it seemed the lesser of two evils, violent certainly, but less random, more controlled than the (wholly typical) incidents just recounted. The custom developed, in part, as a method both of regulating endemic violence and of providing gentlemen with an efficient and immediate way in which their disputes could be resolved and their reputations cleared. Thus, from the very beginning the formal rules of conduct were the most important aspect of duelling. They distinguished the fatal duel from the random murder and, ultimately, the duellist who had killed his man from the common murderer. However, it was not always easy to distinguish the brawl from the duel, as the following example from 1722 shows.

They write from Edinburgh, that Lieutenant Moody, and Captain Chiefly Quarreling, a Challenge was sent, but the former not meeting, the latter Caned him; upon which Moody ran Chiefly into the Body; after which the last drew his Sword and wounded the other, and both are since dead of their Wounds.[15]

Generally, the duellist escaped the penalties prescribed by the criminal law for murder. This was true throughout duelling's history, from the United States to Russia, India to Ireland, but was subject to the very important proviso that the duellist could be shown to have adhered to the accepted rules for the conduct of the encounter. The leniency extended to those duellists who were brought to justice was the result either of the reluctance of courts to convict or of the indulgence of monarchs in offering pardons to those were convicted of these offences. In the latter category, Henry IV of France and Kaiser Wilhelm II were only the most notorious of many inveterate pardoners. This applied, of course, only to those duellists who were tried; many, probably the majority, escaped the clutches of the law altogether. This failure to bring duellists to justice outraged the reformers. Granville Sharp, best known as a campaigner for the abolition of slavery, was also active in the fight against duelling. In a pamphlet on the subject written in 1790, he commented,

> This abominable practice of duelling, which of late years has increased to a most alarming degree, may chiefly be attributed to the improper indulgence which our English courts of justice ... have shewn to persons convicted of killing in sudden affrays and recounters [duels], through a false idea of mercy due to human frailty, in cases of sudden provocation.[16]

With a more robust attitude from the courts Sharp concluded that 'the absurd and depraved notions of honour, and gentleman-like satisfaction, of which I complain, could not possibly exist, if every conqueror in a duel, who kills his antagonist, was sure of being hanged up as an ignominious felon'.[17]

By the same token the German Reichstag was constantly complaining in the years before World War One about the Kaiser's practice of pardoning those convicted of duelling offences. Equally, in the American Old South, particularly in the antebellum era, convictions for duelling offences were virtually unknown; juries simply refused to convict duellists brought before them.

Any suspicion, however, that the rules had not been strictly adhered to, or any inkling of foul play, would expose the duellist, if caught, to the likelihood of much harsher penalties. There were cases that, quite patently, fell on the wrong side of the line between duelling and murder. No amount of clever argument could disguise the fact that the court was dealing with straightforward murder. Take the example of the death of George Reynolds in Dublin in 1788. Reynolds had quarrelled with one Robert Keen and the two men had agreed to fight a duel. As they were going out to fight,

'Mr Reynolds, previous to coming to action, was in the act of saluting Mr Keen with his hat in his hand, wishing him a good morning, the latter fired his pistol, and shot him through the head.'

In a case as blatant as this one, there could be no recourse to a 'duelling defence' nor did the jury have any difficulty in convicting Keen of murder. He was sentenced to death and hanged on 16 February 1788.[18] Likewise, in Mexico in 1926, there was a case that clearly fell on the wrong side of the line. A violent argument had erupted in the Mexican Senate between two senators, Enrique Henshaw and Luis Espinosa, which descended into fisticuffs, whereupon both senators were ejected from the chamber. Once outside, they at once drew their revolvers: Henshaw shot Espinosa dead but was himself wounded.[19] Whatever else this incident might have been, a duel it was most certainly not. By contrast, two young French aristocrats, the comte de Bouteville and the comte des Chappelles – who fought a duel in Paris in 1627 in which one of the seconds was killed – are a rare example of two duellists who adhered rigidly to the protocols yet were still condemned to death. They were victims of Cardinal Richelieu's implacable desire to make an example of a prominent bravo *pour encourager les autres*.

Other cases, in which the suspicion of foul play was less glaring, were more difficult to decide. Several of the best-known English duelling cases contained more than a hint of impropriety: the Hamilton–Mohun case (where one of the seconds faced a charge of murder); Lord Byron's case; and Major Campbell's case. Of these only Campbell's case resulted in a conviction for murder; only Campbell was hanged. All three of these cases will be discussed in greater detail later.

These examples show how important it was for the duellist to pay scrupulous regard to the formalities of the duelling code. If he did so, he would more than likely be able to escape a conviction for murder, assuming he was even brought to trial in the first place. The same held good for the seconds and other accomplices, such as surgeons. On the other hand, failure to observe the prescribed formalities could greatly compromise a duellist's defence in front of a jury. This, too, applied to the seconds. Any whiff of impropriety or foul play in the conduct of the duel would make matters doubly difficult. Let's now look at the immutable characteristics of the duel, characteristics that defined the institution throughout its active life: the challenge, the role of the seconds and the etiquette of the fight itself.

Chapter Two

THE CHALLENGE

All Challenges, whether sudden or deliberate, are a Stain upon one's Honour; because they betray Weakness of Mind, want of Temper, and a Sign that the Person has not the Government of his Spirit.[1]

THE CENSORIOUS OPINION OF Dr Cockburn is greatly at odds with the traditional view of the challenge to a duel, propagated in romantic novels, of the foppish gallant throwing his glove at the feet of his rival in love. In this milieu a challenge, far from betraying weakness of mind or want of temper, was a glorious affirmation of a knightly, chivalrous nature.

The challenge was the first absolute requirement of the duel. Without a challenge, there could be no duel; any subsequent fight would be merely an assault or a brawl. So it was in practice, too. The challenge set in motion the formal protocols of the duelling codes. In fact, there was usually a stage before the sending of a formal challenge: this often took the form of a note, asking for an explanation of the complained-of behaviour or remarks. Such a note, it was hoped, could result in an immediate apology and an amicable settlement of the affair. *The Code of Honor,* written by John Lyde Wilson in 1838, a former Governor of North Carolina and no ardent proponent of duelling, put it thus:

Never send a challenge in the first instance, for that precludes all negotiation. Let your note be in the language of a gentleman, and let the subject
matter of complaint be truly and fairly set forth, cautiously avoiding
attributing to the adverse party any improper motive.[2]

The importance of this step is illustrated by the course of the nego-
tiations prior to the duel between William Wyndham, British Minister in Florence, and Count Carletti in 1798. Wyndham and Carletti
had fallen out due to the latter's habit of publicly dismissing all
Wyndham's utterances on international affairs, casting doubt on his
veracity and integrity. Eventually, the two men met while driving in
their carriages in a park near Florence. Wyndham struck at Carletti
with his whip as the carriages passed each other, although he failed to
make contact. It was an embarrassing loss of temper on the part of the
British Crown's representative in the city, made worse by the fact that
Count Carletti was a favourite of the Grand Duke of Tuscany and held
a position in his household.

Wyndham's subsequent conduct of the affair is a model of propri-
ety, possibly because he was fearful of his diplomatic future. Certainly
in a letter explaining the affair to his brother he is quick to offer the
opinion that his conduct 'is not deserving of a recall from Florence'.
He at once appointed no fewer than four seconds who agreed that a
letter of apology to Carletti, to be read by one of them, was in
Wyndham's circumstances the most appropriate course of action.
Carletti refused to listen to the letter being read, insisting that only a
apology in person from Wyndham would suffice. As Wyndham's
seconds would not consent to this a challenge from Carletti became
inevitable. It duly arrived later that day.[3]

Challenges, of course, arose from insults, real or imagined. These
ranged from the grave to the utterly trivial: from the seduction of a
wife or daughter to a trifling argument over dinner. Indeed, there is
an almost infinite variety of reasons for men to argue and the causes
of duels were equally diverse. However, while there were any number
of duels fought for trivial or outlandish reasons, many disputes, and
this applied from country to country across the centuries, were
sparked off by a small and easily predictable set of causes.

Politics were always a fertile breeding ground for disputes, as men in public life set great store by their integrity: the history of political duels is itself a wide-ranging subject. American congressmen have fought duels; even Abraham Lincoln, that pillar of Yankee rectitude, felt obliged, in his younger days in state politics, to defend his honour on the duelling ground. Four British prime ministers are known to have fought a duel, two of them while in office. Irish MPs were enthusiastic duellists: Henry Flood, a prominent member of the Irish Parliament in the late eighteenth century, fought at least one duel. In 1782 a fellow MP, Henry Grattan, launched a vitriolic attack on Flood during a debate.

> 'You can be trusted by no man,' he thundered. 'The people cannot trust you – the minister cannot trust you; you deal out the most impartial treachery to both. You tell the nation that it is ruined by other men, while it is sold by you.'[4]

No eighteenth-century MP could let such a stream of abuse pass unchallenged, although the duel itself was never fought, as the authorities, alerted to the parties' intentions by the publicity given to the spat, prevented it.

French parliamentarians of the *belle époque* were also notorious for their enthusiasm for duelling. Georges Clemenceau, who twice served as Prime Minister of France, is credited with having fought as many as 22 duels. The late nineteenth century was a turbulent period in French politics: administrations formed and reformed with bewildering regularity, the press enjoyed an unprecedented freedom and the Dreyfus affair polarised society. These factors all gave rise to numerous duels, although fatalities were rare.

Politics continued well into the twentieth century to ignite disputes that could be settled only on the duelling ground. In January 1913 Count Stephan Tisza, president of the Hungarian Chamber, and Count Michael Karolyi, one of the most active of the leaders of the opposition, fought a duel at Budapest. The dispute arose from an exchange of insults about the role of Tisza in securing the ejection of the opposition parties from the Hungarian parliament. The duel was to be fought with sabres until one or other of the combatants was completely disabled. These were regarded as severe conditions, reflecting, no doubt, the importance of the political manoeuvring that lay behind the dispute. When the parties met, they fought 32 bouts before Karolyi was put *hors de combat*; Tisza, who was 20 years older, is reputed to have escaped without a scratch.[5]

Nor was the custom confined to the Old World: the political duel travelled and took root far and wide. In Uruguay no less a personage than the president of the republic fought a duel as late as 1922 with Dr Luis de Herrera. De Herrera had recently unsuccessfully contested the presidential election, which had descended into violent mutual recriminations between the two men. Two pistols shots were exchanged at 25 paces, although neither man managed to hit the other, at which point the fight was stopped.[6]

Disagreements arising from gambling were a rich source of duels. For much of duelling's heyday, men were in the habit of gambling heavily. In eighteenth-century England men routinely won and lost huge sums at cards or on the horses. Nor was betting confined to the tables or the racecourse: according to one historian £120,000 – an enormous sum in the 1770s – was wagered on the sex of the androgynous Chevalier d'Eon.[7] In such a milieu accusations of cheating or a failure to pay a debt might easily result in a duel. Indeed, it is an instructive coincidence that gambling debts were often referred to as 'debts of honour', which, while in part a reference to the fact that they were (and still are) unenforceable at law, is also an indication of the seriousness that attached to them. Not to pay one's gambling debts was conduct unbecoming in a gentleman. The duel between Lord George Bentinck and 'Squire' Osbaldeston in 1836 was fought as a result of a gambling debt, albeit one that had arisen in circumstances that gave rise to suspicions of cheating. Casanova acted as second in a duel arising from allegations of cheating in a game of billiards played for a trivial sum.

Crude insult was, of course, also a frequent cause of duels. They ranged from Daniel O'Connell's wittily insulting description of Lord Alvanley quoted above to more standard fare such as the English General Donkin, who, during the course of an argument in 1813 with Admiral Hallowell, said, 'You are a damned scoundrel and an infernal rascal.' In 1734 the duc de Richelieu fought a duel with the Prince de Lixen. The two men were both serving in the French army besieging the Rhineland city of Phillipsburg. One evening they were dining with the Prince de Conde in the French lines. As the evening wore on Lixen began insulting Richelieu, who took particular exception to Lixen's insinuation that he, Richelieu, had bettered himself by marrying into Lixen's family, one of the oldest and grandest in France. Richelieu, who was not a man to let a slight go unavenged, challenged Lixen to a duel. Lixen, as he was bound to do, accepted; they agreed to meet that night. The duel took place in the trenches before the besieged city at midnight. The two men fought with swords; Lixen was killed, run through the body.

Perhaps the most obvious cause of the disputes that caused men to fight duels was the honour of women. An insult to the honour of a woman who was under a man's protection was the equivalent of an insult to the man himself. Certainly, the rape or seduction of a wife, sister or daughter was not something that could be overlooked. One of the most notorious English duels of the Restoration was the fight between the Earl of Shrewsbury and the Duke of Buckingham and their respective seconds in 1668. Samuel Pepys had no doubt as to the cause of the feud and expressed himself trenchantly:

> ... my Lord Shrewsbury is run through the body from the right breast through the shoulder, and Sir J. Talbot all up one of his arms, and Jenkins killed upon the place, and the rest all in a little measure wounded. This will make the world think that the King hath good councillors about him, when the Duke of Buckingham, the greatest man about him, is a fellow of no more sobriety than to fight about a whore.[8]

In *Anna Karenina*, Anna's husband, Alexei Alexandrovich Karenin, having been told by her of her affair with Vronsky, contemplated challenging his wife's lover to a duel. However, he decided, principally because he was frightened (although Tolstoy allows him more honourable motives for not fighting), not to challenge Vronsky after all. Many men in his position, however, both in the Russia of the mid-nineteenth century and in other places and eras, would have elected to fight a duel in the circumstances, rather than face the ignominy of the situation. The risk of death was in every way preferable to the shame.

This point is reiterated in the tragic tale of Sir Richard Atkins, one of the two MPs for the county of Buckinghamshire. Atkins died in November 1696 of wounds sustained in a duel fought, as he put it in his will, 'in ye defence of ye honour of his family' impugned by the 'calamity of a most scandalous wife'. Atkins's will radiates resentment that he was shortly to be compelled to risk his life in a duel entirely as a result of his wife's infidelities.

> Forasmuch as ye barbarous & whorish behaviour of my accursed wife Elizabeth … is like to ingage mee in several quarrills & disputes which in appearance will bring mee to an untimely end in defence of of my honour & reputation (much dearer to mee then [sic] life) I deem itt fitt … to make this following will …[9]

Atkins's fate is a reminder that the obligation to defend the family honour could, through no fault of one's own, have fatal consequences. In many ways it might have been more appropriate had Atkins been able to challenge his wife to a duel – he had no doubt where the blame for his misfortune lay – but, of course, the code of honour would not permit it, however scandalous her behaviour.

The obligation to protect the honour and reputation of women extended on occasion to taking up their disputes for them. Jacques Richepin, a poet and the husband of the well-known Parisian actress Cora Laparcerie, fought a duel in March 1914 with the playwright Pierre Frondaie. Laparcerie was cast in the lead role in Frondaie's latest play for the Paris stage *L'Aphrodite*. While the play was in rehearsal the leading lady and the playwright fell out; the parties agreed to settle their differences on the duelling ground, Richepin taking up his wife's cause on her behalf. In the duel itself, Frondaie was slightly wounded in the forearm.[10]

Likewise in September 1890 Severine (the pseudonym of an early French feminist journalist) wrote a piece in *Gil Blas* that the Boulangist Gabriel Terrail found offensive. Unable under the codes of honour to challenge the feisty Severine, Terrail instead sought satisfaction from her editor, Georges de LaBruyere. In the subsequent duel, de LaBruyere was badly wounded. His chivalry was not, however, universally appreciated: after the fight Severine was taken to task by a fellow feminist for behaving in such a way that a man had to come to her assistance.[11]

Irresponsibly flighty or merely young, naïve girls could, unwittingly, be the cause of serious trouble. Elizabeth Wynne was about 15 when, attending a ball at Ratisbon in February 1795, she observed the following incident.

> The Count de Lerehenfeld … had put it in his head to serve Mary Blair as he does all the others that pay attention to him; he courted her since three or four balls and Mary that is very foolish and him a pretty and agreeable fellow showed him much preference – he would dance with her nearly the whole evening and as Mr de la Roche had engaged for a dance, that she preferred to dance with the Count Lerehenfeld, the two gentlemen had a great quarrel. Mr de la Roche was insolent and by that got all the wrong on his side – it finished very ill as they would fight. Tomorrow we shall know the end of this sad stories [sic] that gives Mary Blair a very bad name all over the town, as she behaved like a real fool.[12]

In an age when a trivial dispute over dancing partners could result in a fatal duel, it was important that everyone be aware of what, potentially, was at stake.

Politics, gambling and sex were three of the more obvious sparks that, superficially, prompted duels to flare up; after all, most duels were caused by accusing someone of dishonesty. The duelling codes that existed to govern the conduct of duels and to guide combatants through the thickets of etiquette evolved a graduation of insults. The German codes of the late nineteenth century, for example (which themselves followed the comte de Chateauvillard's influential French code of 1838), detected three levels of insult. They were the simple slight, the imputation of shameful qualities and, the most serious, a blow to someone's person. The level of the insult offered dictated which party had the choice of weapon, the mode of combat, distance and so on.[13]

Duelling flourished in military circles, too. This was true throughout its life; indeed, there are good grounds for regarding the military as the nursery in which the etiquettes of duelling were nurtured. As we have seen, it was French soldiers who brought the duelling ethos back with them from Italy in the early sixteenth century. Likewise, it was French soldiers who introduced duelling to the Germanic lands during the Thirty Years War a century later. The officers of the British army were enthusiastic duellists who practised their bloody arts the world over. Indeed, it was the alteration to the Queen's Regulations in 1844, in effect banning duelling in the army, that hastened its demise in Britain as a whole. The officers of the Kaiser's army were some of the most punctilious of duellists right up to 1914.

There is an obvious connection between soldiering and duelling. Both Napoleon and the Kaiser, for example, were of the opinion that duelling fostered a martial spirit among their officers, although Napoleon was more ambivalent about its value when experienced officers were killed. One of the best renditions in fiction of the military duelling ethos is in Joseph Conrad's *The Duel*. The novella tells the true story of two officers, d'Hubert and Ferand, of different hussar regiments in Napoleon's army, who fight a series of duels all over the Continent in a 15-year period.[14]

Officers were, generally, sensitive to questions of honour and rank, even if they did not pursue them to quite the relentless extent that Conrad's two fictionalised officers did. Accusations that one had failed in one's duty or any imputation, however mild, of cowardice, were matters that no officer at any time could allow to pass unchallenged. Numerous duels arose from court-martial proceedings.

The other fertile source of military duels was the obligation amounting almost to a sacred duty for an officer to defend the honour of his regiment or his service. This obligation was the cause of many a duel between officers of rival corps, between officers and civilians and between officers of different armies. Horace Walpole reported the story of a falling-out between two Guards officers, Robert Rich and Captain Vane, who were both serving in Flanders in 1742. As the commanding officer was attempting to heal the rift, Rich came up behind Vane and boxed his ears. The officers in question were immediately arrested but the incident left a more lasting difficulty, as Walpole remarked: 'the learned in the laws of honour say they must fight, for no German officer will serve with Vane till he has had satisfaction'.[15]

In 1787 there was a duel between Chevalier La Brosse of the French army and Captain Scott of the British 11th Foot. Scott had called the French officer out for asserting that 'Officers of the English army had more pleghm [sic] than spirit.' The two exchanged pistol shots at close range, five paces, without effect until one of Scott's bullets hit one of La Brosse's coat buttons. At this point, both parties declared honour to be satisfied and the duel was abandoned.[16]

These, then, were the honourable, even laudable, grounds for fighting a duel. Many duels, however, were fought for reasons that were wholly trivial: a passing disagreement, a casual remark or an unintended slight. Duels fought for trivial reasons, especially if one of the combatants was killed, have a dispiriting sense of waste and futility to them, which clings lingeringly through time to the bare facts of the stories.

Perhaps the best known of all the duels fought for utterly trivial reasons was that between Colonel Montgomery and Captain Macnamara, Royal Navy, at Chalk Farm, then outside London, in April 1803. Montgomery and Macnamara were out riding in Hyde Park, each accompanied by a dog. As the two men passed each other, the dogs started to fight; Macnanmara's dog, being perhaps the stronger of the two, began to get the better of the scrap. Montgomery shouted at the dog, 'Come off, or I'll knock your brains out!' Macanamara retorted, 'If you do, I'll knock your brains out!' whereupon 'very high and warm words arose'. In due course, seconds were appointed, a challenge delivered and the conditions of the duel arranged. The parties met at Chalk Farm at seven o'clock that evening, where Montgomery was hit in the chest at the first exchange of shots. He died shortly afterwards. Macnamara was wounded but survived.[17]

Nearly 40 years later a dog's misbehaving in Hyde Park was once more the cause of a duel. Captain Fleetwood was taking his Sunday constitutional in April 1840 when his small dog rushed into the Serpentine. Having splashed around in the water, the dog emerged onto dry land and, as dogs do, shook itself dry. Unfortunately, he was within range of Mr Brocksopp and two women who were walking with him. The women got wet and the gallant Brocksopp lashed out at the dog with his cane. Inevitably, an altercation with the dog's owner ensued, followed by a challenge to a duel. Mercifully, on this occasion the duel, fought on Wimbledon Common, passed off harm-lessly.[18]

For all the myriad causes of duels there is no doubt whatsoever that the history of duelling would be a much less substantial subject were it not for the influence of alcohol. For much of duelling's history, it was customary in the upper echelons of society to drink much more heavily than is now the fashion. This was particularly true of England in the seventeenth, eighteenth and early nineteenth centuries, when gentlemen regularly drank huge quantities of claret and port. Indeed, it is no accident that the decline of duelling in England in the mid-nineteenth century coincided with a more abstemious attitude to drinking.

So many duels traced their origins to moments when tongues were loosened and tempers inflamed by drink that it will become a leitmo-tiv of the entire book. However, the following tale, from Bedfordshire in 1776, is sadly typical.

> Two gentlemen disputing about American politicks, grew warmer and warmer in their argument as the bottle went round, till at last one gave the other the lye; the expression was immediately returned by throwing a bottle half full of wine at the other's head, which grazed his temples; they immediately retired, procured pistols, and fought before they were sober.[19]

The man who had 'given the lie' was badly wounded in the stomach, in those days an injury that was more likely than not to prove fatal. The report concludes, 'if he dies, he will leave a widow and seven young children'. The anonymous English army officer who, in 1757, wrote a conversation piece aimed at belittling duelling and duellists remarked, 'Were men but more cautious how they chuse their inti-mates, and would drink moderately, duelling would soon grow out of fashion.'[20]

The Irish duelling code of 1777 ('the Clonmel Rules') has little to say about the issuing of challenges. It is more concerned with the conduct of the fight itself. Significantly, however, the only article – of 26 – that deals specifically with challenges has this to say: 'Challenges are never to be delivered at night, unless the party to be challenged intends leaving the place of offence before morning; for it is desirable to avoid all hot-headed proceedings.'[21]

Although the fact that the parties might be drunk is tactfully glossed over, it was clearly in the minds of those who drew up the rules. So if a challenge should not be delivered in the heat of the moment, when should it be delivered, by whom, and in what form? The answer to these questions, in common with other aspects of the duel, varied in detail in different times and at different places but, in all essentials, remained much the same.

The earliest expositions of the honour codes, which were written in Renaissance Italy, set out elaborate procedures for issuing a challenge. Early writers on the duel of honour prescribed that a challenge should normally be given in a document. Of this there were three forms: the first two, the *rogito* and the *manifesto* were not common. The *rogito*, certified by a notary and attested by witnesses, was addressed to the general public but directed at a particular individual. The *manifesto* was also a general notification of intent and was sometimes used in cases where one of the parties was of marginal status. The most frequently employed way of challenging someone to a duel was the *cartello*.

The authorities state that the *cartello* should offer a straightforward recital of the facts, in moderate, unabusive language: it should contain the names and origins of the parties, the signatures of three witnesses and be dated. Originally, a *cartello* would be delivered by a herald, although this custom fell into disuse, not least because heralds were on occasion mistreated by those to whom they were delivering the challenge. It became customary either to post the challenge in a public place or to send it to the court frequented by the knight in question.

For the knight thus challenged, the authorities prescribed three options. He could accept it, ignore it or reply by making some objection to it. Acceptance was usually done by sending a *cartello*; if he chose to ignore the challenge, he was bound to fight according to its terms. An objection, if made, could be valid, of doubtful validity or invalid; here, too, there was a complex set of rules and definitions.[22]

These highly formalised rules evolved to govern the duel of honour, which was often sanctioned by the ruler. In *Richard II* the two feuding barons, Bolingbroke and Norfolk, threw down their gages before the King. This was their formal challenge to each other in the face of the King's authority. However, it was the very nature of the modern duel that it was a secretive, illegal and private affair, in contrast to the late medieval or Renaissance duel of honour, which was a public, officially sanctioned encounter conducted under the aegis of the law. The modern duel, at best frowned upon by the authorities and at worse illegal, evolved a less formalised procedure for challenging an opponent to a duel. After all, if, as was often the case from the seventeenth century, the very act of issuing a challenge was punishable under the criminal law, it was hardly prudent to send a herald to an opponent. This was a parallel development to the decline in the use of the *champ clos* – the closed field on which to settle their differences – that was granted to duellists by their monarch.

From the middle of the sixteenth century – by which time the practices of the modern duel were taking root in France and elsewhere – the normal way to issue a challenge was by way of a letter, or cartel. Clearly, as the name suggests, this was akin to the old-fashioned *cartello* but lacked its formality. It was for the seconds to determine the conditions, time and place of the duel; indeed, as the modern duel developed, the seconds were increasingly responsible for the conduct of the entire affair.

The challenge, whether delivered in person, by a second or in a letter, was required to be politely phrased. No doubt, in the heat of the moment, this convention was often ignored. Pelham, the eponymous hero of Edward Bulwer Lytton's vastly popular novel of 1828, becomes, while in Paris, involved in a duel, as second to his old friend Reginald Glanville. Pelham is deputed, in accordance with custom, to carry Glanville's challenge to his adversary, Sir John Tyrrell. Pelham finds Tyrrell in his club and delivers the letter containing the challenge. Sir John drinks 'a large tumblerful of port wine to fortify himself for the task' of reading Glanville's letter. Having set out the causes of the long-running dispute, Glanville concludes, 'It is for me only to … declare you solemnly to be void alike of principle and courage, a villain and a poltroon.' Sir John, no doubt taken aback by the letter, gives Pelham his reply.

Tell your principal that I retort upon him the foul and false words he has uttered against me: that I trample upon his assertions with the same scorn I feel towards himself; and that before this hour tomorrow I will confront him to death as through life.[23]

The fact that challenging someone to a duel was, throughout the history of duelling, very often illegal meant that a degree of caution was necessary in delivering a challenge. Thomas Moore, poet and raconteur, was told a story about his fellow poet Lord Byron, who delivered a challenge to a senior judge, Chief Justice Best, on behalf of a friend who had been insulted by the judge. Best, having heard Byron out, said, 'I confess, my Lord, that I did say _____ was a great rascal, and I now repeat the assertion to your Lordship; but are you aware, Lord Byron, (he added, laughing) of the consequences you expose yourself to, by bringing a challenge to a Chief Justice?' Byron, we are told, 'was soon made to feel the ridicule of the step, and they parted very good friends, leaving _____'s honour to shift for itself'.[24]

Bryon's bravado in delivering a challenge to a judge was, no doubt, an extreme example but those taking challenges to an opponent had to exercise caution. One reason for this was to prevent the authorities uncovering the intention to fight a duel. The history of duelling is riddled with examples of encounters that were, often at the last minute, averted by the arrival of the police at the duelling ground. In some of these cases the suspicion arose that one of the parties, or someone acting on their behalf, had intentionally tipped off the authorities in order to avoid having to fight the duel. The police would then arrive at the duelling ground in the nick of time, halt the proceedings, confiscate the weapons and arrest the combatants. It may have been embarrassing and humiliating for those concerned, but it did have the cardinal virtue of avoiding death or serious injury in a duel.

Covertly alerting the authorities was considered very poor form, tantamount to cowardice, which was why, if attempted, it had to be done in secret. Where it was done by family or friends it was, of course, actuated by the very best of motives, even if entirely contrary to the precepts of the code of honour.

Arranging for the police to interrupt a duel was but one way of

preventing matters taking their course; in cases of duels between officers the authorities were able to invoke military discipline to prevent
duels from taking place. The long-running animus between Rear
Admiral Sir Benjamin Hallowell and Major General Donkin had its
roots in the siege of Tarragona during the Peninsular War. It is an
instructive tale for the light it throws on a number of aspects of the
duelling code. Although it is an example drawn from British military
circles during the Napoleonic wars, the notions it reveals and the
scruples it exposes would have been recognisable to a much wider
constituency of duellists.

The affair began with Admiral Hallowell accusing General Donkin
of inducing the army commander, Sir John Murray, to raise the siege
of Tarragona quite unnecessarily, thereby abandoning the artillery to
the enemy and disgracing the army. Donkin vigorously denied this
and insulted Hallowell, calling him a 'damned scoundrel and a
damned rascal'. A fortnight later Donkin sent Hallowell a challenge to
a duel.

It was a model challenge, formal, polite and to the point, but in
reply the admiral reiterated his refusal to meet Donkin. He claimed
that his accusations were directed against Donkin's public character,
as a soldier, not against him as a private individual. The accusations
were concerned solely with Donkin's role in persuading Murray to
abandon the guns before Tarragona, thereby disgracing the army. It
was not therefore appropriate for him to fight a duel with Donkin
until the official investigation into the affair had been completed.

However, Hallowell assured Donkin that he would eventually get
the opportunity he sought; Hallowell was not intending to deny
Donkin his duel indefinitely. But Donkin was unhappy. It was the
manner of Hallowell's attack on him that riled; furthermore, the
insult had been delivered in public. It was essential for the maintenance of his reputation, even for his ability to command, that he seek
immediate redress. Moreover, Murray had accepted full responsibility
for the decision; it was not Donkin's fault. But the admiral remained
unmoved and there, for the time being, the matter rested.

Eighteen months later, in January 1815, the court-martial proceedings investigating the conduct of the siege of Tarragona were drawing

to a close in Winchester. Hallowell wrote to Donkin suggesting that the moment the court martial was over they retire to a secluded spot to fight their duel. Donkin replied, with perhaps a touch of melodrama,

> You must be aware, that after what has passed, the interview between us must end fatally for one of the two. I therefore beg leave to propose (out of consideration for the three survivors, for you must know that the Law in this Country considers all parties as principals) that our meeting shall take place on the Continent.

Hallowell replied to this by saying that he could not go to the Continent without the Admiralty's permission; to seek that permission would, in the circumstances, inevitably arouse suspicion. They placed the matter, in the approved fashion, in the hands of their seconds, who exchanged letters on 19 and 20 January. On the evening of 20 January Hallowell received a visit from an ADC to the Prince Regent, bearing a letter from the Secretary for War, Lord Bathurst. The letter informed the admiral that if he challenged Donkin, accepted a challenge from him or acted on any previous challenge he 'will incur His highest displeasure'. On 9 February Hallowell was also commanded by the Admiralty to desist from fighting a duel with Donkin. However, for all the fact that the affair did not result in a duel, it is nevertheless of considerable interest.[25]

The distinction that both men drew between their public and their private personae was one of some importance to the duellist. The extent to which a private individual could call an official to account for the conduct of his public business was a matter of debate. There are instances, for example, of lawyers being challenged by a disgruntled litigant for their conduct of a case in court. John Scott, who later became Lord Chancellor as Lord Eldon, was counsel for the successful party in a long-running case in the 1780s. Once all avenues of appeal had been exhausted, Scott was challenged to a duel by the defeated litigant, one Bob Macretti. Scott, refusing the challenge, reported Macretti to the police; he was summonsed, fined £100 and imprisoned for six months.[26]

The Tarragona case illustrates this point well. Hallowell stoutly maintained that the duel would have to wait until a court martial had finished its business; his accusations were concerned solely with Donkin's advice to Murray and not at all with his character as a private individual. Donkin, on the other hand, had been very publicly insulted and in terms that no officer could afford to ignore. Certainly, he could not allow the insults to stand until the official inquiry into the affair had closed; that might (as indeed it did) take many months, during which time his reputation would be tarnished and, possibly, his authority diminished. There is no obvious way in which the two views could have been reconciled; what is certain is that a duel between two very senior officers during active operations against the enemy would have been very bad for morale and discipline. To the extent that Hallowell's stance prevented this from happening, it was the correct one. There was also some precedent, from both the army and the navy, for delaying a duel until after the court martial. This was one of the circumstances in which it was acceptable for an officer to refuse to fight a duel, although it might well prove impossible honourably to defer it indefinitely.

There was also solid precedent for the military authorities intervening to prevent officers fighting duels, particularly, as in this case, where the officers in question were very senior. But the services had an ambivalent attitude towards duelling as a comparison between this case and that of Ensign Cowell quoted earlier, who was cashiered for failing to fight a duel, shows only too clearly. It is also interesting that Donkin felt it necessary to travel to the Continent to fight.

The twist in the tale is Hallowell's insinuation that it was Donkin who, at the time of the Winchester court-martial proceedings, leaked the news of the intended duel to the military authorities. As the whole story is taken from copies of the correspondence made by Hallowell and, moreover, his insinuation is unsupported by any other evidence, it cannot be taken at face value. Yet, if true, it puts a different perspective on Donkin's blustering insistence that the two men settle their differences at once with a duel in Spain.

This section has attempted to explain the central importance of the challenge to the duel. Without a formal challenge, an armed encounter could not properly be called a duel; it was the challenge that set in motion duelling's elaborate protocols. It is a central contention of this book that, for all the variations in practice and theory that duelling evinced at different times and in different places, its essential nature remained the same over the ages, wherever it occurred. The duel was defined by three immutable characteristics: the challenge, the role of the seconds and the conduct of the fight itself. It is now time to turn our attention to the role of the seconds.

Chapter Three

The Role of Seconds

I am confident that there is not one case in fifty where discreet Seconds might not settle the difference, and reconcile the parties before they came to the field.[1]

THIS WAS the opinion of one of the many writers who produced manuals offering advice to those who acted as seconds in duels. It was a commonplace among duellists and opponents of duelling alike that as many if not more men were killed by the irresponsibility or inexperience of their seconds as by any sword or pistol. What a duellist needed was a sound, experienced, reliable second, a man one could rely upon. When Rawdon Crawley, husband of the ghastly, social-climbing Becky in *Vanity Fair*, caught her *in flagrante* with Lord Steyne, a fracas ensued, during which Crawley insulted Steyne before hitting him and throwing Becky's diamond brooch at him, cutting his forehead.[2] After this, a challenge was inevitable, so Rawdon, who was no stranger to this kind of thing, hurried to Knightsbridge Barracks to visit Captain Macmurdo, 'his old friend and comrade'. Macmurdo was just the man to have on one's side in a tight corner, the perfect second.

Macmurdo proved his worth when, a short while later Rawdon and he met Mr Wenham, Lord Steyne's second. When Wenham put an innocent gloss on the 'assignation' between Steyne and Becky, Macmurdo forced Rawdon to forget the challenge. After all, Macmurdo said, 'If my Lord [Steyne], after being thrashed, chooses to sit still, dammy let him.' Macmurdo may have been a fictional character but he embodied the qualities lacking in many real-life seconds. Beyond the pages of a novel, on the all-too-real duelling ground, the shortcomings of seconds often had fatal consequences. One writer, in offering his advice to would-be seconds, was sure that 'most of the shocking Accidents we read of, are often owing to the Ignorance, or Inattention, of the Seconds'.[3]

The duties of a second were most important. They could make the difference between life and death. When James Paull fought Sir Francis Burdett on Putney Heath in 1807, his second, a Mr Cooper, provided an object lesson in how not to behave as a second. At the first fire when Burdett's second, John Ker, was giving the order to shoot, Cooper 'retreated very precipitately behind a tree at some distance'. For the second exchange of shots, when it was Cooper's turn to give the command to fire, he stood so far out of the line of fire that the principals could not see him. Ker, for the purpose of making the signal, had stood 4 yards to one side halfway between the two men. Cooper also refused to sign the statement declaring what had happened, or to say where he lived or to give any information about himself. The objection to Cooper's dereliction of duty was, of course, that he was putting the life of his principal at risk. Hidden behind a tree he would be unable to supervise the duel or to spot any attempts to take an unfair advantage.[4]

The origins of seconds are obscure; it is probable that they derived from the squire of medieval chivalry. The squire would accompany his master, the knight, to tournaments, helping him to don his armour, to mount his horse and so on. Once the modern duel had begun to develop as an illegal affair, conducted in secret in wooded glades or on sandy heaths, the duellist's need to have a reliable supporter to safeguard his interests was obvious. In the beginning, the seconds normally took part in the duel, fighting the other man's second. Where there was more than one second on each side they would all fight; in these circumstances the duel would become a free-for-all. In sixteenth- and early seventeenth-century French duels, the seconds fought – indeed, sometimes they were killed; in de Bouteville's duel all four seconds joined in. In the duel between Lord Shrewsbury and the Duke of Buckingham (see p. 38) in 1668, each man had two seconds, all of whom fought and one of whom was killed. In the duels fought in the pages of Alexandre Dumas's novels, the seconds always join in.

By the time the modern duel had grown to its maturity, seconds had mutated from active participants into an amalgam of umpire, cornerman and mediator. Once an argument had blown up, it was normal, if a duel was in the offing, to invite one's adversary to name a second, to whom a letter could be sent, and to appoint one's own second. From this point onwards, the conduct of the duel was in the hands of the seconds; in a properly conducted affair, the principals remained in the background until they met on the duelling ground. The American duelling code of 1838 is strict on this point. Indeed, it is adamant that the second must have absolute control over the conduct of the affair. In the dispute between Count Carletti and William Wyndham discussed earlier, Wyndham appoints four seconds to conduct his dispute with the count. He tells his brother that he 'agreed to abide entirely by their counsel, and should consider myself no longer but an Instrument in their hands'.

The authors who wrote manuals offering guidance to seconds in duels were agreed that their most important duty was to seek a reconciliation between the parties. Abraham Bosquett wrote 'A Treatise on Duelling' in 1818; by way of introduction he states, slightly boastfully perhaps, his qualifications: 'I have myself been four times a Principal, and twenty-five times a Second.[5] With all that experience under his belt Bosquett had no doubt that the 'Duty of the Second [was] to interfere and accomodate'.[6] Similarly, the anonymous army officer who wrote the *General Rules and Instructions for all Seconds in Duels* in 1793 thought that the second's main responsibility was to seek a reconciliation: '[H]e is to try, and even rack his Invention, for any new and reasonable Light that can be thrown upon it; in order to reconcile the Party aggrieved.'[7]

John Wilson Lyde, the author of the American code, would have agreed, although he put it differently:

> Use your utmost efforts to allay all excitement which your principal may labor under; search diligently into the origin of the misunderstanding; for gentlemen seldom insult each other, unless they labor under some misapprehension or mistake; and when you have discovered the original ground of error, follow each movement to the time of sending the note, and harmony will be restored.[8]

The duty imposed on seconds to resolve disputes began with their appointment and continued until the duel was over. In 1891 Ferreus published his *Annuaire de Duel: 1880–89*, a duellist's *Wisden*. While all statistics about duelling should be treated with great caution, their very rarity makes them worthy of consideration. Among the statistics in the *Annuaire* are figures that cast some light on the success or otherwise of seconds in preventing duels. Ferreus analysed all the duels reported in the Paris newspapers during the decade and categorised them by the weapons used, noting if one of the principals had been killed. We can also see from the figures how successful seconds were in resolving disputes. In 1880, for example, Ferreus noted 40 occasions on which seconds were appointed following a dispute. Of those the seconds managed to avert a duel on only nine occasions. In 1885, Parisian seconds were less successful in averting duels: in the 61 disputes noted by Ferreus, 50 ended in a duel. In 1889, 62 disputes resulted in 42 duels; seconds had greater success in reconciling their principals in that year.[9]

While it is difficult to know the extent to which one can rely on these statistics, they do suggest that seconds managed to terminate the affair without recourse to a duel in somewhere between a third and a sixth of cases. Ferreus's research was, of course, limited to Paris in the 1880s, when duels were common but rarely resulted in fatalities; in 1885, for example only one duellist was killed in the 50 duels fought in that year. The low chance of a duellist being killed in a duel in France at this time may, of course, have resulted in fewer disputes being settled without recourse of arms, making the seconds' job more difficult.

Similarly, we have many fewer examples of those disputes that were settled before the duel could be fought than we have of duels themselves. This is partly because the fact of two men's having an argument that is resolved before they can fight a duel is notably less newsworthy than the dispute that results in an exchange of shots. In 1924 Raymond Poincare, then Prime Minister of France, was addressing the National Assembly; while he was speaking another member, Monsieur le Provost de Launey, began to barrack him, making unflattering remarks. Poincare took offence and the moment that he left the chamber sent his seconds to de Launey demanding an explanation. De Launey explained his remarks and the matter was amicably settled; the tact of the seconds had averted what could have been a embarrassing and needless duel. One of Poincare's seconds in this episode was, incidentally, the Minister of War, André Maginot, whose work in defending Poincare's reputation was evidently rather more effective than his eponymous line was at defending France in 1940.[10]

In March 1923 *The Times* reported that 'A meeting of composers, impresarios, agents and lyrical artists was held in Rome yesterday in order to study means of furthering Italian music and musical interests, particularly abroad.' The piece concluded, with more than a dash of understatement, that the proceedings were 'rather stormy'. Indeed they were: a row erupted between two delegates, Signori Mascagni and Mocchi, which ended in fisticuffs. Signor Mascagni promptly challenged his assailant to a duel and seconds were appointed. The seconds evidently had calmer heads than their principals, for the following day it was agreed that there was no reason for the two men to fight a duel.[11]

Equally, there were few enough prosecutions of men who fought duels; prosecutions of duellists *manqué* were rarer still, despite the fact that sending challenges was in many countries against the law. In 1831 a London man, Ambrose Poynter, was charged with 'unlawfully and maliciously writing and publishing a certain letter addressed to J. Coverdale Esq., Gray's Inn London, with intent to stir up and provoke the said John Coverdale to fight a Duel with and against him, the said Ambrose Poynter'.[12]

Poynter was arrested and brought before the magistrates, but his case is rare. James Kelly, in his history of duelling in Ireland, produces some rather inconclusive statistics on the number of duels in which seconds intervened. Kelly's figures seem to show that it was rare for seconds to intervene, although his statistics appear to cover only those instances where the parties were reconciled on the duelling ground, rather than at some earlier point in the affair.[13]

Sometimes seconds had a more formal method available to them of achieving a settlement between the parties: the honour courts. The honour courts existed to adjudicate, as the name suggests, on questions of honour that might otherwise be decided on the duelling ground. They existed in various forms in many countries during the life of duelling. The Bourbon kings of France established them in the seventeenth century in order to stem the bloody tide of duels, as did the Hohenzollerns of Prussia. They were regularly constituted in Republican France in the nineteenth century to resolve – or attempt to resolve – the numerous disputes that arose, particularly between politicians and journalists. The idea of the honour court survived into the twentieth century.

In Portugal the government declared duelling illegal in 1911, establishing a court of honour to settle disputes that might previously have resulted in a duel. The court was to have powers to fine, imprison or even to send into exile those brought before it. Men who decided to ignore the court of honour and fight a duel would be prosecuted under the criminal code.[14] A few years later in Uruguay a bill was approved by the Chamber of Deputies suppressing the existing penalties for duelling in cases where the seconds have submitted to an honour court the question of whether an offence justifying a duel had taken place.[15]

As an example of the workings of a court of honour, there is the case of the spat between a French journalist, M. Tery, and a playwright, M. Bernstein, from 1911. Tery considered himself insulted by a letter from Bernstein and challenged him to a duel. The seconds to the two men referred the dispute to a specially constituted court of honour, established to consider the question whether Bernstein was a person qualified to give satisfaction in an affair of honour. In other words, there was some doubt whether he should be allowed to fight a duel or, indeed, whether Tery would be acting properly in fighting him. These doubts arose from Bernstein's conduct in 1898, when, having been challenged to a duel, he had behaved in a way giving rise to suspicions of cowardice. He was also alleged to have deserted from the army. The court considered these questions, holding that Bernstein was not debarred from giving satisfaction because since 1898 he had fought five duels without any objections on the part of his opponents. It also decided that he had made his peace with the military authorities. The court having ruled on these thorny matters of honour, the duel could be fought without loss of face to either party. Neither of the gallant pair was injured in the subsequent duel.[16]

The duty placed on the seconds to strain every nerve to find a solution did not cease when the parties arrived at the duelling ground. Many a duel was averted at the last minute by the intervention of the seconds. In 1842 Abraham Lincoln became embroiled in a dispute with the state auditor, Mr Shields, about the collapse of the State Bank of Illinois. Shields was a peppery individual who demanded an apology of Lincoln for ridiculing him in the press, but the future President refused to apologise and a duel was agreed upon. Lincoln chose broadswords and the parties agreed to meet on an island in the Mississippi, between Illinois and Missouri, since duelling was illegal in Illinois. On the morning of 22 September Lincoln and his second crossed the river to the duelling ground and prepared to fight. Just as the duel was about to begin, the seconds and other friends in common intervened to stop the fight. Shields and Lincoln were induced to settle their differences peacefully; having done so, they shook hands and returned across the river to Illinois.[17]

If the seconds failed to prevent the parties from starting the duel, they were nevertheless still obliged to do everything within their power to bring it to an early and honourable conclusion, preferably before either party could be injured. Any number of accounts of duels end with the formula 'after the first exchange of shots the seconds intervened and the duel was terminated'. In August 1778 the 'Fighting Parson', the Revd. Henry Bate Dudley, fought a duel with Mr De Morande in Hyde Park. The seconds intervened, unsuccessfully, after each party had fired two shots; after the fourth exchange of fire the seconds once more interposed themselves, again unsuccessfully. It was only by threatening to retire as seconds that they managed to prevent the two men firing at each other for the fifth time. Having stopped the shooting the seconds were then able to impose a settlement on the parties.[18] While many duellists were less belligerently obstinate than Bate Dudley and De Morande, nevertheless many seconds can justly claim to have prevented bloodshed (or greater bloodshed) by their prompt intervention.

Competent seconds strove at all costs to avoid the type of duel fought between Mr Munro of the 16th Dragoons and Mr Green at Battersea Fields in 1783. Armed with pistols, they agreed to fight at a distance of 6 yards. They exchanged six shots, the last of which hit Green, who was thereupon asked if he was satisfied. He declared he was not, unless Mr Munro made him a public apology. Munro replied, 'That, now, I will not do.' Whereupon Green rejoined, 'Then one of us must fall.' The two men took up their positions once more and each fired two more shots. Munro was hit in the knee and Green took a shot in the groin, which proved fatal. The available accounts of this sad episode do not say whether seconds were present or not. If they were, they conspicuously failed to do their duty by their principals. If the two men had fought without seconds, their duel stands as a fine example of the type of excess that the presence of seconds could avoid.[19]

A similar situation confronted the seconds in a duel fought between Messrs Barrow and Hogan at Grenville, Jersey in the 1780s. It had been agreed that the parties would exchange six shots. After each man had fired three shots, Barrow's second tried to reconcile them but, failing to do so, departed the scene, leaving Hogan's second 'in charge'. The duel continued and, at the sixth shot, Hogan was killed, shot in the heart. The man left to supervise the fight was, clearly, not equal to the task, as, by the time the last and fatal shot was fired, the two men had encroached to such an extent that they were a mere four paces apart. We cannot say that Hogan would have survived had his opponent's second remained on the ground but his presence might have ensured that the duellists kept their distance. That said, Barrow's second, having tried but failed to bring the duel to a peaceful if not amicable conclusion, no doubt felt himself justified in abdicating his responsibilities.[20]

Seconds were supposed to make every effort to mediate between the parties, to prevent the duel or at least to mitigate its effects. There were all too frequent occasions when they did the exact opposite. Officers of the Austro-Hungarian army in the years before World War One were bound by a strictly observed code of honour. In the early months of 1914 Lieutenant Hadju, attached to the Military Flying Corps, and his brother-in-law, one Babocsay, a civilian, had a falling-out. It was caused by some remarks that Babocsay had made about Hadju to his wife (who was Hadju's sister). These remarks had come to Hadju's notice but, not wishing to challenge Babocsay, he chose to ignore them. However, worried about the inflexible attitudes of the military authorities to matters reflecting an officer's honour, Hadju brought the affair to the attention of his commanding officer. He insisted that a duel was the only course open to Hadju in the circumstances; two officers were appointed to act as his seconds. On hearing of this decision, Babocsay offered to make a full apology on the basis that it was purely a family matter but Hadju's seconds refused to accept the tendered apology, insisting on a duel.

The seconds agreed severe conditions for the duel: pistols at 50 paces and then the duel to be continued with cavalry sabres. Babocsay made further attempts to have the duel abandoned, but Hadju's seconds merely told him that he must fight or risk being considered a coward. The duel eventually took place in the military riding school in Budapest. At the second exchange of shots (the first having missed), a visibly nervous Babocsay shot Hadju in the chest. Hit in the lung, Hadju died on the way to hospital.[21] This family tragedy was caused wholly by the intransigence of Hadju's seconds, who were concerned only with upholding the honour of their caste, with terrible results. The military authorities, however, denied, contrary to Babocsay's story, that pressure had been applied to Hadju to force him to fight a duel.[22]

Although a second's most important duty was to reconcile the parties to prevent a duel from taking place – or from continuing beyond the point at which honour was satisfied – he had other duties that could have an equally critical bearing on the outcome of the encounter, both before the parties met and on the duelling ground itself. These can be collectively described as the duty to ensure a fair and honourable fight. The ideal was absolute scrupulousness in the conduct of the duel. John Ker, whom we met earlier, is a fine example of this honourable impartiality, in marked contrast to the antics of Cooper, James Paull's second. In the statement that he released to the newspapers about the encounter, Ker wrote,

> I should observe, that while they were waiting for the signal, I observed that sir [sic] Francis held his arm raised, and his pistol pointed towards Mr Paull. Knowing that this was not with the view of taking any unfair advantage, but the effect of accident, I said, 'Burdett, don't take aim; I am sure you are not doing so, drop your arm, as you see Mr Paull has his pistol pointed downwards.' Mr Paull then asked me why I advised Sir Francis not to take aim? I said, anyone might see that I could only mean for him not to take aim, or prepare to do so, before the signal, and from desire to see that they were upon equal terms.[23]

There is, in fact, rather more to this account than meets the eye: Ker was not acting solely from a refined sense of fair play. He would also have had in mind that, should Paull have been killed, the fact that Burdett appeared to have been taking aim before the signal to fire was given might have been interpreted as foul play. Ker would have known perfectly well that any suspicion of an unfair advantage could prove highly prejudicial to Burdett's defence – and, for that matter, to Ker's own – should they face trial. Equally, making the incident public once the duel had passed off harmlessly burnished the reputation of both Burdett and Ker as men of honour.

Once the seconds had failed to reconcile the parties, it fell to them to decide the conditions of the duel: to agree upon the time and place of the encounter, the weapons to be used and the duration of the fight. If pistols were to be used, the seconds would have to decide the all-important question of distance. They were often also responsible for procuring suitable weapons and making sure that a suitably qualified surgeon was present.

Folklore has it that duels were fought at dawn in wooded glades or on sandy heaths. There is more than a hint of truth in the stereotype: duels *were* fought in out-of-the-way places, because secrecy was essential. For the most part duelling was illegal, wherever and whenever it occurred; retiring to a secluded spot at dawn was the best way of avoiding the authorities.

Most capital cities had a spot favoured by duellists: in Dublin, Phoenix Park was long popular; in Berlin, the Grunewald and the Tegeler Forest were fashionable; in Washington, disaffected Congressmen crossed into Maryland to settle their differences at Bladensburg; in Paris, the Bois de Boulogne provided cover for any number of duels. What all these places combined was seclusion and accessibility: no duellist wanted a lengthy journey before his ordeal; equally, no duellist wanted to invite intervention by the authorities before matters could be settled. In that respect de Bouteville and his consorts were the exception that proved the rule: they deliberately fought in the Place Royale in broad daylight in order to flaunt their defiance of the King's authority. Another factor to consider in the choice of duelling ground was the need to avoid the legal consequences of duelling. This could necessitate leaving the jurisdiction to fight. Thus Englishmen would cross the Channel to fight on the sands at Calais, Frenchmen would travel to Belgium, Irishmen sail to England and Americans leave their own state to fight in a neighbouring one.

The traditional time to fight a duel was early in the morning. Once again the reason for this was, in part, to help the duellists avoid discovery, but it probably has less bearing on the truth than the tradition of fighting in secluded spots. Duels were, in fact, fought at many different times of the day. The poet Alexander Pushkin's duel with Georges d'Anthes was fought late on a northern January afternoon, not long before dusk. Two Englishmen, Oliver Clayton and Richard Lambrecht, fought each other in Battersea Fields while it was still dark at 6.30 on a January morning in 1830. Indeed, it was so dark that neither man could see the other; marksmanship was purely a question of chance. Clayton was the unlucky one: he was hit in the chest and died. Adolphe Tavernier, the author of a French duelling manual published in the 1880s, positively recommended that duellists should avoid fighting in the early morning, as it was likely to result in their passing an uncomfortable and restless night.[24]

Whatever the time of day at which duels were fought, it was incumbent upon seconds to prevent duellists from taking the field while still in their cups. If a quarrel had arisen during the course of a night's drinking – which, all too often, it did – they should make every effort to postpone the duel itself until morning. One authority found it particularly shocking that seconds should permit drunken duellists to fight. It was both unseemly and potentially lethal when adversaries 'in the most indecent and disorderly State, stagger from the Bottle to the Field'.[25] If it was important that men avoid drunken challenges, it was doubly so that they avoid drunken duels.

There are many stories of disastrous drunken duels; this one from Ireland in 1784 is typical. A Mr Butler, of Co. Kilkenny, and a Captain Bunbury fell out and agreed to settle their differences with pistols. The two men went with their seconds to a tavern, where, 'after ordering supper, and a bottle of hock (as a blind to the people of the house) they began the combat'. Bunbury was hit in the mouth by a ricocheting shot; Butler, less fortunate, was hit in the side and died instantly. The coroner, having examined the case, returned a verdict of murder, prompted by the fact that both men were drunk.[26] This tale also illustrates the point that the law was less likely to look favourably on drunken duellists and the seconds who permitted drunks to fight duels.

The question of the choice of weapons to be used in a duel is more difficult. It is popularly supposed that the man challenged had the choice of weapons. As will be seen later, this was by no means always the case. Indeed, as the challenged party, having given the insult, was often in the wrong, the dictates of equity suggest the reverse might be fairer.

As to the type of weapon that would be used, that was both a matter of local custom and for negotiation between the seconds. For the earliest of the modern duellists, the rapier (often used in conjunction with a dagger) was the weapon of choice; by the mid-seventeenth century, it had been replaced by the more convenient short sword. In England, the duelling pistol all but dominated the scene from the middle of the eighteenth century; by the early years of the nineteenth, it had attained a high state of technical, and aesthetic, development. In *belle époque* France, the foil was the duellists' favoured weapon; at the same time in Italy, however, the vast majority of duels were fought with the small sword (*sciabola*). Similarly in the wilder parts of frontier America, knives, rifles and sporting guns were commonly used. In Virginia, which in the 1820s was hardly frontier territory, even muskets loaded with buckshot are known to have been used.

None of this prevented seconds agreeing to more eccentric weapons, of which the Frenchmen who fought with billiard balls in 1843 is merely one example. Lenfant and Melfont, two inhabitants of the town of Maisonfort, quarrelled over a game of billiards. They drew lots to determine who would be the first to throw the red ball at his opponent's head. Melfont won and, such was the power and accuracy of his throw that the ball hit Lenfant's forehead and killed him outright.[27]

Nineteenth-century France also gives us an altogether more picturesque, eccentric duel, harping back to the high days of medieval chivalry. Under the heading 'Singular Duel', the *Annual Register* tells the following tale of archaic derring-do. It dates from 1826, more than 10 years after the Battle of Waterloo, and a generation after the demise of the *ancien régime*.

> A duel between the marquis Livron and M. du Trone took place at twelve o'clock, in the forest of Senart, very near the chateau of Madame de Cayla. The whole affair had the appearance of an act of madmen, and resembled more a tournament than a modern duel. Du Trone, the young advocate, was habited in the costume of a Greek chief; each was mounted on horseback, and had three seconds. The parties were armed with sabres, and, at the onset, Livron was dismounted by the concussion of the horses. Both were slightly wounded, and the seconds thought it proper to interfere. What adds to the singularity of this duel is, that it took place in the presence of 150 spectators.'[28]

Another account of this strange duel concluded, not surprisingly, that 'This affair will form the subject of the gossips of Paris for weeks to come.'

If the duel fought out in a glade of a French forest recalled the gallantries of medieval chivalry, the fight between two French prisoners of war detained in the hulk *Samson* in the Thames estuary was redolent of the worst excesses of medieval barbarism. Having no swords, the prisoners decided to settle their differences with weapons made by lashing a pair of scissors to the end of a stick. Thus armed, they hacked away at each other until one was too seriously wounded to continue the fight. He had been slashed across the stomach so badly that his guts were hanging out.[29]

An important part of the second's duties in agreeing to the choice of weapon was to make sure that his man would not be fighting at an undue disadvantage. It was difficult to ensure that every duellist was an equally accomplished fencer or accurate shot. There were nevertheless precautions that prudent seconds could take. In 1843 the Hon. William Wellesley was challenged to a duel by Count Hummell, a Belgian, who, being the challenger, had the choice of weapons. He chose swords, which threatened to place Wellesley at a serious disadvantage. At this point his second stepped in:

> on the part of Mr Wellesley it was urged that, not only was he unaccustomed to that weapon, but that an injury to the elbow of his right arm disabled him from fighting with a sword, and he produced a certificate to that effect from M. Cloquet, the eminent surgeon.[30]

They duly fought with pistols.

The second's most important duty was to make a concerted effort to reconcile the parties so that a duel could, within the dictates of the codes of honour, be avoided. If, having failed to bring about a settlement, the duel was to go ahead, urgent duties awaited him on the duelling ground. By now the time and place of meeting had been specified, the weapons chosen, the terms agreed; the final preparations, writing letters to loved ones and making a will, were complete. The second usually travelled to the duelling ground with his principal, not unlike a macabre version of the bridegroom and the best man at a wedding.

Once at the duelling ground, whether it was Hyde Park, the Bois de Boulogne or some more exotic location, the second had much to do. He was there to see a fair fight but also to safeguard the interests of his man (potentially, as we shall see, conflicting duties), to sniff out chicanery and prevent foul play. One writer on duelling recommended that the seconds should aspire 'not only to give to their Friends every honourable Chance of Escape, but also every Latitude for displaying the high Spirit and Generosity of Gentlemen'.

The most important duties of the second before the duel took place were, in the case of a pistol duel, measuring the ground – that is, pacing out the agreed distance between the duellists – and loading the guns. In the case of a sword duel, it was vital to ensure that the swords were of equal length and type. In both cases it was the responsibility of the seconds to see that neither man had a disadvantage on account of the ground – for example, that one duellist was not facing the low sun or did not have loose ground underfoot.

To sample the atmosphere of a duel, its fear and its aggression, its formality and its brutality, let us turn to a second's eyewitness account. It also throws light on the second's role once the parties had arrived at the duelling ground. The man in question was called Moloney; he was an officer in the 5th Dragoon Guards, who had agreed to act as second for Lieutenant Crowther, of the 1st Regiment of Foot. Crowther had had a long-running and complicated dispute with Captain Helsham, which had finally resolved itself into a duel. They had agreed to meet at 11 o'clock on the morning of 1 April 1829, near Napoleon's monument to the Grande Armée on the downs outside Boulogne. It was to be no April Fool.

Shortly before 11 o'clock Moloney and Crowther arrived unaccompanied at the agreed spot, near the tall column. There was no sign of anybody else. Fifteen minutes later, Helsham and his second, Mr O'Grady, rode into view. They were accompanied by a dozen or so other people mounted and on foot. Moloney at once objected to the presence of these spectators; Helsham, who had been spoiling for a fight throughout, told him that he wished them to be present and that they themselves wanted to attend. The seconds then began to prepare for the duel. At this point Moloney takes up the story.

While we were making these arrangements, the prisoner [Helsham] interfered. He would be present, and listened to everything that passed between Mr O'Grady and me. I objected to that several times. Captain Helsham was in the ditch with us when we were loading the pistols, and I observed to him, that it was a very unusual thing for principals to be present when the seconds were loading the pistols, and said, it was contrary to all duelling usage. He said, he did not care a d___n for the usage; he would see the pistols loaded himself ... Mr Grady [sic] and myself arranged about the ground on which the parties were to fire. The distance agreed upon was twelve paces ... The parties were to stand with their pistols even down by their sides, until Mr Grady pronounced the words 'Now, gentlemen'; and those words being pronounced they were to raise their arms, and fire as near together as possible, and no second aim to be taken. The ground had been previously measured, I think, by Mr Grady. He took spring steps as long as he could. When captain [sic] Helsham talked about the rules of duelling, from the rudeness of his manner, I asked him if he wished to quarrel with me. Lieut. Crowther did not at all interfere with the arrangements, but stood at a distance. I then beckoned him to come up, and told him the arrangements ...

Up to this point Moloney's account is very clear as to the second's responsibilities. He objected to the spectators because a duel was supposed to be a private affair and, also, because, it being illegal, the fewer witnesses there were the better. He made sure that the pistols were both properly loaded; loading one but not the other was a stroke that unscrupulous seconds were known to pull. He saw that the ground was paced out, noting with approval that his opposite number erred on the side of generosity in marking the distance. Captain Helsham had interfered, bullyingly, while his adversary, Crowther, had remained calmly aloof from the preliminaries. Moloney noted that he came close to having his own spat with Helsham. Falling foul of the other side was an occasional occupational hazard for seconds. Sometimes it resulted in a separate duel. But now matters were in deadly earnest; the moment of reckoning was fast approaching. Moloney's account continues.

The parties were then placed. Mr Grady pronounced the signal loud enough for both to hear. Lieut. Crowther immediately raised his arm with rather a quick motion, fired, and then lowered his arm. Captain Helsham did not fire till some time after. Not hearing the report of his pistol immediately after that of Lieut. Crowther, I looked about, and I observed captain Helsham's pistol, pointed towards his opponent in a position that, had he fired, the ball would have fallen short, his arm not being fully raised. He leaned his head to the right to get a good view of Mr Crowther, raised his arm gradually, and did not fire for some seconds, until he had fairly covered his man, that is, till he had got his pistol in a direction to Mr Crowther, and was looking along it. He appeared to take a deliberate aim. He fired and Mr Crowther fell ... I should think it was five seconds after lieut. [*sic*] Crowther's fire before it was returned by the prisoner.

The hapless Crowther died shortly afterwards. Helsham was later tried at the Old Bailey for his murder; Moloney's account of the duel given in evidence was one of the main planks of the prosecution's case. In an important exchange Moloney was asked by Helsham's counsel, presumably in cross-examination, why he had not intervened when he saw Helsham taking deliberate aim. He replied, 'I did not like to start objections that could be tortured into a confirmation of that charge [of cowardice].'

During the course of his summing-up to the jury the judge said, 'If parties went out to fight a duel, and death was the result of that meeting, the surviving parties in the transaction were equally guilty of the crime of murder.' Despite this unequivocal statement of the law, the jury returned a verdict of not guilty against Helsham.[31] The jury's verdict was all too typical: even when faced with strong evidence of foul play – as here – and uncompromising directions on the law from the bench, they were reluctant to convict.

But let us now look at Moloney's answer to the question asked of him by Helsham's counsel, for it neatly encapsulates the difficulty that a second faced. He had on the one hand to see fair play; in other words to act in the manner of an umpire: checking the loading of the pistols, ensuring that the distance was correctly measured and the positioning of the duellists was fair to both. But, on the other hand, he had a specific duty to his principal; he was, after all, his second, his support in a moment of supreme crisis. Originally, as we saw in de Bouteville's case, the seconds even joined in the fight with their principals. The resolution of this conflict of duty – the duty to the protocol, to the institution of the duel, as against the duty to the principal – could be, as in this case it was, a matter of life and death. Moloney had, by his own account, two or three seconds to decide what to do. By failing to prevent Helsham taking a deliberate aim he chose the path of honour and reputation, a decision for which Crowther paid with his life.

As Moloney's account makes clear a second had well-defined duties once the parties had arrived on the duelling ground. The anonymous officer who wrote his *General Rules and Instructions for all Seconds in Duels* devoted a section to the duties of the second 'in the Field'. These comprised: the proper choice of ground, loading in each other's presence and determining the distance. He was firmly convinced that 10 yards should be the closest allowed, to be well marked to prevent encroachment.[32] Another English writer on duelling tells us that the duelling distance should always be called in *yards*; he sternly reminds us they are only 'vulgarly but incorrectly called paces'.[33]

Moloney emphasised the importance of the need to oversee the loading of the pistols. Moloney, in giving his evidence, leaves no room for doubt that he supervised closely the loading of the pistols on the duelling ground. It was essential for two reasons. One, to ensure that both guns were properly loaded so that the duellists faced each other on equal terms and, two, to give the seconds the opportunity to check that the guns were within the customary rules. The most common infringement of the accepted rules was for a duellist to use a pistol with a rifled barrel. Rifling gave the duellist a much greater degree of accuracy, thus conferring an advantage over an opponent using a conventional smooth-bored duelling pistol. The Clonmel Rules of 1777 are explicit on the subject:

> Rule 18. The seconds load in presence of each other, unless they give their mutual honors that they have charged smooth and single, which may be held sufficient.[34]

In extreme cases seconds could conspire with each other to ensure that their principals came to no harm. This might be an act of mercy if the duellists were particularly young, inexperienced or foolish. William Hickey in his gossipy memoirs recounts a story of two East India Company cadets who fell out over gambling debts while sailing to India on board the *Hampshire*. When the ship stopped at the Cape, the two young bravoes decided to settle their differences in a duel. However, the duel was reduced to a farce by the fact that the seconds agreed, unbeknown to two cadets, not to load the pistols with ball. The youths faced up to each other; they both fired and one collapsed to the ground, felled, as it transpired, by fear alone.[35]

Another way in which a second could protect his principal from his own belligerent instincts was to collude with the police. As we have seen, this was not considered a legitimate ruse in the best duelling circles but it nevertheless had its advocates. One example will suffice. In 1908 two Russians, M. Markoff and M. Pergament, agreed to fight a duel to settle an argument that had arisen in the Duma. The parties, along with their seconds and accompanied by some reporters, had taken up their positions in a suburban garden. They were about to fire when the police arrived to prevent the duel. 'Ill-natured people', the report says, alleged that the police were not unexpected. Two shots fired by the seconds, supposedly to test the guns, were in fact the signal for the police to intervene.[36]

In 1828 M. Fougère published *L'Art de ne jamais être tue ni blesse en duel sans avoir pris acune leçon d'armes* (The art of never being killed or injured in a duel without taking lessons in self-defence); it is, partly, a parody of the duelling manuals that were so popular at the time but does also, beneath the humour, have something to offer the student of duelling. The author's object was to help his readers avoid duelling altogether, thus guaranteeing the certainty of avoiding death or injury. Fougère set out his advice in 10 lessons. The first step to avoiding a duel, he recommended, is to acquire a reputation for bravery; this will prevent people from challenging you. If you are a military man 'take a cannon, a redoubt, an enemy general'; if you are a civilian, 'perform heroics in a fire'. Failing that, the gist of his advice is that one should do everything one can to avoid causing offence. He suggested behaving in a manner that is 'sweet, polite, considerate and affable to everyone'. If, despite these and other precautions, one is

nevertheless faced with having to fight, Fougère recommends select-
ing good seconds who can extricate one from a tight corner. One
could also try a thoroughly modern-sounding remedy: lunch. Many a
dispute, Fougère maintained, has been settled over a good lunch.
Finally, if all else fails, Fougère has one more ploy up his sleeve. 'We
may think that the age of magic bullets has passed beyond recall but
we are mistaken.' He suggested making imitation bullets, doctoring
them to look like the real thing; one made of cork should do the
trick.[37]

While the second's lot carried with it onerous responsibilities, it
was also, occasionally, not without its dangers. Leaving aside the
dangers inherent when seconds joined in with their principals,
there were other hazards to be faced. Perhaps one of the most
obvious, particularly where a pistol duel was fought with the duellists walking away from each other before turning to fire, was the
risk of being hit by a bullet. Although a second would position
himself out of the straight line of fire, a shot 'on the turn' could
easily be misdirected and place the second in danger. In 1929 a
Mexican man, Miguel Martinez, agreed to supervise a duel between
two friends. They were to fight with pistols at 20 paces; both bullets
hit the unfortunate Martinez in the chest. He died and the duellists
fled.[38]

Few people have written more amusingly about duelling than
Mark Twain. In A Tramp Abroad he recounts the experience of taking
part as second in a duel in France in the 1870s. The duel was fought
between two leading French politicians, Leon-Michel Gambetta and
Marie François Fourtou; it arose from political differences. Twain's
account of the subsequent duel – he was Gambetta's second – and the
formalities preceding it is a masterpiece of melodramatic humour,
largely at the expense of the puffed-up, mock-heroic duellists.

> I now returned to my principal, and was distressed to observe that he had
> lost a good deal of his spirit. I tried my best to hearten him. I said,
> 'Indeed, sir, things are not as bad as they seem. Considering the charac-
> ter of the weapons, the limited number of shots allowed, the generous
> distance, the impenetrable solidity of the fog, and the added fact that one

of the combatants is one-eyed and the other cross-eyed and near-sighted, it seems to me that this conflict need not necessarily be fatal. There are chances that both of you may survive. Therefore, cheer up; do not be down-hearted.

This rallying cry echoing in his ears, Gambetta took up his stance, pistol in hand, with Twain behind him, literally stiffening his backbone. Then,

> I immediately shouted, –
>   One, – two, – three, – *fire!*'
>   Two little sounds like *spit! spit!* broke upon my ear, and in the same instant I was crushed to the earth under a mountain of flesh. Bruised as I was, I was still able to catch a faint accent from above, to this effect, –
>   'I die for ... for ... perdition take it, what is it I die for? ... oh, yes, – FRANCE! I die that France may live!'

It transpired that Gambetta had survived his ordeal completely unharmed, as had his opponent. Indeed, the only person who had sustained injury, including a broken rib that had penetrated his lung, was Twain himself, crushed by the falling bulk of Gambetta.[39]

Before leaving the subject of seconds, we must look briefly at the thorny question of duels fought without them. As it might be asked how an encounter fought without seconds can properly be considered a duel. The answer lies in the fact that such secondless duels are the exceptions that prove the rule; that they were as unusual as they seem to have been shows that the presence of seconds was, generally, considered a *sine qua non*. Certainly, there were a number of duels, well-known ones, too, that were fought without seconds. Lord Byron (the poet's uncle) killed William Chaworth in a fight without seconds in 1765 yet no one would say that their encounter was not a duel. Similarly, Captain Edward Clark RN killed his fellow officer Captain Thomas Innes, also RN, in a duel in Hyde Park in 1749. The lack of seconds apart, this encounter had every characteristic of a duel; indeed, the casual observer would certainly have identified it as such. John Wilkes fought at least two duels without seconds: against Lord Talbot in 1762 and against Samuel Martin in the following year. Again, the absence of seconds apart, these two encounters are immediately identifiable as duels. Likewise the fatal encounter between Major Campbell and Captain Boyd in Ireland in 1809 was fought without seconds.

John Wilkes was evidently as unconventional in his duelling as he was in so many other aspects of his life, but even he realised that it was not the done thing to fight a duel without seconds. That Wilkes was at least aware of the implications of the lack of seconds is made clear in Samuel Martin's account of their duel in Hyde Park.

> As we walked from the Trees of the ring, where I had been expecting him [Wilkes], towards the North Wall of Hyde Park, but inclining to the Left hand Westward. What! said Mr W. are we come without seconds and without previous regulations? – I replied; that I came to risque my life, & was under no apprehension of unfairness. But said he, it is usual upon these occasions to settle some preliminary rules, & indeed it is absolutely necessary. I answered that we would walk from each other half a dozen paces & then turn round and fire. Shall either of us said he receive the others fire or shall we both turn round & fire immediately. I answered we will fire together if we can, or in what other manner each of us shall think fitt. Shall there said Mr W. be any begging of life in case of emergency. Mr M. answered lett that be left to chance, & the occasion when it happens.[40]

Martin, curiously enough, seems the more sanguine of the two at the prospect of fighting a secondless duel. What these duels do show is that duellists who fought without seconds were more likely to fall foul of the law. Clark, Byron and Campbell all ended up in court, charged with murder. While at this distance of time it is impossible to know whether the absence of seconds compounded their sin in the eyes of the law, it certainly could not have improved their prospects. The presence of seconds at a duel was proof that the duellists knew the rules and were prepared to abide by them.

Chapter Four

The Fight

But when the sun had set and it grew dark, he was possessed by a feeling of uneasiness. It was not fear at the thought of death, because while he was dining and playing cards, he had for some reason a confident belief that the duel would end in nothing; it was dread at the thought of something unknown which was to happen next morning for the first time in his life, and the dread of the coming night … He knew that the night would be long and sleepless …[1]

T HUS LAEVSKY, the hero of Chekhov's *The Duel*, contemplated the night before his fight with Von Koren. The anguish of uncertainty, remorse and fear that accompanied the final hours before a duel are a staple of duelling novels. It is a time for sentimental yearning, romantic nostalgia and straightforward guilt. Once Laevsky was alone in his room, his worst fears were realised; he could not settle to anything: 'On the eve of death one ought to write to one's nearest relation' – but the words would not come. Then, as if symbolically, a great storm broke out:

There was a vivid flash of lightning at all three windows, and it was followed by a prolonged, deafening roll of thunder, beginning with a hollow rumble and ending with a crash so violent that all the window panes rattled. Laevsky got up, went to the window, and pressed his forehead against the pane.[2]

The storm at first provoked a torrent of painful memories and remorseful reflections but at length drove him out to visit his mistress, Nadyezhda Fyodorovna, whose behaviour had caused the duel. His visit to Nadyezhda banished the demons of the night, convincing Laevsky once more that life was too precious to lose. Thus strengthened, he can face the trial of the duel with greater equanimity than before.

The anguish of the eve of a duel is also examined in another Russian novel, Mikhail Lermontov's *A Hero of Our Time*, a precursor to Chekhov. Lermontov knew a good deal about duelling having himself fought one shortly before the publication of his novel. Pechorin, the hero, like Laevsky, was tortured by thoughts of his past; his life passed before his eyes. He also worried, almost involuntarily, about the duel itself, unable to sleep and contemplating the possibility of his own demise.[3]

The duelling protagonists of novels were plagued by unwelcome thoughts, beset by fear and worry on the eve of their encounters; one doubts that it was much different for real duellists. Certainly, the authors of the manuals for would-be duellists were anxious to offer advice about the best way in which to pass the anxious hours before the morning rendezvous in the forest. The author of *The Art of Duelling* offers his advice about the 'night before' in a chapter headed 'Precautions to be Observed'. The duellist must treat the matter 'jocosely' and 'declare war against nervous apprehension'. He suggests an obvious solution: 'That his mind may not dwell upon the affair, he ought to invite a few friends to dinner, and laugh away the evening over a bottle of port; or, if fond of cards play a rubber of whist.'

But the duellist and his friends should beware of overdoing it in their anxiety to take their minds off the morning's business. The author, no doubt aware of the anguish that duellists could suffer in the long watches of the night, continued:

> Should he feel inclined to sleep when he retires to rest, and troubled images disturb his imagination, let him take some amusing book – one of Sir Walter's novels, if a lover of the romantic; or, Byron's *Childe Harold*, if he delights in the sublime, and read until he drops asleep ...[4]

Curiously, the novel that Lermontov has Pechorin taking up when unable to sleep the night before his duel was Scott's *Old Mortality*. Sir Walter's novels were evidently well known as the duellists' last comfort from the Home Counties to the Caucasus. Another fictional character, Pelham, Bulwer Lytton's eponymous hero, draws a distinction between a duel fought in England and one fought in France.

> 'Pooh!' said I, 'a duel in France is not like one in England; the former is a matter of course: a trifle of common occurrence; one makes an engagement to fight in the same as an engagement to dine: but the latter is a thing of state and solemnity – long faces – early rising – and will making.'[5]

In August 1780, Warren Hastings and Philip Francis fought a duel outside Calcutta as result of a long-running and acrimonious feud between the two men in the councils of the government of India. It was unusual in that both protagonists left accounts of the duel; in these both refer to the *longueurs* of the day before the duel. Francis comments, laconically, '16th. Employed in settling my affairs, burning papers, etc., in case of the worst. Dull work.'[6]

Hastings, having received Francis's challenge on 15 August and agreed to meet him at Alipur two days later, also spent the intervening hours settling his affairs. Hastings drew up a will, composed a long memorandum on the government of Bengal for the benefit of those who would take over from him in the event of his death and wrote a letter to Marian, his wife. This letter was to be delivered to Marian only should Hastings be killed in the forthcoming duel. 'My Beloved Marian,' the letter begins. 'My heart bleeds to think what your sufferings and feelings must be, if ever this letter shall be delivered into your hands.'[7] In the event, Hastings survived the duel unscathed; it was Francis who was wounded, although he did recover.

George Canning, who fought a famous duel against his Cabinet colleague Viscount Castlereagh 29 years later, also sat down at his desk to bid farewell to his wife and settle his worldly affairs.

If anything happens to me, dearest love, be comforted with the assurance that I could do no otherwise than I have done … I am conscious of having acted for what I thought best for my country; with *no more* mixture of selfish motives than the impatience of misconduct in others and of discredit to oneself …

He then explained his finances and left everything to her, asking only that she provide for his mother, by giving her £1,000 as a lump sum or, preferably, £300 a year.[8]

His long vigil finally over and his affairs settled, it was time for the gallant duellist to make his way to the agreed rendezvous, to meet his fate. Very often this journey was made in company with his second. Of the fighting prime ministers, Pitt jolted down the Portsmouth road from central London to Putney Heath in a chaise with Dudley Ryder, his second; Wellington rode over Battersea Bridge with his second, the one-armed Hardinge, to meet Lord Winchelsea on Battersea Fields. Castlereagh was driven to Putney Heath to fight Canning by his second, Lord Yarmouth, in his curricle. On the way they discussed Catalani, a fashionable opera singer, while Castlereagh hummed snatches from her arias.[9]

Duellists of all eras made their way to their rendezvous, often furtively, with their seconds beside them. Sometimes it was necessary to travel overseas. Edward Sackville and Lord Bruce, Jacobean courtier-soldiers and sworn enemies, galloped along the low-lying Dutch coast for two miles, one behind the other, until they reached their marshy rendezvous. In 1839 Lord George Loftus and Lord Harley made a day's excursion of their duel; they crossed to Boulogne in the morning, exchanged shots, and returned to Dover that day.

France was the most popular place for English duellists who wished to fight out of the jurisdiction. However, when, in 1796, Lord Valentia and Henry Gawlor fell out over Gawlor's affair with Valentia's wife, Britain was at war with France so they were forced to sail to Germany to settle their differences. The two men, accompanied by their seconds and surgeons, sailed to Hamburg, where they exchanged shots in a field outside the city. Valentia was hit in the chest but survived as the ball was extracted on the duelling ground.[10]

In 1819 Captain Pellew of the Life Guards eloped to Paris with the wife of a Mr Welsh, a former officer in the same regiment. Their illicit bliss was interrupted by the arrival in Paris of a vengeful husband who preferred 'what is called the satisfaction of a gentleman to pursuing any legal means of redress' (i.e. a suit for criminal conversation). A duel was arranged, with pistols at 12 paces. Pellew was shot in the head; he 'expired even before his body reached the ground'. History does not relate whether Mr and Mrs Welsh managed to salvage their marriage in the wake of this sad episode.[11]

Sometimes there was a rather unexpected amount of travelling to be done. On Friday, 17 October 1828, one Richard Peters, of Park Street, 'a West Indian, a descendent of one of the original settlers of the island', had agreed to fight a duel with Captain Hutchinson, formerly of the 47th Foot. Their dispute had arisen as a result of their competing for the affections of 'a young Irish lady of great personal beauty and accomplishments'. The pair were attended by a surgeon and by Major Horner, a friend of Hutchinson's. They met at Regent's Park's Gloucester Gate, from where they went to Chalk Farm. However, at Chalk Farm they were observed by passers-by and so were forced to carry on to Hampstead Heath in the hope of finding a secluded spot for their duel. Once on the Heath they did find a suitably secluded spot, near the ponds, where the duel was fought with pistols at 12 paces.

Finally, after a good deal of legwork – Regent's Park to Chalk Farm to Hampstead Heath – the duellists could now get down to business. Peters and Hutchinson removed their coats and took up their positions. Major Horner gave the signal, 'Gentlemen, present – fire!' Hutchinson's ball brushed Peters's hat; Peters himself missed his opponent altogether, whereupon the seconds intervened and the two men were reconciled.[12]

In the golden age of duelling men made their way to the ground by carriage, on horseback, by boat or on foot. By the twentieth century, there was the rather incongruous spectacle of duellists driving to the rendezvous in cars, often, particularly in the case of the more highly publicised French theatrical duels, pursued by a pack of journalists and paparazzi. For a custom that traces its origins to medieval chivalry and flourished in the age of the periwig and tricorn hat, this was odd to say the least. What, one wonders, would Lord Camelford have made of it all?

Once they had arrived at the appointed place, the duellists and their seconds could start preparing for the serious business of the day. As Moloney's account (see Chapter 3) of the preliminaries of the duel between Crowther and Helsham makes clear, there were a number of matters that had to be sorted out. This section will give an overview of the methods that were used to fight duels, pointing out the similarities between duels down the ages, the features that were common to them. A more detailed discussion of particular local variations will emerge as we look at the development of the duel in individual countries. This book will also look at the development of the main weapons used by duellists – swords and pistols.

As far as the sword duel was concerned the organisation of the fight was simple enough. Whichever type of sword was to be used, whether rapier, smallsword, foil or cavalry sabre, the weapons would be compared to ensure that they were the same size (clearly the duellist with the longer blade had an advantage over his adversary). Before the duel in 1613 between Edward Sackville and Lord Bruce the two men had difficulty finding swords that matched. At first Bruce produced one of the same length as Sackville's but twice as broad. Sackville's second advised him to reject Bruce's offering, to find instead a weapon that was similar to his own and allow Bruce to make the choice between them.

In the sixteenth and seventeenth centuries, it was common practice to use a dagger as well as a sword. Camillo Agrippa published a duelling manual, *Scienza d'Arme*, in Venice in 1568, which guides the aspiring fencer or duellist, stage by stage, with the help of numerous engraved illustrations, through the technicalities of swordplay, with particular emphasis on sword and dagger. De Bouteville and his seconds fought their duel armed with sword and dagger; they were also searched before the duel to ensure that they were not wearing armour; this too was common practice.

Once the swords had been checked against each other and the adversaries had stripped for action, there was little more to do than let the fight begin. In earlier centuries the duel continued until one man was killed or disarmed and then spared by his opponent. In later times, where duels were still routinely fought with swords, seconds would agree the terms of the fight. Sometimes they were fought to the point of disablement, sometimes to first blood (*au premier sang*), or sometimes for an agreed number of rounds. The conditions were as severe or forgiving as the seconds chose to make them.

The notorious encounter between Lord Mohun and the Duke of Hamilton in Hyde Park in November 1712 was an example of a duel in which the seconds fought each other; indeed, the most controversial aspect of the duel was the lingering suspicion that Macartney, Mohun's second, killed the duke after his principal had been put out of action. Such was the ferocity of the encounter (and the ill feeling between the parties) that both the duke and Mohun were killed.

By the mid-eighteenth century, it was no longer accepted practice that seconds should join in the fight and gradually the conduct of duels fought with swords became more regulated. By the latter half of the nineteenth century the sword duel was still popular in France and, although perhaps to a lesser degree, in Germany and Austro-Hungary. In Britain and America the pistol had by then long since replaced the sword as the gentleman's preferred weapon. Apart from checking the swords and ensuring that the duellists were not secretly wearing armour, there, in a sword duel, remained the question of the size of the ground on which the duel was to be fought. This was not something that the earlier generations of sword-fighting duellists would have worried about but, in later years, perhaps under the influence of the fencing schools, it became an issue.

In 1913 Georges Breittmayer, a noted authority on duelling etiquette, fought a sword duel with M. Berger at Château d'Orly, near Paris. Breittmayer had originally insisted that the duellists should have only 5 metres of ground behind them – regarded as a severe condition – but, once at the ground, relented and allowed 10 metres of ground for retreat.[13] The importance of the distance of ground permitted behind the duellist lay, of course, in the fact that it allowed space for manoeuvre: the greater the space behind, the greater the freedom of movement.

Also in 1913 two rival Hungarian politicians, Count Tisza, the prime minister, and the Marquis Pallavicini fought a duel. The conditions were severe: heavy cavalry sabres were to be used; the duellists were to have minimal protective equipment and the duel was to continue until one of the combatants was put *hors de combat*. Tisza, we are told, 'enjoys a great reputation as an exponent of swordplay'. The duel had lasted for 11 minutes when, at the end of the ninth round, the surgeons stopped the fight because both men had sustained cuts on their foreheads, the blood from which was interfering with their eyesight. The duel fulfilled its expectations as it 'afforded a fine exhibition of the art of the sabre'.[14]

Rather more typical of the later sword duel – particularly in France – was that fought between M. Leon Daudet and Jacques Ronjon in June 1914. Daudet, who is described as 'a Royalist of a particularly combative disposition', was challenged to a duel by Ronjon for remarks made in the newspaper *L'Action Française*. The duel was fought with swords, but was stopped once Daudet had received a slight wound to his sword hand.[15]

When the duel was to be fought with pistols the most important questions to be decided were the distance, the method of fighting and the signal to be given. The question of the distance was an important one, literally one of life and death, which was discussed briefly in Chapter 3. The distance at which the duel was to be fought was intimately connected with the chosen method of fighting. There were several ways in which, conventionally, a pistol duel could be conducted. The duellists could stand still at an agreed distance from each other and fire as near to simultaneously as they could; this was the method favoured by British duellists. The opponents could stand back to back and walk away from each other, turning to fire at a given signal; this was sometimes known as the 'French' method, although there is no particular evidence showing that it was favoured by duellists in France. The third distinct variation was the 'barrier' duel, whereby the duellists walked in towards a central barrier that divided the ground. There were a number of subvariants of this form of the duel: sometimes the duellists would approach the barrier in zigzags, sometimes straight. Usually, they had to halt before firing and, having fired, remain stationary to receive their opponent's fire (if he was still capable of returning it).

We have seen that in late eighteenth-century England 10 yards was considered by experts to be the minimum acceptable distance. Charles Ellis and Lord Yarmouth, who acted as seconds for George Canning and Viscount Castlereagh respectively at their duel on Putney Heath in 1809, measured 12 paces as being the minimum acceptable distance. The Irish duelling code of 1777 does not specify a minimum acceptable distance, but it merely provides that the challenger chooses the distance.[16] The American duelling code of 1838 pronounces, 'The usual distance is from ten to twenty paces, as may be agreed on, and the seconds in measuring the ground usually step three feet.'[17]

What should be borne in mind is that 10 yards was the distance between the standing positions of the duellists, that is, where their feet were placed. The distance was considerably reduced by the fact that each man held his pistol with an outstretched arm. An average-sized duelling pistol held with an outstretched arm might position the gun's muzzle 3 feet, or 1 yard, nearer the other man; allowing for the same encroachment on the other side, a distance of 10 yards has diminished to 8. The effect of this encroachment is even more marked at shorter distances: a ground agreed at 8 yards would be diminished by a quarter to 6, a range from which, one might have thought, it would be difficult to miss.

The distance considered acceptable varied, according to local custom, the whim of the parties and, sometimes, the severity of the insult. Generally, the more insulting the slur or the more irreconcilable the adversaries the more severe the conditions were likely to be; if the duel was to be fought with pistols, this translated into a short distance. The encounter between Major Chapman and Captain de Lancey, both of the 18th Foot, provides an extreme instance of a duel fought at a short distance. De Lancey is reported to have said that Chapman 'might fire, if he thought proper', but for his own part he was resolved not to discharge his pistol 'until the muzzle of it touched the Major's breast'. To which Chapman replied that he had expected, when he came here to decide their differences, that 'it was to be with a *gentleman*, and not an assassin'. Whereupon Chapman threw down his pistol and, with his second, left the duelling ground.[18]

There is a report in October 1921 of a similar incident from Texas. Norwood Hockaby and Charles A. Williams, who were both scions of old Texan families 'fought a so-called duel from which there was hardly one chance in a thousand that either would escape alive'. The two men entered an old barn at dusk, with a neighbour and Williams's son as seconds. Then, standing toe to toe, with their left hands clasped, they fired at each other with revolvers. Both men, almost inevitably, were killed.[19] From nearly a century earlier, in Virginia in April 1826, we have a brief report of a duel fought with pistols at two paces. Lieutenant Bourne of the Marines was killed; incredibly, given the range, his opponent survived. Bourne's bullet, we infer, passed through the fabric of his coat without doing any injury.[20]

Two French brothers fought at three paces in the Bois de Boulogne in 1827; at this distance, taking into account the encroachment of arm and pistol, the muzzles would have been perhaps 3 feet apart.[21] Messrs Trouett and Prue fought at a almost equally murderous five paces in Louisiana in 1840.[22] Doctors Smith and Jefferies fought a pistol duel at eight paces in Philadelphia in 1830.[23] The German military, too, had an uncompromising attitude to the code of honour and duels between officers were often fought under severe conditions. It was not always merely the extreme close range that made a duel so lethal. Consider the case of Lieutenant von Puttkammer and Lieutenant von Heeringen, both in the 27th Infantry Regiment stationed at Halberstadt: they fought at 15 paces (not an especially short distance) with the additional proviso that they would exchange shots until one or the other was incapacitated. This was almost certain to result in death or, at the very least, serious injury to one (or both) of the principals; it was the unfortunate Heeringen who was shot in the abdomen. It was later reported that he had died.[24]

These are examples of duels fought at such short distances that death or serious injury was very likely to result. Some duellists – or their seconds – were more sensible, electing to fight at longer distances, although mere distance did not guarantee survival. Cilley and Graves, both members of the US House of Representatives, decided to settle their differences with rifles at a distance of 80 yards. The conditions of the duel, fought in 1838, specified that the parties were 'to hold the rifles at arm's length, downwards, the rifles to be cocked, and triggers set …' Despite these conditions, Cilley was nevertheless killed.[25]

Likewise, two officials in the Austrian government, Baron Harmann Widerhofer and Dr Oskar Mayer, in 1910 fought a pistol duel at 35 paces, each man to fire three shots. The unfortunate Widerhofer was killed in the first exchange, shot in the head.[26] A European duelling expert, writing in 1915, recommended that the optimum distance for a pistol duel be 25 metres.[27]

There was also a hybrid form of engagement, where the combatants fought with both pistols and swords. Although it was probably less commonly employed than either of the 'pure' versions of the duel, it nevertheless had an enduring appeal. There are examples of it from the eighteenth century, yet it continues to crop up in the twentieth. The usual practice was to fire the pistols first, before resorting to swords. In November 1773 Count Rice and Viscount du Barry fell out one evening while taking the waters at Bath. A duel was agreed upon so they set off immediately, with their seconds, for the downs above Bath, where, once dawn had come up, they fought. Each man was armed with a pair of pistols and a sword. They began with the pistols; at the first fire Rice was hit in the thigh while du Barry took Rice's bullet in the chest. Undaunted, they both fired again: one pistol misfired; the other missed, whereupon the duellists drew their swords. As Rice was advancing on his opponent, du Barry fell to the ground, pleading for mercy. Rice spared his stricken opponent but the relief was short-lived as du Barry died soon afterwards.[28]

Six years later two British officers, a line infantryman and a Highlander, fought a duel arising out of a dispute over 'the present state of national affairs'. It was agreed that they would fight with pistols and swords. Meeting on Hounslow Heath, they fired the pistols off harmlessly – one into the air and the other into the ground – before setting about one another with swords. At the first pass, the infantryman ran his sword through the Highlander's waistcoat and shirt but, miraculously, failed to do any greater harm. At the second pass the Scotsman hit his opponent's sword arm. The fight continued, the infantryman sustaining two more wounds, before he was weakened by loss of blood and forced to concede.[29] The practice crossed the Atlantic, too. In 1825 the editors of two rival New Orleans newspapers, the *Mercantile Advertiser* and *Argus*, decided to settle their differences in a duel. They chose pistols and swords. Both missed with the pistols; in the subsequent sword fight both men were wounded, the editor of the *Argus* severely, the *Advertiser*'s man slightly.[30] The practice survived into the twentieth century; Leon Daudet, French journalist and incorrigible duellist, for instance, fought at least two duels under the hybrid pistol-and-sword rules.

The question of distance was less clear-cut in the so-called 'French' turn-and-shoot or the 'barrier' duel. In the 'turn-and-shoot' duel the seconds would agree both the form of the signal and the point at which it was to be given. In March 1806 two officers of the 6th Foot, Lieutenant Turrens and Mr Fisher, the regimental surgeon, fought a duel on Galleywood Common near Chelmsford. The parties agreed that they would walk a 'short' distance from each other, turn and fire at once. Turrens was badly wounded and later died. Fisher and both the seconds were convicted of wilful murder; Fisher absconded.

In another example, an unnamed man fought a duel with a clergyman at Salisbury in December 1784. The man of God strongly insisted on a duel; the layman, who had a wife and children, was correspondingly reluctant to fight. In the end the clergyman got his way and a duel was arranged. They agreed to fight by standing back to back, walking away from each other, turning and firing. The clergyman fired first but managed to hit only the sleeve of his opponent's coat. Now at his adversary's mercy, the previously bellicose clergyman fell to his knees and begged for his life. He was spared.[31]

Sadly, we do not know the exact distance over which they shot at each other in either of these encounters. However, it seems that the turn-and-shoot duels were usually fought at much the same distances as the more conventional, stand-and-shoot encounters, somewhere between 10 and 20 paces. The duellists would be allowed to cover the specified number of paces before being given the order to turn and shoot. The difference with the turn-and-shoot duel was that it was, at least in theory, more difficult to aim at one's adversary.

In the case of the 'barrier' duel (or *à la barrière*) distance was a different matter again. Here the seconds would generally mark two parallel lines across the middle of the ground. These lines would be an agreed distance apart, say 12 paces, and represented the 'barrier' beyond which neither duellist could encroach. With this 'barrier' marked in the middle of the ground the duellist would then start at some distance from his side of the 'barrier' and advance towards it. At any point he could stop and fire but, having done so, was normally obliged to remain stationary to receive his opponent's fire.

On 3 September 1783, two Guards officers, Lieutenant-Colonel Thomas and Colonel Cosmo Gordon, met at the Ring in Hyde Park to fight a duel. The quarrel had originally arisen from Thomas's decision to bring Gordon before a court martial in New York a year earlier to face charges of failing to do his duty at the Battle of Springfield. Springfield, fought in June 1780, was a minor engagement of the American War of Independence. The court martial had acquitted Gordon, who promptly challenged Thomas to a duel. In this respect it was a classic example of a duel between officers; accusations of a failure to do one's duty could not be allowed to pass unchallenged, no matter what the official investigation had concluded. It was a matter of personal honour.

The seconds had agreed that their principals would, starting approximately 30 yards apart, advance towards each other, firing at will. Once they had covered about a quarter of the distance, both men raised their pistols. Only Gordon fired; he missed. Thomas thereupon took careful aim and fired, hitting Gordon in the thigh. A thigh wound was often a serious, even fatal, injury but, in this instance, Gordon was lucky: Thomas's bullet had caused only 'a severe contusion'. It may be that Gordon's good fortune owed more to the seconds' 'short-loading' the pistols – that is, making sure that the charge was too weak to enable the bullet to do any serious harm – than to Lady Luck.

Both men then fired their second pistols, without hitting the mark. The seconds then reloaded and the two officers again retreated to a distance of 30 yards and began to close on each other once more. This time Thomas was hit; he later died. The coroner's jury returned a verdict of 'wilful murder' against Gordon.[32]

Although this encounter is a good example of a 'barrier' duel, it would be fair to say that the 'barrier' duel was more popular on the Continent than in the British Isles. The duel in which Alexander Pushkin was killed was fought *à la barrière* in St Petersburg in 1837. Seven or so years before his own death Pushkin completed the verse novel *Eugene Onegin*, in which, by one of those strange instances of literature's anticipating life, Onegin kills Lensky in a duel. Like Pushkin's duel, Onegin's is fought *à la barrière* and, like Pushkin's, in the depths of snowy winter.

> And now the two opponents doff
> their cloaks; Zaretsky's measured off
> thirty-two steps with great precision,
> and on their marks has made them stand;
> each grips his pistol in his hand.
>
> 'Now march.' And calmly, not yet seeking
> to aim, at steady, even pace
> the foes, cold-blooded and unspeaking,
> each took four steps across the space,
> four fateful strides. Then, without slowing
> the level tenor of his going,
> Evgeny quietly began
> to lift his pistol up. A span
> of five or more steps they went, slow-gaited,
> and Lensky, left eye closing, aimed –
> but just then Evgeny's pistol flamed ...

Lensky, shot through the chest, fell to the ground, dead.[33]

Eugene Onegin may be a novel but provides a vivid portrayal of a duel fought *à la barrière*, remarkable for both its descriptive accuracy and the dramatic power it generates despite (or perhaps because of) its spare, unfussy style. It is as good an account as one could hope to find of such a duel and a fine example of the value of literature in helping us to recreate the atmosphere, the *feel* of a duel.

The 'barrier' duel was also widely practised in Germany, where, according to Kevin McAleer, a historian of duelling in the Kaiserreich, it was the most popular form of engagement. In late nineteenth-century Germany, the pistol was the duellists' preferred weapon. As McAleer puts it, 'The greater the danger, the greater the honor; pistols are more dangerous than sabres; therefore pistols are more honorable than sabres.'[34]

While this might seem almost perverse reasoning to the modern mind, it illustrates vividly the impulses that motivated contemporary German duellists. It also goes some way to explaining why the 'barrier' duel was, in Germany, the most commonly used form of engagement: it was considered to provide the best opportunity for a display of personal courage. Once the first duellist had fired his shot, he had to remain stationary, awaiting his opponent's fire; the opponent could, meanwhile, advance to the barrier before aiming and firing. The duellist who had fired first and missed was now a sitting duck – an excellent opportunity, it was considered, to show one's courage and nervelessness. By contrast, in Wilhelmine Germany at least, the duel in which the adversaries fired simultaneously on a signal was looked down upon, as it did not provide a sufficiently good opportunity to demonstrate one's *sang-froid*.[35]

Once the seconds had decided the distance, the next matter was the signal to fire. This in itself depended on the mode of fighting, and prompts the question whether one of the duellists has the right to fire first. As we have just seen, in a duel *à la barrière* the question of the first shot does not arise: the participants, once given the command to start, fire at will. Where the duellists stand facing each other to fire, one man was sometimes granted the right – whether by agreement or as the offended party – to fire first. Casanova acted as second to a Swiss named Schmidt, an officer in the Swedish service, who had been cheated and assaulted by a French officer named d'Ache over a game of billiards. Casanova, who had watched the game in question, had no doubts where his duty lay:

> I know that the law of duelling is a prejudice which may be called, and perhaps rightly, barbarous, but it is a prejudice which no man of honour can contend against, and I believe Schmidt to be a thorough gentleman.

Casanova and his fellow second agreed on pistols and the following morning the parties met in a garden on the outskirts of the town. Casanova takes up the story:

> [Schmidt] placed himself between two trees, distant about four paces from one another, and drawing two pistols from his pocket said to d'Ache, –
>
> 'Place yourself at a distance of ten paces, and fire first. I shall walk to and fro between these two trees, and you may walk as far if you like to do so when my turn comes to fire.'
>
> Nothing could be clearer or more calmly delivered than this explanation.
>
> 'But we must decide,' said I, 'who is to have the first shot.'
>
> 'There is no need,' said Schmidt. 'I never fire first, besides, the gentleman has a right to the first shot.'

D'Ache's second then placed his man in the proper position. D'Ache fired at Schmidt but missed.[36]

In 1787 a Mr Scott, formerly of the 11th Foot, fought a pistol duel against a M. de la Brosse, a French officer, at Kensington gravel pits. They elected to fire alternately, although we do not know who had the right to shoot first. Scott's second shot hit a button on de la Brosse's coat, whereupon the Frenchmen, declaring that he was wounded, fired into the air. The affair was then terminated. The seconds, in their record of the duel, were moved to announce, 'It is necessary to observe, that this affair was a mere point of honour, and did not arise from any difference about a woman.'[37]

The English experts were divided as to the fairness of alternate firing, if not the advantage it conferred on the man who fired first. The anonymous author of *General Rules and Instructions for all Seconds in Duels* (1792) was wholly opposed to this method of fighting. Why, he asked, should 'The Body of a Man ... stand as a Mark, for a cool Shot, without any Interruption, like the Ace of Diamonds?'

Those who worried that allowing alternate firing risked reducing a duel to mere target practice, especially for more experienced shots, need have looked no further than the duel between Schmidt and d'Ache. D'Ache having missed Schmidt once, fired again but missed:

Schmidt, without a word, but as calm as death, fired his first pistol in the air, and then covering d'Ache with his second pistol hit him in the forehead and stretched him dead on the ground. He put back his pistols into his pocket and went off directly by himself, as if he were merely continuing his walk.[38]

The Irish duelling code of 1777 does not envisage that one party should be awarded first fire. On the question of the firing of the pistols it says,

> Firing may be regulated, first by signal; secondly, by word of command; or thirdly at pleasure, as may be agreeable to the parties. In the latter case the parties may fire at their reasonable leisure, but second presents and rest are strictly prohibited.[39]

It is silent on the question of alternate firing. Likewise, John Lyde Wilson's 1838 American *Code of Honor* has nothing to say on the matter. On the other hand, Andrew Steinmetz, whose *The Romance of Duelling* was published in London in 1868, asserts that it was common practice during the reign of George III to toss for first fire. In earlier years, Steinmetz tells us, it was generally the privilege of the challenger to fire first.[40]

In the conventional stand-and-shoot duel, the parties fired simultaneously (or nearly simultaneously) at a given signal, which would be given by one or other of the seconds. By the late nineteenth or early twentieth century the parties sometimes appointed a director or referee to oversee the fight, in which case he would give the signal to fire. If it was the seconds who were to give the command to fire, they would agree who was to perform this important duty. The American *Code* prescribes that the seconds should draw lots for the right to give the signal. In other instances, it was a duty undertaken in turns. In the duel between Sir Francis Burdett and James Paull in 1807, Burdett's second, John Ker, gave the signal for the first shots and Paull's, the timid Mr Cooper, for the second exchange. By contrast in the fatal duel between James Stuart and Sir Alexander Boswell, Boswell's second Mr Douglas 'put it upon' Lord Rosslyn, his opposite number, to give the signal.

The form of the signal to fire varied considerably: it could be given by dropping a handkerchief, by a simple hand signal or, and perhaps this was the most common, by an oral command. Even here there was considerable variation, but the most important thing was that the principals knew what signal was to be given and when they were permitted to fire. The critical importance of this – and it could all too easily be a matter of life or death – is well illustrated by the story of the duel fought in Dublin in March 1830 between Captain Smith of the 32nd Foot and Standish Staner O'Grady, a barrister in his late twenties.

The dispute between the two men originated in an incident on Nassau Street in Dublin. O'Grady was riding up the street towards Merrion Square when he passed a cabriolet containing Smith and a fellow officer, Captain Markham. As the cabriolet drew level with O'Grady it pulled out to avoid another vehicle on its side of the road, forcing O'Grady's horse onto the footpath at the side of the road. This caused O'Grady's mount to lose its footing and slip; O'Grady, to keep his seat, leaned forward in the saddle, causing the light whip he was carrying to strike the hood of the cabriolet. At no point in the episode, which passed in a trice, did O'Grady say a word to either Smith or Markham. O'Grady recovered his balance and continued on his way at a gentle walk, while the cabriolet containing Smith and Markham sped off.

At this point the cabriolet stopped 'as suddenly as its rapid motion would permit'; Smith jumped out and ran back down the street towards O'Grady, where, without warning, he began to set about the barrister with the whip. Smith hit O'Grady many times, before returning to the cabriolet and speeding off once more, pausing only to identify himself as 'Captain Smith, of the 32nd Regiment'. O'Grady repaired to his father's house, from where he sent his second, Lieutenant Macnamara, to challenge Smith to a duel.

The principals and their seconds (there were no other onlookers, by agreement) met at the duelling ground at six o'clock in the morning. The following account of what happened that morning is taken from the evidence of one of the seconds (although we are not told which) at the subsequent trial of Smith and Markham.

At the outset, 'Captain Markham acquainted Mr O'Grady, that the signal to be given was – "Ready! Fire!" ' When all was ready,

> Captain Markham then gave the first signal; but from whatever cause, he did not give it in the terms fixed upon. He said, 'Gentlemen, are you ready?' or 'Are you ready, gentlemen?' Mr O'Grady conceived the word was to be 'Ready! Fire!' and that this was a preliminary inquirey. Capt. Smith, however, did not labour under this mistake; he levelled his pistol, and covered Mr O'Grady for a few seconds. Mr O'Grady, perceiving his antagonist prepared, raised his pistol; but, before he had levelled it, captain [*sic*] Markham, whose eye was upon him, gave the signal. Captain Smith fired, and Mr O'Grady fell.

O'Grady died the following day; Smith and Markham were both subsequently convicted of his manslaughter. They were sentenced to 12 months in prison.

The chain of events just before Smith fired make it clear that O'Grady's misapprehension as to the correct signal, while important, was only partly to blame for his death. It is also evident that Smith and Markham were guilty of, at the very least, sharp practice and, more likely, foul play. The fact that Smith raised his pistol before the signal had been given allowed him those vital few extra seconds to settle his aim. Markham is condemned by the words 'whose eye was upon him', from which we can infer that he gave the signal to fire *knowing* that Smith was ready and O'Grady was not. Seen in this light, the duel was little better than murder. The finger must also be pointed at O'Grady's second, Macnamara, whose spineless failure to intervene at the critical juncture cost his friend his life.[41]

The signal was of vital importance: it had to be clear, audible and properly understood by all parties. The words of command actually used, of course, varied. In the Duke of Wellington's duel it was agreed that the duke's second, Hardinge, would ask, 'Are you ready?' and, on receiving a reply in the affirmative, would say, 'Fire!'[42] In the duel between US congressmen Cilley and Graves in 1838 the seconds agreed that the duellists would be asked, 'Gentleman, are you ready?' If neither said 'No', then one of the seconds would say, in even time, 'Fire! – one, two, three, four'; neither man was to fire before the command 'Fire!' or after the word 'Four'.[43] According to the historian Robert Nye, by the 1880s in France all pistol duels between politicians were of the 'command' variety.

> After being given the order to fire, each man had to raise his arm, aim, and fire before the 'director of combat' counted to three. Since firing after the director uttered 'three' would have permanently dishonored a man, duelers did not really have the luxury of taking careful aim.[44]

Walter Winans, a well-known rifle and pistol shot, double Olympic shooting champion and winner of numerous other competitions, wrote *Automatic Pistol Shooting* in 1915. As its title suggests, it is concerned mainly with competitive shooting, but it does incorporate a chapter on duelling. Winans opines that 'it is not an unmixed blessing that duelling is abolished in England'. In the course of this chapter he gives detailed advice on many aspects of fighting a duel. He recommends that the proper signal be '*Attention! – Feu! Un – deux – trois.*' The duellist must fire between the words *feu* and *trois*. This endorses Robert Nye's opinion of the accepted French practice a generation earlier.[45]

Now that we have seen how a duel was fought, it is time to look at the way in which the duellist himself was expected to behave during and after his ordeal. The ideal was to maintain a cool, unruffled and courteous demeanour at all times.

A stylish insouciance was expected of the duellist. The first thing he had to consider on the morning of his tryst with death was the question of clothing. If it was to be a sword duel, then any clothes would do, provided that they were comfortable and did not restrict movement. No doubt, too, knowledgeable and solicitous friends would recommend a solid pair of shoes, nothing too flashy. As it was the normal practice for sword duels to be fought in shirtsleeves, the principals would discard their coats before taking up their positions.

The English duelling manual written by 'A Traveller' in 1838 offers plentiful advice for the would-be duellists. On the morning of the duel he advises the duellist to drink coffee and eat a biscuit on rising but to avoid a hearty breakfast at so early an hour. If, however, the duel was to be fought with pistols, there were other considerations to be taken into account. He advises his readers not to wear flannel close to the skin, as it can make trifling wounds worse.[46] This was true of most types of cloth, not just flannel, as fragments of the material were carried in the wound by the bullet. Indeed, it was this consideration that induced the odd duellist, often a medical man, to fight naked.

> Humphrey Howarth, the surgeon, was called out, and made his appearance in the field stark naked, to the astonishment of the challenger, who asked him what he meant. 'I know,' said Howarth, 'that if any part of the clothing is carried into the body by a gunshot wound, festering ensues; and therefore I have met you thus.' His antagonist declared that fighting with a man *in puris naturabilus* would be quite ridiculous and accordingly they parted without further discussion.

Howarth, who was at the time (1806) MP for Evesham, and his adversary Lord Barrymore agreed to fight on the beach at Brighton. Howarth's decision to strip naked was prompted no so much by his proximity to the water as by his experiences as a surgeon in the East India Company. He had seen too many wounds complicated by shreds of clothing and had no wish to run a similar risk himself.[47]

For those who preferred not to face their adversaries in the buff, convention dictated sober, dark clothing, reflecting the gravity of the occasion. In the Kaiser's Germany, we are told, black frock coats were considered *de rigueur*; top hats were optional, although many of the pictures that we have of duellists show the participants sporting tall black hats.[48] Sartorial elegance aside, the wearing of dark clothes had the practical purpose, it was thought, of presenting a less well-defined target. Indeed, an Irish duellist, Major Hillas, took this a step further for his duel with Thomas Fenton in Co. Sligo in 1816. Before taking up his position Hillas discarded his coat, revealing what appeared to be a specially made waistcoat with dark sleeves – instead of the normal white – in the hope that he presented a poorer target. Unfortunately for Hillas, his careful preparations were in vain: black sleeves or not, Fenton's aim was true and Hillas was killed.[49] Walter Winans in his advice to duellists agreed that it was conventionally assumed that the duellist should present as dark a target as possible, even turning up his collar in order to avoid showing a white mark to his adversary. However, he was not convinced that the conventional wisdom was sound: 'Personally I should prefer to shoot at an entirely black target without a white collar or white patch anywhere to divert one's eye ...'[50]

If the duellist was expected to arrive looking presentable, his behaviour once he had arrived at the ground was even more important. It was absolutely vital that the duellist be, outwardly at least, calm and collected; displays of nerves, rudeness or aggression were frowned upon and could ruin a man's reputation. 'A Traveller' was able to offer the duellist some no doubt valuable advice. Once at the ground, 'it is always advisable to get the start of his adversary, he should dismount and walk about, coolly puffing his cigar'.

A principal should keep aloof from the preparations for the encounter; the seconds should be allowed to perform their duties without interference.

It was just as important, if not more so, for the duellist to retain his composure in the moments immediately before the exchange of shots. Andrew Steinmetz cautioned the duellist that 'He should also be very careful to remain himself as firm and stiff as a statue – not a muscle in his face or movement of his body should portray any extraordinary degree of feeling or excitement.'[51]

'A Traveller' warned would-be duellists, 'It requires some nerve to elevate the hand, and keep the pistol perfectly steady, when the muzzle of an adversary's weapon is directed upon you.' He conceded, 'The period most trying to a Duellist, is from the time the word "ready" is given until the handkerchief drops. 'Tis an awful moment certainly.'[52]

Still, it was important for the duellist to remain calm for the sake of his reputation. The best evidence for this is the number of duelling stories that finish with a declaration from the seconds or, perhaps, the surviving duellist, that the parties behaved with 'exemplary' courage, 'admirable coolness' or some other suitable words of praise.

Duellists were certainly supposed to behave with a good deal more gravitas than Thomas Winnington and Augustus Townshend could muster when they fought a duel in 1741. Horace Walpole described the encounter thus: 'Winnington challenged; they walked into Hyde Park last Sunday morning, scratched one another's fingers, tumbled into two ditches – that is Augustus did – kissed and walked home.'

Walpole described Townshend as 'a pert boy, captain of an India-man' and Winnington as 'declared cicisbeo to my Lady Townshend'.[53]

If retaining his composure was important for the sake of his reputation, it was equally vital to the chance of survival that he take up the correct stance. This mattered only in pistol duels; in sword fights, evidently, it was irrelevant. One expert reminds the duellist that 'much depended on the position that a man takes when he fights a duel, which is, at least, as one to four, that he is not killed or wounded'.

The prudent duellist should turn sideways on to his opponent, so that he is looking full face over his right shoulder and the right leg is shielding the left. He should pull his stomach in and swivel his right hip to cover the lower abdomen and groin. This, it was held, presented a smaller target as well as allowing the pistol arm to give some protection to the upper chest and neck. The object of the exercise, of course, was to lessen the risk of injury.

For the more portly duellist standing sideways on was not such an advantage. As the amply proportioned Charles James Fox was preparing to exchange shots with William Adam in Hyde Park in 1779, his second reminded him, 'Fox, you must stand sideways,' to which Fox replied, 'Why, man, I am as thick one way as the other.'[54]

'A Traveller' estimated on the basis of a sample of 200 encounters that the odds against being killed in a duel were 14–1, while the odds against suffering an injury were a rather shorter 6–1. Having passed on these statistics, the anonymous author cheerfully reassures the reader with a gruesome tale about a friend of his, a Hanoverian ex-officer, who 'has been twice shot through the head; and, although, minus many of his teeth, and part of his jaw, he survives still, and enjoys good health'.[55]

Adopting a proper position could make a difference between life and death. Captain Harvey Aston, who later perished in a duel, met the notorious 'Fighting' Fitzgerald in June 1790. Aston, according to a report of the duel, appears to have been saved by adopting the side-on stance: 'The ball took a direction so as to glance Mr Aston's wrist, and passed from thence under his right cheek-bone and through the neck. On receiving this wound, capt. Aston [*sic*] called to his antagonist, "Are you satisfied?" the answer returned was, "I am satisfied."[56]

This brief account seems to indicate that it was Aston's pistol arm that saved him; had it not been extended, the ball might well have given him a much more serious wound in the chest. In the days before modern medicine and, particularly, antiseptics, any wound could be potentially lethal, so the more one could do to lower the risk of being hit the better.

The obligation on the duellist to behave with dignity and courage extended to the aftermath of the encounter. Both victor and vanquished were expected to behave chivalrously to their opponent. Many an account of a fatal duel ends with the dying man, his life ebbing away on the dewy, early-morning turf, offering his killer absolution: 'He behaved perfectly', perhaps, or, 'There was nothing unfair about this fight'. Equally, many victors rushed to help their wounded or dying opponents. Gallantry, however, did not excuse a failure to keep a stiff upper lip at all times, even *in extremis*:

> I cannot impress upon an individual too strongly, the propriety of remaining perfectly calm and collected when hit: he must not allow himself to be alarmed or confused, but summoning up all his resolution, treat the matter coolly; and if he dies, go off with as good a grace as possible.[57]

It was an unforgiving code of honour.

Central to the idea of duelling as an equitable method of settling disputes between men was the notion that duellists should meet, so far as was possible, on equal terms. Opponents of duelling regularly pointed out that in practice this was very difficult to ensure. How could one be certain that two men were equally skilled and practised with pistol or sword, or equally fit for the fight? This obvious problem suggested that the duel 'may not always be the infallible criterion of veracity'. Lord Chesterfield illustrated the point with this, presumably fictitious, example.

> A very lean, slender, active young fellow of great HONOR, weighing perhaps not quite twelve stone, and who has from his youth taken lessons

of HOMICIDE from a murder-master, has, or thinks he has, a point of honor to discuss with an unwieldy, fat, middle-aged gentleman, of nice HONOR likewise, weighing four-and-twenty stone, and who in his youth may not possibly have had the same commendable application to the noble science of HOMICIDE. The lean gentleman sends a very civil letter to the fat one, inviting him to come and be killed by him the next morning in Hyde-park. Should the fat gentleman accept this invitation, and waddle to the place appointed, he goes to inevitable slaughter.

Surely, Chesterfield asked, it was better that the portly fellow should send a reply in the following terms.

Sir,

... I must suppose that you will not desire that we should meet upon unequal terms, which must be the case were we to meet tomorrow. At present I unfortunately weigh four-and-twenty stone, and I guess that you do not exceed twelve. From this circumstance singly, I am doubly the mark that you are; but, besides this, you are active, and I am unwieldy. I therefore propose to you, that, from this day forwards, we severally endeavour by all possible means, you to fatten, and I to waste, till we can meet at the medium of eighteen stone.[58]

This type of inequality was often hard to avoid. In 1914 Miguel Almeyreda, a journalist working in Paris, wrote a series of articles traducing André Lebey, a socialist candidate for the Versailles constituency. Lebey challenged Almeyreda; they agreed to fight with swords. It was, however, a thoroughly unequal contest, as Lebey was an accomplished swordsman, the founder of a fencing club, who had won several tournaments. Almeyreda, on the other hand, was 'greatly inferior in the science of arms'. However, when they set to, events took a unexpected turn: 'As so often happens in like circumstances the scientific fencer was the first to be wounded, but his surprise was greater than his injury.' Once Lebey had recovered his poise, he began to gain the upper hand; the fight continued until he managed to inflict a serious wound on Almeyreda, at which point the fight was stopped.[59]

The objection to inequality on the duelling ground was that it allowed the braggart and the bully to throw their weight around, cowing less aggressive souls with their willingness to provoke a duel. It allowed a 'Fighting' Fitzgerald to bluster his way through the world, insulting and threatening with impunity: he was happy to fight and his chances of emerging unscathed from the encounter were, probably, better than his opponent's. Duelling was intended as a way of settling questions of honour between men, not as a method of enforcing one's will on another, justifying relentlessly bad behaviour or killing off one's creditors.

But inequality did not just consist in differing abilities with sword or pistol: it had other sources, gentler but no less worrying. The Revd. William Gilpin wrote a conversation piece in which a soldier, a parson and the local squire discuss the rights and wrongs of duelling. The squire, Sir Charles, told the following tale of a British general officer.

> On receiving a challenge, he went to the challenger, and told him he supposed they were to fight on equal terms; but as things now stand, said he, the terms are very unequal. I have a wife and five children, who have nothing to subsist on but my appointments: you have a considerable fortune and no family: – to place us, therefore, on an equality, I desire you will go with me to a conveyancer, and settle upon my wife and children, if I should fall, the value of my appointments. When you have signed such a conveyance, if you insist upon it, I will then fight you. The deliberate manner in which the general said this, and the apparent justice of the requisition, made his antagonist reflect a little, on the idea of leaving a wife and five children to beggery: and as the affair could not stand reflection, it went off.[60]

Indeed, one of the main arguments of the anti-duelling campaigners was, as we will see later, the distress, emotional and material, of families who lost their menfolk in duels. As one clerical opponent of duelling put it, 'There is no Family secure, but its blooming Hopes, or its main support may not be suddenly cut off.'[61]

Which brings us neatly to the aftermath of a duel, to its effects and results. For the young bloods of de Bouteville's day, duelling was a game, a rite of passage for headstrong aristocrats. It kept them fit and honed their fighting skills; it fostered *esprit de corps*, binding them together in a fellowship, a blood brotherhood. However, the superficial glamour of the duel, the high sentiments and flashing blades should not be allowed to disguise the fact that de Bouteville and many of his fellowship of bravoes met grisly ends in distant glades or, in de Bouteville's case, on the scaffold.

The reformers, from all countries and at all times, never ceased to rail against the toll that duelling took of young, promising lives. In 1807 the Revd. John Williams preached a sermon in the parish church at Stroud in Gloucestershire following the death in a duel of Joseph Delmont, a subaltern in the 82nd foot. Williams described Delmont as 'a young man of a very interesting appearance; truly pleasing in his address, and amiable in his manners; of a liberal education and promising talents'.

Williams, as parish priest, was called to administer the sacrament to Delmont and was with him when he died. In depicting the scene at Delmont's deathbed to his congregation he spared it nothing.

> How distressing it is to a reflective mind, to see a promising youth, of undoubted courage and flattering prospects, cut down in the bloom of his years, like a flower of the field – one, who in maturer years might have been an honour to his country, an ornament to society, and a blessing to his friends.[62]

It was perhaps a blessing in disguise that Delmont was killed in his duel. For those who were maimed, very often all they had to look forward to was an uncertain future of dependence on others, of pain and disability.

Injury was, of course an ever-present threat for duellists and, in the days before modern medicine, the spectre of death stalked close behind. Just about the only serious moment in Mark Twain's wonderfully melodramatic account of 'The Great French Duel' is when Gambetta contemplates the outcome of the encounter.

> I laid it [the pistol], all lonely and forlorn, in the centre of the vast solitude of his palm. He gazed at it and shuddered. And still mournfully contemplating it, he murmured, in a broken voice, –
>
> 'Alas, it is not death I dread but mutilation.'[63]

Even in duelling's later years, when antiseptics and anaesthesia were readily available, danger lurked. In 1925 Senhor Beja Silva, a high-ranking official in Lisbon's city council, and Senhor Antonio Centeno, a director of a gas company, fell out. They agreed to settle their differences on the duelling ground; swords were the chosen weapon. Unfortunately, during the second round, Silva collapsed and died. He had suffered a heart attack.[64]

Other duellists faced the full majesty of the criminal law; the diligence with which prosecutions were pursued varied (as we will see later), as did the severity of the penalties faced by those found guilty of duelling offences. What can safely be said here is that there was, in most countries at most times, a yawning gulf between the theoretical legal position of duellists and the way in which they were treated in practice. Duellists convicted in civil or military courts faced sentences that ranged from the gallows to a mild reprimand. To put it bluntly, with a few notable exceptions, they got off very lightly indeed.

There were other consequences of duelling, not fatal, certainly, but nevertheless serious for the individual concerned. The Count d'Orsay, that flamboyant early nineteenth-century dandy and man-about-town, took part in several duels as second or principal. Just before stepping up to face an opponent he is supposed to have remarked,

> You know, my dear friend, I am not on a par with my antagonist: he is a very ugly fellow, and if I wound him in the face, he won't look much the worse for it; but on my side it ought to be agreed that he should not aim higher than my chest, for if my face should be spoiled, 'ce serait vraiment dommage'.[65]

For a foppish dandy like the count, facial disfigurement would be a fate worse than dishonour or death. The count's remark may seem to us (and probably to his contemporaries too) an outrageous conceit but it is a fine example of the insouciance that duellists were expected to display.

We have now examined in some detail the three foundations of the duel: the challenge, the role of seconds and the conduct of the fight itself. It is these three acts that define the modern duel; there were differences in custom and practice, indeed it would be surprising were this not the case. Duelling, after all, came of age in sixteenth-century France, thrived all over nineteenth-century Europe and was still very much alive in Latin America, among other places, in the twentieth century. There were variations in etiquette, in the weapons used and in way the fights were conducted but the three defining characteristics remained constant and recognisable. The second part of the book will now examine how duelling developed over the centuries in the different countries. It will look too at the opposition to duelling from Church and state, and examine the reasons for duelling's disappearance.

Part II

THE STORY OF THE DUEL

Chapter Five

THE AGE OF THE MUSKETEERS:
1559–1660

I N THE LAST WEEK OF June 1559 Paris was *en fête*, celebrating the signing in April of the Treaty of Cateau-Cambrésis, which brought to an end the Italian Wars between France and Spain. The wars had dragged on, seemingly interminably, since Charles VIII of France had crossed the Alps in 1494 to stake his claim to the Kingdom of Naples. By the late 1550s the principal antagonists, the Emperor Charles V and Francis I (who had died in 1547) had departed the scene, and the new rulers were only too glad to bring the ruinous wars to an end. As was the custom at the time, the peace treaty was accompanied by a brace of marriages, intended to bind the competing dynasties of Valois and Hapsburg closer together. The French king's eldest daughter, Elisabeth, was to marry the recently widowed King of Spain, the austere Philip II. At the same time Marguerite, Henry II's spinster sister, was to marry the Duke of Savoy, Emmanuel-Philibert, a Hapsburg ally.

The young princess was married by proxy in Notre-Dame on 22 June and the tournament forming part of the celebrations of the wedding began a week later. Lists were constructed in the rue Saint-Antoine. The jousting took place over three days in front of galleries of richly dressed courtiers and important foreign visitors from Spain and Savoy. On the third day, in front of the entire court, Henry himself took to the lists. He was victorious in his first two bouts but in the third the King was almost unseated by the young Scottish captain of his bodyguard, the Count de Montgomery. Although it was late in the afternoon Henry was adamant that he be allowed an opportunity to take his revenge on Montgomery, despite his wife, Catherine de Medici, imploring him to stop. The two men took their horses to the entrance of the lists and, levelling their lances, turned to charge towards each other. As they met there was a splintering crash and the King slumped forward over his horse's neck and withers. As he was lifted down from his horse it was immediately evident that the King was seriously injured: splinters from Montgomery's shattered lance had penetrated his jousting helm, causing a terrible wound in his eye and temple. The King was carried to the nearby Château des Tournelles. It was here that, on 9 July, Henry II died, having lingered in great pain for 10 days.[1]

Henry's death opened a new and stormy chapter in French history. His widow, Catherine de Medici, stood behind three young sons in succession as they attempted to rule a France torn apart by factional and religious strife. In circumstances that would have tested much stronger rulers, the last three Valois kings were unable to prevent France slipping into civil war. Chaos and disorder continued until Henry of Navarre established himself on the throne; in 1593 he famously converted to Catholicism, bringing the Wars of Religion to a close. This prolonged period of civil war, disorder bordering on anarchy, was an ideal forcing frame for the new custom of duelling. Weak central authority and a prevailing climate of lawlessness and violence were conditions in which duelling could flourish. The Italian Wars had done much to introduce French fighting men to the new codes of honour that underpinned duelling. Henry's death in a tournament celebrating the end of those wars gave rise to a prolonged period of weak government and strife that allowed the new custom to put down vigorous roots in France.

Henry II's reign ended as it begun, in medieval ritual. The tournament with which the Peace of Cateau-Cambrésis was celebrated was a relic of the medieval knightly culture. Likewise, the judicial combat between Jarnac and La Châtaigneraie in July 1547, three months after

Henry had acceded to the throne, was a hangover from the age of chivalry. The origins of the dispute between the two men stretched back to the previous reign and were intimately connected with the politics and rivalries of the court. Francis had refused to allow the two men to fight, but Henry, relishing the opportunity to preside over such an exhibition of knightly courage and virtue, was only too pleased to grant permission for the two men to settle their differences at the point of a sword.

La Châtaigneraie and Jarnac fought on 10 July 1547 on ground specially prepared for the purpose at Saint-Germain-en-Laye. Around the arena, stands and pavilions had been erected to accommodate all the spectators who thronged the ground, eager to watch the contest. The impending fight had generated a buzz of excitement at court, each party loyal to its man. La Châtaigneraie, whose prowess in combat was well known, was reckoned the favourite. Jarnac, by contrast, was given little chance. However, when the fight took place, before the King, his mistress Diane de Poitiers, the Queen, the entire court and a huge crowd of other, less exalted spectators, the underdog pulled off a spectacular triumph. Snaking in under his opponent's guard, Jarnac slashed La Châtaigneraie behind his knee, slicing through his hamstrings. With his opponent down and at his mercy, Jarnac asked the King for his honour to be restored to him. Eventually, in bad grace, Henry agreed. Jarnac was then content to spare his stricken opponent's life although, in the event, he bled to death. The stroke with which Jarnac felled La Châtaigneraie has been known ever since as *le coup de Jarnac.*

Famous as this encounter is, it was not a duel in the modern sense of the word. Indeed, it serves as a fine example of the differences between the medieval notion of judicial combat and the modern duel. Jarnac's fight was sanctioned by the King and took place in public under the supervision of the monarch. Henry endorsed the result, which was recognised by the parties as binding. It had more in common with the abortive combat between Norfolk and Bolingbroke authorised by Richard II than with the duels of the eighteenth century. The modern duel is a different beast, secretive, private and illegal.

One historian has gone so far as to suggest that Jarnac's 'duel' hastened the disappearance of the judicial combat and the development of the modern, private duel. Henry II's failure, the theory goes, to exercise his authority as 'umpire', resulting in the death of La Châtaigneraie, undermined the concept of the officially sanctioned judicial combat and, perhaps, in the long term, promoted the modern, private duel.[2]

There is no doubt that the nature of duelling changed in the second half of the sixteenth century. By the end of the century the ritual of the quasi-judicial combat had been largely abandoned. No longer were heralds dispatched to issue challenges, nor were fights controlled by royal command. At the same time the role of the second became more formalised: they started taking part in the fight, too.[3] The development of the role of the second was a natural counterbalance to the increasingly secretive, illegal nature of duelling. If a contest is fought in lists in front of the King and several hundred spectators, there is little scope for foul play. If, however, a duel is fought furtively in a distant clearing far from prying eyes, the need for a supporter to guard against chicanery is obvious.

The general lawlessness and violence that infected France in these years was reflected in the atmosphere at court, particularly during the reign of Henry III (1574–89). In these years court was 'no longer a place of great political machinations and manoeuvring; under Henry it became a hotbed of petty hatreds played out with knives, swords and whispered accusations'.[4]

In 1586 Olivier de la Marche published his *Livre des Duels*. The title page reminds the reader that that he or she is about to embark upon a '*Livre fort utile pour ce temps*' ('A most useful book for these times'), and no wonder.

Henry III surrounded himself with a group of young exquisites, known as the *mignons*. They were enthusiastic duellists, so much so that Henry was obliged in January 1578 to issue a decree denouncing the quarrelling and duelling that so disturbed court life. The royal decree was evidently not taken too seriously, as two months later six of his *mignons* fought a bloody duel, three against three, outside the city walls at the Porte Saint-Antoine. The two principals were Quelus and Antraguet; their seconds were, respectively, Maugiron and Livarot and Riberac and Schomberg. The two principals began fighting, whereupon Maugiron and Riberac set about each other. The other two seconds, not wishing to be idle spectators, then joined in. It was a bloodbath. Schomberg, who was German, slashed Livarot's cheek and was promptly run through the body and killed; Maugiron was killed and Riberac mortally wounded. Quelus, badly wounded, lingered in agony for a month before dying.[5]

By the end of the century France's agony was over: Henry IV had ended the Wars of Religion and, with the Edict of Nantes of 1598, begun the process of healing the wounds caused by religious intolerance and persecution. The nation's warring factions may, for the moment, have been quietened but the practice of duelling was by now firmly entrenched among the nobility. The medieval notions of chivalry had now been thoroughly absorbed and updated by a nobility anxious to have a ready means of demonstrating their courage.[6] Henry IV's reign was to witness an explosion of duelling, an unprecedented bloodletting.

* * *

Across the Channel in England the political situation could hardly have been more different. The second half of the sixteenth century was a period of stability and peace at home; Queen Elizabeth's moderate, prudent political instincts prevented the descent into chaos and civil war that so scarred France in these decades. The religious stresses that tore France apart were kept in check in England as the government waged a continual but covert battle against Jesuit priests and popish agents. The threat posed to England by Philip II from the Netherlands was contained until, with the dispersal of the invading Armada in 1588, he was defeated.

However, although the political unruliness infecting the Continent failed to cross the Channel, the ideas on which the duelling codes were based gained a wide currency at Elizabeth's court and in the upper echelons of society. One polemicist writing towards the end of the seventeenth century had no doubt who was to blame for the introduction of duelling to England.

Nevertheless during the League and Civil Wars of France [the Wars of Religion], the overweening heat of that people, brought in vogue amongst themselves, and by a pernicious Contagion propagated amongst their Neighbours, who were silly enough to ape them, the inhuman and barbarous Practice of fighting and murdering one another in cold Blood...[7]

There was no shortage of books explaining to gentlemen how they should conduct themselves or how they should behave in the face of an insult. They were all founded on the new notions of a gentleman's personal honour. These were either translations of foreign (mostly Italian) treatises or home-grown tracts that leaned heavily on the ideas propounded by the Continental authorities. Baldassare Castiglione's *The book of the courtier* was translated into English as early as 1561 and became influential in forming the behaviour of the high-ranking English gentleman of the time. Its influence can be gauged from the fact that Sir Philip Sidney, the epitome of the Elizabethan Renaissance courtier, soldier and poet, is supposed to have carried a copy of Castiglione's book in his pocket. Sidney was responsible for 'perhaps the most famous challenge in Elizabethan England' when he held the Earl of Oxford to account on a tennis court in 1579.[8]

Among other works that an English gentleman aspiring to acquire refined Italian manners could have consulted were the Frenchman Philibert de Vienne's *The philosopher of the court*, which first appeared in English in 1575. In the following year Giovanni Della Casa's treatise on manners and behaviour was translated into English. Stephano Guazzo's *The civile conuersation* was translated in 1586; Annibale Romei's *The courtiers académie* did not appear in English until 1598. One of the earliest English writers to address the subject was Simon Robson, whose *The covrte of ciuill courtesie* was published in 1577.

At the same time as English gentlemen were imbibing these new notions of personal honour, they were also acquiring the skills necessary to put the new ideas into action. An important technical innovation of the period, one that gave a great boost to the science of swordplay, was the development of the rapier. The rapier had originally appeared in Spain in the early fifteenth century; it was 'a slender, double-edged sword, rarely less than four feet long'.[9] The Spanish began to wear these swords with everyday dress and, when Charles V's armies of overran Italy in the early sixteenth century, the rapier went with them. By the middle of the century the rapier had developed into the ideal thrusting weapon: the 'blade was rarely more than three-eights of an inch wide and sometimes as much as fifty inches long, mounted in the classic "swept" hilt'.[10]

By the middle of the sixteenth century, the rapier, usually used in conjunction with a dagger, had become the accepted weapon for duelling in France and Italy, supplanting the broadsword and buckler (or shield). This change in the weaponry used for duelling had two practical results. First, hand-to-hand combat became much more dangerous. Fighting with broadsword and buckler, in the words of one historian, 'allowed the maximum muscular effort and the most spectacular show of violence with the minimum threat to life and limb. Fighting with them was not much more dangerous than all-in wrestling.'[11]

The rapier, by contrast, was a lethal weapon: its sharp point made it all too easy to run a man through his vital organs, killing him. The Earl of Oxford was armed with a rapier when he accidentally killed a man in 1567.[12]

The second consequence of the adoption of the rapier as the principal duelling weapon was the need for instruction. The broadsword and buckler were (at least in theory) an elaborate, formalised method of fighting but the new-fangled rapier required a wholly different technique. The broadsword required, above all else, physical strength, whereas the rapier demanded a much higher degree of skill and dexterity. The much greater level of risk attached to fighting with the rapier persuaded men to master the new art of fencing before putting their lives at stake on the duelling ground.

In 1569 an Italian fencing master, Rocco Bonetti, arrived in England and, in 1576, set up the country's first fencing school at Black-friars in London. Here, courtiers and gentlemen could now learn the new Italian techniques and from the first he numbered important men among his clients, hanging their coats of arms around the walls of his *salle*. Sir Walter Raleigh, for one, was a pupil. In the 1590s,

Vicentio Saviolo and his brother Jeronimo established a second fencing school in London.[13] The brothers were great exponents of the rapier.

Matching, as it were, the fencing schools was the advent of the manual offering technical advice on duelling and the use of the rapier. These drew heavily on the Italian sources, particularly Girolamo Muzio's *Il duello* of 1550. The first to be published in England was the anonymous *The booke of honor and armes* of 1590.[14] However, it was Saviolo himself who produced the most important fencing manual of the period. His book, *His Practice*, was published in London in 1595 and falls into two parts: the first was a straightforward technical manual; the second addressed matters 'of Honor and honorable Quarrles'.[15]

Although Saviolo's book is the best known of the technical manuals, there were two others, at least, published in England in the same decade. Giacomo di Grassi's *His true Arte of Defence* first appeared in English translation in 1594. It deals in great detail with all the different methods of hand-to-hand fighting, including the sword and buckler, the rapier and dagger, the two-handed sword, and the pike and halberd. George Silver's home-grown *Paradoxes of Defence* was published in 1599. Silver was vehemently opposed to the newly imported Italian fencing techniques; he maintained that the traditional sword-and-buckler method was greatly superior to the new-fangled rapier.

William Shakespeare may have taken fencing lessons but we do not know whether he ever became embroiled in a duel. Whether he himself fought, he was keenly aware of the fashionable culture of honour, of the duelling codes and of fencing. His knowledge of the tenets of gentlemanly honour is demonstrated in some of his plays, although his treatment of the subject is usually markedly lacking in respect, if not openly contemptuous. This is amply illustrated by the following lines, uttered by Touchstone, from *As You Like It*:

> As thus, sir: I did dislike the cut of a certain courtier's beard. He sent me word if I said his beard was not cut well, he was in the mind it was. This is called the Retort Courteous. If I sent him word again it was not well

cut, he would send me word he cut it to please himself. This is called the Quip Modest. If again it was not well cut, he disabled my judgement. This is called the Reply Churlish. If again it was not well cut, he would answer I spake not true. This is called the Reproof Valiant. If again it was not well cut, he would say I lie. This is called the Countercheck Quarrelsome. And so to the Lie Circumstantial, and the Lie Direct.[16]

If Shakespeare was here derisive of the refined etiquette of the honour codes, he was no less contemptuous of the duellists' swaggering braggadocio. In *Romeo and Juliet* Tybalt, on behalf of the Capulets, delivers a challenge to the Montagues, in the person of Romeo's father. On hearing of this, Mercutio is withering in his scorn of Tybalt and the duellist's pretensions.

> O, he's the courageous captain of compliments. He fights as you sing pricksong: keeps time, distance, and proportion. He rests his minim rests: one, two, and the third in your bosom; the very butcher of a silk button. A duellist, a duellist; a gentleman of the very first house of the first and second cause. Ah, the immortal *passado*, the *punto reverso*, the *hai*.[17]

When the swords are drawn, however, it is Mercutio who is the first to be killed, by Tybalt, the very model of the modern duellist, who is then himself killed in his turn by Romeo. Shakespeare here is sending up the punctilios of the honour code and the supposed refinement and gallantry of the duellist himself. Nor did the new art of fencing itself escape the dramatist's eye. The denouement of *Hamlet* takes place within the context of a fencing bout between Laertes and Hamlet, supposedly a simple test of skill but in fact subverted to vengeful murder.

The play shows Shakespeare to have been well versed in the formalities and practices of the fencing schools. Reputation in this gentlemanly accomplishment was important. In the play Claudius uses Laertes's renown as a swordsman to draw Hamlet into the bout.

> And gave you such a masterly report
> For art and exercise in your defence,
> And for your rapier most especially.[18]

The fight is arranged as a match, with stopped foils. The King is said to have had a large wager on the outcome. All the customary formalities are observed; the foppish Osric assures the two participants that the foils are the same length. He also acts as umpire. When the bout begins it is fought in the proper sporting spirit. Quickly, however, murderous intent takes over and both men are mortally wounded.[19]

It is clear that the English gentleman of the late sixteenth century who wished to acquaint himself with the codes of honour and the proper principles of duelling had every opportunity to do so. There was no shortage of encouragement for the aspiring duellist. He could buy and read one or more of a number of books in print on the subject. If he lived in London – and, if a courtier, he would for at least some of the year – he could enrol in a fencing school. He could even go to the theatre in the hope of picking up a smattering of knowledge. What is more difficult to determine is the number of duels to which these influences, theoretical and practical, gave rise.

Apart from Sir Philip Sidney's celebrated challenge of the Earl of Oxford in 1579 referred to above, we have very few examples of duels actually fought during Elizabeth's reign. Lawrence Stone, in his classic study of the English aristocracy between 1558 and 1641, asserts that, at first (i.e. in the 1580s and 1590s), the duelling code 'was a useful check upon the insolence of the nobility'. Addressing the question of the number of duels fought in England at this period he says,

> it is worth recording that the number of duels and challenges mentioned in newsletters and correspondence jumps suddenly from 5 in the 1580s to nearly 20 in the next decade, to rise thereafter to a peak of 33 in the next ten years.[20]

These figures represent, of course, only those duels that have come to light, not necessarily all those that were fought and appear to apply to duels and challenges among the gentry and nobility alike. When the focus is narrowed to the peerage alone, the duel becomes, in these years, an even rarer beast. Stone detected a mere 10 duels and challenges to duels between peers in the years 1580–99, or about one every other year.[21] On the basis of Stone's statistics – and I know of no others that cast any light on the propensity of late Tudor gentlemen to challenge and fight one another – it seems fair to conclude that, prior to the end of Elizabeth's reign, duelling in England was not a widespread problem.

* * *

If the second half of the sixteenth century was the period in both England and France when the modern duel put down its roots, the early seventeenth century was the season of its first vigorous growth. Indeed, there are sound reasons for thinking that Henry IV's reign may represent the duel's high-water mark. It witnessed, if the statistics are to be believed, an effusion of blood unequalled before or since. Henry IV reigned from 1589 to 1610, and in this period of just over 20 years it is thought that somewhere between 4,000 and 8,000 'men of quality' were killed in duels. Most modern writers on duelling put forward a figure for the number of duellists killed in this period. Robert Baldick puts the number of deaths at 4,000 in the years 1589–1607 (that is, not quite all of Henry's reign).[22] Richard Cohen follows him, adding that this equates to four or five deaths a week, 'a fatality rate befitting a world war' given the size of France's population at the time.[23] By contrast, V.G. Kiernan plumps for a death toll of 8,000 during Henry's reign (the whole of it, one assumes), while Kevin McAleer prefers to say that more than 7,000 duellists were killed during the same period.[24] The latest historian of duelling, James Landale, does not dip his toe into this particular pool.[25] Whichever figure one prefers, the point remains the same: it was a period of unprecedented bloodletting.

Explaining the reasons for this lethal madness is more problematic. One historian, a Frenchman, ascribes the propensity of Frenchmen to duel – the *furia francese* – to the Gallic temperament. 'We are', he writes, flushed no doubt with chauvinist pride, 'predisposed by national character to duel, therefore we duel.' The same writer does also allow that the political situation in France – as we have seen – was conducive to an explosion of duelling. As he puts it, 'The French path to absolute monarchy and the experience of religious dualism are two roots of the duel's vigour in the Most Christian Kingdom [France].'[26]

While this might be true for a longer view of French history in the sixteenth and seventeenth centuries, it does not necessarily explain why Henry IV's reign became such a bloodbath.

By 1600 there was in France a body of informed opinion that was strongly opposed to duelling. The Catholic Church, as it had for centuries, took the lead in denouncing the practice. The Council of Trent, which sat intermittently from 1545 to 1563, was principally concerned with revitalising the Church to face the challenge of the Reformation. It did, however, in its final session, find time to promulgate a decree against duelling. This forbade princes, under pain of excommunication, from 'granting a field' to duellists (that is, sanctioning a duel). It also condemned all duellists, seconds and other accessories to excommunication as well as banning those killed in duels from being buried in consecrated ground. However, the impact in France of the Tridentine decree against duelling was diminished by the reluctance of the Gallican Church to admit the authority of the Pope.[27] It has also been suggested that the effect of the Council of Trent's decree against duelling was further diminished by the fact that the Counter-Reformation was essentially (at least in social terms) a conservative movement. It tended to align itself with princes, nobles and men of property, the very people who espoused the institution of duelling.[28] Thus, the theory runs, in attacking duelling the Council was running the risk of alienating the very people on whom it depended for support. In France the Estates-General met three times between 1560 and the assassination of Henry IV; on each occasion the clergy recorded at least one formal complaint against duelling.

The Catholic Church may have taken the lead in opposing duelling but there were secular voices raised too against the custom. In 1554 Antonio Massa published his *Contra Usum Duelli*, one of the very first tracts inveighing against the 'modern' duel. It first appeared in Rome in Latin but was sufficiently successful that an Italian translation was published in Venice in the following year. In 1608 Marc de la Beraudiere published an anti-duelling tract that advocated the introduction of 'licensed' duelling in a *champs clos*, under the authority of the King. Although hardly an original idea – the *champs clos* was at the heart of the judicial combat (see Jarnac's fight earlier) – de la Beraudiere proposed it as a way of reducing the number of duels fought in France. The present level of deaths in duels was, the author thought, 'shaming to the nation'.[29]

In 1612 *Anti-Duel ou Discours pour L'Abolition des Duels* was published in Paris. Its author, G. Joly, was a royal councillor and a high-ranking deputy of the Constable of France, so his was an influential voice. Moreover, his book was published with the blessing of the King. It was a two-pronged denunciation of duelling, one aimed at the nobility and the other at the King himself. It is a good example of the type of anti-duelling tract circulating at the time.

Nor did the French monarchy ignore the opposition of the Church and the secular authors; indeed, starting (as we have seen) with Henry III in 1578, it was the source of a stream of edicts against duelling. Henry IV twice promulgated edicts against the practice: at Blois in 1602 and at Fontainebleau in 1609. The edict of 1602 criminalised all duels; the edict of 1609 made duelling a capital offence, moreover explicitly including seconds in its provisions. Not to be outdone, the Paris Parlement weighed in with its own anti-duelling legislation in 1599. So the measures were in place to deal with the bloody scourge of duelling; the problem lay in the lack of will to enforce the law.

The most serious failure of will lay right at the top, with the King himself, for Henry IV was an inveterate pardoner of duellists. We have seen the estimates of the number of duelling deaths during his reign; most writers seem to agree that he pardoned an equal if not larger number of duellists. In other words, Henry granted pardons to around 6,000 or 7,000 duellists over a 20-year period. Clearly, this was not a promising policy for a king bent on eradicating duelling.

Why was Henry so quick to pardon duellists? Or, put another way, why was he so reluctant to let them face the full rigour of the law? The answer lies partly in the political position in which Henry found himself and partly in his own personality.

Henry recognised that duelling was both contrary to the interests of the state and profoundly unchristian. When, however, it came to cracking down on individual duellists Henry was torn between duty and honour, between his role as monarch and his status as a nobleman, albeit a very grand one. As king, he saw the need to eradicate duelling from his kingdom, but the nobleman in him was unwilling to countenance stamping out a privilege enjoyed by his own caste. This ambivalence explained the apparently glaring contradiction between the well-meaning edicts on the one hand and the reckless pardoning on the other. One historian imputes more cynical motives to Henry. V.G. Kiernan suggests that the anti-duelling edicts were intended to impress the bourgeoisie while the promiscuous granting of pardons was to mollify the nobility.[30] Certainly, when Henry came to the throne after decades of civil war he was obliged to heal the rifts in his kingdom; he could ill afford to alienate powerful nobles. Turning a blind eye to their treasured privilege of duelling was, perhaps, a price that Henry was prepared to pay. Others, too, were keen to impute more sinister motives to Henry. Sir George Carew, the English ambassador in Paris, believed that Henry allowed duelling to flourish so as to encourage divisions within the nobility and, at the same time, rid himself of hotheads.[31]

Of the thousands of French noblemen who were killed in this extraordinary bloodletting, one particular individual stands, dripping in blood, head and shoulders above any of his contemporaries: the Chevalier d'Andrieux. He was supposed to have killed 72 men in duels before his 30th birthday. He had the charming habit of forcing his defeated opponents to deny God, on pain of death, before cutting their throats, thereby, as he said, having the pleasure of killing both body and soul at the same time.

* * *

In 1603 Elizabeth I's long reign came to an end and the crown passed to her cousin James VI, King of Scotland. James's reign is an important period in the history of duelling: it witnessed an explosion in the art that, if not on the scale of what was then happening on the other side of the Channel, was nevertheless alarming. One authority has estimated that in the first two decades of the century an English aristocrat had a 40 per cent chance of being involved in a duel at some point in his adult life.[32] There were several notorious duels fought between courtiers that had the effect of stiffening the opposition to the practice. James's reign marks the beginning in England of a concerted opposition to duelling.

We have seen that in the latter years of Elizabeth's reign the Italian honour codes were increasingly in vogue among the English aristocracy and gentry. The fencing schools and the coaching manuals provided men with the practical skills necessary to defend themselves and their honour on the duelling ground. It has been suggested that the outbreak of peace on the Continent following the signing of the Peace of Vervins in 1598 'stimulated interest in the duel'. Englishmen could once again visit France in safety, and, since Paris was the epicentre of the duel, 'knowledge of the art of fencing and the duelling code were standard educational benefits of the Grand Tour'.[33]

Whatever reasons lay behind the growth of duelling during James I's reign it remained, by French standards, relatively modest. One French historian suggests that, while things French were increasingly fashionable among the English upper classes, duelling never caught on in England to the extent it did in France. He suggests that the English aristocracy and gentry had a greater sense of the value of the rule of law and of their own responsibility. He also claims that the English gentry were too busy making money to concern themselves with the finer points of honour. They 'conducted themselves like accountants'.[34]

Although the scale of duelling in England in these years was happily modest by comparison with what was happening in France, there were individual duels that were very far from tame; indeed, their savagery shocked contemporaries. In November 1609 two of James's favourites – Stuart was one of the King's godsons – fought a duel arising from 'light dispute at cards'.[35] A friend's letter tells the story.

> Mr Jas. Stuart and Mr Geo. Wharton have slain each other about the mistaking of a card at play in my Lord of Essex's chamber in Court. Their friends discourse strangely of the humours of those that might have stopped youths' fury [*sic*]. One coach carried them alive to the field and brought them both home dead. They died in Islington Fields.[36]

This sorry tale has two points of interest. First is the wholly trivial cause of the quarrel, a disagreement over a game of cards, one of the players accidentally revoked, perhaps, not something even as serious as an argument over a gambling debt. The second point to notice is the slightly elliptical remark in this letter about 'the humours of those who might have stopped youths' fury'. This suggests that others who were present could and should have made greater efforts to reconcile the two men, particularly as the dispute was over so trivial a matter.

In the following year Sir Hatton Cheke and Sir Thomas Dutton fought a duel at Calais. They were both officers campaigning in the Low Countries, Cheke the senior, and both had a reputation for being hot-tempered and quarrelsome. At the siege of Julich that summer Cheke had given Dutton an order in terms that Dutton resented. Once Julich had fallen, Dutton returned home in a huff and began to circulate rumours about his superior officers. When these came to King James's ears, greatly displeased he ordered Dutton's arrest and trial. He recognised that rumourmongering of this nature was likely to end in bloodshed on the duelling ground. By the end of the year Dutton had returned to the Continent, where he and Cheke were able to arrange to settle their differences. The best account of the duel is Thomas Carlyle's, which, although written more than two centuries after the encounter, has a vivid drama and freshness to it that make it worth quoting.

> And so, on Calais Sands, in a winter morning of the year 1610, this is what we see, most authentically, through the lapse of dim time. Two gentlemen stript to the shirt and waistband; in the two hands of each a rapier and a dagger clutched; their looks sufficiently serious! The seconds, having stript, equipt and fairly overhauled and certified them, are just about retiring from the measured fate-circle, not without indignation that *they* are forbidden to fight. Two gentlemen in this alarming posture; of whom the universe knows, has known and will know nothing, except that they were of choleric humour and assisted in the Netherlands wars! They are evidently English human creatures in the height of silent fury and measured circle of fate; whom we here audibly name once more, sir Hatton Cheke; sir Thomas Dutton: knights both, soldadoes both. Ill-fated English human creatures, what horrible confusion of the pit is this?
>
> Dutton, though in suppressed rage, the seconds about to withdraw, will explain some things if a word were granted. 'No words,' says the other, 'stand on your guard,' brandishing his rapier grasping harder his dagger. Dutton now silent too, is on his guard. Good heavens! after some

ABOVE Medieval jousting was both sport and military exercise. It was the precursor of the modern duel, albeit with important differences.

Tycho Brahe was a sixteenth-century Danish astronomer who lost his nose in a duel and had himself fitted with an early artificial replacement made of copper.

A long-running feud between Warren Hastings and Sir Philip Francis in the councils of the government of India resulted in a duel between the two men in 1780. Francis was seriously wounded but recovered and soon afterwards left India. The suspicion lingers that Hastings deliberately provoked Francis into challenging him to a duel as a way of ridding himself of his presence in the government.

An early English duel dating from the late sixteenth or early seventeenth century.

ABOVE This eighteenth-century American illustration is a stinging indictment of duelling. Both the protagonists have been injured, one, it appears, fatally. Where, the artist asks, is the satisfaction or the honour in this sad, squalid scene?

This engraving is supposed to represent a duel from the 1790s, although by that time in England the pistol was the more usual duelling weapon. In the background is Westminster Abbey.

This nineteenth-century engraving of a pistol duel shows a woman, presumably the object of the rivalry between the two men, fainting in the arms of one of the protagonists.

Russia's most famous poet, Alexander Pushkin, was killed in a duel in 1837. The duel scene in his verse-novel *Eugene Onegin* prefigures to a remarkable degree the duel in which Pushkin was himself killed.

Cut, thrust and swagger in seventeenth-century France: illustration for *The Three Musketeers*, by Alexander Dumas.

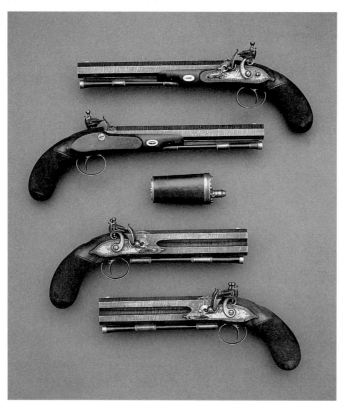

Both pairs of flintlock pistols, dating from around 1804, were made by the celebrated London gunsmith John Manton. The upper pair is typical of the duelling pistols of the day. The lower pair is more unusual, being double-barrelled. As a result, each pistol has two flintlocks, one for each barrel. Between the pairs of pistols is a powder horn.

The *mensur* (or students' duel) was a thriving institution in the universities of Wilhelmine Germany. In this painting from 1894, the two protagonists are wearing extensive head and body protection as well as goggles. Their faces remained exposed and were often slashed – wounds which became highly prized duelling scars.

ABOVE 'Are you ready, gentlemen?' This painting from 1815 depicts the moment of truth: the order to fire is about to be given.

This early nineteenth century engraving shows two women – often known as 'petticoat' duellists – crossing swords. Generally, women did not fight duels, although very occasionally they did.

DI M. CAMILLO AGRIPPA
TRATTATO DI SCIENZA
D'ARME.
ET VN DIALOGO IN DETTA
MATERIA.

In Venetia, Appresso Antonio
Pinargenti. M.D.LXVIII.

Published in Italian in Venice in 1568, Camillo Agrippa's manual *Scienza d'Arme* guides the aspiring fencer or duellist, with the help of numerous engraved illustrations, through the technicalities of swordplay.

brief flourishing and flashing, the gleam of the swift clear steel playing madly in one's eyes, they, at the first pass, plunge home on one another: home with beak and claws; home to the very heart! Cheke's rapier is through Dutton's throat from before, and his dagger is through it from behind: the windpipe miraculously missed; and in the same instant, Dutton's rapier is through Cheke's body from before, his dagger through is back from behind: lungs and life *not* missed; and the seconds have to advance 'pull out the four bloody weapons,' disengage that hell-embrace of theirs. This is serious enough! Cheke reels, his life fast flowing; but still rushes rabid on Dutton who merely parries skips; till Cheke reels down dead in his rage. 'He had a bloody burial there that morning' says my ancient friend. He will assist no more in the Netherlands or other wars.[37]

The duel had an instructive postscript. Six months after Dutton had killed Cheke, he wrote to his patron the Earl of Salisbury bemoaning the consequences of the duel: 'my punishments already have been too great for my poor fortunes to bear'. He had, he said, forfeited the King's favour, suffered a spell of severe imprisonment, lost the command of his company, which had cost him and some friends £600 to raise and equip. To add to his woes, this company had incurred, since the duel, further expenses of £700, which Dutton was in no position to meet. Dutton may have escaped the full censure of the law for killing Cheke but the episode had nevertheless had serious consequences for him.[38]

The duels between Wharton and Stuart and Cheke and Dutton were not isolated examples but, for some reason, 1613 was a particularly quarrelsome year at the court of King James. As Lawrence Stone put it, 'It looked as if the English nobility, like fighting cocks in a ring, were about to indulge in wholesale mutual slaughter.'[39]

The most notorious duel of that year, indeed of the entire period, was that between Edward Sackville and Lord Bruce. The animosity between the two men was said to have arisen over a woman. Sackville has left an unusually detailed account of the affair. Before describing the duel itself he set out the terms that their respective seconds had agreed. The duel was to be fought on the Dutch coast near the border between the United Provinces and the Spanish Netherlands so that the survivor 'might exempt himself from the justice of the country by retiring into the dominions unoffended'.[40]

Clearly, neither Bruce nor Sackville were taking any chances: they had already decided to leave England to fight in order to evade the law, now they were making sure that they would not fall foul of any local provisions against duelling. The seconds also made some very specific arrangements for the conduct of the fight itself. If either duellist should fall or slip, he would acknowledge that his life had been in the other's hands. If one man's sword should break – and this would, it was recognised, happen only through bad luck – it was agreed that neither man would take advantage of the other's misfortune. The adversaries should attempt a reconciliation or, failing that, renew the fight on equal terms.

The duel was fought in marshy ground, at least ankle-deep in water. Sackville's description of his duel is remarkably vivid: he gives such a graphic account of the fight that, nearly 400 years later, we can hear the clanging blades, smell the brackish water and sense the desperation, the finality of the duel. As his account makes clear, there was nothing glamorous about this fight; it was a visceral struggle to the death, fought at close quarters, both men hacking desperately at each other, more akin to a lethal wrestling match than an elegant, gentlemanly fencing bout.

… I made a thrust but came short and in drawing back my sword my arm received a great wound thereon, which I interpreted as a reward for my short shooting, when in revenge I passed into him again, though I missed, then also receiving another wound above my right pap which passed level through my body almost to my back. And so grappling together he got hold on my sword and I on his and there we wrestled for the two greatest prizes we could ever expect trial for – honour and life: in which struggling my left hand having but an ordinary glove on it almost lost one of her subjects (though the meanest) my little finger, which hung only by the skin. But at length, breathless yet keeping our holds, there passed on both side propositions of quitting each other's swords, but where amity was dead confidence could not live, and who should quit first was the doubt, which on neither party either would perform. And so striving afresh with a kick and wrench I freed my long-captivated sword, which incontinently laying at his throat, being still master of his, I demanded if he would ask his life or yield his sword; both which, though in that imminent danger, he bravely denied to do, when myself, being wounded and feeling loss of blood (having three conduits streaming upon me), began to make faint and he courageously persisting not to accord to either of my former propositions remembrance of his former bloody desire and feeling of my present state I strake at his heart but with his avoiding missed my aim yet passed through his body and drawing out my sword, repassed it through again, though in another place, when he cried I am slain! seconding his speech with all the force he had to cast me; but, being too weak, after I had defended his assaults I easily became master over him and threw him on his back, where being over him I demanded if he would request his life but it seemed he prized it not at so dear a rate as to be holden for it, bravely replied he scorned it, which answer of his was so noble and worthy as I protest I could not find it in my heart to offer him more violence, only keeping him down well till at length his surgeon afar off cried out he would immediately die if his wound were not stopped, whereupon I asked him if he desired his surgeon should come in; which he accepted of. And so being drawn away I never offered to take his sword, accounting it inhuman to rob a dead man, for so I held him to be.[41]

Sackville, fearing the worst, sought help from his surgeon. He was being treated when

I escaped a greater danger, for my Lord's surgeon, when nobody dreamt of it, ran full at me with this Lord's sword; and, had not mine with my sword interposed himself, I had been slain by those base hands, although the Lord Bruce, then wallowing in his own blood and past expectation of life, conformable to all his former carriage which was undaunted and noble, cried out Base villain hold thy hands![42]

This, of course, was a serious breach of duelling etiquette on the part of Bruce's surgeon. Had he succeeded in killing Sackville, he would certainly have faced the full rigour of the law, and rightly so.

The two men had made at least one previous attempt to fight their duel. Earlier in the year, Bruce and Sackville had agreed to travel to the Low Countries to settle their differences when Bruce was arrested at

Dover. Sackville and his second evaded the authorities and made the crossing from Newhaven.[43] We also have a glimpse from Paris of the preparations that Bruce and Sackville made for their fight. It was no spur-of-the-moment decision but long contemplated.

> Three days since my lord Bruce ... is gone privately hence having lately bought two swords of a length; we imagine he is come into your jurisdiction to end bloodily that martial difference between him and Sackville. Great pity so brave spirits should receive no worthier trial of their valour.[44]

After the rising tide of duels in recent years the Sackville–Bruce encounter was the last straw for James. The King, a pacific man, was horrified by the bloodletting and determined to do something about it. Sir Henry Hobart, Chief Justice of the Common Pleas at this time, explained why duelling was so repugnant to the rule of law: 'These insolent figures take upon themselves to frame a law and commonwealth to themselves, as if they had the power to cast off the yoke of obedience to peace and justice.'

Hobart's words echo those of any number of anti-duelling campaigners over the centuries. The common law was clear about the responsibility of duellists for their actions: 'Unless a duel was fought in hot blood on a sudden falling out, the man who killed his opponent was guilty of murder; his second, and probably the second of the murdered man, were accessories before the fact.'[45]

The existing law was, however, only partly effective against duellists, as it did not allow for prosecutions for 'acts preparatory to a duel', issuing challenges and so on. The authorities had to wait for a duel to take place before they could bring proceedings. As this clearly hampered attempts to reduce the number of duels, James issued his *Proclamation against Private Challenges and Combats* (1613). This was both an anti-duelling tract and a piece of legislation. It denounced duelling and beefed up the law against it. It made acts preparatory to a duel punishable by fines or imprisonment and gave the responsibility for enforcement to the Court of Star Chamber. These measures were effective in keeping duelling within acceptable bounds, preventing an aristocratic bloodbath along French lines. It might have been more effective had James been less indulgent to his favourite courtiers. Sackville, for example, was exiled by the King for killing Bruce but, within a year, was back at court. James may not have been so free with pardons as was Henry IV across the Channel but he nevertheless undermined the effectiveness of his own campaign against duelling. It was another instance of the ambivalent attitude of early-modern monarchs to duelling.

It was not just the King who was exercised by the problem of duelling: several of his most prominent subjects were sufficiently worried about it to put pen to paper. In 1609 Sir Robert Cotton wrote *A discourse of the lawfulness of combates to bee performed in the presence of the Kinge or the Constable and Marshal of England, etc*. The title of this tract indicates that Cotton was suggesting the revival of the old custom of the officially sanctioned judicial combat as a alternative to bloody private duels. In the same year Sir Edward Coke, the Lord Chief Justice, wrote at the request of Lord Henry Howard *A discourse touchinge the unlawfulness of private combates*. Lord Howard also recorded his experience in resolving a duel in *Duello foil'd* of around the same date. A few years earlier in 1600, a barrister, Francis Tate, wrote a monograph on *The Antiquities, use and seremonies of lawful combates in England*. Again Tate's title indicates that he was promoting a revival of the judicial combat as an antidote to duelling.[46]

We have seen how James I regarded duelling. It seems that his son, Charles I, took a tough line against offenders, as the following story suggests. A quarrel erupted between Lords Newcastle and Holland, two of Charles's senior commanders. Newcastle took exception to his regiment's being assigned to the rear of an expedition. Holland complained to the King, who took Newcastle's side and there, for the time being, the quarrel rested. However, when the army was disbanded, Newcastle challenged Holland to a duel. When the King heard of this, he placed Holland under arrest. When Newcastle and his second turned up at the duelling ground, Holland's second, Sir Edmund Verney, was able to explain his principal's absence. Merely appearing at the duelling ground, although there was no possibility of a fight, was enough to provoke the King into clapping Newcastle into prison, where he was able to arrange a reconciliation between the two peers.[47]

Regulations for the army, forerunners of the Articles of War, issued in the reign of Charles I, imposed harsh penalties for soldiers caught fighting duels.

Charles's favourite prelate, William Laud, Archbishop of Canterbury, was, as one might expect, vigorously opposed to duelling. In his capacity as Chancellor of Oxford University, Laud was responsible in 1634 for providing the university with new statutes. The archbishop included in the new rules governing the conduct of undergraduates articles banning the giving or sending of a challenge or fighting a duel.[48]

During the period there were a number of publications that addressed the question of duelling. In 1610 John Selden published his *The Duello, or Single Combat*, which qualifies as one of the very earliest histories of duelling written in English. More practical advice became available in 1614, when G.H. Gent published his *The Private School of Defence*, a successor to the various fencing manuals that appeared in the late Tudor era. In 1632, during the Personal Rule, John Despagne published *Anti-duello*. Like Selden's history Despagne's book was published in English and is an early example of an anti-duelling tract.

In 1637 Tom Verney, a scion of the Buckinghamshire family, was challenged to a duel. Verney, who was described as a 'picturesque vagabond', was greatly exercised about cutting a dash on the duelling ground. The night before the meeting, he wrote to his brother, asking him produce some suitably fashionable kit in which to fight a duel. Evidently for a certain sort of young bravo, it was as important to look the part as to acquit oneself honourably on the duelling ground.

* * *

After the troubled years of the 1640s, the Civil War and the execution of the King, England emerged as a protectorate under Oliver Cromwell. Cromwell was determined to stamp out duelling, nor did he labour under any of the conflicts of interest that compromised the efforts of other rulers to eradicate the practice. His government had banned dancing around maypoles, an ancient but wholly innocent folk custom, so it was unlikely to tolerate duelling, a jealously guarded aristocratic privilege. In June 1654 Cromwell issued a proclamation against duelling. Describing it as a 'growing evil in this Nation', the Ordinance set out some new, more severe penalties for offenders, addressing both the duel itself and its prelude. Anyone who conveyed or accepted a challenge would be imprisoned for six months, with no grant of bail. Anyone who received a challenge must, within 24 hours, inform the authorities or be deemed to have accepted it. Any death resulting from a duel was henceforth to be treated as murder. Those who fought a duel, whether as principal or second, were upon conviction to be banished from England for life.[49]

It is difficult to know how effective the Ordinance was in eradicating duelling in England; as always in this subject reliable figures are difficult to obtain. What is certain, however, is that the Protectorate would have seemed a period of calm, when relatively few duels were fought, in comparison with what was to follow. The Restoration in 1660 unleashed an unprecedented spate of duels; for the returning Royalists, fighting each other, very often for wholly trivial causes, became an everyday pastime.

*   *   *

We have already seen how notions of gentlemanly honour and the ethos of the duel gradually established themselves in England in the late sixteenth and early seventeenth centuries. It is now time to look at how they took root in other parts of Europe.

On 23 May 1618 a delegation of Czech nobles entered Hradcany Castle overlooking Prague and threw the Hapsburg governors, Jaroslav von Martinez and Wilhelm von Salvata, out of the window, where they landed on a dung heap. The Defenestration of Prague shattered the uneasy peace that had existed in central Europe between Catholics and Protestants and began the long period of religious and dynastic conflict known to history as the Thirty Years War. The Thirty Years War is important in the history of duelling because during that time large areas of central Europe – much of it lying within the Holy Roman Empire – descended into chaos and bloodshed, conditions that were ideally suited to the spread of duelling. It is difficult to exaggerate the extent of the devastation. It was described in unrelenting

detail by Jacques Callot in his cycle of engravings dating from the
1630s entitled *Les Grandes Misères de la Guerre*. Norman Davies, in his
all-encompassing *Europe*, puts it thus:

> Germany lay desolate. The population had fallen from 21 million to
> perhaps 13 million. Between a third and a half of the people were dead.
> Whole cities, like Magdeburg, stood in ruins. Whole districts lay stripped
> of their inhabitants, their livestock, their supplies.[50]

During the decades of fighting and lawlessness that had reduced
Germany to this pitiful state, foreign armies and mercenaries, French,
Spanish, Italian, Danish and Swedish, crisscrossed the country. These
foreign soldiers inflicted untold misery on Germany and its people;
they also brought with them duelling.

In medieval Germany, as in much of the rest of Europe, there
existed, broadly, three institutions that can be seen as the forerunners
of the duel: the feud, the judicial duel and the knightly tournament.
However, as we have already seen, the 'modern' duel is at best a distant
cousin of these medieval forms of combat. The 'modern' duel owed its
existence to ideas that took shape in Renaissance Italy; it was these
ideas that filtered into Germany during the sixteenth and early seventeenth centuries. Charles V's election as Holy Roman Emperor in 1519
introduced the rapier, the duellist's favourite weapon, to the Austrian
court from Spain. Practical assistance for those who aspired to the
new gentlemanly rituals became available in 1558 with the publication
of a German-language manual of arms, *Fechtbuch*, complete with
woodcut illustrations. The extent to which duelling took root in
Germany in these years can be gauged from the fact that the Elector
of Saxony declared duelling illegal as early as 1572. He was the first
German prince to do so. By 1617, the year before the Defenestration,
duelling was a serious enough problem to persuade the Emperor
Matthias to issue an edict condemning the practice.[51]

If the duel and the notions of honour on which it was based had
already taken root in Germany by 1618, the turmoil of the decades of
war served only to strengthen its hold. By the middle of the century,
the 'modern' duel was flourishing in Germany. In 1652 duelling had
reached such pitch in Brandenburg that the Great Elector was

compelled to promulgate the Electorate's first anti-duelling law. It made duelling an offence punishable by death.[52]

In the decades following the Thirty Years War many German states, some of them little more than their rulers' private fiefs, began, quite consciously, to imitate France. As Norman Davies puts it, 'German culture was so traumatised that art and literature passed entirely under the spell of foreign, especially French, fashions'.[53] The French monarchy, embodied by the Sun King, was the glory of the age, and Versailles its holiest shrine. A host of princelings, aping France, established petty absolutisms and built miniature Versailles across Germany. According to one architectural historian, 'Louis XIV becomes the envied prototype for the larger and smaller sovereigns in Germany, and the palace arrangements of Versailles the ideal of court architecture generally'.[54]

The Weissenstein Palace at Pommersfelden, and the palaces at Ludwigsburg, Elligen and Nymphenburg, all of which date from the early years of the eighteenth century, are examples of German palaces that reflect, quite deliberately, the grand French style epitomised by Versailles. This cultural imitation extended to duelling; from the middle of the seventeenth century, German duellists fought and spoke in French.[55] As in France, many German princelings developed a decidedly ambivalent attitude to duellists. While they recognised that it was in their interests to eradicate duelling, they found it difficult not to condone the practice. Many of them were as free with granting pardons as Henry IV had been in France.[56]

✳   ✳   ✳

In Ireland, the Renaissance codes of honour and the duelling ethic were unknown before the English started to colonise the country. In 1541 the Irish Parliament passed an Act declaring Ireland to be a sovereign state, with Henry VIII as its hereditary monarch. During Elizabeth's reign the influence of the 'New English', that is, imported landowners and administrators, became ever stronger. In 1557 the policy of plantation, 'the systematic uprooting of the native population in favour of incoming English colonists', was restarted.[57] It was these incomers from the ranks of the English gentry who introduced to Ireland the notions of honour and the practice of duelling.

There were a number of incidents in the latter part of the sixteenth century that indicated that the notions of honour on which duelling was based were gaining ground. In 1571 Sir John Perrot, the president of Munster, challenged James Fitzmaurice, a rebel leader, to a combat. Although the fight never took place, it was evidence that the duelling spirit was stirring in Ireland. Sixteen years later, Perrot, by now risen to the rank of lord deputy, challenged Sir Richard Bingham, the president of Connaught, to a duel. As in the earlier episode, no duel was fought. James Kelly, the leading modern historian of duelling in Ireland, cited these two examples as evidence of a general trend, rather than as a merely proof of one man's intermittently excitable nature.[58]

The 1640s and 1650s were years of disorder and bloodshed in Ireland. In the autumn of 1641 the Irish rose in revolt against the English but it was not until Cromwell had defeated the royalist armies and the King had been executed that he was able to turn his attention to Ireland. However, when he did so, in 1649, he crushed the resistance of the Irish rebels with utter brutality. The cities of Drogheda and Wexford were stormed and sacked. When Cromwell returned to England at the end of the year 'Ireland lay bleeding, prostrate, and paralysed'.[59] During these years Ireland became an international battleground, attracting mercenaries from England, Scotland and Continental Europe, men who were familiar with the honour codes and with duelling, who were quick to anger and quicker to draw their swords. Sir Edmund Verney perished at the hands of such a ruffian in the aftermath of the siege of Drogheda,[60] which well illustrates the savagery of the Cromwellian conquest of Ireland.

Having crushed the Irish rebellion, Cromwell set about ensuring the political subjugation of the island by means of a huge programme of land settlement. In all he settled around 8,000 Protestant landowners in Ireland, a redistribution of land that dwarfed anything that Elizabeth or James had attempted.[61] In so doing Cromwell created the Anglicised Irish gentry, among whom the duelling spirit would, in time, burn so fiercely.

✳   ✳   ✳

The fifty years between the assassination of Henry IV in 1610 and the emergence of Louis XIV as ruler of his country in 1661 were dominated by two cardinals and two minorities. When Henry IV met his death at the hands of the friar Ravaillac, his son, a boy of nine, ascended the throne as Louis XIII. The commanding figure of French politics during his reign was Cardinal de Richelieu. When Louis died in May 1643, his son was just four years old. During his long minority France was ruled by his mother, Anne of Austria, as Regent, aided and abetted by the Italian Cardinal Mazarin. Following Mazarin's death in 1661 Louis XIV emerged, as a butterfly from its chrysalis, in the full vigour of his early manhood, to take up the reins of government.

Richelieu's power was based on an almost complete dominance of the King, a capacity for hard work and an intelligence network that kept him better informed than any of his enemies. This is not the place for an examination of Richelieu's career, but suffice it to say that he laid the foundations for the absolutism that lasted until the Revolution. His supremacy, which began in the 1620s and lasted until his death in 1642, was a period of consolidation of royal power at the expense of the centrifugal influences of the nobility and the provinces. The Estates-General was dissolved in 1618; it was not to meet again until 1789.

One of the most enthusiastically flaunted of the nobility's privileges was duelling, which cut a bloody swathe through the upper echelons of contemporary French society. The most notorious duel of the age was that between the comte de Bouteville and the marquis de Beuvron, fought in Paris in May 1627. Its story encapsulates the conflict between the modernising, centralising instincts of the monarchy and the deep-seated desire of the nobility to retain their old freedoms and privileges. Louis XIII was a profoundly religious, ascetic man, who deeply disapproved of duelling. Richelieu objected to duelling as a churchman, as a bulwark of royal authority, as an advocate of the rule of law and as a man who had lost his own brother in a duel.

French aristocrats, by contrast, particularly the younger ones, regarded duelling as little more than a game, an inalienable privilege of their caste. François de Montmorency, comte de Bouteville, was the most celebrated duellist of his day. A scion of one of the grandest, most illustrious families of France, he was related to some of the leading figures in the French nobility. Guy de Harcourt, marquis de

Beuvron, was a member of a noble family from Normandy who, if less powerful and well connected than the Montmorency clan, was nevertheless important and influential. Indeed, for several generations they were the King's most important lieutenants in the region.

By the spring of 1627 de Bouteville was skating on very thin ice. He was in exile in Brussels, whence he had fled to escape Richelieu's wrath for having fought yet another duel. His latest, in January, had ended with the death of his second; for Louis this was the last straw. The captain of the royal guard was woken in the middle of the night with orders to arrest de Bouteville and bring him safely to Paris. Three companies of Swiss guards set off to de Bouteville's country estate but they arrived to find the château empty. De Bouteville, forewarned of the danger in the nick of time, had escaped across the border to Brussels.

De Bouteville was accompanied on his enforced journey to Brussels by his cousin, François de Rosmadec, the comte des Chapelles, who, despite a puny physique, was a highly skilled fencer and duellist, a match for the best. Doggedly devoted to de Bouteville, he had acted as his second in the majority of his duels.

The marquis de Beuvron, hearing that de Bouteville had fled to Brussels, decided to follow him. De Beuvron was anxious to avenge the recent death at the hands of de Bouteville of de Thorigny, an old friend. Brussels was the ideal place to settle such a score, away from the prying eyes and long arm of the French authorities. Accompanied by his trusted friend, Chocquet, he arrived in the city soon after de Bouteville. In the 1620s Brussels was the capital of the Spanish Netherlands, which were governed by the Regent, Isabella. On hearing of the arrival of the two enemies, the Regent, fearing a breach of the peace, ordered their arrest. Having given his word to the Regent that he would not fight while in the Spanish Netherlands, de Bouteville persuaded her to petition Louis XIII to allow him to return to France. At first, much to de Bouteville's fury, Louis refused to permit his return. In his anger, de Bouteville swore that he would return to Paris and fight de Beuvron, even in the Place Royale. This would be nothing less than a direct challenge to the authority of the King.[62]

De Bouteville and des Chapelles returned to Paris in secret, heavily disguised and under assumed names. On the eve of the appointed day, de Bouteville and de Beuvron met in the Place Royale to discuss the conditions under which they would fight their duel the following afternoon. De Bouteville nominated des Chapelles and the comte de la Berthe as his seconds; de Beuvron told his opponent that Bouquet and the marquis de Bussy d'Amboise would stand as his seconds. The latter was a hardened duellist who was so keen to assist de Beuvron in his hour of need that he rose from his sick bed to fight.

In choosing the Place Royale – nowadays the Place des Vosges – as their duelling ground, de Bouteville and de Beuvron could scarcely have been more provocative. The Place Royale was one of the most striking of the building schemes that had, since the turn of the century, started to change the face of Paris. From the first it attracted the cream of Parisian society; the houses were soon occupied by nobles, wealthy financiers and the King's ministers. Richelieu himself had lived at No. 21 since 1615. If the two men intended to underline to the King the inalienable right of the nobility to fight duels, they had chosen the right place. Indeed, it is difficult to escape the conclusion that the two men were spoiling for a fight as much with their king and his chief minister as with each other. De Bouteville must have known he had all but exhausted the King's patience; this duel would prove to be the final straw.

De Bouteville and de Beuvron arrived in the Place Royale on the stroke of three o'clock and, anxious not delay any longer, stripped off their doublets – they had agreed to fight in shirtsleeves – and took up their positions. Whether they fought on the *pavé* adjoining the arcades or on the grass in the middle of the *place*, we do not know. What is certain is that they would have been in full view of everyone who happened to be in the Place Royale at the time. The six men spaced themselves out in one line, opponents facing each other so that de Bouteville faced de Beuvron, La Berthe was opposite Bouquet and des Chapelles squared up to Bussy d'Amboise.

The principals, de Bouteville and de Beuvron, were each armed with sword and dagger – as was the custom at the time – and, it is reasonable to assume, so too were the seconds. De Bouteville and de Beuvron began the duel with their swords; both were lethally skilled exponents of the art of fencing and, for all the elements of contrivance in the run-up to the encounter – the journey to Brussels and the enforced reconciliation there – there was no hint of an exhibition bout now. Both men were deadly serious. At the same time the two sets of seconds set about each other.

Accounts of the duel between de Bouteville and de Beuvron vary in the details. There is no obvious way to reconcile them but it seems that, after a passage of swordplay, lunging, thrusting, parrying, testing and probing the opponent for weakness, searching for some all-important advantage – it was now, without any exaggeration, a matter of life and death – they discarded their swords and continued with their daggers. This was an altogether more brutal form of combat, more fitting to an alley footpad than a gentleman duellist. It was, of necessity, fought at very close quarters and some accounts say that the two men had each other by the collar as they struggled, daggers in hand.

At first the outcome of this deadly combat was in the balance, the two men swaying and grappling, each seeking the advantage. Then the more powerful de Bouteville began to get the upper hand: seizing his opponent's dagger in his right hand he held it still, while bringing his own dagger to de Beuvron's throat. De Beuvron was now at his opponent's mercy; de Bouteville could have killed him but, his honour now satisfied, he spared his life.

It is difficult to know how long the duel lasted: estimates vary between a few minutes and an hour. Equally, it is hard to discern what injuries the two men sustained. One account has them both collapsing, weak from exhaustion and loss of blood; another says that they called off the duel, both untouched, after a few minutes of desultory swordplay. The fact that both de Beuvron and de Bouteville were able to flee Paris after the duel suggests that neither was seriously injured. Equally, it is hard to credit that either of them could have escaped without a scratch.

Meanwhile, the two sets of seconds, des Chapelles and Bussy d'Amboise and La Berthe and Bouquet, were fighting their own, as it were, secondary duels. While de Bouteville and de Beuvron threw away their swords and resorted to their daggers, Bussy and des

Chapelles continued with the sword. We do not know how long their fight lasted but, as the two principals were grappling with each other, daggers drawn, Bussy, weakened perhaps by his illness, dropped his guard and was run through the body by des Chapelles's sword. Bussy collapsed to the ground and was dead within a few minutes.

Meanwhile the third pairing, La Berthe and Bouquet, were fighting equally keenly. This duel too ended in bloodshed when La Berthe, struck by Bouquet, fell wounded to the ground. Fortunately, his injury was not as serious as Bussy's and he was taken to the Hotel Mayenne, just across the rue Saint-Antoine from the Place Royale.[63]

The duellists had fought in broad daylight in the most fashionable square in Paris; they could hardly have failed to be noticed. All the participants, particularly de Bouteville, knew that the affair was unlikely to be looked upon leniently by the authorities, nor could it be long before they came to hear of it. To make matters worse, a man was now dead. It was time to get away. De Bouteville and des Chapelles decided to flee to Lorraine, an independent duchy of the Holy Roman Empire, so beyond the jurisdiction of French law. The two men left Paris on the road to Meaux and, riding hard, by late that night had reached Vitry-le-Brûlé in the Champagne country. Here, exhausted and confident that they had shaken off any pursuit, they found a room in an inn and went to bed.

Meanwhile, Louis XIII had heard of the duel, fought so impudently right under his nose. Enraged, he ordered the capture of the fugitives, particularly de Bouteville. The *grand prévôt* – the chief of police – was dispatched to de Bouteville's country estate, only to find the château deserted. De Bouteville had, it seemed, escaped Richelieu's clutches once more. And so, but for a stroke of bad luck, he would have done. A chance sighting on the road out of Paris put the authorities onto their scent and, the following morning the two men gave themselves up. They were brought back to Paris under heavy guard and locked up in the Bastille.

Richelieu, having apprehended the duellists – a rare enough feat in itself – was determined to make an example of them. De Bouteville and des Chapelles were tried by the Paris Parlement and sentenced to death. Before, during and after the trial Louis was subjected to intense pressure to pardon the two men. But the King kept his resolve. On the afternoon of 22 June 1627 they were executed in the place de Grève, in front of the Hotel de Ville. Both men met their death bravely, de Bouteville first, twirling his moustaches.

The main weapon employed by Louis and Richelieu against the duellists was the royal edict. As we have seen, Louis's father, Henry IV, issued two edicts against duelling in seven years; in this regard, at any rate, Louis far outdid his father. He managed to hand down no fewer than seven edicts against duelling between 1611 and 1634. The Paris Parlement, not to be left out, issued its own decrees against the practice in 1640. No swaggering young French noble could have been in any doubt as to the official attitude to duelling and, should he have needed reminding, there was always the example of de Bouteville to stay the sword arm. However, the very frequency with which the authorities issued fresh anti-duelling regulations suggests that they were not effective. Louis XIV, upon achieving his majority in 1651, promulgated yet another edict against duelling. In its preamble, the new king laments the failure of his forebears to eradicate the practice, despite numerous edicts and decrees.[64]

The minority of Louis XIV was marred by the Fronde, a series of rebellions between 1648 and 1652, in which large segments of the French nobility took advantage of the King's minority to reassert their traditional powers and privileges. The aristocrats sensed weakness in the regime of Cardinal Mazarin and the Regent, Anne of Austria (which they were able, conveniently, to stigmatise as foreign) and were determined to reverse Richelieu's centralisation of power. The Fronde was a period of chaos and bloodshed, of armed gangs, private militias, skirmishes and treachery; it was also the era of the Three Musketeers. As such it was probably, in the popular imagination at least, the high-water mark of the sword duel.

Curiously, perhaps the two most famous French swordsmen of the era were historical characters whose exploits were immortalised and embellished in literature. The reputation of Cyrano de Bergerac, in life the Sieur de Bergerac (1619–55), was created by the nineteenth-century playwright Edmond Rostand. De Bergerac did kill at least 10 men in duels but he was, as Richard Cohen puts it, 'far from celebrated in his own time'. Likewise, the historical fame of d'Artagnan, the fourth Musketeer, in life Charles de Batz, owes everything to the novels of Alexandre Dumas, who had in turn poached the idea from another, earlier author. D'Artagnan was, in real life, a member of the elite corps of royal bodyguards known as the Musketeers, as were his three brothers-in-arms, but it was Dumas's romantic confections that conferred on them everlasting fame.[65]

At this point, enter a duellist of a very different ilk, the Cardinal de Retz, one of the earliest, and most elevated, of that curiously incongruous group, the clerical duellists. The cardinal (1613–79) was, as part of a cultivated image, a determined duellist. He was not a natural swordsman, being markedly lacking in athletic prowess. Although he was hardly a dashing cavalier, he fought at least three duels. One of these was against the comte d'Harcourt, whose mistress had laughingly rebuffed de Retz's amorous advances. De Retz fought the nephew of the celebrated marshal Bassompierre, whom he succeeded in wounding, and the *abbé* François de Choiseul. In this encounter both principals and their seconds were wounded.[66]

By the 1650s duelling had become endemic among the French nobility. For Voltaire the situation was alarming: duelling was a 'gothic barbarism' that had become 'a part of the national character'. The right to give and receive satisfaction on the duelling ground was a badge of rank for many in the French nobility, the mark of a caste struggling to retain its ancient privileges in the face of an aggressively assertive monarchy. The process of the emasculation of the French nobility reached its apogee under Louis XIV. The nobility, herded into the gilded cage of Versailles, at Louis's beck and call, was reduced to little more than a bejewelled and bewigged chorus, glorifying Louis at every *levée*, *couchée*, banquet, hunting trip, and masque.

Chapter Six

DUELLING IN THE *GRANDE SIÈCLE:* THE AGE OF LOUIS XIV AND CHARLES II

I N THE AFTERNOON OF 29 May 1660 King Charles II crossed London Bridge and slowly made his way through huge, thronging crowds to his palace at Whitehall. The Interregnum was over, the monarchy restored. Four days earlier the flotilla bearing Charles back from the long years of exile dropped anchor off Dover. Charles had come ashore in a barge to thunderous salutes, and, on reaching the beach, had fallen to his knees to thank God for his restoration.

Returning with Charles was a large number of royalists who had spent the years of exile in poverty and frustrated hope, orbiting the exiled court as it wandered between Paris, Brussels, the United Provinces and Germany. Many of them, moving in the exiles' shadowy *demi-monde*, had acquired the French enthusiasm for duelling. The exiled royalist court took its tone from Charles himself; there was little enough for the King and his courtiers to do, save plot and hope, and the pursuit of pleasure filled the weeks, months and years. Charles's 'extreme susceptibility' to female charm was, as Sir Arthur Bryant put it, 'the Achilles heel of his armour … through that gap every arrow could pierce'.[1] In his dalliances he was aided and abetted by the Duke of Buckingham, the boon companion of his boyhood, described by Bryant as 'the worst rake of his age'.

There is no doubt that Charles's exiled court was a quarrelsome place; frustrated minds were quick to anger and idle hands swift to draw. Indeed, by 1658 the problem was bad enough to spur Charles into taking action. The peripatetic court had temporarily come to rest at Brussels, from where Charles issued an edict against duelling. This 'manifested to the World Our utter dislike of such impious and unlawful Duells'.[2]

Once the returned royalists were re-established in London, the duelling mania exploded. Duels were almost daily events in Leicester or Southampton Fields, the favourite refuge of the Restoration duellist; some even fought in St James's Park, under, as it were, the King's nose. Samuel Pepys, that sharp-eyed observer of the Restoration court, tells of one fracas in 1663.

> Their talk about a ridiculous falling-out two days ago at my Lord of Oxford's house at an entertainment of his ... where there was high words and some blows and pulling off of perriwigs – till my Lord Monke took away some of their swords and sent for some soldiers to guard the house until the fray was ended. To such a degree of madness the nobility of this age is come.[3]

Pepys's opinion of duelling is made abundantly clear in this passage. One of the worst offenders was the Duke of Buckingham, the King's partner in crime during the years of exile. Pepys's account of his murderous duel with the Earl of Shrewsbury was quoted in Chapter 2, but it was by no means the only duel in which Buckingham was involved. Buckingham was one of the most important men in the kingdom, a member of the cabal of ministers and intimate in the councils of the King. If the King expected him to set an example to others, he was to be disappointed, as the duke was constantly and violently quarrelling.

In February 1686, a year after Charles's death, one of his many illegitimate sons, Henry, Duke of Grafton, fought a disastrous duel in the meadows near Chelsea. He had been insulted in 'very unhandsome and provoking language' by Jack Talbot, the Earl of Shrewsbury's brother.[4]

> Poore Mr Talbot was runne through the heart and felle dead upon the place, the Duke was saved by a little buckle belonging to his belt, or some

little picture that hee wore about him. It seems they both thrust att the same time, Mr Talbot's sword hitting on the buckle missed going through the Duke's body and ripped upp all his side. Duncombe was second to my Lord Grafton and Fitzpatrick to Mr Talbot. I hear Mr Duncombe is wounded, but however, they say they are all fled.[5]

Nor was duelling confined to courtiers: as one might expect, the military were enthusiastic duellists. Indeed, on the day that Jack Talbot perished, Harry Wharton killed Lieutenant Moxon of the Duke of Norfolk's Regiment in a duel at the Blue Posts in the Haymarket.[6] Earlier in the reign Pepys had reported the odd military duel and, in July 1666, recorded the complaints of Navy Commissioner Peter Pett, who told Pepys:

> How infinite the disorders are among the commanders and all officers of the fleet – no discipline – nothing but swearing and cursing, and everybody doing as they please; … He himself hath been challenged twice to the field, or something as good, by Sir Edwd. Spragg and Captain Seamour …[7]

Although it might seem to us now that the notorious sexual licence of Charles's court was reflected in its attitude to duelling, there is some evidence that the King was anxious to eradicate the practice. Thomas Hobbes, whose *Leviathan* had been published a decade before the Restoration, poured scorn on the notions of honour that underpinned the duel.

> A man receives words of disgrace, or some little injuries … and is afraid, unlesse he revenge it, he shall fall into contempt, and consequently be obnoxious to the like injurues from others; and to avoyd this, breaks the Law, and protects himself for the future, by the terrour of his private revenge. This is a Crime: For the hurt is not Corporeall but Phantasticall, and … so light, as a gallant man, and one that is assured of his own courage, cannot take notice of.[8]

Practical measures began with the inevitable edicts. Charles had been restored to his throne for under three months when he was moved to take action. The edict's preamble announced:

Whereas it is become too frequent, especially with persons of quality, under a vain pretence of honor, to take upon them [selves] to be the Revengers of their private quarrels by Duel and single Combate, upon slight, and which ought not to be, upon any Provocation.

Motivated by 'Our pious care to prevent unchristian and rash effusion of Blood', the edict reminded Charles's subjects of the penalties prescribed by the criminal law for duelling. However, it introduced two further penalties designed to give even the most blasé duellist pause for thought. The first of these was a permanent disqualification from holding public office for anyone convicted of fighting a duel. In the days when public office often represented a passport to riches, this was, potentially, a severe penalty. This was matched by a permanent banishment from court for all duellists. This was potentially equally disastrous for a man's (or his wife's) career, as it was only at court that one could hope to attract the favour of the King and a share of the rewards that accompanied it. To be banished from court was to be cast into outer darkness.

Charles also specified, purloining an idea from Cromwell's edict of 1654, that these provisions would apply to anyone who failed to inform the authorities of a challenge. Perhaps most tellingly, it expressly forbade 'all Intercession or Mediation' to the King on behalf of duellists. Would-be supplicants were reminded that henceforth no royal pardons would be granted to any duellist, no matter how exalted. Clearly, this was an attempt to relieve the King of the tiresome burden of importunate courtiers pressing for clemency for a favourite or relative.[9]

In 1668 the College of Arms promoted a bill whose object was to suppress duelling. It proposed to appoint the Earl Marshal to resolve disputes in matters of precedence, which were, of course, frequently the cause of disputes between aristocrats. The Earl Marshal's jurisdiction would have been an early form of honour court that might have played an important role in reducing the number of duels and, therefore, of needless deaths. The bill never became law.[10]

In 1679 Charles reiterated his opposition to duelling in another edict. It denounced duelling as 'Scandalous to Christian Religion' and

a 'Manifest Violation of Our Laws and Authority'. It was in very much
the same terms as its predecessor, except that it beefed up one of the
1660 provisions. It specified that anyone who attempted to intercede
with the King (or anyone else in authority) on behalf of a duellist
would themselves face banishment from court. There could be no
clearer indication of the difficulties Charles faced in enforcing the law
against high-ranking duellists.[11]

Five years earlier, Charles had also issued a decree against the
practice in Scotland. This ordered that his grandfather James I's
statute be strictly enforced: it provided that anyone who fought a
duel should face capital punishment as well as 'escheat of their
moveables'. Seconds and other accessories faced imprisonment
and stiff fines. The Scottish edict also contained a declaration of
intent in respect of pardons: 'such persons, who shall be guilty of
the said crime, are not to expect that remissions shall be granted to
them hereafter.' If things had become a little lax, here was due
warning that the authorities had every intention of cracking down
on duellists.[12]

Charles was prepared to take the necessary action against offenders to demonstrate that his edicts were not toothless. In 1666 the Duke
of Buckingham, so often indulged by Charles, went a step too far.

> Upon Tuesday last the Duke of Buckingham and the Marquis of Worces-
> ter were sent to the Tower by reason of a controversy between them at a
> committee. It is said that the Duke took the Marquis by the nose and
> pulled him about.[13]

Such behaviour on Buckingham's part was almost bound to result in
a challenge, so sending the two men to the Tower to cool off was a sensible precaution. The following year a newsletter reported that the
Attorney-General had been instructed to institute legal proceedings
against all duellists 'and especially against Sir Henry Bellasis and Mr
Thomas Porter'. Bellasis was killed a few days later in a duel with
Porter; perhaps had the authorities moved more quickly (and the
argument between the two men was evidently public knowledge) his
life might have been saved.[14]

In 1668, two months after his notorious duel with the Earl of

Shrewsbury, the incorrigible Buckingham was once more embroiled in an argument.

> Sir William Coventry was sent to the Tower on Thursday last for sending a challenge to the Duke of Buckingham; and one Mr Savile that carried the challenge was first sent to the Gate House and after, for honours sake, to the Tower because he was Coventry's nephew.

But the King was determined not to allow Coventry to escape the full weight of his displeasure.

> Coventry is dispossessed of all his employments both Treasury and Councillor, and must be in the Tower to cool himself. It is much wondered at here how he durst attempt such a thing, the world knowing him to be a coward and a knave.[15]

Coventry's fate might have been indicative of Charles's determination to eradicate duelling but, as with so many other monarchs over the centuries, his resolve was compromised by his inability to stop granting pardons. Whatever the royal edicts might have said, the King was nevertheless prone to pardoning duellists, particularly, his favourites. Buckingham was granted a pardon by the King after his duel with Shrewsbury; this aroused the ire of Parliament, no doubt on account of the scandalous and bloody nature of the duel itself. Pepys commented shortly after the duel, 'Parliament ... are likely to fall heavy on the business of the Duke of Buckingham's pardon; and I shall be glad of it.'[16]

By time Charles II died in 1685 he had failed to produce a legitimate heir, so was succeeded by his brother James. James II's reign (1685–8) was brief and inglorious; his attempt to reimpose Catholicism on the nation was deeply unpopular and he was forced to flee the country ignominiously. He was succeeded by the unimpeachably Protestant William of Orange, a Dutchman married to James's daughter Mary. His accession to the throne brought about a new constitutional settlement; his reign was marked by unprecedented commercial development at home, Continental wars and more trouble in Ireland.

Throughout this period, from the Restoration to the beginning of the eighteenth century, there was a steady flow of literature on the subject of duelling, both for and against. In 1692 Sir W. Hope published a fencing guide, *The Compleat Fencing-Master*. It set out to describe 'the whole Guards, Parades and Lessons Belonging to the Small-Sword' but was more than merely a fencing manual, promising 'Directions how to Behave in a Single Combat on Horse back'. The book was illustrated with engravings 'representing the most necessary Postures', in the tradition of the Renaissance instruction manuals. Although published in London it was dedicated to 'The Young Nobility and Gentry of the Kingdom of Scotland'. It was clearly intended to appeal to the duelling classes.[17]

In 1687 a London divine identified only as 'T.C.' published a thunderous anti-duelling tract in which he described duelling as an 'abominable Practice, though it be supported by pretences of Courage and Fantastic Honour; and extenuated by alledging the Fashion of a vicious Age, and many wretched Precedents'. The author set himself to show that the duelling was the 'most impious and dishonourable thing that is openly done among Men that own any Religion' by exploding the arguments used to justify the practice and by pointing out how it offended against every precept of law, scripture and good citizenship. On the whole the anonymous author's arguments are reasonable and of a piece with those employed by other writers. However, there is one point at which he was less convincing. Having asserted that it is the function of the law to resolve differences between men he then declared:

> But if it be such a Offence as the Laws take no cognizance of, as we are
> Gods servants we are obliged to leave the Matter to his Judgment, who
> hath declared and promised, He will right our Wrongs ...[18]

This is a weak argument since one of the justifications given for duelling was that it allowed men to settle disputes that were, at that time, beyond the scope of the law. Indeed, the growth of the rule of law in nineteenth-century Britain is often cited as a reason for the decline of duelling. It was optimistically idealistic to assume that men would allow the Almighty to settle disputes that the law could not resolve when they could fight it out like men of honour.

The author of this tract adopted the conventional, rational

approach to the anti-duelling argument, but a layman writing a few years later, in 1694, used humour to ridicule the practice. The light-hearted approach is every bit as effective as the more earnest, reasoned line of attack. In this conversation piece the author has two characters, Philalethes and Philotimus, engaged in a discussion about duelling.

> Philotimus: 'Why last Night Mr A and I happen'd to fall into a Misunderstanding over a Glass of Wine. At length he told me the Controversy could not be taken up, without giving the Satisfaction of a Gentleman. My Answer was, That I would debate the Matter with him in his own way this Morning. And I am now going to settle some little Affairs before the time of Meeting.'

> Philalethes: 'If you design to make your Will, you are out: For to do that to any Purpose, a Man must be sound in Mind and Memory, which is none in your Case. For the Business you are going about is sufficient to prove you Non Compos.'

Philotimus countered this suggestion with what he no doubt considered a time-honoured justification.

> Philotimus: ''Tis the Custom of Gentlemen, and that is sufficient for my purpose.'

> Philalethes: 'What if it was the Custom to Tilt your Head against a Post, for a Morning's Exercise, would you venture the beating out your Brains rather than be Unfashionable?'[19]

To this, of course, there was no answer.

Thomas Flesher's *The Laws of Honor, or An Account of the Suppression of Duels in France* was published in England in 1685. It is an account, as the title suggests, of the attempts of the French monarchy over the previous century to eradicate duelling. Its interest for us, however, lies in what it reveals about contemporary English attitudes to duelling. Most obviously, it shows that it was considered in right-thinking circles to be a serious problem, 'the effects of a false and spurious Bravour' that resulted in wholly needless deaths. The tract's dedication to the Duke of Norfolk, the Earl Marshal of England, suggests that the author believed duelling to be a problem for the highest level of the King's government. Lastly, it shows that, in the 1680s, France was considered to provide the best example of how to eradicate duelling. The fact that Louis XIV succeeded in stamping out the practice where his father and grandfather had failed was considered an important lesson in the value of firmness and persistence. It was, by implication, a reproof to Charles II for what the author saw as his failure to eradicate duelling from the realm.

*   *   *

In December 1643, the infant Louis XIV had been on the throne for only a few months when two of his most important subjects fought a brutal duel in the Place Royale, the square in which de Bouteville and de Beuvron had crossed swords in 1627. The duel between the duc de Guise and the comte de Coligny was an echo of old sectarian hatreds, for the two combatants were the grandsons of the implacable adversaries of the Wars of Religion, the Admiral Coligny and the then duc de Guise. In 1572 the duke had organised the massacre of the Huguenots and their leader Coligny on St Bartholomew's Day, as they gathered in Paris for the wedding of Henry of Navarre. The rematch, as it were, between the families was not caused by great matters of state or conscience but by drawing-room slanders. If the causes were different, the result was the same, albeit writ small; Coligny was worsted in the duel and later died of his wounds.[20]

By the early 1660s as Charles II was re-establishing the monarchy in England, his cousin Louis XIV was emerging from his long minority to take his place at the very pinnacle of the French state. His minority had been scarred by the Fronde, a period of rebellion and disorder that had witnessed an upsurge in duelling. Indeed, according to one French historian, 'duels were an emblem of the Fronde'.[21] It is significant that Louis (or, perhaps, his advisers) chose to mark his coming of age in 1651 by issuing another edict against duelling. It is a reasonable assumption that the chaos and dangers of the Fronde influenced Louis, strengthening his resolve to combat the aristocratic privilege of duelling. Certainly there was an increasing body of opinion in France that sought to eradicate the practice. The principal conduit for the expression of this opinion was a organisation called the Brotherhood of Passion, whose moving spirit, the marquis de Fenelon, was strongly committed to the abolition of duelling. Gradually, the movement gathered support and received the seal of royal approval when Louis issued the edict of 1651 confirming the pronouncements of his fore-bears banning the practice.[22]

Many of the nobility, to demonstrate their support of Louis's stance against duelling, acting through the Brotherhood of Passion, signed a self-denying ordinance in the same year. Their determina-tion to resist the pressure to fight duels was backed up by the estab-lishment of an 'honour court' under the authority of the Marshals of France. This was intended to act as a mechanism for the peaceful res-olution of the types of dispute that might, normally, result in a duel.[23] According to the latest French historians of the subject the year 1651 was 'unquestionably the start of a new period in the history of the duel'.[24]

The 1651 edict was not the first pronouncement that had been made in Louis's name during his reign. Early in his minority those ruling on his behalf had issued three declarations against duelling, in 1643, 1644 and 1646. Louis himself issued a further decree in 1653 enlarging upon his edict of 1651. In 1657, the Paris Parlement, not to be outdone, promulgated its own decree against duelling. And that, for more than 20 years, was how matters stood.[25]

In August 1679 Louis once again turned his attention to the problem of duelling. That it was necessary to do so after the repeated attempts of the previous 80 years to ban the practice, and Louis's own more recent efforts, shows how deeply entrenched a vice it was. The Edict of Saint Germain-en-Laye was a lengthy piece of royal law-making, running to 36 articles, over many pages of text. It was, at least in theory, a forceful measure. It prescribed the death penalty for all principals and accessories, as well as allowing for the sequestration of property. Aristocrats caught fighting were to be deprived of their noble status – a terrible humiliation – and have their coats of arms defaced and smashed by the public executioner. As if that were not bad enough, duellists killed in the act would be forbidden a Christian burial. Merely sending a challenge was punishable by exile and the confiscation of half of the offender's property. Even servants were brought within the ambit of the law: from henceforth any servant who carried messages for his master or attended him at a duel was to be whipped and branded.[26]

So Louis certainly had the legal powers to mount an effective campaign against duelling. Nor, characteristically, was he shy in proclaiming his role in ridding France of this scourge: the Hall of Mirrors at Versailles has a depiction dated 1662 of Louis stopping 'the fury of duelling'.[27] The question is, however, did he actually succeed in stamping it out during his reign? Contemporaries, at least in England, had no doubt that Louis had successfully eradicated duelling in his kingdom. We have already seen that Thomas Flesher, writing in 1685, held up Louis's anti-duelling policy as an example worthy of emulation. Richard Steele, Addison's collaborator in the *Spectator* and a passionate opponent of duelling, wrote in 1720 – a mere five years after Louis's death – a pamphlet examining the measures that had proved so successful in eradicating the practice in France, then set out to persuade his readers that the French example provided the best hope of extirpating the curse of duelling from the British Isles, where this 'offensive Weed hath taken such a deep rooting'.[28]

However, the view that Louis succeeded in stamping out duelling in France appears to originate with Voltaire, whose *Le Siècle de Louis XIV* was published in 1751. Voltaire gave Louis the credit for largely eradicating duelling from France: 'This horrible custom lasted until the time of Louis XIV,' he wrote in his *Essai sur les moeurs*. It was *'une des plus grandes services rendus à la patrie'*.[29] Voltaire was guilty of giving credit where credit was not due. As we will see, duelling flourished in France for at least another 150 years. Modern authors are inclined to conclude that the Sun King was almost as prone as his forebears to turn a blind eye to duellists, or, if they were silly or unlucky enough to be caught in the act, to pardon them. According to Richard Cohen, Louis pardoned more than 7,000 duellists in a 19-year period, an average of one a day.[30]

No one would now pretend that Louis succeeded in eradicating duelling altogether and there certainly is much anecdotal evidence that the practice was alive and well. The duc de Saint-Simon, whose

Memoirs provide such a vivid portrait of the court at Versailles, admitted that his father fought a duel, probably during Louis's reign.

> A disagreement arose between my father and M. de Vardes ... It was ultimately agreed that upon an early day, at about twelve o'clock, they should meet at the Porte St Honore, then a very deserted spot, and that the coach of M. de Vardes should run against my father's, and a general quarrel arise between masters and servants. Under cover of this quarrel ... the duel took place. M. de Vardes fell, and was disarmed. My father wished to make him beg for his life; he would not do this, but confessed himself vanquished.

The most interesting aspect of this duel is the ruse the two men employed to enable them to fight without arousing suspicion. This suggests that at the very least duelling was, at the time, frowned upon by the authorities. It did not remain a secret for long, however, and was soon the talk of the town. Saint-Simon reports that his father 'was complimented everywhere'; the hapless de Vardes was sent to the Bastille for 10 or 12 days.[31] As both the principals seem, even by Saint-Simon's account, to be equally to blame for the fracas, one wonders whether perhaps de Vardes's real offence was that in losing he was humiliated.

Saint-Simon also refers to two other incidents later in Louis's reign. The first, around 1699, concerned an argument over cards between the Grand Prieur and the Prince de Conti. Conti questioned his 'honesty at play and his courage in war', at which, inevitably, the Grand Prieur 'flew into a passion, flung away the cards, and demanded satisfaction, sword in hand'.

> The arrival of Monseigneur [the Dauphin], in his dressing gown, put an end to the fray. He ordered ... one of the courtiers present, to report the whole affair to the King, and that every one should go to bed. On the morrow the King was informed of what had taken place, and immediately ordered the Grand Prieur to go to the Bastille. He was obliged to obey, and remained in confinement several days. The affair made a great stir at Court.[32]

The second incident reported by Saint-Simon concerned a duel fought between four counts, two French and two foreign. When Louis heard of the duel, he ordered the two French counts to be imprisoned in the Conciergerie. One of them, the comte d'Uzes, gave himself up but the other, the comte d'Albert, was on the run for a long while. Saint-Simon reported that d'Albert 'was broken for his disobedience'.[33] Both of these incidents suggest that the King was vigilant and ready to punish duellists, at least when they fought under his very nose.

Occasionally, humour could percolate through the carapace of even the most touchy of duellists. When M. Madaillon challenged the marquis de Rivard, a veteran soldier who had lost a leg at the siege of Puy Cerda, he received an unexpected reply. As we have seen, duellists were supposed to face each other on equal terms, so the marquis, undaunted, sent his opponent a surgeon, equipped with a case of instruments. The surgeon was instructed to suggest that he should perform a similar amputation on Madaillon. The joke, we are told, was taken in good part.[34]

Some historians now question whether Louis had any quantifiable effect on the incidence of duelling. So far from Voltaire's assertion that Louis eradicated duelling in France, MM. Brioist, Drevillon, and Serna in their 2002 book *Croiser le Fer* (*Crossing Swords*) argue that, by the end of Louis's reign, duelling, at least in military circles, was as prevalent as at any time in the past. They cite the *abbé* de Saint-Pierre, whose writings suggest that the rosy picture portrayed by Voltaire was far removed from the truth. The *abbé* maintained that by 1715 duelling in France was as frequent and as important as ever: 'This scourge continued to kill on a huge scale and to prove the nobility's attachment to the law of honour.'[35]

The *abbé* explained the apparent divergence between his observations and Voltaire's version by saying that, although there was scarcely less fighting than previously, men boasted about it much less. Therefore, much less was heard about duelling, allowing some to conclude, quite wrongly, that it was on the wane. The authors say that, during the reign of the Sun King, 'duelling continued to rage'. The impression of calm was fortified by the fact that there was much less coverage of duelling in the public presses. Deaths attributable to duelling were reclassified as straightforward homicides or simply covered up altogether so that they stopped hitting the headlines.[36]

Duelling was a notoriously dangerous pastime, made worse in the seventeenth century by the rudimentary state of medical knowledge. This was long before the invention of antisepsis or anaesthesia; this was the age in which medical men swore by leeches, the benefits of bleeding patients, and the advantages of trepanning. Louis himself was forced by his doctors in the last days of his life to keep his gangrenous leg in a bath of burgundy. It did not help prolong the King's life and must have ruined the wine. The arrival of a seventeenth-century surgeon could not have been greeted with anything but trepidation by his patients.

*   *   *

In Ireland the Cromwellian plantations had given rise to a significant Anglicised, landowning gentry, who brought with them from the mainland a respect for the law of honour and the duelling codes. It was during the second half of the seventeenth century that Ireland was established as an important theatre for duelling, although the ferocious reputation of Irishmen as inveterate duellists did not acquire its full lustre until the mid-eighteenth century. In the years following the Restoration in Ireland, as we have also noted in England, the authorities adopted a more relaxed attitude to duelling. Similarly, royalists returning from exile with Charles II, brought home with them Continental duelling habits picked up during the long years abroad. One of the most fearless of these was Richard Talbot, who fought a number of duels in France during the years of exile. In 1658, he wounded one Dick Hopton.[37]

In fact, as James Kelly points out, there were at this time (as earlier and indeed later) close connections between the development of duelling in England and in Ireland. Lord Ossory, an Irish peer, was involved in a spat with the notoriously touchy Duke of Buckingham in 1666. However, before the two men were able to settle their differences with swords the King sent them to cool off in the Tower for three days. Charles II was frequently indulgent of courtiers who fought duels – witness his treatment of Buckingham after his notorious duel in 1668 – and the same attitude prevailed in Ireland. When the Earl of Kildare fought a duel with one Talbot, the secretary to the

Earl of Shrewsbury, the Treasurer of Ireland, he was banned 'from the council table'. The ban, however, was short-lived and Kildare was soon reinstated.

Another characteristic that duelling in Ireland and England had in common at this time was the triviality of the causes of many of the disputes. (Indeed, one might add that trifling differences blowing up into lethal confrontations was a salient feature of the entire history of duelling.) In 1667 the Earl of Roscommon and the brother of the Earl of Clancarty quarrelled over precedence at a funeral. In 1670 the authorities failed to prevent a six-man duel in Phoenix Park, caused by a dispute 'at play ... at the Castle Tavern'. One of the seconds, the aptly named Ensign Slaughter, was killed; all the other participants, with the exception of one Captain Savage, were wounded. Even after an incident as brutal as this one evidently was, only one of the five men was convicted of manslaughter: Lord Brabazon, who took part in the duel, received a royal pardon.[38]

Ensign Slaughter's duel was, it seems, entirely typical of the failure of the law to hand down fitting punishments for duellists. In this respect, as in others, there was much in common between England and Ireland. Leniency towards duellists was, it seems, a failing they shared.

In 1685, shortly after his accession to the throne, James II was sufficiently disturbed by the amount of duelling in his army in Ireland to issue a decree against it. It announced that henceforth any officer that 'shall send, receive or deliver any Challenge, or give any real Affront to any Other' shall be cashiered and prohibited from any future employment in the King's service.[39] Five years later William and Mary issued their own decree aimed at putting a stop to duelling in the army. Using almost identical phraseology, it threatened offenders with being cashiered and banned from the King's service.[40] The interesting aspect of these decrees is that they address only the challenge; they do not tackle the act itself of fighting the duel.

The fact that two kings within five years of each other felt compelled to issue decrees against duelling suggests that, in the army at least, it was a problem. Kelly suggests that the increase in military duelling was the result of rising religious tensions during the 1680s.[41]

Certainly, once James II had succeeded his brother in 1685, the issue of religious toleration for Catholics and dissenters alike came to the fore as did the question of the succession. Could the Protestant succession be guaranteed? In Ireland, where there was a small but dominant Protestant ruling and landowning elite and a large, dispossessed, disenfranchised Catholic population, this was a particularly divisive question.

The two decrees seem to indicate that in the army there was an increase in the incidence of duelling. However, as so often in the history of duelling, putting a figure on the number of duels fought is almost impossible. In March 1689 James II, who had the previous year been deposed by William III, landed in Ireland, intent on reclaiming his throne. This was the start of two years of campaigning that resulted in the total defeat of James, at the Battle of the Boyne (July 1690) among other engagements, and the triumph of the Protestant Ascendancy.

Kelly suggests that there was a falling-off in duelling in the quarter-century after the Battle of the Boyne. One reason that might account for this was the flight abroad of a large number of Catholic officers and soldiers following William's triumph. After the Treaty of Limerick was imposed on the defeated Jacobites in July 1691 11,000 of the 14,000 Irishmen in James's army, the 'Wild Geese', followed their leader, Patrick Sarsfield, into exile. Only 2,000 returned to their homes.[42] This gave rise to a large, exiled, rootless population of Irishmen on the Continent, a breeding ground for adventurers, mercenaries and, of course, duellists.

Some of the fleeing Jacobites were notoriously belligerent: for example, Peter Drake fought five duels in France and Spain between 1706 and 1714. One of them, fought at Tournai in France on 1706, was more akin to a skirmish than a duel involving as it did 13 soldiers, of whom three were killed and two were wounded. Had Drake not fled to the Continent, he would, no doubt, have been plying his murderous trade in Ireland.[43]

Another reason for the decline in duelling in these years, Kelly suggests, was the ban, introduced in 1695, on Catholics carrying arms without a licence. This measure was part of the more general penal laws aimed at the Catholic population introduced as part of the Williamite settlement.[44] One historian suggests that the 'carrot-and-stick' application of these laws was responsible for Ireland's quiescence when faced with the incitement to support the Jacobite cause in 1715 and 1745. It is equally possible that the same laws played a part in suppressing duelling in the first decades of the eighteenth century.[45]

For a generation after the Williamite triumph, duelling in Ireland was at a low ebb. From about 1715, however, Kelly detects a revival of the duelling spirit. In the years 1716–19, he notes six reported duels; for the five years between 1725 and 1730, the figure is 16. These years were remarkable for the number of duels fought in which the participants ignored the prescribed etiquettes of duelling. The duel between Adam Cusack, a Dublin JP, and his relative, Lieutenant Brice, in December 1716 is a case in point. The two men argued over dinner, took up their swords, went outside and fought each other to a standstill. Both men died of their wounds. Although the number of duels fought hardly amounted to a murderous frenzy, there were nevertheless several prominent casualties. For example, John Slattery, the MP for Blessington, was killed by Stephen Moore in a duel fought with swords and pistols in November 1726.[46]

The following two decades, the 1730s and 1740s, witnessed a continuation of the steady rise in the number of duels. Kelly found more than 30 reported duels in these years, many of which display the same disregard for the established procedures for the proper conduct of a duel. He cites the notorious duel between Robert Martin and Lieutenant Henry Jolly in Galway in July 1733 as a prime example. As Martin was walking past a coffeehouse he was hit by a lump of phlegm; taking this as a deliberate insult, he drew his sword and entered the coffeehouse, demanding satisfaction of whomever was responsible. Captain Edward Southwell, who was playing billiards with Jolly, owned up and offered an apology. Martin refused to accept the proffered apology and demanded that Southwell, who was unarmed, go to fetch his sword, so that they could settle the matter like gentlemen. Southwell left to do Martin's bidding. Meanwhile, Jolly made some disparaging remarks that prompted Martin to

advance towards him in a threatening manner. Jolly, feeling intimidated, held a chair up to protect himself; this, however, provoked
Martin to thrust repeatedly at and through the chair. Jolly received
wounds from which he later died.

This outrageous case of gratuitously aggressive violence resulted in
Martin's being charged with murder. The case was even transferred
from Galway, where the defendant had considerable local influence,
to Dublin, but it made no difference. The jury acquitted him.[47]
Indeed, the criminal justice system in Ireland throughout the 50 years
to 1750 seems to have been remarkably passive in dealing with the
threat posed to law and order by the duellists. James Kelly, in the
period 1716–60, has found that there were only 19 trials for causing
death in a duel. These trials produced 18 convictions for manslaughter and just two for murder.[48]

This gloomy picture of ruffians ignoring the etiquettes of duelling
and of a somnolent legal system is relieved by a least one shaft of light.
Captain Dudley Bradstreet (1711–63) was an Irish adventurer, rogue
and philanderer. When he came to write his memoirs he had a wealth
of material at his disposal, gleaned from a misspent youth and a life-
time of adventure and dissipation. Among the bawdy tales is Bradstreet's account of how he was cured for ever of the duelling bug. He
and some friends had been dining, somewhere in Ireland, with 'a
Gentleman remarkable for unlimited Hospitality', and were on their
way home.

A silly Dispute happen'd on the Road between one of the Gentlemen and
me, tho' in the closest Friendship before, which was very near ending
fatally, for we agreed to determine it instantly with the Pistol I had in my
Furniture, the other Gentleman delivering each of us one of them, and
fixing us on the Ground gave the Signal. I instantly snap'd at my Antagonist, the Powder of which only flash'd in the Pan; he embraced me
without further Ceremony ... About a quarter of an Hour afterwards, I
prim'd the Pistol again and fired it at a Door, through which it drove a
Brace of Balls.

This lucky escape prompted the captain to reflect on his good
fortune: '... from that Time to this, which is about fifteen Years, I

seldom drank to Excess, nor enter'd into warm or fruitless Arguments'.[49]

And, it appears from the remaining memoirs, that Bradstreet kept his resolve, as least as far as duelling was concerned. This was despite his rackety existence, his perpetual shortage of money and acting as a government spy during the Jacobite Rising of 1745, all circumstances that would have exposed him to belligerent duelling types.

Chapter Seven

DYNASTIC RIVALRIES: DUELLING IN THE AUGUSTAN AGE

THE FIRST DECADES of the eighteenth century in England were years of great cultural vigour. The literary world was illuminated by Swift, Pope, Addison, Steele and Congreve; it was an age of satire and polemic when writers were politically engaged and literature was a vital part of the political process. At the same time, England's architects were creating some of the most enduringly beautiful buildings in our history. It was the age of the English Baroque, of Wren, Vanbrugh, Hawksmoor and of the Palladian Colen Campbell; its legacy is Blenheim, Castle Howard, the City churches and Chiswick House. These were the years of the Earls of Creation. It was also a period of momentous happenings on the political stage. The Union with Scotland, the advent of the Hanoverian dynasty, the growth of the Jacobite menace and, abroad, continuing war with France, all of which helped to raise the temperature of domestic politics. The divide between Whig and Tory was never so bitter or so keenly felt.

For all the cultural distinction of these years – which was confined to a tiny fraction of the population – England remained a violent society. Life was, for the most part, unforgiving and men quick to quarrel. A taste for violence was deeply embedded in the English psyche. A German traveller in England reported watching a prize fight in London in the early part of the eighteenth century.

They had taken off their coats and tied only a handkerchief round their heads. First they bowed in every direction, and then showed their swords all round. These were very broad and long and uncommonly sharp. Each of the combatants had his second by him with a large stick in his hand; they were not there to parry blows, but only to see that there was fair play on all sides. They began the fight with broadswords. The Moor got the first wound, above the breast, which bled not a little. Then the onlookers began to cheer and call for Wood; they threw down vast quantities of shillings and crowns, which were picked up by his second. This seemed to me quite the wrong way round, as one should have compassion on the fellow that is hit, especially since the winner receives two-thirds of the money that is taken as the gate. In the second round the Englishman, Wood, took a blow ... of such force that, not only did his shirt hang in tatters, but his sword was knocked out of his hand and all the buttons on one side of the open breeches he wore were cut away.

Then they went for each other with sword and dagger and the Moor got a nasty would in his hand, which bled freely. It was probably due to this that, when they had attacked each other twice with 'sword and buckler', that is to say with broadsword and shield, the good Moor received such a dreadful blow that he could not fight any longer. He was slashed from the left eye right down his cheek to his chin and jaw with such force that one could hear the sword grating against his teeth. Straightway not only the whole of his shirt front but the platform too was covered with blood. The wound gaped open as wide as a thumb, and I cannot tell you how ghastly it looked on the black face.[1]

The onlookers' delight in this gruesome spectacle is all too evident, nor was the taste for violence confined to the unsophisticated lower orders. While it is impossible – as always – to say whether there were more duels in these years than previously, there does not seem to have been any appreciable letting up. The upper classes seemed as willing as their fathers and grandfathers to settle their differences, no matter how trivial, on the duelling ground, with equally bloody consequences. In 1721 two young Irishmen, Richard Grantham and Mr Fitzgerald, fought a duel in Temple Gardens, in which Fitzgerald received horrific injuries: 'a Wound appearing in his Belly, large enough to receive a Man's Fist, and another in one of his Arms very monstrous'. Fitzgerald, not surprisingly, did not survive. The two men had been, we are told, 'most affectionate Friends'; the duel was occasioned by dispute over the correct spelling of a single Greek word.[2]

The heightened political passions of the period frequently boiled over into violence: Whig or Tory mobs rarely hesitated before attacking their enemies. Riots, destruction of property and pitched battles between rival factions were common occurrences on the streets of London at this time. The political rivalries that inflamed the mob had much the same effect on the duelling classes. Indeed, the most notorious duel of the age, the fight to the death in November 1712 between the Duke of Hamilton and Lord Mohun, was between men from opposite sides of the political divide, one a Whig, the other a Tory. Disputes about the Jacobites, a potent cocktail of divided loyalties, dynastic, political and religious, was another issue that never failed to cause tempers to run high.

In 1716, the year after the first rising in favour of the Stuart kings, Dudley Ryder, a young law student, witnessed at first hand the animosities kindled by the Jacobite question.

> This [10 June] being the Pretender's birthday it was given out before that his friends would wear white roses and green favours to distinguish themselves. A great many soldiers patrolled about the streets and were ordered to take away any white roses they saw ... [an] abundance were taken away and many quarrels happened upon it. Particularly an officer, one Mr Musgrave, saw a gentleman walking in Gray's Inn Walks with a white rose on. He took it away from him, upon which they drew their swords and the officer wounded him ...[3]

Later in the year Ryder reported some coffeehouse gossip of a quarrel in Paris between Sir Samuel Garth and another, nameless Englishmen. The latter said, provocatively, that he supposed a toast to 'The King' referred to James III (that is, the Stuart Pretender), whereupon Garth at once slapped him across the face. Both men then drew their swords but, happily, were separated before they could do each other any serious harm. The French authorities, however, were not amused and ordered the man who proposed the toast to 'James III' to the Bastille.[4]

The period opened in 1700 with the trial of John Cowland for the murder of Sir Andrew Slanning. Cowland and some friends, other *bons vivants*, we are told, while in the Drury Lane theatre, ran into Slanning, 'who had made a temporary acquaintance with an orange-woman'. After the play, Slanning and his new friend left together, followed by Cowland and his companions. After a few yards, Cowland put his arm around the orange girl's neck, whereupon Slanning, claiming that she was his wife, asked him to stop pestering her. Cowland, who knew that Slanning was married to 'a woman of honour', gave him the lie. Both men drew their swords but a fight was averted by the prompt intervention of some passers-by.

Slanning and his orange girl and Cowland and his companions then withdrew to the Rose tavern; it appeared that the parties had been reconciled and that any bad feeling had subsided. However, as the party was making its way upstairs in the tavern for a drink, Cowland drew his sword and stabbed Slanning in the belly. He collapsed, shouting, 'Murder'; Cowland was arrested and disarmed but the damage had been done; Sir Andrew died soon afterwards.

This was as plain a case of an unprovoked assault as one could wish to see and, not surprisingly, Cowland was indicted for murder. At his trial there was little prospect that Cowland's lawyers would be able to run a successful 'duelling' defence and so it turned out. His sword was produced in evidence: it was bloodied to the depth of five inches. When the jury convicted him of murder, he was executed at Tyburn, despite great efforts to secure him a pardon. Cowland's case is an unedifying tale, all too common in the history of duelling, in which bravado, temper and, probably, drink sparked off a fatal brawl. It stands as fine example of what cannot be – or ever was – considered to fall within the definition of a duel. It was a murderous attack and, rightly, the jury saw it as such.[5]

So far, little has been said about the places where English duellists fought. Ideally, as we have already seen, the contending parties would agree to meet in a secluded spot, a woodland glade or deserted heath. This was because duelling was illegal, nor did anyone wish to run the risk of the meeting being disrupted by the authorities. In London, this meant one of the parks or some other out-of-the-way spot.

The Duke of Grafton fought his duel against Jack Talbot in 1685 in the fields near the village of Chelsea, then some miles from London itself. Others fought in Islington Fields, in Southampton Fields, in Leicester Fields. The Earl of Shrewsbury was killed by the Duke of Buckingham at Barnes Elms in 1668. Gradually, the growth of London compelled duellists to go further afield to fight, as the old 'inner city' sites were built over. Southampton Fields, for example, an area corresponding roughly to modern Bloomsbury, had become too public by the latter part of the eighteenth century. By the nineteenth century, the duellists had moved out to Battersea, Chalk Farm and Wimbledon Common. But that is to anticipate.

The following account of an encounter between two army officers in 1748 gives an excellent sense of the importance of London's geography as a backdrop to a duel. It conveys a strong impression of the physical being of the city, its layout, its buildings and byways. The two officers in question, L___k and D___n (John Dawson), had had an argument during a long night's drinking; they had previously been close friends. A man identified only as P___k had agreed to act as L___k's second. 'Bagnio' was an eighteenth-century term for a brothel.

About Eleven the next Morning the Captain and P___k took Coach, and went to the Coffee-House, where they tarried but a few Minutes, and all three coming out together, they walked to Leicester-Square, where they took Coach, and drove to Montague-House Gate in Great Russel-Street, having been watch'd all this while by one C___ D___, a Waiter at Spring-Gardens Bagnio, who had Orders from his Mistress to observe wherever D___n went to.

They quitted the Coach at the End of Southampton-Row next the Fields, and took the Path that leads to Tottenham-Court Road, the Waiter still dodging them at about two or three hundred Yards Distance.

After passing thro' the first Field, D___n observes D___ and L___k shaking Hands, and stooping as if they were taking up their Swords from the Ground, but observed nothing else particular till the two Gentlemen, the Duellists, were in that Part of the Field which is against the Wall of the Gardens of Montague-House; and being then about 300 Yards from them, P___k comes to him, and tells him, he was desired not to proceed that Way, or Words to that Effect. The Waiter saying he hoped there would be no Mischief done. P___k making answer, he would use his Endeavours to prevent it. By the Time P___k had got half of the Way (about 150 yards) from the Waiter to his Company, D___n and L___k were parrying, P___k run with all the Speed he could towards them, drawing his Sword as he run, and beckoning his Hand to the two Gentlemen who were walking in the Fields, tho' not in Company, to come up, they being, tho' at a considerable Distance, Spectators of the Engagement.[6]

Captain Dawson was killed in the fight; his adversary, L ___ k, was subsequently convicted of manslaughter.

This story is an fine example of what one historian has called the 'conventional half-concealment' of duelling. He was discussing the later half of the seventeenth century but his remarks apply equally to later periods.[7] Everyone knew that duelling was illegal but nevertheless it took place, semi-secretly, as it were, under the nose of the authorities. Men frequently fought in, for example, Southampton Fields yet no attempt was made to prevent the duels from happening there. It amounted to 'turning a blind eye' to the custom. Equally, the duellists themselves were guilty of an identical connivance as they rarely bothered to fight in places that would be truly private. That would be too troublesome. It was easier to opt for the 'conventional half-concealment' of, say, Islington Fields, just a short carriage ride from town, safe in the knowledge that there was little danger of falling foul of the criminal law.

Another favourite rendezvous for duels was London's parks. In the seventeenth and eighteenth centuries these presented a different aspect from what we see now. A German visitor to London in 1710 recorded his, slightly mystified, impression of St James's Park: 'Since not only some of the finest English cows but also a considerable number of red deer graze there, it is called a park, although there is no real woodland but merely avenues.'[8]

The Swiss traveller Cesar de Saussure also took in Hyde Park during his visit to London, in the mid-1720s. It was, he wrote, about five or six miles in circumference, and is closed in by high walls. It contains several avenues and a quantity of elm and lime trees, planted irregularly and forming little woods. A small river or stream flows through the park and forms an ornamental pond. In this park is a place called the 'Ring'. It is a round place, two or three hundred feet in diameter, and shut in by railings. This ring is surrounded by fine trees …

Both observers recorded that the parks were fashionable meeting places. Sometimes, we are told, as many as 200 coaches were to be seen.[9] In St James's Park things were different: 'During the week gentlemen of the highest fashion are to be met here and, moreover, on foot, for none but a few persons of the Court may enter the park in their coaches.'[10]

By the early eighteenth century St James's Park was regarded as rather too public a place to fight a duel. Hyde Park, however, was a different matter, particularly if one met early in the morning, being both large enough and close enough to London to combine seclusion and convenience. It was a popular rendezvous for duellists at all times of the day, as was made clear by the following curious report from 1722.

> Since the Duel that happened last Week in Hyde-Park, Orders have been given, that the People of the victualling and drinking Booths about the Camp, shall put out their Lights every Night by Ten a Clock.[11]

It was in Hyde Park that the most notorious duel of the age was fought on 15 November 1712. The combatants were James, 4th Duke of Hamilton, and Charles, 4th Baron Mohun. There was a long history of animosity between the two men, who were nevertheless related to each other by marriage. The background to the duel is extremely complicated; indeed, it forms in its own right the subject of an entire book.[12] Their feud centred on a disputed claim to an estate in Cheshire called Gawsworth Hall, the subject of litigation that had ground glacially on since 1702. However, their relationship was further clouded by the fact that they stood on different sides of the political divide. Hamilton, being a royalist and a Scotsman, was an ardent Tory and long suspected by the Whigs of Jacobite sympathies.

Charles Mohun, who was 19 years younger than Hamilton –

curiously, they shared a birthday, 11 April – had as a young man acquired an extremely unsavoury reputation as a rake and duellist. Duelling was evidently in his blood: his father had died when little Charles was only five months old from injuries sustained in a duel. Mohun himself became involved in a number of duels and brawls, some of which ended fatally. By his 22nd birthday he had already been tried twice by his peers in the House of Lords for murder; he was acquitted on both occasions. He was spared facing his peers on a third occasion, again on a charge of murder, by the timely arrival of a royal pardon. Politically, Mohun's position was bolstered by his friendship with King William III, who was firmly identified with the Whig interest.

Matters came to a head during a court hearing between the parties in November 1712 at which Mohun considered his honesty to have been impugned by Hamilton. The following day, he sent his second, General George Macartney, to challenge the Duke to a duel. Early in the morning of Saturday, 15 November, the two men and their seconds – the Duke's was his kinsman, Colonel John Hamilton – met near the Ring in Hyde Park. What followed was more akin to a footpad's brawl than an aristocrat's duel: Mohun and Hamilton slashed viciously at one another, each managing to wound his adversary. Meanwhile, the two seconds drew on each other but Colonel Hamilton, despite sustaining a wound to his foot, succeeded in disarming Macartney. Meanwhile, the Duke had inflicted a serious wound on Mohun but was himself, in Mohun's last desperate attack, stabbed in the chest. As Mohun collapsed dying, the Duke's life, too, was ebbing away. Within a few minutes both men were dead.

News of this disastrous duel spread as quickly as the two seconds, both now in deep jeopardy, went into hiding. Contemporaries were shocked by the prominence of the duellists. But what really caused a sensation was the version of events given by Colonel Hamilton after he emerged from hiding a few days later. The colonel asserted that Macartney, once Mohun had expired, had turned on the duke, killing him with a thrust of his sword. This, clearly, put a wholly different complexion on the affair: far from being a duel between two gentlemen to settle private differences, it now looked like a murderous conspiracy with sinister political overtones.

The hacks and presses at once began working overtime to produce partisan pamphlets stating each side's case. *A True and Impartial Account of the Murder of his Grace the Duke of Hamilton and Brandon* published in Edinburgh shortly after the duel. It belied its title, alleging that Macartney, having seen Mohun die, stepped in to finish off the duke. *A Letter from Mr Macartney to a Friend of His in London* put Macartney's defence.[13] Both the seconds were tried for their part in the duel, Hamilton a month after the event but Macartney not until 1716. Both men were acquitted of murder.

In certain quarters the response to the duel was immediate and uncompromising. A week after the two peers had hacked one another to death in Hyde Park, Queen Anne, attending divine service at Windsor, heard a fiery denunciation of duelling from her chaplain, Edmund Chishull.

He took as his text one of the anti-duellists' favourite pieces of scripture: 'Dearly Beloved, avenge not your selves; but rather give place unto Wrath: for it is written Vengeance is mine; I will repay, saith the Lord' (Romans, xii, 19).

Chishull then launched into an impassioned tirade against duelling. The duel, he thundered,

> is that wild decision of the private Sword: that effort of mistaken and unmanly Courage; exerted always against true Honour which it boasts so much, as well as against true Religion which it little minds.

Duelling was an impious deed, which flouted God's law.[14]

In the early years of the seventeenth century there was a noticeable stiffening of the sinews among those opposed to duelling. One of the leading lights of the opposition was Sir Richard Steele. Steele, born in 1672, the son of a Dublin lawyer, was sent to school at Charterhouse, where he began a lifelong friendship with Joseph Addison. He later went up to Oxford, although he left without taking his degree and went into the army. It was as a serving officer that, in 1700, Steele fought the duel that would convert him into so staunch an opponent of the practice. He campaigned against the practice relentlessly, employing all the lines of attack that his varied career made available.

As a playwright he used the stage to ridicule duelling, or the 'Force of a Tyrant Custom, which is misnamed a Point of Honour', as he called it. His proselytising against duelling started with *The Christian Hero* (1701), his early play *The Lying Lover* (1704), finishing only with his last play, *The Conscious Lovers* (1722).[15]

But it was as a journalist that Steele achieved his lasting reputation as an implacable opponent of duelling. In partnership with Addison he wrote the *Spectator*, a daily essay sheet, between March 1711 and December 1712. Edition No. 9, of 10 March 1711, was a satirical discourse on male clubs. Among the institutions mentioned – No. 9 was in fact written by Addison – was the 'Club of Duellists', founded in the reign of Charles II, 'in which none was to be admitted that had not fought his Man'. Its rules had been drawn up, it appeared, in defiance of any notions of civilised behaviour or common sense.

> The President of it was said to have killed half a dozen in single Combat; and as for the other Members, they took their Seats according to the Number of their Slain. There was likewise a Side-Table, for such as had only drawn Blood, and shewn a laudable Ambition of taking the first Opportunity to qualifie themselves for the first Table. This Club, consisting only of Men of Honour, did not continue long, most of the Members of it being put to the Sword, or hanged, a little after its Institution.[16]

In June 1711 Steele wrote two *Spectator* essays, Nos 84 and 97, calling for official action to ban duelling. They appear as conversation pieces between a king of ancient Gaul, Pharamond, and Eucrate, one of his favourite courtiers. Eucrate, it transpires, has killed a dear friend in a duel and implores the king to take action to stamp out the vice of duelling. He urged that to eradicate a 'Crime which had so long prevailed and was so firmly fixed in the Opinion of the World as great and laudable' only extreme measures would suffice:

> the most severe and vindictive Punishments, such as placing the Bodies of the Offenders in Chains, and putting them to Death by the most exquisite Torments.[17]

Pharamond, however, disagreed, proposing instead that 'Poverty and Shame' are sufficient deterrents to would-be duellists. Accordingly, he published an edict against duels. It provided a draconian system of fines and confiscations for duellists. For instance, any one who was convicted of killing in a duel shall not only be put death but 'his whole Estate ... shall from the hour of his Death be vested in the next Heir of the Person whose Blood he spilt'.[18]

It is telling that Steele attributes these ideas to an ancient king of Gaul – the edict is dated 'Blois, the 8th of February 420' – since we have already seen that he regarded modern France as the leading example of how to stamp out duelling. In 1720 Steele published a pamphlet 'on the Occasion of the Bill now depending in Parliament relating to Duels', an overt attempt to rally support for the anti-duelling cause. As Steele was himself a Member of Parliament at the time, his pamphlet was an obvious attempt to influence the debate. He proposed to reduce the bloodshed by compelling the quarrelling parties to submit their differences to arbitration by a panel of local worthies in each county. In taking this line, which we have seen surfacing elsewhere in the form of the 'honour court', Steele was recognising that 'no Law ... [MPs] can make will prevent Duels, unless they authorize them, unless they make lawful; provided the Duellists first apply to the Magistrate'.

Under Steele's proposed system of 'licensed' duelling these local worthies, should they fail to reconcile the parties, would be responsible for supervising the duel. They would nominate the weapons to be used and ensure a fair fight. Official oversight of the duel extended, in Steele's scheme, even to transport: the adversaries were to be 'carried in close Coaches, with Wooden Windows, to the Place set apart for fighting'. This was, presumably, in order to deny the duellist his moment of glory.

The keystone of Steele's proposal, again clearly actuated by the need to prevent duelling and its practitioners acquiring a false lustre in the public eye, was that fights should take place behind closed doors in specially constructed buildings. Steele hoped that by regulating duels in this way, by making them so deliberate, so utterly devoid of any romance, spirit or spontaneity, they would simply wither away. After all, what was the attraction of a licensed fight to the death, under official supervision, in a cold drill hall?[19]

Sir Richard's was, however, by far from being the only voice raised against duelling at this time. We have already encountered Dr Cockburn's hostile history of duelling, published in 1720. Isaac Watts, a prominent dissenter and hymnist (composer of that perennial favourite 'Our God, our help in ages past', among more than six hundred others, now mostly forgotten), was, as one might expect, implacably opposed to duelling. He spared his readers nothing in sulphurously denouncing the practice.

> But if you are obstinately resolved to dye for a Point of Honour, go rush into the other World by the Sword or by the Gibbet, and make your *Appeal* for injured Honour to the most righteous and supreme Tribunal of Justice there ... you will be sentenc'd to everlasting Infamy and Shame, as a Punishment to your Pride.[20]

A more measured, secular attack was launched at duelling in 1750 by William Webster. It was presented as a conversation piece, between a clergyman and a gentleman. The clergyman asks:

> Is there any Proportion, in this Way of deciding the Controversey, between the Crime and the Punishment? Does a Piece of ill Manners deserve Death? Because a Gentleman has affronted and slighted you, is it right to do him the greatest, an irreparable, Injury; to send him reeking hot out of the World ... with all his sins about him?

As his answer, predictably, was 'no', he suggested that duellists should be locked into neck stocks, directly facing one another, 'like two Game-cocks upon a Stage'. On the stocks would be hung a board carrying the legend, 'These are Gentlemen of Honour, Who stand here to receive proper Satisfaction'.[21] If Watts aimed to terrify would-be duellists with fire and brimstone, Webster aimed at death by ridicule.

Nor was criticism of duelling restricted to metropolitan sophisticates. In 1720 an author describing himself only as 'a Gentleman of Wales' published in Shrewsbury a pamphlet entitled *The Humour of Duelling, Considered, Its Pretences examined into And Exploded*. The author's lucubrations on the subject were prompted by a recent duel in the county in which, it was feared, one of the participants had lost his life. It seemed to him an 'impertinent and Senseless' practice: 'Among all the Ridiculous Customs that this unthinking Age falls into so easily, there is None so absurd as the Humours of fighting a Duel upon every little quarrel, & trifling occasion.'[22]

We have seen how men fought their duels in the England of the first half of the eighteenth century and looked at the objections of those who opposed them. We now need to examine why they fought, and put these reasons into some historical perspective. According to one historian, 'Duelling is for the eighteenth century what trials for witchcraft are for the seventeenth', all too often dismissed as an 'inconvenient and anachronistic' relic of an earlier and less civilised age.[23] However, the fact is that men fought duels; they chose to ignore the strictures of the Church and the prohibitions of the law. Why?

> Custom has made it a maxim, that we must defend what we call our honour: for to suffer under the imputation of cowardice, is worse than being buried alive.[24]

There is no doubt that gentlemen did feel, and feel acutely, a sense of honour. It was a defining characteristic, passed on and nurtured from generation to generation, governing their society. To defy it risked social ostracism. There were those, of course, who sought to give duelling a more convincing, less visceral, justification. One such was the anonymous author of *A Hint on Duelling in a Letter to a Friend*, published in London in 1752. This anonymous apologist maintained that duelling allowed 'a Manly Decision of ... Differences ... or an Honourable Punishment of Injuries inoperable by the Magistrate'. He then resorted to the well-worn line of argument that the abolition of duelling would have worse consequences than continued connivance.

> The Leviathans of Riches and Power ... would be thereby let loose to Insult and Oppress the Gentry of moderate Fortunes ... Every Brute of high Condition, when influenced by Insolence or quotidian Wine, might disturb with Impunity the proposed Amusement of Thousands ... And the libidinous Villain destroy with Boasts the Peace and Honour of Families, by the insidious corrupting of Maids and Matrons.

In short, for him, duelling was the lesser of two evils.

✶ ✶ ✶

By 1700 the Grand Tour was firmly established as an essential part of a young gentleman's education; 'an ideal finishing school', as Christopher Hibbert put it.[25] Moreover, during the course of the eighteenth century, the numbers of young Englishmen undertaking a Grand Tour greatly increased. 'Where one Englishman travelled in the reign of the first two Georges,' wrote one observer in 1772, 'ten now go on a grand tour.'[26] The Grand Tour was, of course, undertaken to broaden the minds of young aristocrats, to visit Paris, the greatest city of the age, to see Rome and, most importantly, to acquire that veneer of Classical culture considered so essential in the well-rounded gentleman. If, while in Rome, they managed to sit for Pompeo Batoni, then so much the better.

However, the Grand Tour was also an opportunity for young men to acquire rougher habits or fall into bad company. In the late 1740s Lord Chesterfield felt the need to warn his son of the dangers that lay in wait on the Continent for the unwary. In Rome, he counselled, the exiled Jacobites were a notorious source of trouble to visiting Englishmen. Equally, in Paris, it was all too easy to fall into quarrels with touchy Frenchmen. In either case, a duel was likely to be the result.

James Boswell, travelling on the Continent 15 years later, and perhaps lacking the advice of a protective father, came within a whisker of having to fight a duel in Berlin. He became embroiled in an argument with an artillery officer named Durand, who called Boswell a 'scoundrel' in public. 'This last word gave me a blow to the heart,' wrote Boswell in his journal, and no wonder, since he knew there was now only one honourable solution. 'It was a clear affront that could not be put up.' Boswell, after a certain amount of wrestling with his conscience, duly demanded satisfaction of Durand. Happily, a duel was averted when both men were persuaded to make 'equal' public apologies.[27] The episode ended harmlessly but it illustrates the need for caution.

The French and the Italians were enthusiastic duellists. Sir

Horace Mann represented the British government in Florence for many years in the middle of the century, from where he carried on an interminable correspondence with Horace Walpole. He told Walpole of a duel fought there in March 1743. Gino Pasquale Capponi

> has fought with a Lorrain officer. The latter was the aggressor; they both behaved well. Gigi was wounded first in an odd place. The sword went into his codpiece, wounded what it met there, and then pierced his thigh. He bled much but would not leave off, it being said his blood could not wash out the affront he had received, so fought on till he had wounded his adversary in the hand. Then, there being blood on both sides, they kissed, and went home to bed, where Gigi remains still under the surgeon's hands.[28]

It was all too easy to get into trouble while abroad. One of Sir Horace's successors as Minister at Florence, William Wyndham, was compelled to fight a local aristocrat, hardly model diplomatic behaviour.

Indeed, one of the skills that young men frequently acquired during the course of their Grand Tour, to complement the Classical learning, was fencing. The hero of Quebec, James Wolfe, perfected his fencing skills in the 1750s while on a prolonged period of leave in Paris. Boswell took fencing lessons in both Berlin and in Holland during the course of his Grand Tour in the 1760s. His Dutch fencing master was, one suspects, unusual: 'He is ninety-four years old. His father taught William III, Prince of Orange, to fence ... He was at the famous Battle of the Boyne.' Despite his immense age he was 'as healthy and spry as a man of thirty' and could fence 'with all the agility in the world'. Furthermore, Boswell reported that his hand was stronger than his own. 'We tried it, and he won.'[29]

It would be wrong to claim that the Grand Tour alone was responsible for inflaming the duelling spirit among Englishmen. It was already firmly instilled in English minds by the time Grand Tour became an established custom. Equally, it is obviously the case that a number of young 'men of quality' did, during the eighteenth century and beyond, come into contact with duelling while travelling on the

Continent. And, along with their souvenirs of Classical Rome and
their Batonis, they brought it home with them.

*   *   *

When Louis XIV died at Versailles on 1 September 1715 after a monu-
mental reign lasting 72 years, he was succeeded by his five-year-old
great-grandson. As Louis XV was a child, the reins of government
passed to his cousin, Philippe d'Orleans. The death of the old king
and the advent of the Regency marked the start of a new era in the life
of the French court. Philippe moved back to Paris, away from the stul-
tifying formality of Versailles. The new age took its lead from the
Regent: a man of many contradictions, thoughtful yet dissipated,
scholarly yet buffoonish. The abrupt change of tone was, as so often,
reflected in architecture and painting. Escaping the dead hand of Versailles for the freedoms of Paris, aristocrats abandoned the baroque
pomposities that had dominated architecture for two generations,
and joyfully embraced the carefree curlicues of the rococo. They
exchanged the grandeur of Versailles for the intimacy of Parisian town
houses. Watteau was the painter of the age; his frivolous *fêtes cham-
pêtres* superseding the ponderous history painting and portraiture
that had held sway under Louis XIV.

When Philippe d'Orleans died, aged 49, in 1723, the young
Louis XV took over at least nominal responsibility for the running of
the government. His long reign – he did not die until 1774 – was a
period of stagnation at home dominated by frequent and expensive
wars abroad. Louis's reign is now probably best remembered for
Madame de Pompadour, of the fripperies of François Boucher, and
for its exquisitely elaborate furniture, known as Louis Quinze. Many
of the champagne houses whose names are still familiar to us were
founded during Louis's reign. It was also the Age of the Enlightenment, whose leading figure was Voltaire. Louis was succeeded by his
grandson, Louis XVI, who was, as it turned out, the last of the *ancien
régime* monarchs. On the day the storm that was to wash away the old
order broke, 14 July 1789, Louis's entry in his diary was '*Rien*'. Four
years later he lost his head on the guillotine.

In many ways duelling was a quintessential custom of the *ancien régime*: its aristocratic character, its pride, its love of honour, protocol and precedence and its touchiness all chime with the spirit of the age. This section charts the history of duelling in the last 75 years of the *ancien régime*, from Regency to Revolution.

If there was one figure who embodied the spirit of the *ancien régime* in the eighteenth century it was Louis-François-Armand, duc de Richelieu. When he was born, the Sun King had nearly 20 years still to reign but he did not die until the year before the Revolution. A great-nephew of the cardinal, he inherited a vast fortune, yet, as a result of his extravagance, he was plagued by financial difficulties. He was a legendary philanderer and a man of great charm, characteristics that, according to some observers, disguised his other shortcomings. Thomas Carlyle vividly described him as having 'an old dissipated mastiff-face'.[30] According to Lord Chesterfield, Richelieu was a man 'without a grain of merit, knowledge or talents' who had nevertheless risen to the pinnacles of the French state.

Even Louis XV referred to Richelieu as '*mon amiable vaut-rien*' (my lovable good-for-nothing). Despite this evident lack of solid talent he was showered with honours, entrusted with embassies and promoted to the command of armies. He was in command of the abortive expedition to support the Jacobite rising against the English in 1745. More successfully, Richelieu led the French force that captured Minorca from the English, a defeat for which the hapless Admiral Byng paid with his life. Incongruously, one might think, he was nevertheless a friend of Voltaire. He was also an inveterate duellist.

His most celebrated duel was the affair, already noted, in which, goaded by his new wife's family's snobbery, he killed the Prince de Lixen in 1734. Two year later he fought a duel with the comte de Pentiriender. The dispute was entirely characteristic of Richelieu as it was caused by his having taken Pentiriender's mistress. The duel was fought at Les Invalides in Paris; the hapless Pentiriender was killed. The Duke had himself earlier unwittingly been the cause of one of those rare happenings, a duel between two women. The comtesse de Polignac and the marquise de Nesle were both infatuated with the young Richelieu and competed simultaneously for his affections. By Richelieu's own, somewhat smug, account the comtesse de Polignac was 'madly enamoured of my coquetry'; enraged by jealousy and the Duke's insouciance, she challenged the marquise de Nesle, who was only one of her many rivals, to a duel. They agreed to meet in the Bois de Boulogne, where they were to fight with pistols to decide, as Richelieu complacently put it, 'which should have me if they were not both killed'.

When they met, in the Bois de Boulogne, the two ladies, dressed in riding habit, gave a preliminary curtsey and then exchanged pistols shots. People came running up when they saw Madame de Nesle fall to the ground, with blood flowing over her bosom. But on examination it was found that the blood was coming from a scratch on her shoulder, the bullet having only grazed Madame de Nesle's skin.[31]

Duelling in the final decades of the *ancien régime* was a distinguishing attribute of the French nobility, as Carlyle's memorable description makes clear:

> Ever since that period of the *Fronde*, the Noble has changed his fighting sword into a court rapier; and now loyally attends his King as ministering satellite; divides the spoil, not now by violence and murder, but by soliciting and finesse. These men call themselves supports of the throne: singular gilt-pasteboard *caryatides* in that singular edifice! ...
>
> These people, of old, surely had virtues, uses; or they could not have been there. Nay, one virtue they still are required to have (for mortal men cannot live without a conscience): the virtue of perfect readiness to fight duels.[32]

If aristocrats were the duellists *par excellence* of the *ancien régime*, it was entirely appropriate that one of the most elevated of all aristocrats, no less a personage than the King's brother, a Prince of the Blood, should fight one of the most celebrated, and most ridiculous, duels of the period. The comte d'Artois, who later ascended the throne of France as Charles X (when supposedly he was the last man in Europe to wear a powdered wig), fought a duel with the duc de Bourbon in 1778. D'Artois, to a greater extent even than Richelieu, embodied the very essence of the feckless French aristocrat. One of his biographers wrote of him:

Artois grew older without growing up. He flitted with impunity from one folly to another, exhibiting not the slightest curiosity in anything, happy to be lazy, scatterbrained and amiable.[33]

He was also, like Richelieu, an inexhaustible womaniser. The contretemps between Artois and the duc de Bourbon had its origins at a Shrove Tuesday masked ball held at the Opéra. Artois, arriving with Mme de Carillac on his arm, ran into the duchess de Bourbon. The two women cordially loathed each other: Mme de Carillac had been the duc de Bourbon's mistress, but had lately transferred her affections to Artois. According to one version of events, the duchess's jealously of Mme de Carillac stemmed not from the fact that she had been her husband's mistress but, deliciously perversely, that she had *ceased* to be her husband's mistress and was now occupying Artois, on whom the duchess herself had designs. The two women sniped at each other; Artois, flushed with wine, decided to pretend – it was a masked ball – that he thought the duchess was a prostitute and made a lewd suggestion to her. The duchess, outraged, said, 'Only M. de Artois or a dirty old man could speak to me like that!' and, grabbing his mask, pulled it off. Artois, furious, retaliated by crushing the duchess's mask onto her face before escaping into the crowd.[34]

Behaviour of this kind was bound to cause trouble and so it proved. While Artois continued to make tactless remarks about the incident, the King washed his hands of the whole affair. The person who was most embarrassed was the duc de Bourbon. Honour dictated that as the duchess's husband he should expunge this stain on her reputation but to do so entailed challenging his old partner in crime Artois, who was, moreover, the King's brother. Bourbon's father, the Prince de Conde, was pressing his son to uphold the honour of the family; certainly all the court gossips anticipated a duel to resolve the matter. Eventually the two men did meet, in the Bois de Boulogne, but it is difficult to believe that the subsequent duel was fought in earnest. Indeed, it barely merits being called a duel.

Once all the usual formalities had been observed – including moving to a spot where the sun was not in Artois's eyes – the two

men began a some rather half-hearted swordplay. After a few lunges
Artois's sword was seen to pass under the duke's arm, at which point
the seconds intervened to stop the bout. Bourbon pronounced
himself satisfied and the two men, instantly reconciled, leapt into
each other's arms.[35] They might have thought that their efforts
would satisfy the punctilios of honour and propitiate public
opinion, but these testy gods were not so easily assuaged. The
duchess, for one, saw through the whole charade. Nor has history
taken the duel too seriously: Artois's biographer called it a 'parade'.
Carlyle was even more scathing: 'Monseigneur d'Artois pulls the
mask from a fair impertinent; fights a duel in consequence – almost
drawing blood.'[36]

It has been argued that the more relaxed atmosphere of the
Regency, after the long reign of Louis XIV, gave rise to a resurgence in
duelling. One of the most important figures of the Regency, the Scots
financier John Law, was a known duellist. Law, a great favourite of the
Regent, ran the Bank of France and presided over the French equivalent of the South Sea Bubble. Earlier in life, before emigrating to
France, he had killed his man in a duel in disreputable circumstances.
However, it is doubtful that Louis XIV was as successful at eradicating
duelling in France as was previously imagined. In this view, therefore,
the Regency represents not so much a resurgence of duelling as business as usual.

The traditional view holds that, after the excitements of the
Regency years, duelling gradually began to fall from fashion in France.
Artois's farcical encounter in the 1770s served to show how degraded
the once noble institution of duelling had become. Horace Walpole
observed in 1765 that, 'Diderot said, the French were so changed, that
it had been said lately, that Louis XV would find it as difficult to re-
establish duels, as Louis XIV had to suppress them.'[37]

This felicitously phrased opinion has been used by historians as
evidence to support the theory of duelling's decline during the
period.[38] However, even Walpole's own correspondence contains evidence, albeit anecdotal, suggesting that duelling, far from being in
decline, was in rude health. In the year that he recorded Diderot's
epigram he received a letter from an English friend in Paris.

It is not only in England that they fight duels; Lady Hertford, Mr Hume and myself were melancholy eye-witnesses to one last week between two French soldiers in which we saw one killed before our window as we sat at dinner.[39]

A few years later Walpole received another letter from Paris, this time from a French correspondent, telling him that 'The madness of the duel is reinvigorated; there have been two in the last fortnight.'[40]

Recent research suggests, however, that far from declining in the first half of the eighteenth century, there was a steady increase in the number of duels fought, reaching a peak in the 1740s and 1750s. The research, conducted by three French historians, looks at the criminal appeal records for the Paris Parlement for the whole of the eighteenth century. There were in total 333 cases, a figure that, of course, does not represent the total number of duels fought, merely those that reached the appeal court.[41] Other research conducted into the records of the Paris municipal morgue lends support to the theory that the levels of duelling peaked at the same time.[42] M. Barbier, a lawyer who practised in the courts of the Paris Parlement, recorded in one year alone, 1753, 11 reported cases of duels between nobles. So the evidence, empirical and anecdotal, suggests that, far from tailing off, duelling was on the increase in the first half of the eighteenth century.

If this was the case it does not speak volumes for the authorities' continuing efforts to eradicate duelling. Louis XV marked the start of his majority in 1723, as his great-grandfather had done 70 years earlier, with an anti-duelling edict. Promulgated at Versailles in February 1723, it reiterated that all the anti-duelling edicts of Louis's ancestors remained in force. But his attempts to stamp out duelling in France were no more effective than those of his forebears.

The mid-eighteenth century was the Age of the Enlightenment, the age of Diderot, Montesquieu, and Rousseau, the *philosophes* whose writings promoted a more modern, secular view of the world, one which would most certainly not include duelling. The most famous of the *philosophes* was Voltaire, who, as we saw earlier, derided duelling as a 'gothic barbarism' and credited Louis XIV with having stamped it out in France. Yet Voltaire himself came within a whisker of fighting a duel. This was despite having what his latest biographer calls 'a deep-seated aversion to physical violence'.[43] One evening at the Opéra, the Chevalier de Rohan-Chabot, a 'feckless and degenerate scion' of one of France's oldest aristocratic families, baited Voltaire about his change of name (from François-Marie Arouet). When a couple of days later Rohan-Chabot repeated his jibe, Voltaire deliberately insulted the chevalier, who only just managed to restrain himself from thrashing Voltaire on the spot with his cane.

Rohan-Chabot was determined to have his revenge on Voltaire but, as he did not consider him a social equal, would not contemplate fighting a duel with him. So the chevalier laid a trap for Voltaire by sending him an invitation to dinner with the duc de Sully. During dinner Voltaire was called to the entrance and there set upon by three or four heavies bearing cudgels; Rohan-Chabot looked on while they beat him before calling them off and retiring. Voltaire, having failed to enlist any help in bringing Rohan-Chabot to book for this outrageous assault, decided he had no option but to challenge him to a duel. Rohan-Chabot got wind of Voltaire's intention and made himself scarce. Once Voltaire had eventually succeeded in delivering his challenge to the chevalier, he was again outwitted by Rohan-Chabot, who had arranged for his arrest and confinement in the Bastille. So the famous *philosophe* never fought his duel.[44]

Did the *philosophes'* advocacy of enlightened, modern thought make men more reluctant to duel? After all, in the long term, it was the advance of modern manners and the rule of law – ideas that the *philosophes* wholeheartedly embraced – that finally consigned the duel to history. Moreover the statistics quoted earlier do seem to suggest that the incidence of duelling declined gradually after peaking in mid-century.

Sadly, it is a question that is difficult, if not impossible, to answer. We have seen, for example, that Voltaire was intellectually opposed to duelling, yet in practice was quite prepared to fight to restore his honour. The question was tackled, albeit in a slightly different form, by an anonymous pamphleteer from The Hague. Writing in 1751 he posed the question whether the literature of the Enlightenment had had a greater effect against duelling than the rule of law. There follow

50 pages of discussion, at the end of which, perhaps not surprisingly, he concludes that the answer is yes.[45]

Away from the high-minded philosophising of the Enlightenment, the last decades of the *ancien régime* was a period, like many in the history of duelling, rich in eccentrics. Two in particular stand out. The first is the character known to history as the Chevalier d'Eon, who, as the subject of no fewer than 16 biographies, is clearly irresistible to writers. The chevalier has also found his way into most histories of duelling, despite the fact that, so far as can be discerned, he never fought a duel. The secret of the chevalier's appeal lies in the fact that he was a transvestite in an age when such traits were considered scandalous. The excuse for including the chevalier in histories of duelling, titillation apart, is that he was an exceptionally fine swordsman. Born in the Burgundian town of Tonnerre in 1728, the chevalier when young learned to fence brilliantly before entering the service of Louis XV as, variously, a soldier, diplomat and secret agent. He had early in life manifested a marked liking for dressing up in women's clothes and, by all accounts, looked the part. The chevalier sat for numerous artists, including Angelica Kauffman, who painted him as a woman, a portrait that achieved a wider audience as a stipple engraving by Francis Hayman in the 1780s.[46]

The question of the chevalier's sex confounded and fascinated his contemporaries. Huge sums were bet on it in the St James's clubs and the latest odds quoted daily on the stock exchange in London.[47] In 1777 there was a judicial investigation into the question of the chevalier's gender at the Guildhall in London. Presided over by no less a figure than the Chief Justice of the Court of King's Bench, Lord Mansfield, the court, having shied away from the necessary anatomical examination, failed to reach a conclusion. In 1764 Casanova, while on a visit to London, dined with the French ambassador, where he met the chevalier. Casanova, who could reasonably be considered an expert in such matters, was completely fooled – he was certain the chevalier was a woman. The chevalier died in 1810 at the age of 81. After his death a postmortem was conducted that proved, incontrovertibly, that the chevalier was, anatomically at least, a man.

The second figure is the Chevalier Saint-Georges, a mulatto from

Guadeloupe. Born in 1745, he was the progeny of a French planter and a local woman. He was a cultivated man, a sufficiently accomplished musician to be able to earn a living as a virtuoso, conductor and composer. Saint-Georges, like the Chevalier d'Eon, figures in most histories of duelling but, in his case, with rather more justification. He was a highly skilled fencer and a duellist with a fearsome reputation. He fought many duels, usually, we are told, as the insulted party. Indeed, 'he was never known to avail himself of his reputation to insult anyone less skilled in the science of destruction'. This talent had other, more pleasurable rewards: 'His skill in arms and his numerous duels rendered him such a favourite among the ladies, that his dark complexion and wooly head were forgotten.'[48]

Such was the fame of these two exotic creatures that a fencing bout was arranged between them at Carlton House in 1787 in front of the Prince of Wales and his friends. There is a splendid engraving by James Gilray of the match, which shows the two fencers in action, with Prinny and friends looking on from a safe distance.[49]

The two chevaliers were far from being run-of-the-mill individuals but they were honourable; neither of them would have cheated for advantage in a duel. There were, as always, plenty of men who would; these were the rogues and ruffians, men who gave not a whit for the rules or for good manners. Here, from 1769, is an example of one (who should have known better) who failed to abide by the rules.

> The sieur Chelais, member of parliament in France, was condemned to be broken upon the wheel, for the murder of the sieur Beguin, captain of the legion in Flanders, by challenging him to fight, covering himself with armour, and coming into the field so fortified, and when his antagonist's sword was broke in the attack, most treacherously assassinating him, by stabbing him when he was down. He has, however, made his escape for the present; but, it is hoped, no state will protect him.[50]

At the opposite end of the spectrum is an incident recorded by the Prince de Ligne in his memoirs. The Prince de Ligne was an immensely wealthy and cultivated noble, a gilded leviathan of the *ancien régime*, a man who knew everyone and was invited everywhere. Carlyle described him as 'that brave literary De Ligne the Thundergod of Dandies'.[51] He is credited with the famous jibe about the Congress of Vienna, '*Le congrès ne marche pas, il danse.*' ('The Congress does not work, it dances.')[52]

> One evening [the prince recalled] when it was pouring, Segur and I left Madame de Polignac's house. There was no cab in sight; no one to find one for us. 'Let us pretend to be fighting,' said I; 'a patrol of the watch will come by, will arrest us, and will fetch a coach to take us to the police-station.' We drew our swords and made a terrible clashing and then, when we shouted: 'Are you dead or wounded?' the watch passed and, frightened at our appearance, did not arrest us; so, in addition to the fatigue of walking home, we had that of our fight.[53]

Although de Ligne here exhibited a light-hearted attitude to duelling, there was, as he explained, a more serious side to it.

> I have been, at times, so indiscreet, so imprudent, so foolish even, both when I was young and now, for the sake of a joke – though, I must admit, never for a spiteful or backbiting one – that I wonder I have not been involved in a dozen duels.[54]

In eighteenth-century France, as in other countries at other times, there were many men around who were quick to take offence. Those who wished to avoid having to fight for their lives did well to take care what they said.

Before we leave *ancien régime* France we must return to the subject of female duellists. The example quoted earlier of the two *grandes dames* who fought over the young duc de Richelieu is a rarity in the history of duelling. Women, by and large, did not fight duels. While some might say that they had more sense than to risk their lives for something as ephemeral as honour, the truth was that women did not duel. It was not the done thing. We have seen many examples of a man taking up sword or pistol to defend the honour of his wife, sister or daughter. It happened often, throughout the history of duelling; it was, as it were, a transferred but nevertheless unavoidable responsibility. The man was the head of the family, the provider and protector; if there was duelling to be done, he would do it. And, in the vast majority of cases, that was what happened.

There were, of course, exceptions to the general rule – they were known as 'petticoat duels' – and two of them crop up in the 1770s. The first, from 1772, was a most unladylike encounter, more like a brawl in an alley than a formal, considered duel. 'Two ladies of quality', a Mlle de Guinges and a Mlle d'Aguillon, quarrelled about their position in the order of precedence. The argument reached such a pitch that they repaired to the garden and fought with knives. One was wounded in the arm and the other in the neck.[55] Five years later a French naval officer got his comeuppance.

> A young woman at Paris, enraged at being abandoned by her lover; after many useless reproaches, at length waited on him a few days ago, and told him, that being unable to survive his perfidy, she was determined to fight him, and that she had brought two pistols with her for that purpose. The gentleman took one, and, making light of the matter, fired it into the air; but she, not imitating his example, and become perfectly mad through despair, fired hers at him, and wounded him dreadfully in the face.[56]

The French opera singer Maupin, who was at her peak at the end of the seventeenth century, was a fiery character who was not in the least afraid of taking on the men. She had an advantage in that one of her lovers was the celebrated fencing master Serana who, besides his other duties, gave her fencing lessons. Confident in her ability to defend herself, when an actor called Dameny insulted her, she called him out. He declined to give her satisfaction so, in revenge, she purloined his watch and snuffbox as trophies. Another actor who aroused Maupin's ire but also refused her satisfaction was forced to go down on bended knee and beg forgiveness. Then, finally, at a ball she got the opportunity to put her fencing skills to the test.

Maupin, having been rude to a fellow female guest, was asked to leave the ball. This she agreed to do, provided that the men who had stood up for the object of her scorn accompany her from the ball. This they did. Once outside, we are told, Maupin challenged them all to a duel and, one by one, killed them all. Louis XIV pardoned her and she left France to live in Brussels, although she did return to Paris to sing at the Opéra before her death in 1707.[57]

*　*　*

When Frederick William, Elector of Brandenburg, the 'Great Elector', died in 1688 he was succeeded by his son Frederick. The Great Elector had issued Prussia's first anti-duelling law and his son, on succeeding to the electoral dignity, promptly followed suit. Frederick III (he later became Frederick I, King of Prussia) was solidly against duelling, an attitude reflected in the stringent provisions of his edict. It defined duelling as an evil influence in two different ways. First, it impoverished the state by depriving it of important servants; and, second, it arrogated to itself the administration of justice, which, rightfully, was the preserve of the courts. Neither of these was an original idea and both would be seen again elsewhere, but they demonstrated that the new Elector was serious about eradicating duelling. This statement of principle was backed up with severe penalties. Sending or accepting a challenge was punishable, for government employees, with dismissal; all other offenders were liable to have their income confiscated. The edict also promised the introduction of judicial reform so that such disputes could be settled in the courts, rather than at the point of a sword. Moreover, if a duel actually took place, the death penalty was imposed. In 1695, as a sign of earnest, a 60-year-old duellist and the corpse of his victim were publicly hanged in Berlin.[58]

Frederick William I ascended the throne of Prussia on the death of his father in 1713. He is known to history as the 'Soldier King'; a man of ascetic habits, his abiding interest lay in his army. During the course of his reign he doubled the size of the Prussian army, and immersed himself in the minutiae of military life.[59] His particular obsession for recruiting abnormally tall soldiers was notorious throughout Europe. Perhaps not surprisingly, Frederick William was more forgiving of duelling; indeed, according to one historian, he was responsible for sealing the (somewhat obvious) connection between duelling and militarism in Prussian society. It had long been recognised that duelling could foster the martial qualities desirable in an officer. He reduced the penalty for non-fatal duels from ten to eight years but did continue his father's deterrent policy of publicly hanging the corpses of the losers.

Frederick the Great, who succeeded his father in 1740, was the archetypal monarch of the Age of Enlightenment. A brilliantly

successful general with a large, well-oiled military machine at his disposal, he was able to pursue an aggressive, expansive foreign policy at
the expense of his neighbours. Yet he was a man of wide learning and
culture, a prolific author, who designed the exquisite palace of Sans
Souci, played the flute and befriended the *philosophes*; in 1750 Voltaire
became a paid 'writer in residence' at Frederick's court. These apparently contradictory aspects of Frederick's character were reflected in
his attitude to duelling. In theory, as one would expect of a monarch
as influenced as Frederick was by the thinkers of the Enlightenment,
he thoroughly disapproved of the practice. As a general, however, he
admitted that it was, in part, responsible for promoting a martial
spirit among his officers, while conceding that it did result in a steady
wastage of talent.

In 1783 Paolo Vergani published his *De l'Énormité du Duel* in
Berlin, in a French translation of his original Italian. As the title suggests, it was work that denounced duelling. The dedication to Frederick the Great promised a book that would leave no stone unturned in
proving even to the most obstinately prejudiced that duelling was an
antisocial menace.

The German historian Ute Frevert has analysed the attitudes to
duelling that prevailed in eighteenth-century Germany. Criticism of
the practice can, she says, be conveniently summarised in six heads.
First, duelling was irrational. Critics pointed out that duellists were
merely observing unquestioningly a social convention, anathema to
the enlightened mind. Second, it was unchristian and immoral,
infringing the sixth commandment, 'Thou shalt not kill', and the basic
Christian precepts of love, reconciliation and forgiveness. Third, it
was illegal. Fourth, it was a feudal privilege of the aristocracy, contrary
to the modern view that privilege derived from merit and achievement. Fifth, it was a caste mark of the officer corps and, therefore, a
symbol of the inferiority of civilians. Officers settled their disputes on
the duelling ground; civilians had recourse only to law. Lastly, duelling
was a crime condoned by the state. Although duelling was illegal, the
authorities appeared all too often to turn a blind eye to it. None of
these criticisms is unique to mid-eighteenth-century Germany;
indeed, all of them, in different guises, appear in anti-duelling

literature over the whole period. But they do constitute a comprehensive summary of the arguments employed against the duel.

These criticisms spurred duellists to construct a rational defence of the practice. It was not enough in the Age of Reason to rely on the fact that it was a practice sanctified by tradition; more persuasive arguments were needed. Frevert groups the justifications in seven heads. First, duelling was an essential outlet for personal honour, a conduit for self-assertion and self-respect. Second, it was a civilising influence, acting as a restraint against rude, aggressive or unseemly behaviour. Third, duelling was not so much an instrument of revenge as a medium for achieving reconciliation. The concept of a 'brotherhood of gentlemen' was central to this idea: the duellists were not merely adversaries but, potentially, friends as well. There are many examples of duellists who, having resolved their differences with sword or pistol, were amicably reconciled. It was, in such cases, as if the duel washed away the animosities that had existed between the parties. Fourth, duelling was the shield for a gentleman's personal integrity; it was the only way in which one could restore one's traduced honour and reputation. Fifth, duelling was one of the last remaining bastions of individual freedom, something beyond the reach of the state and the criminal law. Sixth, it established social equality between men. The duelling code was a unifying element in an aristocracy not otherwise notably equal in wealth or living standards. Lastly, it was a heartily masculine activity, that encouraged men to be men.[60] These justifications for duelling, like its criticisms, are not specific to Germany in the eighteenth century. Indeed, at one time or another, they all make an appearance in pro-duelling literature.

We now turn to the exploits of two famous figures, both roués of international standing in eighteenth-century Europe. The first is Frederick Augustus, known as the 'Strong', Elector of Saxony (1694–1733) and twice King of Poland (1697–1706 and 1710–23). His reputation as a philanderer of unquenchable enthusiasm is well deserved: he sired eight illegitimate children by five different women as well as an heir by his wife. One of his illegitimate sons, Maurice, later achieved fame as the French general, the Marechal de Saxe. The Elector had countless affairs as he progressed around the courts of

Europe and was clearly a man of eclectic taste: the mother of two of his illegitimate children is known to history as Fatima the Turk.

Much of Augustus's reputation is based on a racily scurrilous biography written shortly after his death by the courtier Karl Ludwig von Pollnitz. *The Amorous Adventures of Augustus of Saxony* (titillatingly subtitled *Several Transactions of his Life not mentioned in any other History Together with Diverting Remarks on the ladies of the Several Countries thro' which he travell'd*) is as prurient and sensationalist a piece of writing as can be found in any twenty-first-century tabloid newspaper and almost certainly not a reliable historical record.[61] Von Pollnitz was himself a chancer and a rogue, who wrote purely for money, with scant regard for truth or accuracy. However, what this entertaining book does show is that, if one was going to embark on a career of seduction on this scale, it helped greatly to be Elector of Saxony. From our point of view, not the least benefit was that Augustus was able to avoid the sort of trouble that dogged other serial womanisers of the time. There was the ever-present risk of being called to account by cuckolded husbands or disappointed rivals; often this would result in a duel. Augustus managed to steer clear of such dangers although, according to von Pollnitz, there were one or two close shaves.

One such episode occurred while the Elector was in Spain. He fell for the young and impressionable Marchioness of Manzera and, after a great deal of scheming and amorous intrigue, was eventually able to complete the conquest. Unfortunately the marquis was a 'very jealous Husband' and, seeing the lovers together, decided to take his revenge on the Elector. To this end he hired four ruffians to assassinate his wife's lover. They attacked the Elector as he left the Marchioness's apartments but he was able to hold them off – he was carrying a pair of pistols – until his guards arrived, at which point a fight broke out in which three of the hired assassins were killed.[62]

Augustus had another narrow escape in Warsaw. He had succeeded in seducing the virginal Henrietta Duval, a 'great Beauty', but, as he made his way home from her house, his secretary and confidant, Rantzau, was attacked by a jealous rival, who supposed him to be Henrietta's lover. The Elector looked on until another man joined the fray against his long-suffering secretary, at which point Augustus leapt in and, with a single stroke, disarmed him. The episode ended bloodlessly but might easily have been much more serious. Although Augustus did challenge the Duke of Mantua to a duel over some aspersions cast by the duke on the Elector's athletic prowess, it was never fought.[63]

The second figure is Giacomo Casanova. Casanova, whose very name has passed into the language, was perhaps the most famous philanderer of them all. He led a very eventful life: he was constantly on the move, travelling far and wide in Europe – sometimes of necessity; he consorted with crowned heads and was at home among the *beau monde* in many capitals; he was an incorrigible gambler; and, of course, he was an indefatigable lover of women. It comes as a surprise, given his sexual appetites and his cavalier attitude to money, to learn that he apparently fought only one duel in his life, although he had, as we have seen, acted as a second. Certainly, he had none of the advantages that the Elector of Saxony enjoyed when it came to avoiding duels.

The duel that Casanova did fight took place in Poland. Casanova had arrived in Warsaw in 1765, when Stanislaw Augustus had been on the throne for two years. Casanova worked for the King and entertained hopes of becoming his secretary. However, in March 1766, Casanova had a falling-out with Xavier Branicki, colonel of the Uhlans, courtier and favourite of the King. The two men had been arguing about their lovers when Branicki called Casanova a 'Venetian coward'. This, of course, could not be allowed to go unavenged so Casanova, having waited for 15 minutes, sword in hand, outside the theatre for Branicki to emerge, wrote a note challenging him to a duel. As there was a *starostia* (decree) in force banning duelling within four leagues of Warsaw, they agreed to travel out of the ban to fight.

Casanova gave a rambling account in his *Memoirs* of events leading up to the duel, of the duel itself and its aftermath. He was, at least by his own account, a model of unruffled calm before the duel. The two men had agreed to fight with pistols and then, in the event of both missing, with swords. Casanova was not entirely happy with this arrangement: he considered that 'a pistol duel is a barbarous affair'.

The Italian and the Pole travelled out of Warsaw together in Branicki's coach-and-six, accompanied by two aides-de-camp, two hussars and two grooms leading saddle horses. After half an hour they arrived at a suitable spot and, once the pistols had been loaded, prepared to face each other. Casanova takes up the story.

> I took the first pistol that came to my hand. Branicki took the other, and said that he would guarantee upon his honour that my weapon was a good one.
>
> 'I am going to try its goodness on your head,' I answered.
>
> He turned pale at this, threw his sword to one of his servants, and bared his throat, and I was obliged, to my sorrow, to follow his example, for my sword was the only weapon I had, with the exception of the pistol. I bared my chest also, and stepped back five or six paces, and he did the same.
>
> As soon as we had taken up our positions I took off my hat with my left hand, and begged him to fire first.
>
> Instead of doing so immediately he lost two or three seconds in sighting, aiming, and covering his head by raising the weapon before it. I was not in a position to let him kill me at his ease, so I suddenly aimed and fired on him just as he fired on me. That I did so is evident, as all the witnesses were unanimous in saying that they only heard one report. I felt I was wounded in my left hand, and so put it into my pocket, and I ran towards my enemy who had fallen. All of a sudden, as I knelt beside him, three bare swords were flourished over my head, and three noble assassins prepared to cut me down beside their master. Fortunately, Branicki had not lost consciousness or the power of speaking, and he cried out in a voice of thunder, –
>
> 'Scoundrels! have some respect for a man of honour.'
>
> This seemed to petrify them. I put my right hand under the pistoli's armpit, while the general helped him on the other side, and thus we took him to the inn, which happened to be near at hand.[64]

Casanova had been hit in the hand but Branicki, it turned out, had sustained a much more serious wound in the abdomen. Casanova's bullet had gone right through the Pole's guts, entering on his right and exiting on the left. It looked dangerous. However, Branicki remained magnanimous.

'You have killed me,' he said, 'so make haste away, as you are in danger of the gibbet. The duel was fought in the ban, and I am a high court officer, and a Knight of the White Eagle. So lose no time, and if you have not enough money take my purse.'[65]

For once, a duel had a happy ending. Casanova was pardoned by the King, despite having seriously wounded one of his favourites in a duel fought within the ban. Both men eventually recovered fully from their wounds. Casanova had had a lucky escape from Branicki, who was a crack shot. Casanova was told, after the duel, that

the only thing that saved your life was your threat to aim at Branicki's head. This frightened him, and to keep your ball from his head he stood in such an awkward position that he missed your vital parts. Otherwise he would undoubtedly have shot you through the heart, for he can split a bullet into two halves by firing against the blade of a knife.[66]

Chapter Eight

HONOUR EXPORTED: DUELLING IN
THE COLONIES

I N THE COURSE of their long colonial history the British exported
from these islands many institutions that have subsequently taken
root and flourished on distant shores. The common law, railways,
Anglicanism, cricket and, most important of all, the English language
have all survived the end of the colonial era and, to a greater or lesser
degree, continue to prosper to this day in many parts of the former
empire. The soldiers, administrators and merchants also took with
them the habit of fighting duels. Duelling flourished in the colonies
from the seventeenth until the mid-nineteenth centuries. Wherever
the Union Flag was planted, duels were fought: America, Canada, the
West Indies, Gibraltar, Malta, the Cape Colony and, above all, India.

In the so-called 'settler' colonies of North America, the custom survived the achievement of independence, acquiring a life of its own
under the republic. By contrast in India, the custom was confined to
the British ruling class, never catching on among the indigenous population. The custom also prospered in the colonies of other European
powers, notably France and, much later, Germany. This chapter looks
at duelling in the colonies from the seventeenth century until the
custom died out. In the British colonies duelling had, following the
lead from home, largely died out by the middle of the nineteenth
century. This was not necessarily the case in the colonies of countries

where duelling survived into the twentieth century. This chapter will cover duelling in the 13 American colonies only up to the moment of independence.

India

The Honourable East India Company was granted its Royal Charter on 31 December 1600. At first it was a trading company, a purely commercial venture; it was only later that the Company's responsibilities expanded into government and administration. The Company's first trading post – or 'factory', as they were known – was established at Surat, up the coast from modern Bombay. The first of the three great cities of British India, Madras, was founded in 1640. The second, Bombay, passed into British hands as part of Catherine of Braganza's dowry when she married Charles II in 1661. Seven years later the swampy, mosquito-infested archipelago that lies under the teeming, modern city was transferred to the East India Company. The last to be founded, Calcutta, in 1690, became in time, thanks to the wealth of Bengal, the capital of British India. By the end of the seventeenth century the British were well established on the peripheries of the subcontinent. The young men – for they were, at this time, mostly men – who made the hazardous voyage to India to seek their fortunes in the service of the East India Company took with them few enough habits from home. One that did survive the move eastwards was duelling; indeed, it seems that it positively flourished in Indian conditions as the following excerpt from the Consultation Book at Fort St George (Madras) shows.

> Monday 1st April, 1697. Mr Cheesely, having in a Punch house upon a quarrell of words drawn his sword (but were parted and put up without any mischief done) and being taxed therewith, he did both own & justify the drawing of the sword, and alleges that he had received provoking language which he thought himself obliged to resent.

For this display of aggression Cheesely was ordered to desist from wearing his sword and reminded that under local law anyone giving or receiving a challenge shall be fined. Such quotations from the

Consultation Book 'could easily be duplicated many times over.'[1] In Calcutta there are reports of duelling as early as the first years of the eighteenth century when a Mr Hedges, joint chairman of the Calcutta Council, was obliged to make the following entry in the council's minute book: 'Is either of the Chairmen obliged to answer the challenge of everybody that pretends to be affronted and challenges him to a fight?' Hedges entered this question into the minutes as a result of having been challenged by a Captain Smith, who took umbrage at the fact that the fort guns had not fired a salute upon his arrival in port.[2] Life in India was uncertain enough without the addition of this kind of hazard.

An article in a military magazine contained the following observation about the popularity of duelling among the English in India: 'The duello being pretty nearly as much a matter of recurrence to them, as a dish of curry at the mess table.'[3] The article in question was written in 1844, when duelling had all but died out in Britain. According to one historian of the Raj, 'duelling was common until about the time of Waterloo in India'.[4] Another historian, writing in the 1880s, was of the opinion that duelling was rife in the military in India in the 1840s and later; there was, he concluded, considerable peer pressure to 'play the duelling game'.[5] There were a number of reasons why duelling was so prevalent in India – although, as always, reliable statistics are hard to find – many of them common to the colonial, expatriate experience in other imperial outposts.

As elsewhere, the military in India was a bastion of duelling. In British India the distinction between the 'King's officers' and the 'Company's officers' was a cause of friction throughout the period. (It was only in 1858, after the Mutiny, that the East India Company's army was transferred to the British Crown.) Most glaringly, officers of the Company's army always ranked below officers of the King's army of the same grade. This inequality extended beyond mere questions of precedence of rank. A parliamentary inquiry into the affairs of the East India Company in the early 1830s heard that jealousy between Company officers and King's officers was commonplace. One witness put it down to the fact that officers in the King's army enjoyed better prospects in

…the means of obtaining rank through merit, favour and staff services. I think also that His Majesty's officers obtain rewards and honours which are sometimes bestowed on the Company's officers, but are not a necessary consequence of their relative claims.[6]

Little wonder, then, that the Company's officers perceived themselves to be second-class citizens.

While this distinction was an aggravating factor unique to India, most of the other military punctilios had successfully made the journey east. One such was the unspoken expectation, amounting almost to an absolute requirement, that officers would defend their honour on the duelling ground. In January 1791 Lieutenant-Colonel S.H. Showers faced a court martial at Calcutta, accused of conduct unbecoming the character of an officer and a gentleman. His accuser was a Lieutenant O'Halloran, who alleged that Showers was guilty of a 'deliberate infamy' in that he seduced the daughter of his most trusted friend before giving his consent to her marriage to O'Halloran. Showers hitherto had protested the 'highest esteem and regard' for O'Halloran. However, the nub of O'Halloran's complaint was that Showers had refused him satisfaction – that is, declined to fight a duel with him – for this betrayal of trust. Showers was found guilty by the court martial of the offence charged, a breach of the Articles of War. The court recommended that he be discharged from the service. In effect, Showers was cashiered for failing to fight a duel.[7]

William Douglas, author of *Duelling Days in the Army* cites another example of this attitude, which amounted to an official endorsement of military duelling, from as late as 1843. Ensign Frederick Dacre of the 1st Bombay European Regiment – so an East India Company officer – was brought before a court martial in Poona for failing to seek redress for having been repeatedly struck and assaulted in his quarters by Ensign Markham of the 78th Foot – a Queen's officer. Dacre was found guilty of conduct unbecoming an officer and suspended from the rank and pay of an ensign for six months. Like Showers, Dacre was punished for failing to challenge his assailant to a duel.[8]

One of the worst problems of service in India was isolation and the boredom that could so easily arise from it. Drinking and gambling were two diversions that helped to while away the days but they created their own problems. Except in the big cities, military (and civilian) life could be very circumscribed; in many upcountry cantonments there were only a few European officers, who lived cheek by jowl for months, even years, on end. One could ill afford to fall out with one's fellows. The price of doing so is illustrated by the sad tale of Captain Bull.

Captain Bull transferred from a cavalry regiment into the 34th Foot, which was at the time, 1828, posted at Vellore, an upcountry station in the Madras Presidency. Bull was engaged to an English girl who was soon to join him in India and was, therefore, trying to make economies. As the 34th's officers were most unfriendly towards him and lived extravagantly Bull withdrew from their mess. His brother officers decided to treat this as a collective insult so nine of them drew lots to determine which would challenge Bull to a duel. A Lieutenant Sandys drew the short straw and duly challenged Bull to a duel, who accepted but, as he had no injury to redress, resolved to fire into the air.

At the appointed time, Bull met Sandys and his second, Yeatman, to settle the affair. He was killed by Sandys's first shot. Sandys and Yeatman were taken to face trial in Madras, where, much to everyone's surprise, they were acquitted. No one was more taken aback than the judge, who, on hearing the verdict, exclaimed, 'Not guilty! A most merciful jury! Prisoners, had you been found guilty, you would never have seen the sun rise again.' The jury, which was composed of 'Madras shopkeepers', acquitted the defendants because, according to some, it feared the consequences to their trade of convicting two British officers. Not surprisingly, the case 'excited universal indignation throughout the whole Presidency'. In the end, however, justice was done as Sandys and Yeatman were found guilty by a court martial and cashiered.[9]

The problem was exacerbated by the fact that not only were individual European communities close-knit, even claustrophobic, but the whole European population in India was small. This meant that gossip travelled quickly. As Thomas Williamson, a writer on life in India explained in 1810, 'in India, where an individual is *cut* at one station, he will rarely experience common civility at any other; his character generally preceding him by many a day's journey!'[10] In such circumstances, it was even more important than it was at home that a gentleman should do everything in his power to ensure that his escutcheon remain untarnished. This, without doubt, encouraged men to fight duels to expunge slurs on their reputations.

Another factor common to duelling in Europe and in India was drink. The eighteenth and nineteenth centuries were, in Britain at least, a period when men routinely drank huge quantities. Those that went to India enthusiastically continued the custom, despite a climate that was less forgiving of heavy drinking than that of northern Europe. In the seventeenth century at the British factory at Surat the per capita ration was set at a quart of wine and half a pint of brandy a meal.[11] Another frequent cause of disputes, and one that often had to be settled at the point of a sword, was gambling. This was as true in India as in England. The sahibs were able in India to indulge their love of racing and betting; they also whiled away the long evenings playing cards.

Cherchez la femme has always been a phrase for those interested in duelling to keep in mind. It might be less important in India than elsewhere if only because, during the period (until about 1850), there were relatively few European women in India. From the end of the first quarter of the nineteenth century the numbers of European women coming to India did start gradually to increase; until then the long voyage around the Cape and the supposedly unhealthy climate did act as a deterrent. Women started coming to India in greater numbers after the opening of the Suez Canal in 1869 radically reduced the time it took to travel to India.

For all that, there were inevitably still duels fought that had their origins in disputes over women. Lawrence James quotes the example from 1836 of the young Irish wife of a 60-year-old cavalry major who had been seduced by a young officer in his regiment. When the major surprised the pair *in flagrante* he challenged his wife's lover to a duel. When they fought, the young officer, as the offending party, initially refused to return the major's fire but did return fire in the second exchange, killing the major. The death was officially attributed to cholera.[12]

This tale – and James quotes another instance when cholera was blamed for a duelling fatality – is evidence of how the authorities in British India turned a blind eye to duelling. Further proof of this is provided by Thomas Williamson's *The East India Vade-Mecum*, published in 1810. Williamson's book, which filled two volumes, running to more than 1,000 pages, provides a mass of information, and there is hardly an aspect of expatriate life in India he does not touch upon; yet it is striking that he says nothing at all about duelling. This was despite the fact that a young man in India, whether a civilian or a soldier, in the early years of the nineteenth century, would have been likely to come upon it. The clue to his silence lies in the dedication; this was a book for which Williamson wanted official endorsement, so it was better not to rock the boat by mentioning that duels were a common feature of life in India. It was something that the authorities preferred to have swept under the carpet.

There are many tales of duels from India. Perhaps the saddest (because it was such a waste) is the story of the duel in which Colonel Henry Hervey Aston, the commanding officer of the 12th Foot, was killed. He was, it must be said, an inveterate duellist, having fought at least three duels in England before he was posted to India, including one against the notorious 'Fighting' Fitzgerald. He fought Major Allen, also of the 12th Foot, at Arnee on 23 December 1798; Aston was hit in the abdomen and died a week later. The duel was the result of a complicated series of events, notable for the prickly pride displayed by the participants; only Aston behaved reasonably but only he was killed. Aston, who was a friend of the Prince of Wales, was buried with full military honours. One junior officer in the 12th remembered that 'His beautiful Arab charger was hung with crape [*sic*], and his boots pendent from the holsters.' The horse itself, he noticed, almost seemed to realise the loss of his master.[13]

By the late eighteenth century, 'political' duels in Britain were becoming more common and the habit migrated to India. In September 1784 George Macartney, Governor of Madras, fought a duel with Anthony Sadleir, another member of the Madras administration, in which he was wounded. Macartney's period in office in India resulted in a second duel, this time against General Sir James Stuart, although the meeting took place in Hyde Park. Stuart bore a grudge against Macartney for having dismissed him as commander-in-chief in India in favour of Sir John Burgoyne.

The most notorious duel fought in India, that between Philip Francis and Warren Hastings, was a 'political' duel *par excellence.* Hastings had taken office as Governor of Bengal in 1772, but, when the administration was restructured by Lord North's India Act of 1773, Hastings was promoted to Governor-General, to govern with the help of a council of four. Francis was one of the four original members of this council; from the start, in alliance with two other members of the council, Francis did everything he could to discredit Hastings and limit his freedom of action. Francis does not come across as a sympathetic character; one historian described him as 'a man rancorous and unforgiving, a wellspring of venom'.[14] These rivalries in the councils of the government resulted in prolonged periods of administrative paralysis. However, when the war against the Marathas of western India resumed at the beginning of 1780, it was evident that decisive leadership was needed; it was vital to resolve the impasse.

To this end a compromise was patched up between the two men, allowing Hastings the freedom to conduct the war. Francis agreed 'not to oppose any measures which the Governor-General shall recommend for the prosecution of the war'. However, it soon became evident that Francis had no intention of abiding by the terms of the compact. In the first six months of 1780 Francis opposed Hastings on several operational questions that were clearly covered by the agreement. Eventually, Hastings lost patience and, in early July, wrote an extremely hostile, provocative minute for the council's consideration, setting out his complaints about Francis's behaviour. Hastings considered that, by the terms of the agreement of February 1780, he had 'a right to his implicit acquiescence.'

> I do not trust to his [Francis's] promise of candour, convinced that he is
> incapable of it, and that his sole purpose and wish are to embarrass and

defeat every measure which I may undertake or which may tend to promote the public interest, if my credit is connected with them.[15]

This was fiery stuff but Hastings continued:

I judge of his public conduct by my experience of his private, which I have found to be void of truth and honour. This is a severe charge, but temperately and deliberately made ...[16]

When eventually this was delivered to Francis, he had no option but to challenge Hastings to a duel. Both men have left accounts of how they whiled away the hours before the fight (see Chapter 4); this is Hastings's description of the duel itself, fought early in the morning of 17 August 1780.

The next morning Colonel Pearse by appointment called on me, but before the time, at about a quarter after 4. I laid down again on the couch for half an hour. Then dressed and went with him in his carriage ... Arrived at Belvedere exactly at the time proposed – at 5.30, found Mr. F. and Colonel Watson walking in the road. Some time was consumed in looking for a private place. Our seconds proposed that we could stand at a measured distance which both (taking a recent example in England) fixed at 14 paces, and Colonel Watson paced and marked 7. I stood to the southward. There was (as I recollect) no wind. Our Seconds (Colonel W. I think) proposed that no advantage should be taken, but each choose his own time to fire – I should have said that Colonel Pearse loaded my pistols on the ground with two cartridges which he had prepared. I had resolved to defer my fire that I might not be embarrassed with his. He snapped, but the pistol missed fire. The Second put a fresh priming to it and chapped the flints. We returned to our stations. I still proposed to receive the first fire, but Mr. F. twice aiming and withdrawing his pistol, I judged that I might seriously take my aim at him. I did so and when I thought I had fixed the true direction I fired. His pistol went off at the same time, and so near the same instant that I am not certain which was first, but believe mine was first, and that his followed in the instant. He staggered immediately, his face expressed a sensation of being struck, and his limbs shortly but gradually went under him, and he fell saying, but not loudly, 'I am dead.' I ran to him, shocked I own at the information, and I can safely say without any immediate sensation of joy for my own success. The Seconds also ran to his assistance. I saw his coat pierced on the right side, and feared the ball had passed through him; but he sat up without much difficulty several times and once attempted with our help to stand, but his limbs failed him, and he sank to the ground.[17]

Francis made a sufficiently rapid recovery from his wound that he was able to return to Calcutta on 24 August and attend a council meeting on 11 September.

It is hard to avoid the conclusion that, with his stinging council minute, Hastings set out deliberately to provoke Francis to a duel. Given Hastings's language in the minute, it is hard to see how Francis could have remained in his position on the council had he not challenged Hastings. In the event, Hastings achieved his aim of ridding himself of Francis, who decided shortly after the duel to return home. When he left India on 3 December 1780, the boil of six years of festering resentment was lanced. However, not only was it a thoroughly disreputable use of the duelling code, it was an act of gross irresponsibility on Hastings's part to fight a duel while the government of which he was the head was at war.

The duel did not, however, result in any kind of reconciliation between the two men. Back in England, Francis was determined to take his revenge on his adversary. He became one of the moving spirits of Burke's campaign against Hastings and his administration in India, and one of the principal progenitors of the interminable impeachment proceedings brought against the former Governor-General.

Before we leave India we should look at a duel – if the fight in question can be dignified as a duel – that is as far from the scrupulous formality (ignoring for a moment its suspect motives) of the Hastings–Francis encounter as could be. There were elements to it that seem to exemplify the madness that the boredom, disease or drunkenness of Indian service could bring on. At Surat in the early hours of the morning of 12 November 1784 Captain Edward Nugent, of the 1st Battalion of Sepoys, forced his way into the bedroom of Lieutenant Stephen Dods. Nugent drew his sword and demanded a meeting. Dods, no doubt startled by this bizarre nocturnal intrusion, agreed but asked for time to settle his affairs. Dods also demanded that they fight with pistols, as he knew Nugent to be a much superior swordsman.

The duel was delayed by, first, the parties being arrested and, second, by Nugent's failure to equip himself with a second. Eventually, however, the two men did meet, in a garden. As they prepared to face each other, Dods told his second that he would not fire at Nugent, as they had been close friends; he would receive Nugent's fire without returning it.

> But previous to the word fire being given, Captain Nugent, in an unprecedented manner, twisted one end of his hankerchief round his right hand, and bringing the other end round his neck into his mouth, levelled his pistol over the other arm, and with his arm thus steadied, was taking deliberate aim at Mr Dods. This conduct obliged one of the seconds to interpose, and remind Captain Nugent that such a proceeding was so contrary to all rule and right, that it could not be permitted.

Despite 'such an unequivocal indication of Captain Nugent's unfair intentions', Dods did not change his mind about not returning his opponent's fire. When the order was finally given, Nugent fired at Dods but missed. Dods's pistol went off accidentally, luckily also missing its target. He told his second that the hair trigger was responsible for the accidental discharge of his pistol. However, his second refused to continue to act, as he was of the opinion that Dods had broken his word not to fire at Nugent, nor could he be persuaded by Dods's offer to allow Nugent a second shot at him. Once Dods's second had withdrawn, Nugent's second felt he could not act alone, so he too withdrew. This left Dods to suggest that they should arrange another meeting with different seconds. Nugent, realising that he had been thwarted, became very angry and an unseemly scuffle broke out.

> [Nugent] caught at the pistol which was in the hand of his own friend, and declared he would fire it at Mr. Dods, if he did not then stay, and give him satisfaction: but his friend observing, by the symptoms almost of madness which Captain Nugent was seized with, how unfit he was to be

trusted with a pistol, withheld it from him; and left. Nugent still struggling to get it from his friend, Mr. Dods seized on the pistol also, and by an effort of strength, forced it with his knee, below the level of his body, at which Captain Nugent was directing it, and in this state, Captain Nugent, in some period of the struggle having cocked the pistol, fired it, and the ball passed between the calf of Mr. Dods's leg and his thigh, grazing his cloaths.

The gun fired so close to Dods's leg left 'a mark of the powder on [his] breeches and stocking, as large in circumference as a common-sized tea-saucer'. Nor was this the end of the matter. Dods's observation that 'You act more like an assassin than a man of courage' 'excited in Captain Nugent such a degree of irritation, that he really foamed at the mouth'. Dods persisted in his offer to afford Nugent satisfaction but, as neither of the seconds would agree to remain, nothing came of it. Nor did Nugent arrange another meeting; perhaps once the red mist had receded, wiser counsels prevailed. In January 1785, Dods resigned his commission and left India.[18]

Social mores in India, as in many other colonies, were usually noticeably less advanced than those prevailing at home. By the 1840s in England duelling was considered *passé* in most circles, although it was not entirely moribund. It seems more than likely that, following the lead from home, duelling in India was in decline in mid-century. The shock of the Indian Mutiny in 1857 applied the *coup de grâce*.

The Cape Colony

Until the opening of the Suez Canal in 1869 the main route to India was via the Cape of Good Hope. By the early nineteenth century individuals or small groups could take the shorter route via the Mediterranean and the Red Sea, but this entailed disembarking and crossing the isthmus between the two. For the troopships the passage to India was always by way of the Cape. It was a long, tedious and sometimes perilous voyage during which passengers lived cheek by jowl in ships that seem to us now unimaginably small and cramped. After several weeks cooped up on board, arrival at the Cape was a blessed relief.

The Dutch were the first to colonise the Cape of Good Hope, but, as the British interest in India became ever greater, so the Cape took on a larger strategic significance. There was an abortive attempt by the British to capture the colony in 1781, but, once the Dutch had become enforced allies of the French in the 1790s, the importance of the Cape loomed large in the minds of the British planners. The government was warned by a naval officer that 'What was a feather in the hands of Holland will become a sword in the hands of France.'[19] With this in mind an expedition was dispatched in 1795 to capture the Cape, which, in September, it did. The colony was returned to Holland (and therefore, in practice, to France) under the terms of the Peace of Amiens in 1801 but was recaptured by the British in January 1806, this time for good.

To passengers bound for India, a stopover at Cape Town was a welcome opportunity to get ashore, to stretch the legs and to eat fresh food. Thomas Williamson enthused that the Cape offered the traveller:

> The liberty of taking exercise in a fine climate, abounding with the most delicious fruits, the choicest vegetables, and that kind of social intercourse, which, chasing away the recollection of former langour, gives energy to meet succeeding dulness [sic] and inactivity.

He did add one note of caution, warning that the 'Dutch are most offensively avaricious' and 'think of nothing but money-making.'[20] That apart, Cape Town made a very pleasant break in an otherwise tiresome journey.

There was one form of social intercourse for which the Cape became notorious, about which Williamson is silent: the duel. The longueurs of the voyage from England (or India, for that matter) provided ample opportunity for men to fall out and plenty more time for the quarrels to blow themselves out of all proportion. The landfall at Cape Town very often provided the first opportunity for the bickering parties to settle their differences.

The Annual Register of 1775 reported a duel between a Captain David Roach and a Captain Ferguson, both officers in the service of the East India Company. During the course of the long voyage to the

Cape the two had had a number of arguments and, a day or two after their arrival, they fought with swords. Ferguson was killed. Roach was taken back to London and tried for Ferguson's murder. At his trial he ran the defence that, as he had already been tried for and acquitted of the same offence, albeit under Dutch law, in the Cape, he could not be retried in London. In the event, it was of no consequence, as the jury acquitted him anyway.[21]

In 1802 the *Annual Register* reported another fatal duel at Cape Town, the result, it said, of a quarrel that started on board the *Hindoostan*, the ship in which both men were sailing. In this instance, Lieutenant Rae of the Royal Marines killed Mr Bremen, who was a member of the *Hindoostan*'s company.

From Cape Town comes an account of a novel way of escaping liability for a duel. Captain Hussey was killed in a duel on Table Mountain by Lieutenant Osbourne, both officers in the same regiment, the 38th Foot. Hussey having died instantly, the 'seconds then placed him erect against a tree, and dropping an anonymous note in one of the officer's rooms, the body was found as described.'[22]

The reports of duels at Cape Town seem to agree that they were, almost universally, the result of quarrels at sea. The most spectacular example of seaborne animosities erupting into armed combat on the dry land of the Cape occurred in 1827. Two civilians, a J. Williams, a barrister, and a J. Noble booked themselves a passage to Hobart, Tasmania, via the Cape, on the *Harvey*. Also on the *Harvey* was a detachment of the 55th Foot, commanded by Captain Elrington, which included three subalterns, Lieutenants Wilson, Bonnis and Peck. The *Harvey* sailed from Plymouth but before she had left the Channel the two civilians had fallen out with the subalterns; Williams, it seems, had made some derogatory remarks about the military. These animosities festered during the long voyage and, by the time the ship reached Cape Town, the two camps were irreconcilable. One report of the saga explained that 'It appears they had some dispute during the passage, which was increased to the most deadly hatred by the intermeddling of some of the passengers.'[23]

Upon arrival in Cape Town, Williams was challenged, in succession, by Bonnis, Wilson and Peck. The barrister, with admirable *sang-froid*, promised them all that 'he would not fail to accept their invitations in due order, if he had life enough left in him to do so'. He duly fought all three subalterns in turn, 'wounding one, very nearly quieting the second, and not returning the fire of the third'. Wilson and Bonnis did not, however, consider their honour satisfied by these encounters so challenged Noble as well, despite a warning from Williams that 'Mr Noble was a man not very likely to make child's play of such matters'.

Wilson was the first to take the field against Noble, who had done everything in his power to avoid a new round of duels. They exchanged shots, after which Wilson, having sustained a slight wound, declared himself satisfied. Now it was Bonnis's turn, but he was not so lucky. Noble's first shot hit him in the temple, killing him instantly. Williams and Noble stood trial but were both acquitted for lack of evidence.[24]

The Mediterranean: Gibraltar and Malta

Gibraltar and Malta, islands of great strategic importance in the Mediterranean, both came to Britain as the spoils of war. Gibraltar was captured for Britain from the Spanish by Admiral Rooke in 1704 and was confirmed as a British possession by the Treaty of Utrecht in 1713. The Rock withstood three sieges in the eighteenth century, proof, if proof were needed, of the strategic importance of its position. Spain maintains her vexatious claim to Gibraltar to this day, despite the fact that the population has shown itself, whenever asked, to be resolutely against severing its ties with Britain. Malta was likewise captured in war, in her case from the French in 1800, after a two-year siege.

Malta had been ruled by the Knights of St John until they were dispossessed by Napoleon in 1798. While the Knights ruled, Malta was one of the few places in the world where duelling was legal, albeit closely controlled. As the Knights of St John traced their origins directly to the age of chivalry, this was perhaps more than a colourful anachronism. One author, writing in 1773, opined that to abolish duelling in Malta would be inconsistent with the 'wild and romantic principles of chivalry' on which the place was founded. Duelling was, at this time, reportedly still a relatively common occurrence. The same author counted about 20 white crosses in the streets of Valetta, each one commemorating the death of a knight in a duel.[25]

Gibraltar, as a British naval and military base, had its fair share of duels. A British officer was killed in a duel during the siege of the Rock in 1727. In April 1819 there was a spate of duels, perhaps as many as three in a single day, between British officers of the 64th Foot serving in the garrison and American officers of the US naval vessel *Erie*. The origins of the dispute lay in the supposed mistreatment of an American merchant captain, Taylor, by the members of the garrison. He was arrested and refused bail; he was denied a pen and paper and when he protested at his detention he was ignored. When eventually he was released he tried to challenge Captain Johnson, of the 64th Foot, to a duel but Johnson declined to accept, as he did not consider Taylor to be worthy of fighting. Taylor then left the island but a few days later an American naval squadron sailed into port. The squadron's officers had heard of Taylor's treatment at the hands of the British and were anxious to salvage American pride. They drew lots to decide who would challenge Johnson; a Mr Bourne was chosen and duly exchanged shots with Johnson. Bourne was slightly wounded.

However, that was not the end of the matter, as the officers of the garrison managed to offend the Americans to such an extent that further duels became inevitable. One can only suppose that the ill feeling between the two navies was a hangover from the war of 1812. The British further enraged the Americans by again refusing to face them in a duel, thereby implying that they were not gentlemen. This reduced the Americans to accusing the entire 64th Foot of cowardice, at which point Captain Frith stepped up to defend the honour of the regiment. In the subsequent duel with Mr Montgomery, the surgeon of the *Erie*, Frith was hit in the hip. The authorities then stepped in to calm this outbreak of duelling frenzy. The Governor of Gibraltar ordered that no officer should leave the precincts of the Fort; while, for his part, Captain Ballard of the *Erie* issued orders confining his officers to the ship. Despite these precautions, Captain Johnson and Mr Stockton of the *Erie* managed to exchange shots before being arrested. Soon afterwards, the *Erie* left Gibraltar bound for Algeciras.[26]

A nineteenth-century American historian of duelling, Lorenzo Sabine, asserts that this spate of duels in Gibraltar was not an isolated episode. According to him, duels between British and American naval officers serving on the Mediterranean station were commonplace at this time. Indeed, Sabine states that US naval vessels were banned from Gibraltar in 1819 because of the incidence of duels between the two services.[27]

North America

Just as the Europeans who established trading posts and garrisons in India and the Far East during the seventeenth century took the habit of duelling with them, so too did those who travelled west across the Atlantic. The Pilgrim Fathers sailed from England in 1620, hoping to join the English colony of Virginia (founded 1607), but, landing further to the north, founded a new colony, Massachusetts. They were fleeing from religious intolerance in England, in search of a land where they could establish their own Puritan community.

Evidently, however, earthly corruption quickly insinuated itself into the new God-fearing colony, for the first recorded duel on American soil was fought at Plymouth, Massachusetts, in June 1621, less than a year after the Pilgrim Fathers had set foot in the New World. Beyond the fact that the combatants were two Edwards, Doty and Leicester, nothing is known about the duel. Although duelling made a rapid appearance in the new colony, it was not until 1719 that a law was enacted against duelling in Massachusetts.[28]

The colony was also home to the first recorded fatal duel in America. On 3 July 1728 Benjamin Woodbridge and Henry Phillips fought a duel to settle a dispute that had arisen over a game of cards at the Royal Exchange tavern. The duel took place on the common in Boston; they fought with swords and Woodbridge was killed.[29]

Duels were not confined to New England; indeed, by the nineteenth century the South was widely considered to be the home of American duelling. Georgia was the southernmost of the 13 colonies that rebelled against the British and it was here that some of the South's most energetic and deadliest duellists were to be found. This formidable reputation was established in the eighteenth century. Duelling was brought to Georgia by the first settlers; one of the first recorded duels was fought in 1740 between Ensign Tolson and a military surgeon, one Eyles. In the same year Peter Grant, a citizen and freeholder of the town of Savannah, was killed in a duel by Mr Shanton, an army cadet. Grant thereby became the first of a long list of men of Savannah to be killed in duels.

By the time of the War of Independence, duelling was well established in Georgia. In 1777 General Lachlan McIntosh was challenged to a duel by a local nabob, Button Gwinnett. McIntosh had the command of three battalions of infantry and some dragoons, which Gwinnett, who had been elected commander-in-chief of Georgia, coveted. His frustrated military ambitions embittered relations between the two men and, when McIntosh denounced Gwinnett in public as a scoundrel, a duel became inevitable. They faced each other with pistols at the murderously short distance of four paces; both men were hit in the thigh, McIntosh survived but Gwinnett did not.[30] They would, perhaps, have been better served concentrating their energies on fighting the British. Gwinnett County in Georgia is named after him.[31]

Another enthusiastic Georgian duellist of the period was James Jackson, the so-called 'Chief of the Savannah Duellists'. He settled in Georgia in 1772, aged 15, and fought against the British, rising by 1780 to the rank of major. In March 1780 Jackson killed George Wells, the Lieutenant-Governor of Georgia, in a duel. He fought another duel against a wealthy Savannah lawyer, Thomas Gibbons. He has also left an account of a fracas in 1796 with a political opponent, Robert Watkins, which illustrates how near to the surface violence was in late eighteenth-century Georgia. For all the public pretensions of constitution and the rule of law, it remained a rough and ready society. It serves too to illustrate the dividing line between a duel and a murderous assault. The attack took place as Jackson was leaving the state capitol in Louisville.

I rose and my blood rose with me – I made at him [Watkins] & was told he had pistols. This made me recollect one I had carried, apprehensive of an attack from John Greene who I had been under the necessity of telling was a damned lyar a night or two before, & I immediately exclaimed, 'Tis well, we are on a footing. Clear the way.'

It was proposed by Fournoy, one of his partisans, for us to fight in the morning – I replied that I never fought a base assassin but on the spot. I met him & ordered him to take his ground.

I should have killed him, for I fired as soon as we were open to each other, but my hand was knocked up by one of the party, & as soon as I fired he ran at me with a bayonet at the end of his pistol. We closed and twice I threw him.

I soon found that I was his Master as to strength & was beating him handsomely, when a scoundrel by the name of Wood turned Watkins on me and the Assassin strove to gouge me. Driven to necessity I was compelled to put one of his fingers in my mouth which made him relinquish his attempt after skinning my eye.

He then sprung another bayonet, for the first one was either taken from him or returned to him, & he had a pair on purpose, & stabbed at me repeatedly. I was all the time unarmed. He stabbed me in the left breast which fortunately entered my collar bone and ran me through my shirt and grazed my ribs a second time – a half inch lower in the breast the Doctors pronounced, would have finished my business.[32]

Since Jackson rose to become Governor of Georgia and a member of the US Senate, a reputation as a hard fighter at this time was evidently no bar to political advancement.

Nor was duelling during the War of Independence restricted to the colonists: as might be expected, the British continued to fight duels among themselves even as their colonies slipped from their grasp. Two English officers, Captain Pennington of the Coldstream Guards and Captain Tollemache, fought a duel in New York, probably in 1777. The quarrel arose, with splendid refinement, from a sonnet that Pennington had written which Tollemache considered cast aspersions upon the wit of his wife. The duel began with the two men each firing a brace of pistols but failing to score a hit, whereupon they drew their swords. It was, clearly, a savage fight: Tollemache was killed, run through the heart; Pennington was wounded seven times.[33] At the top of the chain of command, the French general the marquis de Lafayette, who was fighting on the American side, challenged the Earl of Carlisle, the British Commissioner, to a duel.

The Earl of Carlisle was the head of the British Peace Commission, charged with negotiating terms with the American rebels. In August 1778 Carlisle issued a manifesto inviting Congress to consider the proffered terms. In this document the Commissioners said that France 'has ever shown itself an enemy to all civil and religious liberty'. They added that 'the designs of France, the ungenerous motives of her policy, and the degree of faith due to her professions, will become too obvious to need any further illustration'.

Lafayette, as the senior French officer serving with the Americans, wrote to Carlisle as head of the Commission, demanding an apology for the calumny or satisfaction. Carlisle replied, loftily refusing to offer an apology or fight a duel. He refused the challenge on the grounds that, one, he was answerable solely to king and country and, two, that it was a public, not a private, matter.[34] Lafayette's challenge to Carlisle has resonances of the ancient custom of champions, whereby the fate of two opposing armies hung on the outcome of a trial between two individuals. This was, or could have been, the legend of David and Goliath re-enacted in the wilderness of the New World.

Further north, in what is now Canada, the French were the first European colonial power. The Breton sailor Jacques Cartier penetrated up the St Lawrence River as far as modern Montreal on his voyage in 1534–5, thereby staking France's claim to a vast area of northern America. Gradually, civilisation followed in the footsteps of the fur trappers and the traders; Quebec was founded in 1608 and Montreal in 1642. The colonists of New France were, like their British counterparts to the south and their compatriots at home, enthusiastic duellists.

The first reference to duelling in New France dates from 1646; it concerns a confrontation between two men at Quebec. The first recorded fatal duel in the colony occurred in April 1669 at Trois Rivières when François Blanche killed Daniel Lemaire. Blanche was hanged in July and his property donated to the Quebec hospital. In the 1670s Montreal acquired an unsavoury reputation as 'a brawling, unruly place, quite out of character with the religious ideals of its founders'. Until the mid-1680s, duelling in the colony had been an infrequent occurrence. However, with the expansion of the population and an increase in the numbers of troops stationed in the colony, to counter the Indian menace and in expectation of war with the English to the south, duels became more common. There were at least four in the colony between 1687 and 1691. It is interesting to note that drink is frequently reported as a contributory factor in many colonial duels. Enforcement of the laws against duelling was patchy too, just as it was in Europe.[35] The New World had already acquired some decidedly Old World habits.

It was against this background of a gradually rising tide of violence that the authorities in New France were forced into action. In February 1691 two well-considered army officers, Guillaume de Lorimier and Pierre Payan de Noyan, fought a duel in Quebec in which both were wounded, de Lorimier seriously. Immediately after the trial of the two officers, the Sovereign Council ordered that Louis XIV's *Édits des Duels* of 1679 be published in all the towns of the colony. For a while the edict succeeded in restraining duellists from taking up their swords but the calm was shattered by an ugly incident in Quebec in 1698, and by the early years of the eighteenth century duels were once more regular events.[36]

French rule along the St Lawrence came to an end in 1759 when the British, commanded by the daring General Wolfe, took Quebec and claimed the colony for their own. In due course this vast area, extending from the mouth of the St Lawrence to the Great Lakes, was divided into Upper and Lower Canada. More immediately, however, the British conquest of Canada had two important consequences for duellists in the colony. The first was that the pistol replaced the sword as the customary weapon for settling disputes. This development mirrored, as we will see, changes that were taking place in Europe, where, particularly in England, the pistol duel was becoming the norm. There are those who have maintained that the fact that the English adopted the pistol duel while the French continued to settle their disputes with swords betrays a deep-seated difference between the two nations. What is certainly true is that it required a good deal less skill to use a pistol competently than it did to fence properly. As a result, the advent of the pistol broadened the appeal of duelling by making it easier to take part.

The other change that came about as a result of the British conquest of Canada was legal; with British administration came the common law. One historian of duelling in Canada claims that although there was little difference, so far as duelling was concerned, between the British and French law, 'enforcement differed markedly'. The French government before 1759 took a much stiffer line with duellists than did the British after they took control. It has to be said that he does not adduce much in the way of evidence for this proposition.[37]

What is indisputably true is that Canada was, and remained after the British conquest, a rough and ready society with more than a whiff of the frontier about it. Benjamin Roberts, who was a subordinate of Sir William Johnson, the head of the British Indian Department, had constant contact with the ruffians who drifted round the frontier. Roberts wrote to Johnson telling him of one unpleasant episode at Montreal in 1769, when he was accosted by a man called Rogers in the street demanding that he fight a duel there and then. Roberts, seeing that Rogers had a pair of pistols hidden under his coat, insisted on his right to choose the weapons and nominate a meeting place. They agreed upon a time and a place to meet but, when Roberts arrived at the duelling ground, there was no sign of his opponent. Having told Roberts 'he'd blow my brains out & and not give me any fair chance for my life', once there was an even chance between the two, he avoided the meeting. Roberts, fearing assassination, thereafter always carried pistols.[38]

*　*　*

It is a central contention of this book that duelling differed little from the sixteenth to the twentieth centuries. There were, of course, from time to time, local variations in procedure and etiquette, as there were in the weapons used: pistols, revolvers, smallswords, foils, sabres and more eccentric arms were all pressed into service at one time or another. But the basic formula remained constant. This was as true for colonial duelling as it was for the metropolitan version. Whether the duellists fought by the Hoogly River, in a coconut grove in the West Indies, in the shadow of the Table Mountain or in the desolate forests of North America, they were all following the same, universal code.

The only aspect that did differ was longevity. In this respect, as in many others, colonies took the lead from the mother country. Hence, duelling in the British Empire had largely died out by the second half of the nineteenth century, whereas elsewhere, in the colonies of more belligerent countries, duels continued into the twentieth century. As late as 1884, for example, two French Marine lieutenants fought a duel at Saigon. Armed with revolvers, loaded with three rounds each, they both missed with their first shots. At the second exchange of fire, one of the two was shot and later died.[39]

Chapter Nine

HIGH NOON: DUELLING IN GEORGIAN AND EARLY VICTORIAN ENGLAND, 1760–1860

THE LONG REIGN OF George III (1760–1820) is often considered the high-water mark of duelling in the British Isles. During the period duelling attained new heights of popularity and acceptability. Army officers, naval officers, aristocrats, swells, young bloods, old stagers, even clergymen – they all took to the duelling ground to restore their good name. In particular it was the era of the political duel: prime ministers, members of the Cabinet and myriad MPs fought duels. It was as if duelling had become a parliamentary custom, a rite of passage in a political career.

Contrastingly, it was also a period of ever-increasing opposition to the practice from pulpit and pen. Well-intentioned laymen formed earnest societies to campaign for duelling's abolition; modernisers and reformers ridiculed this 'Gothic barbarism'. Poets and dramatists weighed in to the debate, too; duelling transferred well onto the stage but could easily be sent up at the same time. The prologue of the comedy *The Duellist*, which opened in London in November 1773, was unequivocal:

Deaf to the Bar, the Pulpit, and the Throne,
And aw'd, if aw'd, by Ridicule alone,
The daring Duellist, in captious Pride,

Hath long his Friend, his King, his God defied.
Thrice happy we, if Laughter from the Stage
Should cure this frantic Folly in the Age.[1]

In the end, of course, the opposition achieved its goal: duelling in Britain died out. What is remarkable is the speed with which the custom disappeared from the scene. In 1829 no less a figure than the Prime Minister, the Duke of Wellington, felt obliged to fight a duel. In 1840 the bullying Earl of Cardigan fought one of the most notorious of all duels, yet by 1850 the custom had virtually died out. The last officially recorded fatal duel in England was fought in 1852 near Windsor between two French *émigrés*, M. Barthelemy and M. Cournet; Courbet was killed. In Scotland, the last fatal duel was fought a generation earlier, in 1826. The speed with which duelling was eradicated from English society is as much a part of the story as its furious, bloody heyday.

During this period duelling in Britain underwent a fundamental change. In the early eighteenth century the majority of duels had been fought with swords; by 1800, sword duels in England were a rarity. Most men fought with pistols. The principal reason for this is that it ceased to be fashionable for men to wear swords with everyday dress. Opinion is divided as to when this change came about; some writers suggest that it did not happen until the 1790s, others prefer to say that it began to gather momentum in the 1750s. It is safe to say that it was a change that occurred gradually over a long period. In the 1740s the sword was still a powerful symbol. Henry Digby Beste, priest, traveller and author, recalled, in 1829, an engraving owned by his father of five 'dandies' from the end of George II's reign. It depicted

> light rapier swords too; some of them pendent in splendid uselessness from the sides of the wearers, and others, innocently laid on distant chairs. The sword, though in these times not a belligerent, was a great political engine; it inspired respect; it distinguished the gentleman; it raised its wearer from the pedestal to the capital of the social order.[2]

The young James Boswell was certain enough in 1764 that a sword was still an important accessory for a fashionable young buck to spend five guineas buying one from the King's sword cutler, Mr Jeffery of the Strand. Equally, two years later the following letter, signed only 'Derrick, jun.', was published in the *Public Advertiser*.

> At the Rooms in Bath, and all other Places of public Resort, Gentlemen lay aside their Swords, why should not the same Regulation take place at Ranelagh; where numerous Inconveniences to the Fair Part of the Company arising from Sword-Hilts, viz. torn Aprons, etc., etc., seem to make it absolutely necessary? ... Perhaps you will cry that out that a Sword is a necessary Appendage to a Gentleman; but consider how it is prostituted; Taylors, Hair-Dressers, and Lawyers Clerks, promiscuously assume it.[3]

By the end of the Napoleonic wars it was becoming increasingly acceptable for men to wear trousers rather than breeches and stockings for everyday dress.

This sartorial shift did, over time, affect the way in which duels were fought. The change in fashion was a gradual process; so too was the change in duelling custom. Pistol duels took place before 1750 but sword duels were rare by the nineteenth century. As early as 1711 Sir Cholemy Dering, MP for Kent, was killed in a pistol duel by Mr Thornhill. In 1749 two Royal Navy captains fought a notorious duel in Hyde Park with pistols: Captain Clark killed Captain Innes with a single shot at six paces. In 1772 Richard Brinsley Sheridan fought Mr Matthews with swords on the downs above Bath.

The decline in the fashion for men to wear swords resulted not only in the virtual demise of the sword duel but, more positively, in greater degree of restraint among would-be duellists. With weapons no longer immediately to hand, duels became, if not less rashly impetuous, at least more trammelled by etiquette. It was not possible, for civilians at least, to fight then and there. Once men no longer wore swords with everyday dress, the type of incident described by Horace Walpole in 1743 became a thing of the past. Walpole's uncle, another Horace and a Member of Parliament, had 'high words' one day with William Chetwynd, a fellow Member, behind the Speaker's Chair in the House of Commons. Chetwynd took Walpole by the arm and led him out into the lobby to settle their differences. Walpole, alarmed at the prospect of fighting a duel in so public a place, said, 'We shall be observed, we had better put it off till tomorrow.' 'No, no, now! now!' insisted Chetwynd. When they reached the bottom of the stairs, Walpole said, 'I am out of breath, let us draw here.' Drawing their swords they began to fight. After a couple of passes Walpole had driven Chetwynd against a post and might have run him through had not a clerk arrived to beat down their swords. Chetwynd, slightly wounded, went off to find a surgeon, while Walpole, apparently wholly unruffled, returned to the Chamber to speak in a debate. Horace the nephew was thrilled at 'this new acquisition of glory to my family'.

> 'Don't you delight in this duel?' Walpole asked. 'I expect to see it daubed up by some circuit painter on the ceiling of the salon at Woolterton.'[4]

Once swords were no longer part of everyday dress, duels could not be fought, like Walpole's, on the spot. They had to be arranged. This in turn gave rise to a greater willingness to conform to the etiquette of duelling, to appoint seconds – who should attempt to reconcile the parties – and to fight once hot heads had cooled somewhat. Lord Byron's celebrated duel with William Chaworth in January 1765 is another example of what could happen on the spur of the moment when men were as a matter of course carrying swords. It is worth remembering that Byron (the poet's uncle) and Chaworth were attending an informal dining club of fellow landowners from Nottinghamshire in the Star and Garter Inn in Pall Mall, it was a run-of-the-mill evening yet they had swords to hand, with fatal consequences. The two men had had an inconsequential argument about game birds but tempers seemed to have cooled by the time Chaworth got up to leave. Byron followed about 10 minutes later, only to run into Chaworth on the stairs. Chaworth, who was clearly intent on fighting Byron there and then, asked a waiter to show them into an empty room and put a candle on the table. 'I imagine', he said, 'this room is as fit a place as any other to decide the affair in.' Byron, in his evidence at his trial, gave the following account of the duel.

> Then turning round, [Chaworth] said, he would bolt the door to prevent any interruption, or any body interfering, or words to that effect.

Accordingly, he went to the door and fastened it. In the mean time, his intention being but too manifest, … I went round on the further side of the table, towards the most open part of the room, which … is about sixteen feet square, and the furniture did not leave a vacant space of more than twelve feet in length, and as I believe, five feet in breadth, where it was my unhappy lot to be obliged to engage.

Mr Chaworth was now turned round from bolting the door, and as I could not any longer continue in doubt of his intention, it was impossible for me in such a situation to avoid putting my hand to my sword, and I believe I might at the same time bid him draw ….

Mr Chaworth immediately drew his sword, and made a thrust at me, which I parried; he made a second, which also missed …: and then finding myself with my back against the table, with great disadvantage of the light, I endeavoured to shift a little more to the right hand, which unavoidably brought us nearer to each other, and gave me an opportunity to perceive that [Chaworth] was making a third pass at me. We both thrust at the same time, when I found Mr Chaworth's sword against my ribs, having cut my waistcoat and shirt for upwards of eight inches; and I suppose it was then, that he received the unlucky wound …'[5]

Chaworth died the following day.

Side by side with the decline in the carrying of swords as part of everyday dress came the development of duelling pistols. Whether gunsmiths started making these specialist weapons as a result of the growing popularity of duelling with pistols or whether their increasing technical sophistication encouraged men to use them to settle their affairs of honour is open to question. What we do know is that specially made duelling pistols began to appear in London in about 1770.[6]

The early flintlock duelling pistols were more accurate than their ordinary service or general-purpose cousins. This was due to three factors. They were better balanced in the hand and greater care was taken to ensure that the bore was even and highly polished. Care was also taken to ensure better loading; in particular this meant ensuring that duellists used better-made ammunition. 'Windage', that is the minuscule gap between ball and barrel (necessary in a muzzle-loading firearm), was the cause of much of the notorious inaccuracy of smooth-bore weapons. By doing as much as possible to eliminate windage, gunsmiths hoped to improve the accuracy of their weapons. Some duellists took to casting their own ammunition so as to be sure of its size and quality. On the duelling ground this could make the difference between life and death.

Among the prominent early London gunsmiths were Griffin and Tow of Bond Street and John Twigg. Twigg is credited with the introduction, before 1775, of the octagonal barrel, which became a distinctive characteristic of the duelling pistol. Henry Nock and Durs Egg, who set up independently of each other (although they later amalgamated their businesses) as gunsmiths in 1772, were responsible for the introduction of the gold-lined priming pan and touchhole. This innovation was directed at reducing the incidence of 'flashing in the pan', that is, where the flint sparked the gunpowder in the priming pan but failed to ignite the charge in the barrel, resulting in a misfire. Nock and Egg were also responsible for the introduction of hair triggers in duelling pistols.

Around the year 1780 John Manton, H.W. Mortimer and Robert Wogden all started in business as gunsmiths in London; all three became famous for the aesthetic as well as the functional quality of their duelling pistols. By the latter years of the eighteenth century, duelling pistols had become, as well as instruments of lethal efficiency, objects of great beauty. The octagonal barrels were often burnished with a characteristic steely blue and the silver or gunmetal mountings on the body and stock of the gun frequently chased with intricate patterns. Duelling pistols usually – for obvious reasons – came in pairs, and usually in cases. The cases, often fashioned from mahogany, have an appeal all of their own, equipped as they were with powder horns, miniature ramrods for loading, and even the wherewithal for casting bullets.

Wogden is credited with having developed a technique for improving the accuracy of his pistols at the commonly used duelling distance of 12 yards. It involved a correction to the alignment of the barrels to compensate for the inaccuracy inherent in the separation of eyeline and barrel. By 1800 heavier pistols were becoming more fashionable, epitomised by the guns made by Joe Manton, younger brother of the Dover Street gunsmith John.

By the turn of the nineteenth century, the flintlock duelling pistol had reached an advanced state; it was, within the limitations imposed by the flintlock mechanism itself, as reliable as it was possible to make it. It was much more accurate than had been the case three decades earlier and, at the same time, had developed into an object of great beauty. But, for all the advances, even the most expensive guns still suffered from unreliability. This potentially lethal shortcoming was due to the fact that a spark still had to pass from the priming pan through the touchhole to the charge in the barrel. The touchhole could easily – it was a tiny aperture – become blocked, clogged with damp or burnt powder; this would prevent the spark from the flint firing the gun.

However, a solution to this problem arrived in 1805 in the unlikely form of the Revd. Alexander Ferguson, a Scottish cleric. A keen fowler, Ferguson invented the percussion cap as a way of preventing damp from affecting the firing mechanism of his guns. A percussion cap was a method of firing a gun without having to rely on powder in the priming pan. Ferguson patented his new invention in 1807 and the following year set up in business in London making percussion weapons.

In due course, the copper percussion cap was developed; by 1820 it had been incorporated into duelling pistols. It was a much more reliable firing mechanism and, eventually, completely superseded the flintlock. Definitive proof of the superiority of the percussion cap to the flintlock was provided by a firing test conducted at the Woolwich Arsenal in 1834. One platoon of soldiers fired 6,000 rounds from flintlock muskets, while another fired the same number of rounds from percussion muskets. It was found that the flintlocks misfired, on average, twice in 13 rounds, whereas the percussion muskets misfired only once in every 166 rounds. Moreover, the percussion weapons were more accurate, could be reloaded and fired more quickly and achieved greater penetration on targets of green elm.

Duelling pistols were valuable, prized possessions, lovingly tended and passed down through families. In *Vanity Fair* Rawdon Crawley

drew up his will the night before joining his regiment for the Waterloo campaign. Included in the inventory of his possessions are 'my
duelling pistols in rosewood case (the same [sic] I shot Captain
Marker), £20'.[7] A few months later, after Waterloo, Rawdon was
delighted to discover that his wife's domestic economy was such that
they could survive the winter in Paris without pawning his precious
pistols.[8] Two Irishmen fought a duel in the late eighteenth century, at
least in part over the ownership of a fine pair of pistols. William Pitt,
having exchanged shots with George Tierney in May 1798, gave his
second, Dudley Ryder, the pistols; they are still in the possession of
Ryder's descendants.[9]

Some pairs of pistols, perhaps not surprisingly, were used several
times over. The pistol with which Aaron Burr killed Alexander Hamilton on the banks of the Hudson River in 1804 was part of a pair that
had already been used at least twice in earnest. They belonged to
Hamilton's brother-in-law, John Church, who had used them in a
duel with Burr himself in 1799. They had also been used in the duel in
which Hamilton lost his eldest son Philip in 1801.[10] In England a single
pair of pistols saw service in two political duels within four months of
each other. Colonel Fullarton used his own pair of duelling pistols in
his duel with the Earl of Shelburne in March 1780, in which the latter
was wounded. In November the previous year William Adam MP had
borrowed the colonel's pistols for his duel with Charles James Fox.
Fox was slightly wounded. As Horace Walpole reflected, 'It was odd
that the same pistols gave both wounds.'[11]

The chosen method of fighting duels in England may have
changed between 1750 and 1800, but the principal reasons for its doing
so did not. Men fought to clear their reputations. The need to do so
often arose from having, as the phrase went, 'been given the lie', that
is, accused of dishonesty. This was the case throughout the history of
duelling, from sixteenth-century France to twentieth-century
Hungary. One could, of course, be given the lie in any number of ways
but in late eighteenth- and early nineteenth-century England the
gentry's propensity for heavy drinking and reckless gambling was a
fertile breeding ground for disputes. It was also the age of the political duel.

Gambling was, perhaps, the vice of the age. Many of the luminaries of the period were addicted and profligate gamblers, whether at cards or on the horses. The Prince of Wales and Charles James Fox were merely the tip of the iceberg; both routinely won and lost large sums in a night's play, accumulating huge debts. Fox is supposed to have lost £140,000 (possibly £10 million nowadays) at cards in three years. In the febrile political atmosphere of the time, this addiction to high play was widely regarded as a distinguishing characteristic of the Whigs, although, of course, it was by no means confined to that clique. Georgiana, Duchess of Devonshire (a leading light of the Whigs), one of the most notorious gamblers of the age, was dogged by debts built up at the tables. In 1776, when she was only 19, she had amassed gambling debts of at least £3,000 (perhaps £200,000 in today's money), a sum that represented three-quarters of her annual income.[12] Sometimes, then as now, an addiction to gambling turned to tragedy. Sixty years later Berkeley Craven committed suicide 'after losing more than he could pay' gambling on the horses. A contemporary commented that 'It is the first instance of a man of rank and station in society making such an exit.'[13]

There were many duels caused by gambling, arising often from accusations of cheating, which were, of course, with such large sums at stake, always likely to cause tempers to flare. However, one will have to stand for them all: the encounter in the spring of 1836 between Lord George Bentinck and 'Squire' Osbaldeston.[14] It is a racy tale of sporting skulduggery, which gives us taste of the shenanigans that were an accepted part of racing in the early nineteenth century. Lord George Bentinck was a younger son of the 4th Duke of Portland, a man who was, by all accounts, arrogant, sensitive to criticism and lacking humour. After an early stint in a cavalry regiment – during which he came within a whisker of fighting a duel with a brother officer – he devoted his life to racing as an owner, administrator, gambler and member of the Jockey Club. George Osbaldeston, nicknamed 'the Squire', was the finest sportsman of his day, a magnificent shot, an all-conquering cricketer, a fearless huntsman and a shrewd horseman.

The dispute between the two men arose from a controversial race at the Heaton Park meeting of September 1835. Heaton Park was the

Lancashire estate of the Earl of Wilton; every September, in the week following the St Leger Meeting at Doncaster, a race meeting was held there. The meeting was, even by the standards of the time, a byword for sharp practice. The earl was a keen racing man and did all he could to ensure that his runners enjoyed every advantage. The handicapper, as a guest of the earl for the week, was expected to allot favourable weights to his Lordship's runners. John Scott, the earl's trainer, was allowed the use of the gallops at Heaton Park, while other trainers were forced to use inferior facilities elsewhere. While some owners debated boycotting the meeting, Osbaldeston hatched a plan to teach the earl a lesson. He bought a Irish colt called Rush and brought him over to England in time for the St Leger meeting of 1835, where he was able to give the horse a trial against decent opposition.

Now certain that in Rush he had a useful horse, Osbaldeston went to Heaton Park races full of hope. Rush was entered in a race on the first day of the meeting; Lord Wilton had a runner in the same race, a filly called Lady de Gros. Osbaldeston, riding his own horse, succeeded in muddying the waters by finishing last. He had deliberately, but undetectably, stopped his mount. Lady de Gros, conceding a stone to Rush, finished second, well beaten. The two horses were due to meet again the following day in the big race of the meeting, the Gold Cup. This time de Gros, on account of the previous day's result, was two stone higher in the handicap than Rush.

Supporters of Rush were confident of victory and his odds had, by the start of the race, tumbled from 10–1 to 2–1. Bentinck, a guest of Wilton's, had decided, equally confidently, that Rush was no good and busied himself taking bets against the horse. One of the last bets he took was from Osbaldeston himself, from the saddle as the horse was cantering to the start. The Squire had £100 on his horse at Lord George's 2–1. Needless to say, Rush won easily, Lady de Gros finishing second. Bentinck, never a good loser, was furious but the bet stood.

There, however, the matter rested until the following spring. As the bet had still not been settled, the Squire approached Lord George in the betting ring at Newmarket and asked for his money. Bentinck, evidently still rankled by the Heaton Park affair, replied, 'I wonder you have the impudence and assurance to ask me for that money.' He accused Osbaldeston of deceiving the public but was nevertheless obliged to pay up. Osbaldeston, for his part, having been insulted in public, was determined to clear his name. Despite frantic efforts to reconcile the parties by those who feared for Lord George's life in a duel with one of the best shots in the land, a meeting was arranged.

The two men met at Wormwood Scrubs at six o'clock on an April morning. Osbaldeston had had difficulty in finding someone who was prepared to act as his second, eventually persuading a Mr Humphreys to accompany him. Lord George's second was Colonel Anson. What exactly happened that morning is shrouded in mystery but it seems likely that the seconds, in their anxiety to ensure that Lord George survived unscathed, deliberately failed to load the pistols with ball. As a result they discharged noisily but harmlessly. The Squire was always convinced – and he was a very experienced shot – that his pistol had never been properly loaded.

The importance of drink in the history of duelling has already been noted; nevertheless, it is true to say that it had a special significance in late eighteenth- and early nineteenth-century English society. This was the age of the 'three-bottle man', an era in which gentlemen routinely drank vast quantities of alcohol. William Hogarth's *A Modern Midnight Conversation* was painted in the early 1730s (it was subsequently, and very successfully, sold as a print) but would have been equally apposite had it appeared half a century later. It depicts a gentlemen's drinking bout in full swing. It is after midnight; under a side table is a pile of empty bottles; on the table are more bottles and a large bowl of punch. The revellers are in varying states of disarray: one has just fallen over, smashing the bottle he had in his hand; another is staggering uncertainly around the room; two others appear to have fallen asleep.

One of the reasons why men drank so much so often was that they had the chance to do so. Dinner was taken early, leaving plenty of time afterwards for tippling. This had been the custom in the 1780s in the better households in England, as a French visitor confirmed. Dinner began – he was staying with the Duke of Grafton at Euston – at four in the afternoon. It was, he discovered 'one of the most wearisome of English experiences, lasting as it does, for four or five hours'. Once the food had been eaten the table was cleared, wine produced, and, after a while, the ladies retired.

> It is then that the real enjoyment begins – there is not an Englishman who is not supremely happy at this particular moment. One proceeds to drink – sometimes in an alarming measure.

The French visitor then noted the effects that this prolonged drinking had on the conversation.

> Conversation is as free as it can be, everyone expresses his political opinions with as much frankness as he would employ upon personal subjects. Sometimes conversation becomes extremely free upon highly indecent topics – complete licence is allowed ... [15]

It is not difficult to see how such prolonged drinking bouts might all too easily have ended in high words, quarrels and, perhaps, challenges.

The duel between Major Campbell and Captain Boyd in June 1807 was one of the very few of the period that resulted in the death sentence being carried out. At dinner after a regimental inspection the two officers began to argue about a reproof the inspecting general had delivered to Campbell earlier in the day. As the officers became increasingly drunk the dispute heated up, resulting, eventually, in a duel. They fought then and there, in a room in the mess; Boyd was killed. Campbell owed his conviction and subsequent execution to the dubious circumstances in which the duel was fought. There is no doubt that drink played a large, if not vital, part in the story. It was all too common a tale at the time. A nineteenth-century historian commenting on this duel, wrote, 'It was in the hard-drinking days ... when no officer was supposed to be fit to command a company that was not able to consume three bottles of port or more during dinner.' [16]

Frequent heavy drinking was a feature of both military and civilian life in this period. Politicians on both sides of the political divide were notoriously bibulous. The Whigs boasted Fox and Sheridan, legendary topers both, while for the Tories the Prime Minister, William Pitt, and his Scottish drinking crony, Dundas, would no doubt have been able to match the opposition glass for glass. The eighteenth-century gentleman drank port and, it would seem, drank it to get drunk. According to Andrew Barr, the port that was consumed in the late eighteenth and early nineteenth centuries was not the sweet drink that it is today. Generally, it was drunk throughout the meal. Its popularity lay not in its sweetness but in its strength. 'It satisfied,' Barr writes,

> the demands both of drinkers who wanted a wine for drinking after meals that would make them drunk, and of diners who called for a strong dry wine to wash down the vast quantities of meat that they consumed.[17]

French table wines, from Bordeaux, Burgundy and the Rhone, were, according to Barr, virtually unknown in England during the period, even among the wealthier classes. The popularity of port was, in part, due to its strength and taste but was also a consequence of the long periods of war with France. During time of war, French wines were not only difficult to obtain but were, no doubt, considered unpatriotic; Portugal, with whom England had long-standing treaty and trading arrangements, was an altogether sounder source of supply.

To the modern eye, the eighteenth-century concept of the 'three-bottle man' is a great mystery. How did they manage it? Anyone frequently drinking three bottles of port a day nowadays would spend his life in the grip, alternately, of a drunken stupor and a miasmic hangover. Yet many of these men had successful careers as soldiers, politicians and so on. Did our forefathers simply have a much greater capacity to hold their drink? Perhaps the capacity of modern man to drink on a titanic scale has declined. Or, perhaps, the answer lies elsewhere.

William Hague, in his recent biography of Pitt the Younger, looked into this question and concluded that the epithet 'three-bottle man' misleads the modern reader. The standard size of bottle used in the eighteenth century was smaller, holding little more than half the volume of liquid of a modern 75cl wine bottle. Moreover, the port itself was not as alcoholic as it now is. It was fortified with brandy – a process that stopped the fermentation, increased the strength of the wine and helped it survive the long journey from Portugal – but not to the extent that it is nowadays. So the port that Sheridan, Fox, Pitt and their contemporaries drank in such quantities was weaker than the modern version and they were drinking it from significantly smaller bottles. On this basis Hague concludes that the 'three-bottle man' of the late eighteenth century was consuming the modern equivalent of one and two-thirds of a bottle of strong table wine.[18] This would be enough wine to make for a convivial evening, certainly, but not so much as to be stupefying even when consumed regularly. Nowadays, however, it would no doubt be considered excessive for any politician let alone the leader of a political party.

We have seen that, in eighteenth- and nineteenth-century English society, gambling and drinking were tolerated, indeed encouraged, to a degree that would be unacceptable in the more straitlaced age in which we now live. However, while drunken arguments, accusations of card-sharping or dishonourable treatment of women could all too easily provoke a duel, they alone were not a sufficient trigger. There had to be a pre-existing willingness among men to fight or, at the very least, an acceptance that, in certain circumstances, it was the only honourable course to take. 'Our ancestors were men of their hands who regarded a duel as the natural issue of a quarrel,' wrote the historian G.O. Trevelyan.[19] The notion of the duel was deeply embedded in the psyche of the upper-class man of the eighteenth century; it was the drunken insult, the gambling debt or the seduction of a daughter that brought it to the surface.

Central to an understanding of the English duellist of this era is the concept of 'bottom'. The historian T.H. White explained it thus:

> In the eighteenth century, but particularly under the Regency, a gentleman was expected to have 'bottom'. It was a word of composite meaning, which implied stability, but also what the twentieth century calls 'guts'. It meant being able to keep one's head in emergencies, and, in a financial sense, that one was backed by capital, instead of being an adventurer. Bottom, in fact, was synonymous with courage, coolness and solidity. The metaphor was derived from ships.[20]

'Bottom' was an admirable quality, one, incidentally, that was still valued in certain circles of the Conservative Party as recently as the 1990s. According to White, for the eighteenth-century gentleman, 'The duel was the final test of Bottom.' 'Bottom' was the courage to risk one's life in the first place for a question of honour; it was the *sang-froid* to receive one's opponent's shot without flinching; it was the magnanimity to say, when one's life was ebbing away, that one's adversary had behaved well, that he was not to blame. It was 'bottom' that Horace Walpole was commenting on when he wrote that William Chaworth, having received a wound 'fourteen inches deep' in his body during his duel with Byron, 'was carried to his house in Berkeley street, – made his will with the greatest composure, and dictated a paper, which they say, allows it was a fair duel, and died at nine this morning.'[21]

Five years later Walpole returned once more to the subject of duelling, this time to the meeting between Lord George Sackville and Colonel Johnstone. Lord George had become notorious as 'The Coward of Minden' as a result of his alleged failure to obey orders during that battle and eventually Johnstone succeeded in provoking Sackville into challenging him to a duel. Walpole described the affair in a letter to a friend.

> Lord George behaved with the utmost coolness and intrepidity. Each fired two pistols, and Lord George's first was shattered in his hand by Johnstone's fire, but neither was hurt. However, whatever Lord George Sackville was [he had changed his name], Lord George Germaine is a hero.[22]

For all Lord George's supposed failings during the Battle of Minden, his duel with Johnstone demonstrated incontrovertibly that he possessed 'bottom'.

Duelling had always exercised a special fascination over the military mind and the period between the accession of George III and 1850 was no exception. Indeed, duelling continued to flourish in the military to such an extent that the army (and to a lesser extent the navy) came to be seen as a bastion of the practice. The custom persisted in the armed forces after it had started to lose its kudos among the civilians but, once it was effectively outlawed in the army in 1844, it very quickly faded from the scene altogether.

The attitude of the army to duelling during this period is important because, as a result of prolonged wars – for more than half of

George III's long reign Britain was at war – the military came to occupy a more prominent position in society that had perhaps previously been the case. More men than ever before were exposed, especially during the Revolutionary and Napoleonic wars, to the military way of life. The raising of local or national defence forces, yeomanries, militias or fencibles brought the army to the shires. As the number of part-time officers grew, so did the number of men who considered themselves entitled to defend their honour on the duelling ground.

The army continued to display an ambivalent attitude to duelling. It remained an offence against military discipline to fight a duel; indeed, it was expressly forbidden to challenge a more senior officer. Officers were cashiered by courts martial for fighting a duel or even for behaviour that was likely to provoke one. In July 1813 Ensign T.R. Delannoy, of the Royal Perthshire Militia, was tried by a court martial for 'disgraceful conduct, unbecoming the character of an officer' for calling Captain Macduff of the same regiment 'a coward'. It is interesting to note that the officers who figured in this case were both officers in a local militia. Similarly, Lieutenant Dominic French of the 82nd Foot was tried in 1811 for 'unofficerlike and ungentlemanly conduct in using abusive and provoking language to Assistant-Surgeon Scott, tending to incite him to fight a duel'. French had given Scott the lie. He was found guilty and cashiered.[23]

Yet, at the time, the army disciplined officers who failed to uphold the honour and reputation of their rank or regiment. We have already noted instances of officers who faced a court martial on these grounds. In 1809 Captain Griffin of the 14th Foot was brought to a court martial charged with 'scandalous and infamous behaviour, unbecoming the character of an officer'. Although he was acquitted the significance of the tale lies in the fact that he was tried at all.[24] This ambivalence in the army to duelling extended right to the top. The Duke of Wellington himself, field marshal and national hero, was a strict disciplinarian yet not only fought a duel himself (albeit in a private capacity) but appeared to condone the practice.

In 1824 Lord Londonderry fought a duel against Mr Battier, who was a junior officer in the 10th Hussars, of which regiment Londonderry was colonel. Battier considered that he had been insulted by

Londonderry at a mess dinner and, after an acrimonious correspondence in which Battier accused his colonel of lying, he transferred out of the regiment. He then promptly challenged Londonderry to a duel. They duly exchanged shots but neither man was wounded. The interest of the encounter lies in a phrase contained in a letter that Wellington wrote to Londonderry after the duel. Having delivered the mildest of reproofs, the Duke considered the future of Londonderry's regiment: 'I think it is not impossible that they [the 10th Hussars] may have to fight a duel or two. *But that I consider of no consequence*'[25] (my italics). If that was the attitude of Britain's most revered soldier to duelling, it can hardly be a surprise that it flourished so vigorously in the army.

Duelling was at least tolerated in armies because it was recognised that its detrimental effect on discipline was, potentially, offset by its usefulness in fostering the fighting spirit among officers. However, particularly in time of war, duels between officers on the same side could have a deleterious effect on the proper conduct of operations. The long-running saga during and after the Peninsular War between General Donkin and Admiral Hallowell quoted earlier is a good example. More serious, potentially, was the dispute between Admiral Lord St Vincent and Vice-Admiral Orde. The two men, both very senior and experienced officers, had agreed to fight a duel on 7 October 1799.

The duel had arisen from Lord St Vincent's decision as commander-in-chief of the Mediterranean Fleet to appoint Nelson to command the squadron sent to attack Napoleon in Egypt in 1798. We know now, with the advantages of hindsight, that it was the correct decision: Nelson located the French in Aboukir Bay and, in an action as brilliant as it was daring, completely destroyed the enemy fleet. From Orde's point of view, however, it was the wrong decision: Orde was serving in the Mediterranean Fleet at the time, was senior in rank to Nelson and should, according to service custom, have been given command of the squadron, rather than Nelson. On hearing of Nelson's appointment, Orde wrote querulously to the First Lord of the Admiralty 'Sir Horatio Nelson, a junior officer, and just arrived from England, is detached from the Fleet in which we serve ... I cannot conceal from your Lordship how much I feel hurt.' As a result of St Vincent's perverse preference for Nelson, he, Orde, had missed the opportunity to cover himself with glory. Nor did Orde bother to conceal his feelings from St Vincent, who, after a stormy interview, ordered him home.[26] Whether, had he been given the command, Orde would have executed his orders as brilliantly as Nelson did, we shall, of course, never know.

The disgruntled Orde, sent home in disgrace, nurtured his grievance against Lord St Vincent. He complained to the Admiralty and attempts were made, unsuccessfully, to mollify him. Having failed to obtain redress through official channels Orde decided to take matters into his own hands. Accordingly, when St Vincent arrived home from foreign waters Orde sent him a challenge. St Vincent accepted and a rendezvous was agreed for 7 October.

However, word of the admirals' intention had been passed, by whom it is not recorded, to Mr Justice Ford, who promptly issued a warrant for their arrest. Orde was arrested at Durant's Hotel in Jermyn Street and bound over by Ford to keep the peace in the sum of £2,000. He was also ordered to provide two further sureties for his good behaviour of £1,000 each. Mr Justice Ford then set off to Lord St Vincent's country seat at Brentwood, where, on arrival, he found the admiral preparing to set out for his rendezvous with Orde. The judge, arriving in the nick of time, bound St Vincent over to keep the peace in identical terms. So, by acting promptly, the authorities had averted a duel with potentially disastrous consequences in time of war. Lord St Vincent was one of the most important men in the navy; it is no exaggeration to say that he was a vital figure at a crucial time in the defence of the realm against the French. To have lost him in a duel with a fellow officer would have been most unfortunate.[27]

The Admiralty may have had a secret hand in averting the duel between two of its most senior serving officers but, when it came to dealing with more junior officers, it had no qualms about openly flexing its muscles. Captain Thomas Fremantle had served in 1801 and 1802 as captain of HMS *Ganges*, in which a certain Harry Rice had served as a lieutenant. Rice harboured a grudge against Fremantle for having recommended to the Admiralty his removal from the *Ganges*, considering his action to have been motivated by personal animosity and malice. On 16 July 1802, he wrote to Fremantle challenging him to a duel on the grounds 'that your conduct to me, when First Lieutenant of H.M.S. *Ganges* was unlike a gentleman, unmanly, Base and dishonourable'. Fremantle, on receiving this letter, informed the Lords of the Admiralty of the challenge, and they immediately commenced criminal proceedings against Rice.[28]

The armed services may have been a bastion of duelling in this period but it was the politicians whose duels caught the public eye. Members of Parliament were, as a group, the most enthusiastic of duellists. Although it is likely that we have received an exaggerated impression of their propensity to fight duels, their duels being reported when others' were not, the fact remains that parliamentary proceedings were a fertile breeding ground for disputes. Parliamentary privilege, which was then in its infancy, protected members from the laws of defamation but did not afford any protection from the outraged sensibilities of fellow members. MPs were free to call their political opponents to account on the duelling ground for utterances made in the Chamber and frequently did so. Political duels were not of course confined to the late Georgian period: we have seen a number of such encounters from earlier periods, for example the fight between Walpole and Chetwynd in 1743. But it did produce a vintage crop.

John Wilkes was a controversial figure, an outspoken libertine, who delighted in insulting political opponents. He used his magazine, the *North Briton*, to attack his enemies and it, in turn, got him into trouble. He attacked Samuel Martin, who was MP for Camelford and secretary to the Treasury, in the most forthright terms in an edition of the *North Briton*, accusing him of corruption. Wilkes renewed (although the articles were anonymous) his attack in a later edition (No. 40), in which he described Martin as 'the most treacherous, base, selfish, mean, abject, low-lived and dirty fellow that ever wriggled himself into a secretaryship'.

This sort of insult could clearly not be allowed to pass unchallenged, so, having extracted from Wilkes an admission – which he was only too glad to give – that he was the author of the offending passages, Martin challenged Wilkes to a duel. In the letter challenging Wilkes to answer for his words Martin wrote, 'I must take the liberty to repeat that you are a malignant & infamous scoundrel, & that I desire to give you an opportunity of shewing me whether the epithet of cowardly was rightly applied or not.'[29]

They agreed to meet in Hyde Park at one o'clock in the afternoon of 16 November 1763. Martin left a account of the duel, written (curiously, in the third person) shortly after the event.

> Mr. W[ilkes] then stepped forward (I think he ran) several paces. Mr. M[artin] retreated a pace or two facing Mr. W. & with his remaining pistol pointed at Mr. W. and when he saw that Mr. W. presented his second pistol, Mr. M. fired; Mr. W. snapping ye pistol in his hand in ye same moment at Mr. M. Mr. W. threw this pistol immediately upon the ground and said he was wounded: and unbuttoning his Surtout, Frock & waistcoat shewed Mr. M. a large patch of blood upon his shirt about the middle of his belly. Mr. M. said upon seeing it, I have killed you, I am afraid. Mr. W. Buttoning up his clothes walked to the rail before mentioned, & stooping under it, went on with a hasty pace to the upper ground of Hyde Park, making ye best of his way towards Grosvenor Square Gate. Mr. M. gathered up the four pistols into two long pockets in the lining of his frock & followed him.[30]

Not surprisingly, this duel excited a great deal of comment. Horace Walpole, who was an amused yet detached observer of many of the political duels of this era, had this, cattily, to say about Wilkes's injury:

> Don't be frightened, the wound was not mortal – at least it was not yesterday. Being corporally delirious today, as he has been mentally some time, I cannot tell what to say to it. However, the breed will not be lost, if he should die. You still have countrymen enough left; we need not despair of amusement.[31]

Such was Wilkes's notoriety that rumours started to circulate after the duel that Martin had been put up by the government to challenge Wilkes. The government could thereby rid itself of a tenacious and tiresome critic. Wilkes later discovered that £40,000 had been paid to Martin from government funds for 'secret and special service' in the

12 months before their duel. This proved, at least to Wilkes's satisfaction, that Martin was a tool of the government.[32]

In 1779 Charles James Fox, then the young firebrand of the Whigs, fought a duel with a Scottish member about a remark that Fox had made during a debate. Adam demanded that Fox publish an explanation, absolving Adam from the speech's criticisms. This Fox refused to do so Adam called him out. They met in Hyde Park on 29 November; Adam slightly wounded Fox, who, having no quarrel with his opponent, fired into the air. Walpole described it to a friend.

> Of all the duels, on true or false record, this was the most perfect! So much temper, sense, propriety, easy good humour, and natural good nature, on a base of firmness and spirit, never were assembled. For Mr. Adam, I cannot describe him, as I never extracted malevolence out of the fogs of the Highlands.[33]

Fox displayed 'bottom', whereas Adam, it seems, did not.

Four months later, in March 1780, two more politicians were squaring up to each other in Hyde Park: this time it was Colonel Fullarton and the Earl of Shelburne. Shelburne, who was briefly Prime Minister three years later, had offended Fullarton, the MP for Plympton, by daring to question 'with all the aristocratic insolence' that made Shelburne so unpopular the patriotic loyalties of Fullarton and the regiment he commanded. This was a red rag to a bull for a serving army officer. Shelburne was challenged and the two met early in the morning of 22 March. Both men – they were 12 paces apart – missed with their first shot; Shelburne, having first refused to shoot, fired only once Fullarton had fired at him. The colonel then fired a second shot, which hit Shelburne in 'the right groin'. Shelburne then discharged his second shot into the air.[34]

Horace Walpole, as always, had the best tale to tell of the affair. In recounting the story of the duel to a friend Walpole wrote, of Shelburne's wound, that 'he was so cool, that having asked how he did, he looked at the place, and said "Why, I don't think Lady Shelburne will be the worse for it." '[35]

There was, however, a serious side to all this knightly parliamentary posturing. On the very afternoon that Shelburne and Colonel

Fullarton had faced each other in the grey dawn of Hyde Park, Sir James Lowther rose to speak in the House of Commons. He observed that the fighting of duels arising from parliamentary business 'seemed to be growing into such a custom' that the House ought to take action against it. It was, he said, important that the House intervene to prevent duels becoming a habit, as this would gravely threaten the freedom of speech. The *Annual Register*'s report of Lowther's speech continues:

> If free debate was to be interpreted into personal attack, and questions of a public nature, which come before either house, were to be decided by the sword, the British parliament would be at once reduced to the condition of a Polish diet. In such circumstances, he thought it would be better for the members totally to give up all ideas of parliamentary discussion, to abandon the senate and resort at once to the field; where, without further trouble, they might have recourse to arms, as the sole arbiter of political difference of opinion.[36]

This was, of course, an important point but not one that appeared to cut much ice with MPs, who continued regularly to call one another out. In 1794 Edward Bouverie MP was killed in a duel by Lord Tankerville.

Political duels continued well into the nineteenth century. As late as 1835 Mr Roebuck MP fought a duel over a newspaper article and four years later the Marquis of Londonderry (the man who fought Mr Battier in 1824) exchanged shots with Henry Grattan's son as a result of a political slur. The political upheaval surrounding the passage of the Great Reform Act of 1832 did, as expected, give rise to a spate of duels between Whigs and Tories. One of the first of the so-called 'Reform' duels was fought on 18 June 1831 between Charles Tennyson d'Eyncourt and Lord Thomas Cecil. D'Eyncourt, the Whig member for Stamford, had taken umbrage at some remarks made by Cecil in a speech at a public meeting in the town. D'Eyncourt asked Cecil for an explanation, which was refused, so he called him out. The two men met at Wormwood Scrubs, where each fired a single shot. Neither was injured. D'Eyncourt wrote the following day to his father, admitting, 'It is a silly way of settling a dispute – but under all circumstances it was the only mode of terminating this.'[37] Two days later d'Eyncourt told his father what the Westminster wags were saying about his duel: 'It is said that this only No.1 of a series of Reform Duels, & it is thought a very proper thing that The Clerk of the Ordnance [Cecil] should commence the Shooting Season.'[38]

Before we leave the subject of British political duels we must at least glance at the three most celebrated examples of the genre: the duels involving William Pitt, George Canning and the Duke of Wellington. They are a class apart in that Pitt and Wellington were Prime Minister when they went out; Canning was a Cabinet minister – and much later became Prime Minister in his turn – when he fought another member of the Cabinet, Viscount Castlereagh. The details of all three duels are so well known that I do not propose to recount every detail of each dispute or give a blow-by-blow account of each duel. The interest in these three famous duels lies in the reactions, public and private, that they provoked. They speak volumes about contemporary attitudes to duelling. Of particular interest is the fact that, as the high standing of the participants provoked a reaction in each case from the King, these duels give us a glimpse of the royal view on duelling.

The first of the three to take the field was William Pitt. In May 1798 Pitt had asked the House to vote through some amendments to the rules governing naval recruitment and, in the subsequent debate, George Tierney, the *de facto* leader of the Whig opposition, questioned the way in which Pitt had brought the measure before the House. Pitt, in turn, cast aspersions on Tierney's motives in opposing the Bill, in effect accusing him of a lack of patriotism in time of war. This, of course, was more than any eighteenth-century politician could be expected to tolerate, and the following day Pitt received a challenge. The two men met near the gibbet on Putney Heath on 27 May; both missed with their first shot, Pitt firing his second into the air. They then returned to London. The affair, not surprisingly, caused a sensation.

The newspapers were quick to express their disapproval of the duel; no one involved escaped the torrent of righteous indignation. Tierney was censured for issuing a challenge that could hardly be refused, Speaker Addington for failing to keep the debate under control. William Wilberforce, the reformer, was 'more shocked than almost ever' and gave notice of his intention to propose a Commons motion 'Against the Principle of Duels'.[39] But to most critics, the most reprehensible aspect of the affair was the fact that the Prime Minister had risked his life at a time of national crisis.[40] Many regarded it as an act of gross irresponsibility. The King agreed, as the brief letter he wrote to Pitt on hearing news of the duel shows.

> 30 May 1798.
>
> I trust what has happened will never be repeated. Perhaps it could not have been avoided, but it is a sufficient reason to prevent its ever being again necessary. Public characters have no right to weigh alone what they owe to themselves; they must consider also what is due to their country.
>
> G.R.[41]

This terse rebuke left no doubt about the King's view of the duel.

Eleven years later Pitt was dead but Britain was still at war with France; Trafalgar had finished the war at sea but in Spain and Portugal the two countries were evenly matched. The year 1809 was notable for three duels between prominent members of society. In February the 9th Viscount Falkland was killed by Mr Powell following a trivial, drunken dispute. In May all of London was agog with excitement when Lord Paget fought a duel with Colonel Cadogan. It arose from Paget's scandalous affair with Cadogan's sister, Lady Charlotte Wellesley, the wife of one of the Duke of Wellington's brothers. And then, as if that were not enough, in September there was further excitement when a long-running Cabinet row exploded very publicly in a duel between Canning and Castlereagh.

When Lord Portland formed a government after the collapse of the Ministry of All the Talents in 1807, Canning become Foreign Secretary and Castlereagh Minister of War. By 1809 Canning was disillusioned with the government's conduct of the war, and with his colleagues' shortcomings as ministers. At the same time the government was shaken by the 'Duke and the Darling' scandal, involving allegations of the sale of commissions by the commander-in-chief's mistress. From the early summer Canning began to agitate for Castlereagh's removal from the War Office. Portland was reluctant to lose Castlereagh's support, so various compromises were mooted, none of them effective. In July the British expedition to attack Walcheren, an island off Holland, sailed. It was soon evident, however, that it was a disaster, another nail in Castlereagh's coffin so far as Canning was concerned. All the while, however, Castlereagh had been kept in the dark. The failure to inform Castlereagh of the manoeuvring against him can be blamed on Portland and the Lord President, Camden. On 7 September Camden told Castlereagh of the plot against him. On 19 September, having brooded on the news for nearly a fortnight, he challenged Canning to a duel in terms that could be not be refused. Canning accepted the challenge 'cheerfully', despite the fact that many, including Canning himself, considered that it was either Portland or Camden who should be facing Castlereagh.

Both men resigned from the government in order to fight the duel; Canning did not return to office for seven years. They met on Putney Heath at six o'clock in the morning of 21 September. Twelve paces was agreed as the minimum acceptable distance; pistols were the weapons. Charles Ellis, Canning's second, confessed Canning's inexperience to his opposite number, Lord Yarmouth: 'I must cock it for him for I cannot trust him to do it himself. He has never fired a pistol in his life.'[42] Both men missed at the first exchange; at the second Canning missed again but Castlereagh's shot hit home in the 'fleshy part of the thigh'.

Over a period of about a fortnight the details of the Cabinet intrigues that lay behind the duel filtered out into the public domain. *The Times*, which supported Canning in his efforts to improve the efficiency of the ministry, was unable to defend the machinations that caused the duel.[43] The *Annual Register*, in its review of the affair, came close to accusing Canning of duplicity in his scheming against Castlereagh. Wilberforce, who had been so horrified at Pitt's duel, was predictably scandalised by this new outbreak of political violence. He described Castlereagh's challenge as a 'cold-blooded measure of deliberate revenge'. The Duke of Portland, whose government had been rent apart by this duel, dutifully informed the King of events. George III replied loftily, the Duke must be sensible that as it is his M[ajest]y's duty not to countenance in any manner such transactions, it must be equally his wish to abstain ... from any comment except an expression of the sincere concern with which he must ever view this event.[44]

Neither of the combatants comes out of the affair with much credit, but there remains a question mark over Castlereagh's motives for fighting the duel. The day after the duel he wrote to his brother saying that he considered his reputation was buried 'in the ruins of Intrigue, Shabbiness and Incapacity'.[45] It is strange that Castlereagh should still think this after the duel, the purpose of which, after all, was to clear his reputation of the aspersions made against it. It leaves open, therefore, the possibility that Castlereagh fought the duel not to clear his name but to take his revenge on Canning. This was not at all an honourable motive for fighting a duel.

The third of these famous political duels was fought nearly 20 years later. It pitted the Duke of Wellington, the victor of Waterloo, national hero and now Prime Minister, against the Earl of Winchelsea, an eccentric peer of extreme Protestant sympathies. The duel was fought against the background of the debate on Catholic Emancipation. The dispute between the two peers blew up over the foundation of King's College, London, of which the Duke was a leading promoter. Winchelsea cancelled his subscription and wrote a highly charged letter to a newspaper alleging that Wellington was intending to use the foundation of the college as an instrument for 'the introduction of Popery into every department of the State'.[46]

Winchelsea's inflammatory letter had appeared on 16 March, following which the Duke twice wrote to him requesting a public apology. Winchelsea refused to apologise unless Wellington stated publicly that he had not contemplated Catholic Emancipation when he founded King's. This, of course, was unacceptable and, on 20 March, the Duke sent Winchelsea a challenge. Seconds were appointed, Sir Henry Hardinge for Wellington and Lord Falmouth for Winchelsea. They agreed that the parties would meet, with Mr Hume, a surgeon, in attendance, in Battersea Fields the following morning. Once the parties had arrived, the seconds paced out the ground.

Hardinge, who had lost his left hand at Waterloo, delegated the important task of loading the Duke's pistols to Hume. Falmouth, shakily, loaded Winchelsea's pistols.

With the two parties now ready to exchange shots, Hardinge berated Winchelsea and Falmouth for allowing matters to reach such a pitch. He then gave the order to fire. Wellington, seeing Winchelsea's pistol arm firmly down by his side, fired deliberately wide; Winchelsea then fired into the air. Winchelsea had been in a quandary before the duel. He had refused to back down, thus blowing the affair up into a matter of honour and precipitating a duel, yet the prospect of wounding or, worse, killing the Duke was too dreadful to contemplate. We now know that he had decided before the duel not to fire at Wellington. But he went through with the duel rather than apologise for the letter, which he admitted he was wrong in publishing, because not to duel would expose him 'to imputations which would have made life to me utterly worthless', that is, cowardice.[47] This was the dilemma that faced many a duellist.

Honour satisfied, Winchelsea was now able to apologise, whereupon Falmouth produced a draft 'expression of regret', which, initially, Wellington was unwilling to accept: he wanted to see the word 'apology'. Hume, the surgeon, rectified the situation by adding 'apology' to the text in pencil. Wellington then bowed to Winchelsea and his second, touched his hat and, bidding the company 'Good morning, my Lords', rode back to London and the business of government.

One of the first to hear the news was the Duke's mistress, Mrs Arbuthnot. Interrupting her during breakfast, he asked, 'Well, what do you think of a gentleman who has been fighting a duel?'[48] The reaction, public and private, was incredulous. The diarist Charles Greville recorded that 'Nothing could equal the astonishment caused by the event.'[49] Greville was not sure that the Duke was right to challenge Lord Winchelsea, who was a 'maniac' but nevertheless generally held to blame for the duel. Jeremy Bentham, the philosopher and an ardent opponent of duelling, wrote to Wellington, 'Ill-advised Man! think of the confusion into which the whole fabric of government would have been thrown had you been killed …'[50]

The duel caused a sensation in the public prints. At first 'the event appeared so improbable that it obtained very little credit' but gradually the details came out. Unlike most duels, it was, as it involved the Prime Minister, an event of national significance, with potentially far-reaching effects. Yet, as 'providentially' the Duke survived unscathed, disaster was averted; the financial markets remained 'perfectly steady'. *The Times* opined that the affair was unnecessary and ridiculous.

> [T]he Duke of Wellington is the last man on earth who could be called upon to defend himself by duel against any attack on his public character. We must also add, that of all men existing, Lord Winchelsea is precisely the one from whom nobody need think of demanding satisfaction for offences arising out of the Catholic question.[51]

Within a few hours of exchanging shots with Lord Winchelsea, Wellington went to Windsor for an audience with the King, and went through public business before mentioning the duel. According to *The Times*, the King had not seen a copy of Winchelsea's letter, so a newspaper was brought, Wellington withdrawing 'to afford leisure for its uninfluenced perusal and consideration'. Having seen the offending letter, George said that he thought it was a matter of personal honour and feeling and that, 'being a soldier, his Grace might be perhaps more sensitive on such points than an individual of a different class of society'. The duel, the King thought, had been 'unavoidable'.[52] According to another source, however, 'the King was delighted with the duel and said he should have done the same'.[53] George IV did not share his father's severe disapproval of duelling, even when it was his Prime Minister who had put himself at risk.

When *The Times* wrote two days after the duel that 'it may at least have a tendency to calm the violence of the partisans throughout the remainder of these discussions', it was, albeit unknowingly, Hinting at the Duke's motivation for fighting. He had never before fought a duel, indeed he did not own any duelling pistols, but was prepared to make an exception in this case because he considered it necessary for political ends. As Wellington explained to the Duke of Buckingham:

The truth is that the duel with Lord Winchilsea was as much part of the Roman Catholick question, and it was as necessary to undertake it … as it was to do every thing else that I could do to attain the object which I had in view.[54]

In other words, he did not consider it purely (or at all) a private matter: it was an adjunct of his public policy. This was diametrically opposed to the view taken by the other duelling Prime Minster: Pitt's justification for his duel was that Tierney had insulted him as a private individual not as a public figure.

Before we leave the Duke's duel it is interesting to note that in the following year, 1830, the Manchester and Liverpool Railway was opened for passenger use, with Stephenson's *Rocket* pulling the train. The Duke himself cut the ribbon but tragedy occurred when William Huskisson, MP for Liverpool, ran onto the line and was crushed to death. The contrast between the medieval ritual of the duel and the all-too-modern phenomenon of fatal railway accidents is striking. The modern world was arriving rapidly, while the old world faded slowly away.

Chapter Ten

WANING MOON: DUELLING IN GEORGIAN AND EARLY VICTORIAN ENGLAND, 1760–1860

THE HISTORY OF duelling bristles with rogues, ruffians and romantics but none of them surpass the fighting parsons for sheer incongruous eccentricity. Duelling clergymen were preeminently a British, and Irish, phenomenon and, moreover, one confined almost entirely to the Georgian period. While it is unfair to bring modern sensibilities to bear on the standards of the Georgian priesthood, it was nevertheless true that even the most worldly, cynical clergyman was supposed to respect the Ten Commandants. The sixth commandment is 'Thou shalt not kill'.

The first duel involving a clergyman in the period was the meeting between the Revd. Mr Hill and Cornet Gardiner in Epping Forest in 1764. Gardiner was an officer in the Carabineers, Hill the chaplain of a regiment of dragoons. Hill was wounded in the duel and died two days later. An obituary described him as being 'of good address, great sprightliness, and possessed of an excellent talent for preaching', all promising attributes for a clergyman. But, the obituarist concluded, he had one flaw that proved his undoing: 'he was of rather too volatile a turn for his profession'.[1]

In 1782, the Revd. Mr Allen fought a duel with an American, Lloyd Dulaney, in Hyde Park. Dulaney was described as 'a gentleman of a most respectable character, and large property in the province of Maryland'. Allen was, as well as being in holy orders, a journalist for the

Morning Post. He wrote a piece for this newspaper entitled 'Characters of Principal Men in Rebellion', in which he referred to Dulaney as 'a liar and assassin'. It took Dulaney three years to call Allen to account for his remarks and, when he had done so, they fought with pistols at 8 yards. Dulaney was killed. Allen and his second absconded after the duel; the magistrate at Bow Street offered a reward of 10 guineas each for the arrest of the two fugitives. Allen was eventually tried for his crime, found guilty of manslaughter, fined a shilling and imprisoned for six months. There was some rather vague evidence at the trial that Allen had been practising his pistol shooting the day before the duel. The whole episode passed off, it was said, without 'incurring any ecclesiastical censure, though Judge Buller, on account of his extremely bad conduct, strongly charged his guilt upon the jury'.[2]

As this example shows, the Church authorities were not as strict about clergymen fighting duels as one might have expected. However, there were some bishops who were determined to eradicate this ungodly practice from among their priests. After a duel fought in Salisbury between a clergyman and a layman the following item appeared in a newspaper.

> Since this, the affair, we are told, has been taken up by the Bishop, who, not being of the Church Militant, is determined to have no fighting Parsons, and will therefore make an example of him.[3]

The previous year Captain Leeson and the Revd. Mr Dunbar fought a duel on a Sunday morning in a field near Battersea Bridge. Both men missed with their shots and the matter was promptly settled. Then, having finished his business with Leeson,

> the Reverend duellist went to perform divine service at a parish church to which he has lately been appointed curate. In this we think there is nothing wrong; for after trying to take away the life of a fellow creature, nothing can be so proper as to go to prayers, and to make peace with the Deity.[4]

In 1828 the Revd. Mr Heaton de Crespigny fought a duel against Mr Long Wellesley on the sands at Calais. This was different from the other examples given in that it is the only one in which we know that the clergyman was the challenger. The confrontation had its origins in some

remarks made by Wellesley about de Crespigny's father: he alleged that
de Crespigny senior had had an illicit affair with an unnamed woman.
They repaired to Calais to fight because Wellesley had been bound over
to keep the peace in England at the time.[5] De Crespigny had served in the
Royal Navy (where perhaps he was exposed to duelling) and came under
fire, before taking orders. Having been ordained, in 1820 he sensibly
married the daughter of the Bishop of Norwich; soon afterwards he
became Rector of Stoke Doyle in Northamptonshire.[6] One wonders
what his father-in-law would have made of his escapade on Calais sands.

For all these tales of fighting parsons there were (no doubt many)
occasions when priests performed their more traditional functions,
spreading peace and harmony rather than discord and confrontation.
One such was reported in the public prints in 1783.

> On Sunday morning, about ten o'clock, two officers, with three gentlemen,
> their friends, met in a field near Bayswater, to fight a duel, when the Revd.
> Mr Swaine, coming to town to perform his duty, observing their inten-
> tions, kindly interfered, and having seen them to London, by appointment,
> met them again in the evening, and through the wise and salutary admo-
> nitions and advice of the benevolent clergyman and another gentleman,
> the difference was amicably and finally adjusted.[7]

The best-known duelling clergyman was the Revd. Sir Henry Bate
Dudley; indeed Sir Henry was so notoriously bellicose that he was
widely known as the 'Fighting Parson'. After ordination he acquired a
living in Essex but abandoned it in favour of London and journalism.
In 1775, he became the editor of the *Morning Post* and, in 1780, started
the *Morning Herald* in competition with the *Post*. His journalistic
activities earned him both influence and notoriety. A contemporary
described him, in a memorable piece of verse, as

A Canonical Buck, Vociferous Bully
A Duellist, Boxer, Gambler & Cully ...
A Government Runner of Falsehood a Vendor
Staunch Friend to the Devil, the Pope and Pretender
A Manager's parasite, the Opera Writer
News paper Editor, Pamphlet Indictor.[8]

Bate Dudley's reputation as the 'Fighting Parson' was founded on his prowess both as a duellist and a pugilist. His fist fight with Captain Miles in 1773, which became known as the 'Vauxhall affray', established Bate as a man not to be trifled with. He also fought at least three duels. The earliest was against Captain Andrew Stoney over some derogatory remarks that Bate had made in the *Morning Post*. The duel was fought, most irregularly, in a room in the Adelphi tavern in the Strand, with pistols and swords. Both men received slight sword wounds; also one of the pistols was fired – it smashed the mirror in the room. The suspicion lingers that the duel was a 'put-up job', arranged to increase the widowed Countess of Strathmore's infatuation with Stoney. To the extent that they married a few days later, the ruse succeeded. Suspicions of collusion were aroused by the facts that it was fought in private behind locked doors, that the seconds – one of whom was a very dubious character – waited outside, that the wounds were both superficial and that only one of the pistols had been fired.[9]

There was no hint of collusion attaching to Bate Dudley's duel with Mr De Morande in August 1778. Indeed, it was all the seconds could do to dissuade the two men from taking a fifth shot at each other. The two principals have left a vivid account of the duel in the form of a draft statement to the press. They composed it between them in the Turk's Head coffeehouse in the Strand, immediately on their return to town from Kilburn Wells, where the duel had been fought. I have retained the original liberal use of abbreviation in order to preserve the immediacy of the account, the sense of Bate and De Morande sitting at a table in the Turk's Head, sipping their coffee, working out their story together, oblivious to the fact that an hour earlier they had been trying to kill each other.

The time fixed to settle the Dispute in Hyde Park being 5 o'Clock, Mr Bate, attended by Captn. Baillie & a surgeon, & Mr Demorande by Mr Austin, arrived there a little before that time, when each of the seconds seeing the adverse Party load his Pistols, Mr Bate got out of his Chaise, & took his Ground, Mr Demorande immediately followed from his, and being told by Captn. Baillie 'that he might advance as near as he pleased' that Gentn. did so; and both fired within twelve Paces of each other, without Effect. Mr Demorande then advanced two or three Paces & discharged his second Pistol wch. was returned by Mr Bate witht. either Shot takg Place. Both of them then expressed a Desire to proceed, wch was attempted to be over-ruled by the seconds, who made use of every Argument they cod. think of to prevail upon them to desist; but Mr Bate parlarly insisted he was not satisfied, they instantly agreed (to avoid being broke in upon by some people who were by this time assembling in the Park) to go along the Edgware Road & terminate the Affair in some convenient Spot on this Side [sic] Kilburn Wells; – for this purpose they went abt. a Mile, where Mr Bate & his Friend got out, & immediately Mr Demorande & his Friend followed into an adjoining Field. Mr Demorande receivg the same Intimatn. again from Captn. Baillie to advance as near as he thought proper, he snapped his Pistol which missed Fire; on this Mr Bate fired & slightly wounded Mr Demorande on ye upper part of ye Head. Mr immediately sd. 'You are wounded, Sir!' to which Mr Demorande rejoined 'not materially' & fired his second Pistol which was returned by Mr Bate's other Fire, witht. either taking Effect. The Seconds here again stepped in, & sd. ye Matter must not be carried on further, as each had given the fullest Proof of his Courage. Mr Bate replied, that it was not to ascertain the Courage of either that he came out, it was to have the fullest Recantatn. of what Mr Demorande had advanced in the public Prints against him partarly in certain Queries, which he expected wod. be apologised for in the fullest manner, or he must Insist on proceeding till one of them dropped, Mr Demorand [sic] not chusing to comply with this, they reloaded their Pistols, & went into a Field a little further, but just as they were about to renew their Fire, the seconds again warmly interposed, & threatened immediately to retire, observg to Mr Demorande yt as he had given the strongest proofs of his personal Courage, it cod. be no Impeachment of it to do Mr Bate the ye Justice he seemed otherwise inclined to ...[10]

Bate also fought a duel against Joseph Richardson, one of his co-proprietors at the *Morning Post*, as a result of which Bate left to start up the *Morning Herald*.

Bate and De Morande had started their duel in Hyde Park but were forced to move to Kilburn Wells in order to settle their dispute in private. This reflected a more general centrifugal migration of London duellists. Leicester Fields, Southampton Fields and the other open spaces immediately around London, so popular with Restoration duellists, had been built over or had become insufficiently private. By 1760, the duellists were moving westwards. Hyde Park remained popular but Kilburn, Regent's Park, Hampstead Heath and Chalk Farm, as we have seen, all had their adherents, as did Marylebone Fields, Tyburn and Blackheath. The fatal duel between Colonel Fawcett and Lieutenant Monroe in 1843 that caused such a brouhaha was fought at Regent's Park. Lord Camelford fought his fatal duel with Captain Best, as we have seen, behind Holland House in Kensington.

With the construction of the bridges across the Thames, the duellists' choice of a suitable rendezvous to the south of the river expanded. Until 1750s the only bridge across the Thames in the metropolitan area was London Bridge; further west, access to the south was by ferry only. This clearly was not ideal for duellists, as even the most obtuse ferryman could not fail to spot the purpose for the crossing. Westminster Bridge, opened in 1756, was the first addition, followed by Blackfriars Bridge in 1760 and Vauxhall Bridge in 1816. The first Battersea Bridge stood between 1771 and the 1880s.

Battersea Fields and Wimbledon Common were popular among duellists because they were, in the early nineteenth century, accessible from London via the new bridges yet sufficiently secluded to prevent interruption. Battersea Fields were drained and filled in the 1850s but until then had been low-lying agricultural land and the site of a notoriously licentious fair. When the Duke of Wellington and Lord Winchelsea arrived there on the morning of their duel in 1829, they were observed by a labourer whetting his scythe.

Wimbledon Common – then part of a larger area of common land that included Putney Heath – was, for the same reasons, a favoured resort for duellists. It was close to the relatively well-maintained Portsmouth road – an important consideration when roads generally were in an atrocious condition – yet large enough to enable duellists to achieve privacy. Pitt fought Tierney on Putney Heath in 1798; Colonel

Lenox had exchanged shots with the King's brother, the Duke of York, on Wimbledon Common in May 1789. Many of the later duels fought on the Common took place near the famous windmill, built in 1817. Indeed, it was the miller, Thomas Dann, who, in his capacity as a constable, arrested Cardigan after his duel in 1840 with Harvey Tuckett.

London was not, of course, the only place in Britain that duellists fought, although it was probably the scene of more duels than any other part of the country. Scotsmen fought in fields, on moors and in Edinburgh. According to Sir Walter Scott, writing about the 1730s, Holyrood Park was a duellist's delight, the perfect place to fight, a 'deep, wild, grassy valley, scattered with huge rocks and fragments'.[11] Sir George Ramsey was mortally wounded, for a row over a footman, by Captain Macrae on Musselburgh Links in 1790. Englishmen too fought by the seaside: on the beach at Brighton, at Gosport, at Southsea, at Deal and at Plymouth. They fought, in fact, wherever was most convenient: at Osterley Park, at Cowes and at Carisbrook Castle on the Isle of Wight, on Bagshot Heath, at Liverpool, at Bridlington, at Epping Forest, on the downs above Bath, wherever there was an open space away from prying eyes and officious constables. The Welsh fought the odd duel, too. The bourgeois calm of Tenby was ruffled by a long-running property dispute that erupted into a duel in 1839. In 1799 Sam Fortune was killed in duel at Haverfordwest fought for a row over a triviality. It seems that one John Benyon killed his man in suspicious circumstances in a duel near Newcastle Emlyn in 1814.

Hyde Park remained, however, at least until the end of the eighteenth century, *the* place to fight a duel. It was close to the smart residential areas of Mayfair, yet offered sufficient privacy to allow duellists to settle their differences. In 1763 Wilkes and Martin both walked from home to their rendezvous in Hyde Park. Around 1760 we are told that the 'Park was notorious as a place where footpads prowled, and where duels took place without much danger of observation or interference'[12]. Captain Gronow, writing his memoirs in the 1860s, left a description of Hyde Park as it was in his youth.

[It was] far more rural in appearance in 1815 than at the present day. Under the trees cows and deer were grazing; the paths were fewer, and none told of that perpetual tread of human feet which now destroys all idea of country charms and illusions. As you gazed from an eminence, no row of monotonous houses reminded you of the vicinity of a large city, and the atmosphere of Hyde Park was then much more like what God had made it than the hazy, gray, coal-darkened, half-twilight of the London of today.[13]

A German visitor to London in the early nineteenth century confirmed Gronow's recollections of rustic charm and was impressed with the ostentatious display in the park on Sunday afternoons, when, 'The fashionable world drives, rides on horseback, or simply walks there.' She informed her readers that it was estimated that as many as 100,000 people thronged the park on these occasions.[14]

For all the rustic delights of Hyde Park in the early nineteenth century, it does seem that it was falling out of fashion with duellists by the turn of the century. Captains Clark and Innes fought in Hyde Park in March 1749, although, perhaps, had they chosen to go further afield to fight, Clark might have escaped the clutches of the criminal law. As we have seen, Wilkes and Martin fought in Hyde Park in 1763 and Bate Dudley and De Morande in 1778, although in both cases they were interrupted by passers-by and had to move on. By 1800 duellists preferred to fight elsewhere; Hyde Park had become too risky.

Pitt fought Tierney on Putney Heath in 1798, as did Canning and Castlereagh in 1809. Montgomery and Macnamara fought at Chalk Farm in 1803, although their dispute had arisen in Hyde Park. Lord Paget and Colonel Cadogan exchanged shots on Wimbledon Common in 1809, while in the same year Lord Falkland died at the hands of Mr Powell at Chalk Farm. As if to confirm the fact that Hyde Park was no longer the haunt of duellists one Thomas Smith published a pamphlet in 1836 called *Historical Recollections of Hyde Park*, which contained the stories of the better-known duels fought in the park. So far as Smith was concerned duelling in Hyde Park was, by 1836, a thing of the past, confined to the realms of history.

In the Georgian period the failure of the criminal law to take a stronger line against duelling was highly controversial. Of the legal

position of the duellist there was no theoretical doubt. Sir Fletcher
Norton, the Attorney-General, in opening the Crown's case against
Lord Byron in 1765, restated the law to the House of Lords.

> It is clear ... if there be a quarrel, and the parties afterwards have time to
> cool, and after that they fight, and one falls, he who survives is guilty of
> murder; or if the manner in which the fact was done bespeaks a deprav-
> ity of mind, and a wickedness of intention, that will make it murder.[15]

This was as clear as could be. Moreover, as duelling etiquette prescribed that quarrels should not be fought out immediately, duellists
who followed the codes would of necessity fall foul of the criminal law.
The rationale behind the etiquette was to prevent enraged, possibly
drunken, duellists fighting on the spur of the moment; a hiatus in proceedings would allow for the appointment of seconds and for time in
which the dispute could be settled. But the law was clear that, if a
cooling-off period was allowed, then the duellist was guilty of murder.

However, juries were reluctant to convict men of murder for fighting a duel where it could be shown that the proprieties had been
observed. This was the case even when the duellists had had ample
time – days in some cases – to cool their heels, thus bringing the
encounter squarely within the law's definition of murder. Indeed, it
was a further complication of the paradox that the duels that tended
to arouse a jury's suspicions were those fought in the first flush of
anger. It was in those circumstances that Major Campbell was convicted of the murder of Captain Boyd in 1808. Yet it was these duels,
in theory at least, to which the law turned a blind eye. Thus, on the
face of it, the law condoned the drunken brawl in which someone was
unfortunately killed yet condemned the duellists who observed the
etiquettes.

In January 1830 Richard Lambrecht killed Oliver Clayton in a duel
in Battersea Fields. The duel was fought in the dark; neither man
could see his target but Clayton was nevertheless killed. Lambrecht
and the two seconds, Frederick Cox and Henry Bigley, were subsequently tried at Kingston Assizes for Clayton's murder. There was no
dispute that Lambrecht had fired the fatal shot and the judge, in
summing up, told the jury that there were no grounds that would

justify reducing the verdict from murder to manslaughter. Despite this the jury returned a verdict of not guilty.[16]

This reluctance by juries to convict is well illustrated by two Scottish cases of the 1820s: the trial of James Stuart for killing Sir Alexander Boswell in a duel in 1822 and the trial of David Landale for killing George Morgan in a duel in 1826. In both cases the jury acquitted the defendant without hesitation. In Stuart's case, the jury did not need to retire to consider its verdict. Similarly, in Landale's case, the jury delivered its verdict 'immediately and unanimously' without needing to retire. The jury's task in this case was made easier by the judge, Lord Gillies, who, in his summing up, virtually instructed the jury to acquit Landale. This was despite the fact that there was no suggestion on the part of the defence that Landale had not killed Morgan.[17] These three cases show how difficult it was for the prosecution to secure convictions in duelling cases.

The extent of the difficulty faced by those who wished to eradicate duelling is shown by some statistics that say that there were 172 reported duels during the reign of George III. Of the 344 principals, 69 were killed and 96 wounded, leaving 179 who survived unscathed.[18] These figures are trotted out by historians of duelling and, although there is no means of testing their accuracy, they do nevertheless make a telling point about the ineffectiveness of the criminal law at dealing with duellists. Or, put another way, they show the extent to which duelling was condoned by the authorities in Britain under George III. Of these 172 duels spread over 60 years only 18 resulted in trials; from this group seven defendants were found guilty of manslaughter and only three of murder, of whom two were executed.[19] In the opinion of Granville Sharp, a reformer writing in 1790, 'the Indulgence allowed by the Courts' in duelling cases was 'indiscriminate and without foundation in Law'. He went on to assert that the impunity that duellists appeared to enjoy in the eyes of the law was 'one of the principal causes of the continuance and present increase of the base and disgraceful practice of duelling'.[20] On any view of the statistics it is hard not to agree with him.

Even when only one-tenth of duels attracted prosecutions and barely half of those resulted in convictions, there were yet further obstacles in the path of those who wished to see more duellists

convicted of murder. The first, an ancient legal anomaly, raised
Grenville Sharp's hackles: benefit of clergy. The benefit of clergy was
originally designed to protect the clergy from harassment by the
secular state, particularly when the Church had its own legal system.
As the ability to read was in medieval England considered sufficient
evidence of someone's being in holy orders, 'pleading' benefit of
clergy was simply a matter of reading (or reciting parrot-fashion) a
verse from the New Testament. By a statute of 1547 all peers could
invoke benefit of clergy without even the necessity of being branded
on the hand (which had been introduced to make sure that laymen
could plead the benefit only once). What this anomaly meant for
duellists was that, provided the jury could be persuaded to convict of
the lesser offence of manslaughter, the offender would get away scot-
free. The existence of this loophole, the reformers maintained,
encouraged juries to convict duellists of manslaughter (that is, killing
without malice aforethought). Edward, Earl of Warwick, a crony of
Lord Mohun's, had pleaded the benefit of clergy when convicted of
manslaughter in 1699. Lord Byron had taken advantage of it to escape
any penalty under his conviction for the manslaughter of William
Chaworth. Various attempts were made, from time to time, to reform
the benefit of clergy but it remained on the statute book until its abolition in the reign of George IV. It continued to exist for peers until
finally abolished in the 1840s.[21]

If the duellist had been unlucky enough to be prosecuted and convicted of murder (for which the plea of benefit of clergy was not available) there was always the hope that a royal pardon might be
forthcoming. Captain Clark was convicted by a jury at the Old Bailey
in 1750 of murdering Captain Innes in circumstances that suggested
foul play. Shots were exchanged at very close range – perhaps four
yards apart – but, most significantly, Clark's pistols were vastly superior to those used by Innes. The jury, having convicted Clark of
murder, recommended him as a suitable subject for mercy.[22] George
II was duly pleased to spare him the gallows.

Andrew Steinmetz wrote in the 1860s that 'George III furnished
intending duellists with a "pardon" beforehand, which they carried in
their pockets to the ground – as in the case of Earl Talbot and John

Wilkes, of which the latter was aware.'[23] Whether this was literally true – as, according to Wilkes, it was in the case of his duel with Lord Talbot – is open to doubt, but Steinmetz clearly had grounds for believing that most duellists could expect a pardon from George III in the event that they killed their man. The duelling statistics quoted earlier suggest (in so far as they suggest anything) the reverse: only one of the three men convicted of murder in the reign was not executed, which hardly represents a promiscuous use of the royal power of mercy. Those statistics suggest much more strongly that the duellists' principal guarantee lay in the reluctance of the authorities to prosecute in the first place and then in juries' reluctance to convict rather than in the expectation of a royal pardon. What the statistics do not tell us is how many duellists were pardoned at an earlier stage of the proceedings against them.

There is, however, evidence that George III did take an active interest in duelling, particularly between officers in the armed forces. This evidence indicates that, far from adopting a lenient line with duellists, he was inclined to do all he could to prevent duels from happening. Douglas quoted two cases in which the King had intervened in court-martial proceedings. In one of them Major John Browne, of the 67th Foot, was tried by a court martial in Antigua. The president of the court, Lord Frederick Cavendish, reported that there was 'much heat and animosity' between the parties and that 'without some timely interposition, consequences may be expected subversive of military order and discipline'. Lord Frederick was ordered by the King to effect a reconciliation between the warring officers. The King similarly intervened to procure a reconciliation between General Murray and Sir William Draper. Ill feeling had flared up between the two as a result of a letter written by Draper that accused Murray of lying. The King ordered that the court martial trying Murray should reopen in order to reconcile the officers. It did.[24]

In the wake of the Duke of York's duel with Colonel Lenox in May 1789, Lords Dover and Amherst, the colonels of the regiments of Life Guards, were asked for their opinion of how best to deal with any recurrence of the dispute. They advised that George III should 'exert your Royal authority to check these alarming and increasing evils by manifesting in the strongest manner your displeasure with them'. This should include, their Lordships thought, a statement that any officer offending against these rules and the Articles of War would be dismissed the service.[25] Three years earlier the Home Secretary, Lord Sydney, had enlisted the King's help in preventing a recurrence of the long-standing dispute between Lord Macartney and General Stuart.[26] In 1788 George III had been so appalled by Captain de Lancey's murderous brutality in his duel with Major Chapman (see Chapter 4) that he ordered him to be struck off the army list permanently.

The King was also involved in the hue and cry that followed the conviction of Major Campbell for killing Captain Boyd in a duel in June 1807. As we have already seen, the circumstances of the duel were decidedly suspicious. Campbell was tried for Boyd's murder by Judge Mayne and a jury at Co. Armagh assizes in the summer of 1808. Campbell's defence relied upon his good character as an officer and a man of honour. However, when Mayne came to sum the case up to the jury – and he had a reputation as something of a hardliner when it came to duelling – he omitted to defend the code of honour. He also resisted any attempt to enlist the jury's sympathy for Campbell; in other words, he was not seeking to influence the jury in the defendant's favour, as the judge did, for example, in Landale's case in Scotland a few years later. As a result, the jury convicted Campbell of murder – as we have seen, a rare verdict indeed at the time – and Mayne sentenced him to death by hanging. However, it was widely and confidently expected that he would be pardoned. The Grand Jury of Armagh petitioned the Lord Lieutenant, the Duke of Richmond, (who had himself, as Colonel Lenox, fought two duels 20 years earlier) for mercy but Judge Mayne undermined the appeal by failing to certify Campbell as a suitable case for a pardon. The execution of the sentence was suspended pending an appeal to the King himself.[27]

On 16 August 1808 Lord Hawkesbury (who, as Lord Liverpool, was later Prime Minister) wrote to George III about the Campbell case. He advised the King that it was the opinion of His Majesty's confidential advisers that it was not an appropriate case for the King to intervene. In other words, he should let justice run its course and allow Campbell to go to the gallows. Hawkesbury's reasons for this were threefold.

First, the provocation was not sufficient to warrant such a departure from the usual duelling rules. Second, that it was clear from the evidence that Campbell had forced Boyd to fight at once, against his will, depriving him of the opportunity to recruit a second or settle his affairs. Third, Hawkesbury was of the opinion that the fight took place long enough after the provocation for cooler heads to have prevailed. The King accepted his minister's advice.[28] And there, despite a personal appeal by Mrs Campbell to the King and another appeal to the Prince of Wales, the matter rested. Campbell was executed on 24 August 1808.

The Campbell case was one of the most notorious duelling cases of George III's long reign, one that was accompanied by strenuous efforts to secure a pardon for Campbell. Yet the fact that George III did not bow to pressure to pardon Campbell suggests that perhaps he was not as indulgent of duellists as has been suggested.

*   *   *

Dr Johnson was a qualified defender of duelling. In 1773 Boswell (whose own son was to be killed in a duel) reported Johnson's offering the following opinion:

> that if publick war be allowed to be consistent with morality, private war must be equally so. Indeed, we may observe what strained arguments are used, to reconcile war with Christian religion.[29]

Ten years later the doctor was still persuaded that 'a man may shoot the man who invades his character, as he may shoot him who attempts to break into his house'.[30]

Johnson did not, however, for all his fame and learning, represent the undivided views of the educated classes on duelling. There were many voices, particularly in the universities and in the clergy, raised against it. The examinees for Cambridge University's Seaton Prize, an annual literary event, were for two consecutive years, 1774 and 1775, given duelling as their set topic. Clearly, duelling was a subject that exercised the minds of the dons who administered the Seaton Prize. George III, incidentally, had in his library a copy of Charles Layard's winning entry of 1774, a flowery anti-duelling tract written in verse in the epic style.[31] Whether he ever read it, however, we do not know.

The last phase of duelling in England, from 1790 to 1850, poses a problem for historians. There is little doubt that the end of the eighteenth century and the first two decades of the nineteenth witnessed an increase in the number of duels and a gathering acceptance of duelling as a way of settling quarrels. As we have seen, it was considered – at least in certain influential quarters – *de rigueur* for prime ministers, Cabinet ministers and MPs, the nation's political leaders, to resolve personal political differences on the duelling ground. Soldiers and aristocrats equally regarded it as part of their birthright. As late as 1829, the Prime Minister, the Duke of Wellington, fought a duel for avowedly political reasons. Yet within 20 years duelling had faded away. It was simply no longer acceptable. This section will attempt to explain this remarkable, and remarkably rapid, transition.

We have seen how George III reacted to the news of Pitt's duel; his son was less forthright in his condemnation of his Prime Minister's duel. Indeed, as we have seen, he almost appeared to approve of it. Lord Auckland told Henry Brougham:

> The fight was a silly business that ended well. The King told the Duke that if he had read the letter he would have called on the Duke to resent it. Probably by this time he thinks that he has been out himself or was second at least.[32]

Nor was it just the King who was a state of excitement about this outbreak of gallantry. Lord John Russell reported that 'All the ladies are in heroics about the Duke's duel – such flummery you never heard.'[33] By contrast, the Whig politician Thomas Spring-Rice told Brougham of his view that the fact that the successful applicant to a judgeship in Ceylon had been a second to O'Connell in one of his many duels must have harmed his prospects of securing the appointment (which he did secure).[34] The contrary view is that it speaks volumes for official insouciance in respect of duelling that he could land the job at all. Certainly it does not seem that a reputation as a duellist was a bar to political advancement. Colonel Lenox, who fought two duels in a fortnight in the summer of 1789 (one against the King's brother) later, as the Duke of Richmond, held high office as Lord Lieutenant of Ireland and Governor-General of Canada.

We have already looked at the 'Reform' duel between Lord Thomas Cecil and Charles Tennyson d'Eyncourt in June 1831, but its aftermath provides an interesting insight into the attitude of the new King, William IV, to duelling. Four days after his duel d'Eyncourt attended a levee at court, where he was received by the King in a 'most highly gratifying' manner so far as his 'late affair' was concerned. There is no suggestion of any degree of disapprobation of his duel, indeed in the following year he was appointed to the Privy Council. William IV, at least in this instance, seems to have shared his brother's uncensorious attitude to duelling.

While these examples of a decidedly tolerant attitude to duelling do not represent the attitude of the nation as a whole, they are significant in that they are indicative of the attitude of the ruling elite to duelling. It is no exaggeration to say that in 1830 the ruling elite were (still) prepared to turn an indulgent blind eye to duelling. As late as 1842 Craven Berkeley MP and Captain Boldero MP fought a duel near Osterley Park; their seconds were also both MPs.[35]

That duelling was allowed to survive into the railway age is in itself a remarkable thing, something that is not altogether easy to explain. It was partly because it was an ancient privilege of the ruling elite itself, a long-established right, sanctioned by custom, which it saw no need to end. The reluctance of juries to convict duellists is clear evidence of the acceptance of duelling by the lower echelons of society as an aristocratic (or at least gentlemanly) privilege. Its longevity is also partly explained by the enthusiasm with which the military embraced the duel; the army was a stronghold of duelling and would remain so right to the end. Indeed, as we have seen, this positively encouraged officers to fight duels at least as much as it discouraged them from doing so.

Another reason for the longevity of duelling was the feeling among the upper classes that there were certain sorts of insult that could be settled only in a duel. The law, which awarded damages calculated in money, could not provide an adequate remedy. The kind of slight that was so serious as to fall into this category was the seduction of a wife, sister or daughter. No sum of mere money, however substantial, could requite such an insult. Lord Paget's duel with Colonel Cadogan took place after a jury had awarded Henry Wellesley £20,000, an enormous sum in 1809, in damages in an action for criminal conversation (or 'crim. con.', to give it its accustomed truncation). Paget had allowed judgment to be entered in default, thereby admitting the adultery.

In 1823 Lord Brudenell (as he was known before he succeeded to the earldom of Cardigan) eloped with the beautiful, wilful, quick-tempered Mrs Elizabeth Johnstone, wife of Captain Johnstone. In 1824 Captain Johnstone sued Brudenell for damages for crim. con., the first step in the complicated process of procuring a divorce. Brudenell was represented by counsel but did not appear, putting himself at the discretion of the court in the matter of damages. The jury awarded Johnstone £1,000. After the trial Brudenell sent a messenger to Captain Johnstone offering to 'give him satisfaction' in a duel. Johnstone, having burst out laughing, replied to the messenger, 'Tell Lord Brudenell that he has already given me satisfaction: the satisfaction of having removed the most damned bad-tempered and extravagant bitch in the Kingdom.'[36]

Nearly 20 years later the Earl of Cardigan was again sued for crim. con., this time by Lord William Paget, the son of the Lord Paget. Cardigan, chastened perhaps by the Tuckett affair, which we shall look at later, refused to fight a duel. When the action for crim. con. opened, it promptly collapsed, amid recriminations that Paget's principal witness had been bought off by Cardigan.[37] When the trial did eventually restart, it promptly collapsed once more. This time it was Cardigan who was able to acquire the higher ground by alleging that the action had been nothing more than an attempt by the notoriously spendthrift Paget to extract money from a 'wealthy nobleman, unpopular with the public'.[38]

While the ruling classes continued to condone duelling on the grounds that the civil law did not provide an adequate remedy, it was also given an extended lease of life by the inadequacies of the criminal law. We have looked at length at the unwillingness of juries to convict duellists but there was, some reformers believed, a matching failure to beef up the criminal law so that it could deal adequately with duellists.

In March 1844 Captain Polhill MP gave notice of his intention to move an amendment to a Bill to suppress duelling on the grounds, according to Hansard, 'that it is inexpedient to interfere with the existing law on the subject, which was already sufficiently stringent – (a laugh).'[39]

'Titus', an anti-duelling author, commented,

> Why, what practical law, stringent or not stringent, does there exist against duelling, except that which would hang the survivor of a meeting without seconds, and either proved or strongly inferred to have been unfair on the slayer's part ... Did Captain Polhill ever know ... of a gentleman's being hanged for having 'killed his man' in the conventionally allowable form, even when the parties fired across a handkerchief [?][40]

In other words, even as late as 1844, the reformers believed that the existing criminal law was inadequate for the purpose of eradicating duelling. Yet, as we can now see, it had already practically withered away before their very eyes. Another criticism that 'Titus' levelled at the criminal law concerned the Campbell–Boyd case of 1808. 'Titus' believed that the extreme rigour of the application of the law in Campbell's case – he was hanged – paradoxically gave rise to the idea that, had he 'obeyed the rules', he would have escaped punishment. In time, according to 'Titus', 'it gave an almost avowed sanction to the ordinary practice.'[41] It is ironic that the reformers should have devoted so much energy to decrying the law's failure to punish duellists severely yet when, in a bad case, the full treatment was meted out, they should complain that it has the effect of encouraging duellists.

There is another, rather more metaphysical, reason for the long survival of duelling: the rise in interest in all things medieval and chivalric. The late eighteenth and early nineteenth centuries in Britain witnessed a revival of interest in medieval history and medieval architecture. It became fashionable to remodel one's house in the Gothic, castellated style, to hang scenes from medieval history on the walls and to collect armour. It also became pre-eminently fashionable to read the novels of Sir Walter Scott, the greatest, most popular novelist of the day and the leading proselytiser of things medieval. While no one would pretend that this widespread resurgence of such interest was in any direct or tangible way responsible for the contemporaneous revival of duelling, it is illogical not to make some, perhaps subconscious, connection between the two. After all, duelling was, however distantly, founded on medieval ideas of chivalry, and an interest in the chivalric ideal was a strong element of the medieval revival.

Between 1787 and 1789 Benjamin West painted a cycle of seven pictures for the King's Audience Chamber at Windsor illustrating various episodes from the reign of King Edward III. The series represents a glorification of the chivalric values of the medieval knight: Edward III and his son, the Black Prince, are depicted as the very essence of the knightly ideal, powerful and victorious yet solicitous, courteous and merciful.

West's imaginative and idealised reconstructions of scenes from English medieval history had their equivalents in architecture. A taste for the picturesque – Turner's early watercolours of Tintern Abbey spring to mind – led to a fashion for building castles in the medieval style or at least remodelling existing buildings with keeps, battlements and moats. Robert Smirke built both Lowther Castle in Westmoreland and Eastnor Castle in Herefordshire in the first decade of the nineteenth century, both splendid medieval pastiches. And there were others, but the most ambitious scheme was the remodelling of Windsor Castle for George IV from 1823 by Jeffrey Wyatville in the Gothic style.

Another manifestation of the penchant for things medieval was the fashion for collecting armour, an obvious link with and reminder of the ideals of the age of chivalry. The first recorded sale of armour in England was at Christie's in 1789. In 1824 Samuel Rush Meyrick published his three-volume *Critical Inquiry into Antient Armour*, the first comprehensive study of the subject. In between these two dates the enthusiasm for armour resulted in the formation of numerous collections and, occasionally, the construction of purpose-built armouries for their display.

*   *   *

We have looked at some of the reasons why duelling persisted in England for as long as it did; we now need to examine the second part of the conundrum posed earlier: why did it fade from the scene so quickly and so completely? The short answer is that public opinion would no longer sanction its continuance. The longer answer lies in the various influences that bore upon that shift in opinion.

The pamphleteers had, by 1830, been attacking the justifications advanced for duelling by its proponents for decades. In particular, they aimed their fire at the contentions that (1) duelling remedied deficiencies in the law; (2) duelling promoted good behaviour in society; and (3) it was founded on notions of honour. However one looked at it, it had no redeeming features: 'among the advocates of duelling are principally found, the idle, the dissipated, the debauchee, the gambler, the seducer and the adulterer!'[42]

According to one writer duelling was by 1807 a 'degenerate relick' which disgraced society, 'a pernicious and an impious custom'.[43] The author's maxim was 'That the Christian's best Rule of Action are the Dictates of his Religion and the Englishman's best Standard of Appeal the Laws of his Country.'[44] The anonymous 'Senex Observator', writing in 1810, railed against this

> awful practice, which appears to be gaining ground, not only among young and inconsiderate persons; but has also lately been practised, by those, whose exalted situations in life, it might be supposed, would not have been actuated by a practice so inexpressibly subversive of good policy.[45]

This was a thinly veiled dig at Lord Castlereagh and George Canning, who had fought the previous autumn, but it shared with other tracts the opinion that duelling was, at this time, on the increase. Indeed, a pamphleteer writing as late as 1835 was convinced that 'much yet remains to be done before this national sin can effectively be eradicated'.[46] John Dunlop, an anti-duelling campaigner as well as a leading proponent of temperance, estimated in 1843 that the 'duel-exposed class' (as he infelicitously put it) numbered perhaps 70,000 (or 0.3 per cent of the total population of 23.8 million reckoned in the census of 1851). Dunlop proclaimed his figure to be a 'tolerable guess' made from 'taxation returns of persons keeping carriages and riding horses, and the amount stated of capitalists and educated men in certain public reports'. A large majority of the 70,000 would, he sur-mised, be happy to see the end of duelling. For Dunlop duelling was not a gentlemanly practice: 'it gives the treacherous mysteries of saloon pistol practice and blackguardism an undue advantage over all true excellence and innocence of character'. Dunlop's solution to the problem was a 'negative association' – that is a combination devoted to not doing something – to combat duelling. An association of the 'duel-exposed' gentlemen would adopt a pledge against duelling.[47]

The reformers realised as the nineteenth century progressed and as the population grew rapidly (and became increasingly urbanised) that it was the pressure of popular opinion that would bring about the end of duelling. In 1822 the Revd. Peter Chalmers wondered, 'If, there-fore, the tide of public opinion were made to flow in an apposite channel, would not this odious and destructive practice ... be abol-ished from our land?' Chalmers recognised the power of public opinion and its usefulness in the fight against duelling.

> It is from private, and even obscure persons, that the aggregate of society is formed; and there is none so isolated and unimportant, but the weight of his judgment, insignificant as it may be in itself, tells upon the whole.[48]

In June 1830 Philip Crampton delivered a speech at a public meeting of the Association for the Suppression of Duelling in Dublin. Strongly supporting the aim of the association, he said, 'Sir, let your society be the burning-glass to collect, combine, and concentrate into one focus the rays of all that is good and manly in the nation.'[49]

That is, in the modern political jargon, to focus public opinion. In 1844 'Titus' observed that there was a 'fast-forming public opinion' against the 'abominable and foolish practice' of duelling.[50]

The fact was that, as the pamphleteers recognised, public opinion was indeed moving. Politically, in the 1830s, things were beginning to change in England. The slave trade had been abolished in 1807, fol-lowed by the abolition of slavery itself in 1833. The Catholic Emanci-pation of 1829 relieved Roman Catholics of most the disadvantages imposed upon them since the Reformation. The repeal of the Test Acts the previous year (a preliminary step towards emancipation) also relieved nonconforming Protestants of many of the more repressive civil disabilities that had long affected them. There was a Whig government for the first time since the 1780s (excepting the short-lived venture of 1806–7), which set about introducing a measure of parliamentary reform. The Great Reform Act of 1832 could scarcely be said to have introduced democracy in the modern sense, but it did start chipping away at the oligarchic practices of rotten boroughs and closed electorates.

Best of all, the country had a new, young monarch. When, in 1837, Princess Victoria ascended the throne she was barely 18 years old and determined to rid the court of the louche characters and easy morals of her uncles' reigns. Her marriage to the high-minded, ascetic Albert in 1840 merely added impetus to this process. Royal seaside holidays would from now on be spent wholesomely at Osborne on the Isle of Wight, which was spiritually, if not geographically, far removed from the exotic fleshpots of Brighton. Duelling, an anachronistic relic of a self-indulgent age, was unlikely to be tolerated by the new regime. And so it proved.

The country was moving into a more modern age in other important ways, too. The effects of the Industrial Revolution had transformed huge areas of Great Britain, creating the satanic mills but generating colossal wealth and an industrial bourgeoisie. The increasingly urbanised population had espoused evangelical Christianity. Wilberforce, the great evangelical, had expressed outrage at the duels fought by Pitt and by Castlereagh, nor could his fellow Evangelicals be expected to smile upon the practice. The historian Donna T. Andrew has written, 'In contrast with the competitive and social life of the man of fashion, Evangelicalism preached a life of sobriety, co-operation and concern only for the approbation of God.'[51]

This was not an environment in which the duellist was likely to be accepted or tolerated. Equally, as Andrew points out, the ever-increasing influence of business and industry in the nation's life militated against duelling. It increased the importance of and respect for the rule of law. In a commercial society, individuals do not resolve their differences on the duelling ground: they go to law. In the 1830s and 1840s Britain was becoming increasingly modern; mass industrialisation was arriving; the railway boom was under way; duelling was looking ever more archaic and doomed. As *The Times* put it, 'The shackles of the ages are falling off and the human intellect is rising up ...'[52]

If the rising tide of modernity formed the background to duelling's demise, there were three events which hastened it along the path to extinction. James Brudenell, the 7th Earl of Cardigan, was a magnificent anachronism, a Regency buck born 20 years too late and so condemned to live much of his life in the soberer world of early Victorian Britain. Vastly rich, immensely stupid and possessed of a chilli-hot temper, he was an inveterate philanderer and duellist. It was his duel with Captain Tuckett on Wimbledon Common on 12 September 1840 and the events surrounding his subsequent acquittal that raised an unprecedented outcry against duelling. The events leading up to the duel were complicated but, in essence, revolved around Cardigan's hatred of the so-called 'Indian' officers in his cavalry regiment, the 11th Hussars. In 1834 Cardigan had been removed from the command of the 15th Hussars, but only two years later had secured command of the 11th. When Cardigan bought the command of the 11th in 1836, it had been stationed in India for 17 years. The earl sailed to India to take up his command and, although he spent only a few weeks with his regiment, it was time enough for him to form a strong aversion to 'Indian' officers.

'Indian' officers were those who had served with the regiment during its long stint in India. In Cardigan's eyes they were socially inferior, insufficiently smartly turned out and slack in the performance of their military duties. Nor did he make any attempt to conceal his contempt for them on the parade ground or in the mess. They were not the sort of officers he wanted in his regiment. By the summer of 1838 Cardigan and the 11th Hussars were back in England.

It was the affair of the 'Black Bottle' in May 1840 that brought the relations between Cardigan and the 'Indian' officers to a head. An 'Indian' officer, Captain John Reynolds, was spotted by Cardigan at a mess dinner given for a visiting general drinking from a black bottle. Bottles in general were banned from the mess table by Cardigan, who insisted on decanters, but black bottles raised his particular ire, as they often contained porter, the preferred tipple of the hated 'Indian' officers. Reynolds was severely reprimanded and refused the opportunity of clearing his name in a court martial. Thereafter relations between Cardigan and his 'Indian' officers went from bad to worse.[53]

On 4 September 1840 the *Morning Chronicle* carried an anonymous letter, under the headline 'To the Officers of the British Army', attacking Cardigan 'with intimate knowledge and extraordinary virulence'. It accused the earl of grossly insulting his officers in the mess and of sheltering behind his rank as commanding officer to avoid a duel when called to account for his behaviour.[54] It was an open secret that the author was Captain Harvey Tuckett, an 'Indian' officer of the 11th, who had recently resigned his commission. Cardigan sent a friend to Tuckett demanding an apology and, as none was forthcoming, a duel was arranged.

Lord Cardigan and Harvey Tuckett met near the windmill on Wimbledon Common at 5 p.m. on Saturday, 12 September 1840. They were accompanied by their seconds, Douglas and Wainwright respectively, and by the eminent surgeon Sir James Anderson. A distance of 12 paces was measured out and shots were exchanged. At the first fire both missed but at the second Tuckett was hit in the back part of the lower ribs. At this point Thomas Dann, the miller who doubled as a constable, appeared on the scene. Seeing Cardigan still holding a smoking pistol, he arrested him and Douglas for a breach of the peace. Tuckett, who was bleeding from his wound, was taken away.

The law ground into action and in due course a grand jury at the Old Bailey committed Cardigan and Douglas for trial on three counts of intent to murder, or maim or cause grievous bodily harm to Tuckett. Cardigan, as was his right, elected to be tried by his peers in the House of Lords. The prospect of the trial aroused great excitement, for no such thing had happened for 60 years. Elaborate and expensive preparations were made: 'several scores of carpenters, upholsterers, labourers, etc.' were pressed into service to make the necessary alterations to the Painted Chamber, where the trial would take place.[55] Three-quarters of the total costs of the trial were taken up by the refurbishments.[56] Tickets for the trial, for which there was a voracious demand, were allocated on a strict basis; lists of witnesses were announced. *The Times* could not resist offering advice to the

House of Lords. Their Lordships should, the newspaper advised, take the opportunity to register a 'fearless unqualified expression of your united abhorrence of the unhallowed system of duelling'.[57]

On 16 February 1841 the eagerly awaited trial, presided over by the Lord Chief Justice, Lord Denman, opened. The proceedings began at 11 o'clock; by five, Cardigan had been unanimously acquitted on a submission by his counsel of no case to answer. The evidence called by the prosecution had failed to establish that the person named in the indictment as the victim was in fact the Tuckett referred to by their witnesses. Tuckett himself did not give evidence. It was, by any standard, a gross technicality and the response was predictable. *The Times* could barely contain its outrage. The case, it spluttered, 'reflects deep disgrace upon the present state of the English law, and suggests very grave doubts as to the manner in which the officers who represented the Crown … have discharged their duties'.

The evidence was 'perhaps the clearest and most convincing, ever submitted to a court of justice', yet Cardigan had been acquitted. It was now plain for all to see 'how much more important names are considered in British jurisprudence than things [and] how omnipotent quirks, and quibbles, and pettifogging objections are in Westminster-hall'.[58]

That evening, when Cardigan appeared in a box at the theatre in Drury Lane, there was a near riot. Such was the noise that it was impossible for the performance to begin.

The Cardigan case is significant because of the public outrage it provoked. It showed that the law was not willing or able to deal with the archaic, privileged practice of duelling. The facts of Cardigan's case appeared to fall neatly within the provisions of a recently enacted anti-duelling statute; indeed, he had even been caught with a smoking gun in his hand. Yet he had been acquitted. It seemed that duellists, of which Cardigan was a prime example, enjoyed a licence, tacit or otherwise, to break the law that was not granted to less exalted folk. However, the Cardigan affair was about more than merely an unjust, even an outrageous, acquittal. It was about the old world and the modern world. Cardigan was a representative *par excellence* of the old world, of privileged wealth, of unfettered arrogance; a man who considered that his position entitled him to do whatever he wanted, whenever he wanted. Cardigan personified the evil of duelling. People saw that duelling was more than just an antisocial, unchristian and illegal hangover from earlier times: it was a symbol of what Lord Cardigan and his ilk represented. It was not to be tolerated in the modern world.

The last word on the Cardigan case should perhaps be given to J.W. Croker, Tory politician and formerly Secretary to the Admiralty. He had innate conservative sympathies as well as considerable experience of public affairs. Cardigan's counsel, Sir William Follett, took Croker's advice while preparing his client's defence. Croker recommended that Follett should not defend the institution of duelling should it become necessary to 'parry an attack on the general system'. Instead Follett should defend Cardigan by urging that more stringent legislation be passed to eradicate duelling rather than penalising an individual for adhering to custom.[59] The eradication of duelling was a small price to pay for maintaining intact the 'general system'.

While Cardigan's duel provoked a general feeling that duelling had had its day, the duel between two brothers-in-law, Lieutenant Munroe of the Blues and Colonel Fawcett of the 55th Foot, prompted action. On 1 July 1843 the two men met near the Brecknock Arms in Camden Town to fight a duel. The dispute had arisen as a result of a minor argument over the management of property. The colonel was hit in the chest and died a lingering death two days later. According to Andrew Steinmetz, at 'the report of this duel the public were greatly shocked' and, as a consequence the Anti-Duelling Association was formed.[60] A similar body, the Association for the Discouragement of Duelling, had been formed a year earlier, in 1842. Founded on the conviction that 'the practice of Duelling is both sinful and irrational, and alike contrary to the laws of God and man', it boasted a distinguished membership. Twenty-eight peers and 24 MPs were joined by an impressive roll call of generals and admirals as well as a large number of officers from the lower reaches of both services. Among the civilians was a decent sprinkling of JPs, barristers and medical men.[61]

The following year, 1844, the government introduced legislation into the House of Commons to amend the Articles of War. The Prime

Minister, Sir Robert Peel, intended to eradicate duelling by storming its principal bastion, the army. The amended Articles were published on 15 April; they included a number of provisions aimed at reconciling quarrelling officers, thereby preventing duels.[62] They also provided that all parties implicated in a duel be liable, on conviction by a court martial, to be cashiered. But the setting trick for the government was the provision preventing the widow of any officer killed in a duel from collecting a pension. This, it was hoped, would force would-be duellists to consider the likely consequences of their actions to their nearest and dearest before agreeing to fight.

The government hoped that if duelling could be abolished in the army it would rapidly wither away in civilian society. And so it proved. From the date of the amendment of the Articles of War there were no more than a handful of duels fought in England. A year later Lieutenant Hawkey of the Royal Marines killed Mr Seton of the 11th Hussars in a duel fought on a beach near Gosport. Andrew Steinmetz thought this was 'the last duel of Englishmen in England; at any rate, I have been unable to find the record of any other'. He also suggested that the last duel – and a fatal one – fought in England was the encounter in October 1852 between two refugee Frenchmen, Cournet and Barthelemy. It was Cournet who was killed.[63] For V.G. Kiernan it was George Smythe and Colonel Romilly in 1852 who fought the last duel in England.[64]

One of the remarkable things about the demise of duelling was the speed with which the custom withered and died. Having enjoyed vigorous life in England for two and a half centuries, it disappeared as a serious undertaking in a matter of a few years. Legal abolition and practical extinction were almost contemporaneous. In 1852 a Mr Hayward was insulted while dining at the Carlton Club. The insult was both cutting and unequivocal and Hayward immediately wrote his traducer a note requiring him, in the time-honoured fashion, to name a friend. However, once the seconds had met, the affair unravelled very rapidly indeed. By the following morning it was agreed that both parties would make 'a complete and unqualified withdrawal' of everything that had been said. So much for the fighting spirit.

A few days later Hayward wrote to a trusted friend to tell him the story of the contretemps in the Carlton Club. It is a remarkable letter as, in describing the course of the dispute, it shows how unacceptable duelling had become in just a few years. A dispute that perhaps 10 and certainly 15 years previously would have ended on the duelling ground now ended in grovelling apologies and promises of silence. The letter makes it clear that there was no question of any duel whatsoever happening in England; if the parties were to fight, it would have to be in France. It was also agreed that 'no memorandum should be made for fear of publication'.[65] Gone were the days when the parties to a duel issued a statement to the press describing the encounter. One cannot imagine the Revd. Bate Dudley and Mr De Morande, as they sipped their coffee in the Turk's Head, sheepishly deciding not to compose a memorandum of their duel, 'for fear of publication'.

That was in 1852 but the straws were already in the wind. In 1836 Lord de Ros had been accused of cheating at cards. In the first six months of the year rumours were circulating in the clubs of St James's that de Ros habitually cheated at cards by means of a sleight of hand known as *sauter la coupe*. In time these rumours found their way into a publication called the *Satirist* and thence into the press at large. De Ros, of course, denied everything and sought to clear his name. He decided to do so by suing for libel. In December 1836 de Ros wrote to his accusers, 'I shall neither be deterred by your reasonings, nor intimidated by your numbers, from the course I have been advised to pursue. That course is to prosecute the *Satirist*.'[66]

John Cumming, one of the group of men who harboured grave doubts about de Ros's probity, replied, discussing de Ros's chosen course of action, 'Your Lordship prefers a legal one – a legal one let it be, but one where I can prove my own allegations, call my own witnesses, and appoint my own legal advisers.'[67]

Cumming's letter amounts to a very strong hint that the affair could be settled in a duel. This shows that in 1836 the duel was still very much regarded as an acceptable way of resolving questions of honour such as allegations of cheating. Nevertheless, de Ros chose to vindicate himself through the courts.

On 1 June 1891, a trial for defamation began in London that was to prove 'in many respects the most sensational of the Queen's reign'.[68] The plaintiff, Sir William Gordon Cumming, a wealthy baronet, was lieutenant-colonel of the Scots Guards and a long-standing crony of the Prince of Wales. He was suing the defendants for slander for saying that he had cheated at cards, specifically baccarat. The allegations had arisen the previous autumn during a house party at Tranby Croft in Yorkshire for Doncaster races. The principal guest at Tranby Croft was the Prince of Wales; Gordon Cumming was, among others, also staying in the house that week.

On the first evening, the guests played baccarat after dinner. One or two members of the party noticed that Gordon Cumming appeared to be cheating by covertly increasing his stakes after the cards had been declared. They said nothing to him but did alert some of the other players so that when, the following evening, the party again sat down at the baccarat table, there were more pairs of eyes watching him. Again, it appeared that Sir William was cheating. This time he was confronted and, although he hotly denied any sharp practice, he was eventually induced to sign a piece of paper. This paper recorded an undertaking by Gordon Cumming that he would never again play cards. In return for this undertaking, his accusers promised that they would keep the whole affair a secret.

Inevitably, the story leaked out – the finger of suspicion is often pointed at the Prince of Wales – and the rumours and gossip began to circulate. Now that the allegations were public knowledge, Sir William decided to sue for slander. He had been branded a cheat and was determined to clear his name. His counsel at the trial, Sir William Clark, opening the case to the jury, said of the accusation of cheating, 'It is a serious question, involving his honour, his reputation, his whole career.'[69]

Clark's oratorical flourish makes abundantly clear what was at stake in that courtroom. The case was not about baccarat, or about the mores of late Victorian high society, or even about the gambling habits of the Prince of Wales. It was a matter of honour. If Gordon Cumming failed to clear his name, it was no exaggeration to say that he would be ruined. This was just the kind of dispute that 60 years earlier would have been settled with pistols. Moreover, the guests at

Tranby Croft were precisely the rich, leisured, hearty, military types who would, in earlier years, have had immediate recourse to a duel. This was the milieu in which duelling had, in its heyday, thrived, yet Sir William Gordon Cumming chose to clear his name through the courts. The Tranby Croft affair showed, beyond any doubt whatsoever, that duelling in England was dead.

Chapter Eleven

The Ascendancy of the Pistol: Duelling in Ireland, 1760–1860

IT WAS IN THE LAST 30 years of the eighteenth century that duelling in Ireland reached its apogee. The 1770s and 1780s were the years of the so-called 'Fire-eaters', an amorphous group of Irishmen whose bloody deeds have been glorified by some of duelling's chroniclers, most notably Sir Jonah Barrington. In reality, they were more akin to murderous ruffians than elegantly composed gentlemen duellists, but their careers – and the stories that have grown up around them – have done much to foster the notion of Ireland in those years as a duellists' paradise.

The history of duelling in Ireland in these years followed a similar but not identical trajectory to its history in England. While there was a steady rise in the number of duels fought in England until, say, 1820, followed by a sharp and terminal decline, the Irish graph described a sharp upturn in the numbers after 1760 followed by a falling-away after 1800. The importance of two statutes, the Octennial Act of 1768 and the Act of Union of 1801, in the history of duelling in Ireland cannot be ignored.

The period opened in Ireland (as in England) with the death of King George II. In Ireland the death of the King precipitated parliamentary elections. However, they had an added significance, as, unlike the case in England, there was no provision for elections at any other time. So with a young king coming to the throne – George III was 22 when he succeeded his grandfather – the elections could determine the political landscape for decades. This added spice to the elections that followed George II's death. Against a background of renewed vigour in Irish politics after a period of torpor and of rising prosperity, duelling took on a new lease of life. For the next 40 years politics was the most fertile source of duels in Irish society. This was greatly, if unintentionally, assisted by the passing of the Octennial Act, which prescribed Irish parliamentary elections at least once every eight years. As elections were a frequent cause of disputes between candidates, the Act did much to promote duelling. The first elections held under the new octennial regime were those of 1768, which gave rise to a number of duels. By the same token, the Act of Union of 1801, by transposing Irish parliamentary politics to Westminster, removed, at a stroke, the biggest single cause of duelling.[1]

There were a number of other factors that helped duelling to become more widespread in the late 1760s and early 1770s. As always in the history of Irish duelling the proximity to and connection with England was important. The publication of pamphlets in Dublin about well-known English duels was one way in which the word was disseminated. Two such pamphlets, both referred to by James Kelly in his history of duelling in Ireland, were those dealing with the trials in London for murder of Edward Clark in 1750 and Lord Byron in 1765. Both (discussed earlier) were notorious cases, which attracted a good deal of publicity in England; the publication in Dublin of the sensational stories of the fights helped to widen the appeal – if that is the right term – of the duel in Ireland.

The rising tensions in politics and the newsworthiness of some of the more notorious duels from England may have contributed to an increase in the number of duels fought in Ireland but they were fertilising already productive pastures. We have already encountered (see Chapters Five and Six) the Anglicised and Anglican gentry who were established in Ireland by the various plantations of the sixteenth and seventeenth centuries. By the middle of the eighteenth century this class of Protestant landowners was firmly rooted in Ireland and busily devoted itself, for the most part, to a life of hunting, gambling and drinking. It was a hard-living, unreflective society, an ideal milieu in which the duel could flourish. Furthermore, according to Kelly, there was a growth in economic prosperity from around 1745, which encouraged more men to think of themselves as gentlemen and, therefore, to consider themselves able to give and receive satisfaction on the duelling ground. Many of these were, in Sir Jonah Barrington's memorable phrase, 'half-mounted gentlemen', men who nevertheless considered themselves able to defend their honour with the duel.

Kelly also points to three celebrated duels that, coinciding with the developments discussed above, helped to prepare the ground for the excesses that were to follow in the later 1770s and 1780s. On 25 August 1769 Henry Flood met Mr Agar at Dunmore and, with his first shot, killed him. The dispute was, broadly, political in origin. Flood was a prominent member of the 'Patriot' party in the Irish Parliament; the families had a history of rivalry over control of the parliamentary borough of Callan. Indeed, the two men had travelled to England to fight a duel in 1765. The immediate cause of this conflict was the defection of an important elector from Flood to Agar and a dispute about a pair of the latter's duelling pistols. Flood was tried for killing Agar but convicted only of manslaughter, which meant that he escaped prison.

The second duel was between Lord Townshend and Lord Bellamont, fought in London in February 1773. The fact that Lord Townshend had recently completed a term of office as the Lord Lieutenant of Ireland lent the duel its notoriety. The dispute had trivial beginnings but came to represent the rivalries that characterised Irish politics. To many the fact that Townshend had been called to account personally for actions taken during a period of public office was an unwelcome development. The duel itself was fought in Marylebone Fields; both men were armed with swords and pistols. Townshend fired first, hitting Bellamont in the groin.

The third duel was between Sir John Blaquiere and Beauchamp Bagnall, who had a reputation as an enthusiastic duellist. The episode has parallels with the two other duels mentioned above. The animosity between the two men was of long standing and the dispute arose out of Blaquiere's conduct of public business. They exchanged shots in Phoenix Park, Dublin, in February 1773, three days after Town-shend and Bellamont had done so in London.[2]

It seems likely that the 1770s and 1780s saw a tangible increase in the number of duels fought in Ireland. A reliable statistic is, as we have seen, a rare beast in the history of duelling. However, James Kelly has produced some about duelling in late eighteenth-century Ireland. Between 1751 and 1760 Kelly found a sample of 36 duels; in the following decade the figure was 47. The majority of these were fought in Dublin and its environs. The same statistics show that, as the century wore on, the pistol gradually replaced the sword as the duellists' preferred weapon.[3] This mirrors the anecdotal evidence we observed when looking at duelling in the Georgian period in England.

However, after 1770 there is a marked increase in the number of duels fought. Kelly's sample for the decade from 1771 rises steeply to 159 duels, more than a threefold increase over the previous 10 years. Between 1781 and 1791 it remains roughly the same at 147. The figures appear to show that the majority of duels were fought in and around Dublin; they also show that, after 1770, the pistol was the most popular duelling weapon.[4] The statistics support the idea that from the 1790s there was a falling-off in the number of duels fought in Ireland. This trend was reinforced by the Act of Union, which removed much of the politicking from Dublin to London, thus reducing the number of political duels in Ireland. Kelly's statistics reveal a sample of 113 duels for the decade 1791–1800, a decline of more than one-fifth from the previous decade. In the 10 years following the Act of Union of 1801, the sample declines further to 81 duels. This suggests that, by the first decade of the nineteenth century, there were only about half the number of duels that were fought just 30 years earlier in the furious years of the 1770s. The statistics also show that after 1800 duels were fought exclusively with pistols.[5]

It was against this rising tide of violence in the 1770s and 1780s that duelling in Ireland became more closely governed by etiquette. The high point of this process was the formulation of the 'Clonmel Rules'. The preamble announced, 'The practice of Duelling, and points of honor, settled at Clonmell summer assizes, 1777, by the gentlemen delegates of Tipperary, Galway, Mayo, Sligo and Roscommon, and prescribed for adoption throughout Ireland.'[6]

The 'Rules' were signed by Crow Ryan, James Keogh and Amby Bodkin, three self-appointed experts, and are best seen as an attempt at self-regulation by the duelling fraternity. It may also be significant that the 'Rules' were formulated at the assizes, because a duellist's chances of evading the gallows if he killed his man were greatly enhanced if it could subsequently be shown in court that he had 'played by the rules'. That this was the case is borne out by the experience of duellists on both sides of the Irish Sea and further afield. The 'Rules' were an attempt to keep duellists out of trouble rather than to reduce the number of duels.

The 1770s and 1780s was the era of the so-called 'Fire-eaters'. The 'Fire-eaters' were, by and large, 'thoroughly disreputable figures', violent and persistent duellists, not men who were inclined to obey the 'Rules'.[7] The best known of them is George Robert Fitzgerald, known to history as 'Fighting' Fitzgerald. His career amply illustrates all that the 'Fire-eaters' stood for.

Fitzgerald was born in 1748 of an aristocratic family: his mother was Lady Mary Hervey, sister of the Earl-Bishop of Armagh.[8] According to William Douglas, having attended Eton and Trinity College, Dublin, Fitzgerald was a quiet, reflective young man as well as highly educated. All this changed when he had part of his skull shot away in a duel, as a result of which he became 'choleric, cunning, and cowardly'.[9] William Hickey related some anecdotes about Fitzgerald in his memoirs: 'In person he was uncommonly slim and delicate, his address mild and insinuating in an uncommon degree, yet in temper and behaviour at times ferocious beyond measure.' Hickey reported that a silver plate had been inserted in his skull, where he had received a bullet wound.[10]

In 1772 Fitzgerald married an heiress and left Ireland for an extended honeymoon in France, where he succeeded in gaining the entrée to the court at Versailles. Fitzgerald was immensely extravagant, even by the standards of a spendthrift age. He loved display.

'On any journey he travelled in state, his servants dressed in blue hussar uniforms faced with yellow and carrying huge sabres, while he himself always wore in his tricorn a hatband of diamonds or oriental pearls.'[11]

By the time he returned to Ireland in 1775, his extravagance had saddled him with huge debts, perhaps as much as £120,000.

Fitzgerald is credited with having fought a large number of duels, perhaps as many as 27, by the time of his return to Ireland from France in 1775.[12] James Kelly, the latest authority on the subject, suggests that perhaps he had fought 12 duels by the time of his execution in 1786.[13] As his duelling career shows all too clearly, he had no interest in abiding by the conventions. He was open to any ruse that might help save his skin: crouching down to present a smaller target, wearing hidden armour or, most effectively, simply fleeing the duelling ground. Kelly concluded that for Fitzgerald duelling 'was nothing less than a quasi-legal means of assassination or of exacting vengeance for perceived insult'.[14]

Eventually, Fitzgerald's violence and his disregard of the conventions caught up with him. He was arrested and tried for his part in the assassination – it could not by any stretch of the imagination have been called a duel – of Patrick McDonnell. His trial opened at Castlebar on 11 June 1786 before the Lord Chief Baron and a jury. Prosecuting counsel was the Attorney-General, John Fitzgibbon, with whom Fitzgerald had once fought a duel. Whether Fitzgibbon had any sympathy for Fitzgerald's plight we do not know but the jury certainly did not. 'Fighting' Fitzgerald was convicted and hanged.[15] A Dublin newspaper treated its readers to a lurid description of the state of Fitzgerald's body shortly before his execution.

> Every part of Fitzgerald's body was scarred with wounds, which he had received in the various ... duels he had been engaged in. There was a large hole where a ball had lodged in one of his hips, another in the small of one of his legs; his head had been trepanned, and his right side was so perforated with the pricks of a small sword that if had an appearance not easy to describe.[16]

By the early years of the nineteenth century the character of duelling in Ireland had begun to change. Until then it had been largely the preserve of the Protestant landed gentry. This was partly the result of the ban on Catholics carrying weapons which had been in force since the Williamite settlement of the early 1690s. Horace Walpole recounted the story of an Irish duel, in a letter in 1751. Setting the scene, he wrote, 'Taafe is an Irishman, who changed his religion to fight a duel, as you know in Ireland a Catholic may not wear a sword.'[17]

Whatever one thinks this conversion has to say about the strength of the mysterious Taafe's religious and moral convictions, it would by 1800 no longer have been necessary. The law was changed in 1793; thereafter Catholics were allowed to bear arms legally. This, of course, made it easier for them to fight duels and many of the leading Catholics enthusiastically embraced the code of honour. The question of emancipation for Catholics from the civil disabilities under which they had laboured since the Reformation was a more important question in Ireland (where there was a much larger Catholic population) than in England. The Act of Union had been forced through on a promise of emancipation for Catholics, motivated in part by fear of a repeat of the French-backed invasion attempts of the 1790s. But the promise was not honoured and emancipation became one of the most important political issues of the first quarter of the nineteenth century on both sides of the Irish Sea and the cause, as we have seen, of many a duel.

It was against this background that Daniel O'Connell (1775–1845) rose to prominence in Irish politics. O'Connell was a barrister by profession and a tireless campaigner for the rights of Catholics. He founded the Catholic Association, which became 'the most effective political lobby of the day'.[18] O'Connell was also a man of splenetic temper, whose intemperate outbursts frequently got him into trouble. On occasions, this resulted in a duel. O'Connell had a deep-seated dislike of Sir Robert Peel, the future Prime Minister, which dated from Peel's days as Chief Secretary in Ireland between 1812 and 1818. As Peel was vehemently opposed to Catholic Emancipation, he became the target of O'Connell's barbs. In a debate in 1813 he had ridiculed Peel:

> that ludicrous enemy of ours … 'Orange Peel'. A raw youth, squeezed out of the workings of I know not what factory in England … sent over here before he got rid of the foppery of perfumed handkerchiefs and thin shoes … a lad ready to vindicate anything, everything.[19]

Small wonder, if he was in the habit of using such language, that O'Connell got himself into trouble. Two years later there was a further exchange of insults between the two men, which resulted in a duel being arranged at Ostend. However, the authorities, alerted to the affair by the publicity it had generated, had O'Connell arrested as he crossed London on his way to the Continent.

In the February of the same year, 1815, O'Connell fought a duel with Mr d'Esterre near Dublin. It was a dispute that also had its origins in the divisions between Protestants and Catholics. O'Connell had insultingly referred to the 'beggarly Corporation of Dublin'. D'Esterre, a Protestant member of the Corporation, took exception to O'Connell's words and wrote to him seeking clarification of his remarks. O'Connell wrote back assuring d'Esterre 'that no expression which language could furnish was sufficient to convey the sentiments of contempt he had for that body'.[20] The contretemps between d'Esterre and O'Connell created an extraordinary degree of publicity and excitement. D'Esterre swore to horsewhip O'Connell for his impudence, an indication perhaps that he did not consider O'Connell a man with whom he need fight a duel. So for the best part of a week between the exchange of letters and the duel itself, d'Esterre, whip in hand, pursued O'Connell between his house in Merrion Square and the law courts.

The two seconds, Major Macnamara for O'Connell and Sir Edward Stanley for d'Esterre, arranged a rendezvous at Bishopscourt, Naas. Duels were conventionally fought away from the public eye but O'Connell and d'Esterre fought in front of a sizeable crowd of onlookers. Purcell O'Gorman, who accompanied O'Connell to Naas, reputedly counted no fewer than 36 pairs of pistols among the 'Orange' contingent, supporters of d'Esterre, who had come to the ground. Macnamara, as a competent second should, prepared O'Connell for the duel. He removed a large bunch of seals that hung from O'Connell's fob and replaced his white stock with a black one. Both precautions were intended to make O'Connell a lesser target.[21] A local newspaper reported the event.

At forty minutes past four the combatants were on the ground; they both displayed the greatest coolness and courage. The friends of both parties retired, and the combatants, having a pistol in each hand, with directions to discharge them at their discretion, prepared to fire. They levelled, and before the lapse of a second, both shots were heard. Mr d'Esterre's was first, and missed. Mr O'Connell's followed instantaneously, and took effect in the thigh of his antagonist, about an inch below the hip. Mr d'Esterre of course fell, and both the surgeons hastened to him.[22]

O'Connell's shot had passed through both d'Esterre's thighs, causing 'an immense effusion of blood'. He died on 3 February. After the duel O'Connell, perhaps knowing that d'Esterre had been on the verge of financial ruin when he fought the duel, offered his widow a pension; she refused it. He did, however, persuade one of the dead man's daughters to accept an annuity, which was paid regularly until O'Connell's death.[23] The long-term result of O'Connell's duel with d'Esterre was that he swore (although not for a while, as the episode with Peel later that year demonstrates) never to fight another duel.

Unfortunately, O'Connell's determination not to fight duels was not matched by a resolution to curb his tongue. In April 1835 he insulted Lord Alvanley in a 'coarse attack' in the House of Commons, describing him as 'a bloated buffoon, a liar, a disgrace to his species and heir-at-law to the thief who died upon the cross'.[24] Alvanley sent a letter to O'Connell demanding an apology or satisfaction and received a letter back from Morgan, O'Connell's son and substitute. Alvanley decided, after a good deal of discussion, to fight Morgan. So with his second he set off to meet O'Connell junior. Charles Greville recounted the story in his diary for 17 May 1835.

> The only other persons who came near them were an old Irishwoman and a Methodist Parson, the latter of whom exhorted the contestants in vain to forego their sinful purpose, and to whom A. replied 'Pray sir, go and mind your own affairs, for I have enough to do to think now of mine.' 'Think of your soul' he said. 'Yes' said Alvanley 'but my body is now in the greatest danger.' The Irishwoman would come and see the fighting, asked for some money for her attendance. Damer seems to have been a very bad second and probably lost his head; he ought not to have consented to the third shots upon any account. Alvanley says he execrated him in his heart when he found he had consented to it. Hodges acted like

A nineteenth-century English caricature depicting a device designed to stiffen the resolve of even the most irresolute of duellists. Notice the seconds cowering behind a nearby tree, well out of the line of fire.

The tearful woman is trying to prevent her lover from going off to fight a duel. The picture suggests that he has just caught her *in flagrante* with another man. An oil painting by the nineteenth-century Italian artist Silvio Faccioli.

Wellington was Prime Minister when he fought this duel over Catholic emancipation in 1829. Lord Winchelsea is the figure on the far right of the cartoon, ostentatiously firing his pistol into the air. Three other British prime ministers fought duels: Shelburne, Pitt the Younger and Canning, although of these only Pitt was in office at the time.

A more conventional view of this celebrated duel.

Georges Clemenceau, journalist and radical politician, was twice prime minister of France. An enthusiastic duellist in his youth, he is credited by some with having fought as many as 22 duels, although the real figure is probably lower. His duel with the nationalist politician Paul Deroulede in Paris in 1892, shown here, arose out of allegations of corruption made against him by Deroulede and was fought on St. Ouen racecourse.

When Benjamin Constant and Forbin des Issarts met to fight a duel in the early nineteenth century, they faced each other seated in chairs.

LEFT The two leading French politicians Paul Deroulede and Jean Jaures fought a duel on the Spanish frontier in December 1904. That Jaures, the 'Apostle of Peace' and a man of deeply held socialist beliefs, should fight a duel shows the strength of the compulsion to fight to clear one's name in early twentieth-century France.

BELOW A cartoon from 1907 entitled *Une Erreur* depicts one second saying to the other 'Good Lord! A bullet through his hat! But we didn't load the pistols!' The cartoon is making fun of the supposed innocuousness of the contemporary French duel.

UNE ERREUR

— Nom de Dieu ! Une balle dans son chapeau ! Et nous n'avons rien mis dans les pistolets !...

ABOVE Two Russian generals, Smirnoff and Fock, settle their differences in a riding school, 1908.

Two Parisian taxi-drivers slug it out with whips. This may be more akin to a brawl than a duel.

Duelling has always appealed strongly to novelists, playwrights and film-makers. This scene is from the 1936 film of *Romeo and Juliet*, with Basil Rathbone as Tybalt defending the honour of the Capulet clan.

This duel between the Marquis de Cuevas (left duellist) and Serge Lifar (right duellist) in 1958, conducted in a blaze of publicity, arose out of a dispute over a ballet. Lifar was obliged to concede defeat when he was slightly wounded on the forearm.

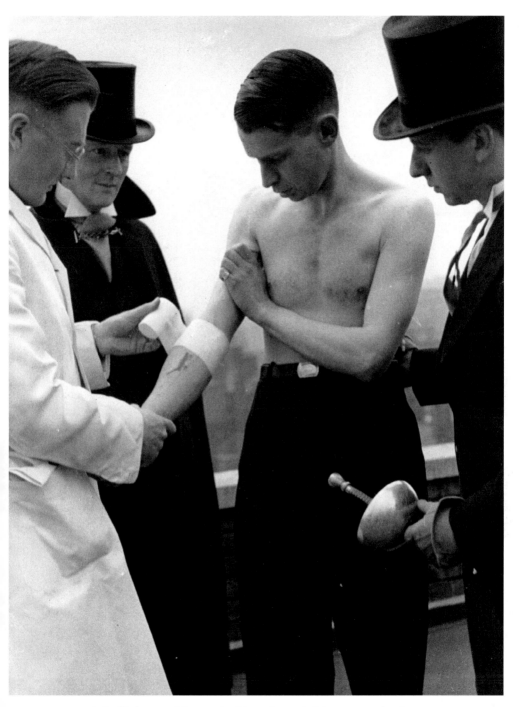

A duellist's wound is examined by a doctor in May 1939, under the watchful eyes of the top-hatted seconds. The injury does not appear to be life threatening.

LEFT Ridley Scott's award-winning 1977 film *The Duellists* is based on Joseph Conrad's novella *The Duel*. It follows the fortunes of two officers of Napoleon's army as they fight a series of duels against one another across Europe over a period of fifteen years. Here Keith Carradine (d'Hubert, right) and Harvey Keitel (Ferand, facing the camera) cross swords, with the seconds looking on.

BELOW In July 2004, Douglas Hamilton and Antonio Burr, descendants of Alexander Hamilton and Aaron Burr, re-enacted the famous duel of 1804, clad in period costume on the banks of the Hudson River, near the spot where Hamilton was killed. The re-enactment was intended as an act of reconciliation and was broadcast on national television.

a ruffian, and had anything happened he would have been hanged. It is impossible to know if the first shot [by O'Connell] was fired by mistake or not. The impression on the minds of Alvanley's friends is that it was not, but it is difficult to believe that any man would endeavour to take such an advantage. However no shot ought to have been fired after that. The affair made an amazing noise.[25]

It is said that Lord Alvanley, returning home from this duel, was in such high spirits that he overtipped the coachman, giving a guinea. The driver, surprised at his passenger's largesse, said, 'My Lord, I only took you to—' Alvanley interrupted him, 'My friend, the guinea is for bringing me back, not for taking me out.'[26]

At the same time O'Connell was involved in spat with the young Benjamin Disraeli. During the course of the Taunton by-election in the spring of 1835 – which Disraeli had contested, unsuccessfully, in the Tory interest – it was reported that Disraeli had traduced O'Connell. The reports were, as it happened, inaccurate, but O'Connell was enraged by them and, at a meeting in Dublin, 'let himself go in one of the most ferocious pieces of invective which the annals of British politics can furnish'. 'He dwelt on Disraeli's "superlative blackguardism", "impudence", "assurance", and "gratuitous impertinence" ... Disraeli himself was "a vile creature", a "living lie", "a miscreant" and "a reptile".'[27]

O'Connell concluded:

> He has just the qualities of the impenitent thief on the Cross and I verily believe, if Mr Disraeli's ... genealogy [be] traced, [he] would be discovered to be the heir at law of the [thief] ... I forgive Mr Disraeli now, and as the lineal descendant of the blasphemous robber who ended his career beside the Founder of the Christian Faith, I leave the gentleman to the enjoyment of his infamous distinction and family honours.[28]

Reference to the 'thief upon the Cross' was clearly the favourite barb in O'Connell's lexicon at the time, his 'insult of the month'. Disraeli lost no time in writing to Morgan O'Connell challenging him to answer for his father's words. Disraeli argued that, as Morgan had so recently fought Lord Alvanley for insulting his father, he should be allowed satisfaction from Morgan for insults suffered at the hands of O'Connell Sr. A duel was arranged but before it could take place, the police intervened.[29]

O'Connell 'The Liberator' is a revered figure in Irish history, and can share much of the credit for the coming of Catholic Emancipation in Great Britain. Yet his antagonistic turn of phrase and his preparedness to fight his political battles on the duelling ground mark him out as a man apart. At least one contemporary, Thomas Moore, a fellow Irishmen and, earlier in life, a duellist too, harboured reservations about O'Connell on this score. While discussing duelling with a friend in 1833 (that is, while O'Connell was still alive) Moore

> remarked that one of the worst things, perhaps, that O'Connell had done for Ireland was his removing, by his example, that restraint which the responsibility of one man to another under the law of duelling imposed, and which in a country so little advanced in civilization as Ireland was absolutely necessary. We see accordingly that the tone of society there is every day growing lower and lower, and men bear blackguarding from each other in a way that to an Irishman of the good old school, or to a gentleman of any school, seems inconceivable.[30]

Whatever Thomas Moore thought of O'Connell's influence on Irish manners, his belligerence clearly rubbed off on one of his closest parliamentary colleagues, E.S. Ruthven, a fellow MP for Dublin. There was an unusually lengthy inquiry into the results of the 1835 elections in the Dublin constituency. While the scrutiny was continuing, so while Ruthven's seat was 'in jeopardy', the House listened with some impatience to his speeches. This 'discourtesy' usually took the form of persistent coughing. One night Ruthven took the barrackers to task: 'I don't know that within this House I can offer any cure for the cough by which honourable members are affected, but outside I shall not have far to seek for a remedy.' To show that he was in earnest, Ruthven exchanged three shots with Alderman Perrin, presumably one of the 'coughers'.[31]

Away from the big stage of national politics, duelling in Ireland, as elsewhere, continued to exist as part of the fabric of everyday life, in both town and country. It threw up tales of tragic waste of life, of lucky escapes, of happy endings; sometimes amid the pride and touchiness there was a flash of humour. In February 1816 *The Times* carried a copy of a report from a Galway newspaper of a duel fought between a Mr P. Dillon and a Mr B. Kane in which Dillon was killed. The article reported that the dead man had previously fought several duels, all of them with Kane as his second. Remarkably, Dillon's father had also been killed, at the same age, in a duel fought at more or less the same spot. *The Times* was unable to resist passing judgement: 'We cannot say that we feel much sympathy: a professed duellist appears to have met with a very consistent fate.' [32]

The Times may have been unable to summon up any sympathy for the fate of Mr Dillon, but it reported an incident thirteen years later which must have elicited some sense of regret from even the stoniest-hearted journalist. On 11 July 1829 two friends fought a duel at Jackson's Turret, Co. Limerick. One of them was hit in the hip at the first exchange of fire. The ball subsequently found its way into the victim's abdomen and, by evening, he was dead. On the day that the dead man's remains were buried, his wife gave birth to their son. [33]

Two years earlier, in Dublin, a man was killed in a duel in circumstances that could act as a universal cautionary tale. It showed how careful one had to be in a society in which duelling was an accepted norm. One sentence, one word even, out of place could spell a premature and painful death. A Mr Bric, a barrister, journalist and aspiring politician, was standing in the colonnade of the post office in Dublin, chatting to a friend while he waited for the results to arrive of an election in Cork. Bric remarked that he had heard that 'that rascal' Callaghan had been voted out of office in the Cork poll. Unfortunately, standing within earshot of Bric was one Hayes, a solicitor from Cork, who not only acted as Callaghan's agent but was his cousin as well. Hayes, on hearing Bric's words, retorted, 'Anyone who called Mr Callaghan a rascal was a damned ruffian.' Bric promptly challenged Hayes. A duel was arranged in which Bric was hit in the chest; he died instantly. [34]

Daniel O'Connell, of all people, told a touching tale of a happy ending to a duel in a letter to his son Morgan.

Did you hear of the great duel in Ennis between Charles O'Connell and Mr Wall? The latter abused a relation of Charley's, a Mr Blood, and Charley knocked Wall down. They then fought, fired a shot each, came home safe and arm-in-arm together, got tipsy in company with each other, went together to the ball and danced till morning.[35]

* * *

We have already examined at length the way in which the laws against duelling were (or were not) enforced in England. Much of what was said there applies, *mutatis mutandis*, to Ireland. During the Georgian period Ireland had substantially the same system of criminal law as England and much the same method, trial by jury, of enforcing it. There was also much common ground in the view that judges and juries took of duelling cases. In Ireland, as in England, juries tended to acquit or convict of manslaughter (in which case the defendant often walked free) unless there was evidence of foul play. In other words, only the really blatant cases fell foul of the law. The Campbell affair in 1808 (discussed in the previous chapter) was actually an Irish case: the duel happened in Ireland and Campbell was tried by an Irish jury. It was one of the few examples on either side of the Irish Sea of a duellist suffering execution. We have already seen that an Irish jury had no hesitation in convicting 'Fighting' Fitzgerald in circumstances that clearly did not admit of a duelling defence. Similarly, the jury in Keen's case in 1788 (see Chapter 1) had no difficulty in convicting in circumstances that amounted to straightforward murder. None of the usual formalities, such as loading the weapons, agreeing the signal or measuring the ground, had been observed; Keen simply shot Reynolds dead.

But these cases were, in Ireland as in England, the exception. The general expectation in duelling cases was neatly summed up in an Irish case reported in 1779. The report

imagined the jury, as usual, would bring in their verdict of manslaughter. But the Barrister found himself mistaken – they deemed the intentions of the two men going out premeditated to fight, to be malice aforethought, and to the astonishment of the court brought the prisoner in guilty – death.[36]

This story succinctly makes the point that, in the normal run of duelling cases, where the formalities had been observed, juries would not convict.

Another Irish case, that of Rowan Cashel, was equally typical. Cashel had killed Henry Arthur O'Connell in a duel at Tralee in August 1815. Cashel, it was alleged, was not only 'not unpractised in the art of duelling' but had been 'positively and systematically inured to it'. Cashel had held his fire for a considerable while after the command to fire, then he had taken a pace forward, levelled his pistol, taken 'cool, deliberate and premeditated aim' and shot the hapless O'Connell. But, despite the fact that the case looked like a deliberate revenge killing, an assassination, almost, the jury acquitted Cashel.[37]

The case of Lord Kingsborough from the 1790s is another example of a failure to adhere to the duelling etiquette that did not result in a conviction for murder. Kingsborough killed Colonel Henry Fitzgerald, his illegitimate nephew, in a fight that was more akin to a brawl than a duel. The dispute had arisen as a result of Fitzgerald's having eloped with Kingsborough's daughter Mary. It is an involved story – at one point Kingsborough's son Robert fought a duel with Fitzgerald in London – which reached its climax in Ireland when Kingsborough and his son sought Fitzgerald out and demanded satisfaction. A brawl ensued, during which Kingsborough shot Fitzgerald dead. As it was wholly beyond the bounds of acceptable behaviour as prescribed by the duelling codes, both Kingsborough and his son were, potentially, in serious trouble. Both, however, escaped scot-free. Robert was acquitted for want of prosecution at Cork assizes; his father elected trial by his peers in the House of Lords, where he too was acquitted when no evidence was offered against him.[38]

The law in Ireland and that in England seemed equally willing to condone duelling. In England few if any senior members of the judiciary had fought duels, whereas in Ireland several had done so. According to James Kelly, Marcus Paterson and John Toler, both at different times the Chief Justice of the Common Pleas, each fought at least one duel. John Scott, who presided as the Chief Justice of the Court of King's Bench, fought a duel, as did Peter Metge, a Baron of the Court of Exchequer.[39] We saw earlier that John Fitzgibbon, the

Attorney-General who prosecuted 'Fighting' Fitzgerald in 1786, had himself fought a duel. Daniel O'Connell was a barrister who enjoyed a thriving practice in Dublin. Nor was the propensity confined to the upper echelons of the legal profession. *The Times* reported in April 1840, under the headline 'Affair of Honour', a duel between two magistrates. The duel arose from a dispute on the bench at Cashel sessions. As both men had already been bound over to keep the peace in their own county they crossed into Co. Kilkenny to fight. It speaks volumes for contemporary attitudes in Ireland that two magistrates were prepared to settle their judicial differences on the duelling ground.

It is difficult to know, and yet more difficult to quantify, the effect on the administration of justice of the 'fighting' judges. It is impossible to prove that their experiences predisposed them to treat duellists leniently. What we do know, however, is that some judges were vigorously opposed to duelling. One such was Edward Mayne, a judge of the Court of Common Pleas. A 'serious, solemn man and a rigid moralist', he was known as the leading anti-duellist on the Irish bench.[40] We have seen already his role in condemning Major Campbell to the gallows in 1808. In the same year Judge Mayne presided at another duelling trial, this time of William Hammond. Hammond had fought a duel against one William Foley at Sixmilebridge, in which Foley had been killed. Hammond had fired the fatal shot but, as the duel had been conducted in accordance with the prescribed etiquette, the jury had no hesitation in returning a verdict of manslaughter. This would normally have allowed the defendant to walk free. Mayne, however, instructed the jury to consider bringing in a more serious verdict. This the jury refused to do so, but Mayne still sentenced Hammond to 12 months' imprisonment and to be branded on the hand.[41]

Before leaving the subject of duelling and the law, we should not overlook the humorous common sense of an anonymous judge who, in 1815, fined both principals and both seconds 25 guineas each for fighting a duel. He then ordered that the money 'be applied for [the benefit] of the Lunatic Asylum, as being, from its nature, an institution best entitled to a fine derived from such a source'.[42]

✳   ✳   ✳

'The rage of duelling had of late much revived, especially in Ireland, and many attempts were made in print and on the stage to curb so horrid and absurd a practice.'[43] Thus wrote Horace Walpole in the 1770s – nor, as we have seen, was he far from the truth. We have already examined in Chapter 10 the opposition to duelling in the Georgian era and the contributions made by the clerical and lay critics to hastening the demise of the practice. In the course of the discussion a number of Irish examples were invoked, as the English and the Irish opposition to duelling took, broadly, similar forms. In essence critics on both sides of the Irish Sea maintained that duelling was against God's law and the civic law – in other words, it was unchristian, unlawful and antisocial. The principal difference between the English and the Irish critics was that the Irish were slower into their stride. The first Irish cleric to publish a reasoned attack on duelling was William Butler Odell in 1814.[44] By contrast, as we have seen, the English critics were in full cry long before the turn of the century.

The year after Odell published his tract the Revd. John Davies preached a sermon attacking duelling at the York Street Chapel in Dublin. The sermon was delivered in response to a recent duel, this 'melancholy event'. 'It is evil, and only evil,' Davies thundered, 'and the welfare of the society, and the happiness of the world call loudly for its abolition.' He then launched into purple flights of rhetoric, sparing his congregation nothing in impressing upon them the horrors of duelling, before considering how duelling might best be prevented. First, the existing law should be more strictly enforced; second, parents should be more aware of their duty to look after their children; and, third, 'society at large' had a obligation to express its abhorrence of duelling.[45] In 1822 another clergyman, the Revd. Charles Bardin, published an anti-duelling sermon that he had preached at St Mary's Church, Dublin. It attacked the practice as contrary to Christian, scriptural teaching.[46]

In 1823 the first serious secular work attacking duelling in Ireland was published. It appeared under the pseudonym 'A Christian Patriot' but was in fact the work of Joseph Hamilton. Dedicated to 'the Mothers, Sisters, Wives, and Daughters of the Nation', it attacked duelling as much on grounds of common sense as for religious or moral reasons. First, it exposed the fallacy that duelling placed men on an equal footing; there were too many variations of nerve, strength and skill for that to be a reasonable supposition. Second,

> it is as imprudent to give a man, who has already wronged me, an opportunity of doing me a further injury, as it would to trust with one thousand pounds a person who had already run away with ten.[47]

Third, fighting a duel with a 'worthless man', merely degraded one's own character. Lastly, it was 'imprudent to chastize at the hazard of my life, the abuse, rudeness, or injustice' of any man, no matter who he may be. Hamilton realised that duelling would wither away only when men no longer paid heed to the notions of honour that underpinned it. He was therefore keen to put forward an alternative conception of honour. True honour

> is derived from pious and patriotic actions and is generally the sentence of the wise and the virtuous, pronounced upon the citizen whose conduct squares with the laws, morals and religion of his country.[48]

Duellists should ponder the fact that 'Magnanimity, fidelity, justice, and generosity' have always been considered as the marks of an honourable man. 'There is,' he concluded, 'more honour in withstanding this vile custom than in slaying one hundred adversaries in as many combats.'[49]

Hamilton was, however, sufficiently worldly to realise that, as duelling would not disappear overnight, steps should be taken in the interim to mitigate its effects. To this end he republished as an addendum to his pamphlet the tract *General Rules and Instructions for all Seconds in Duels*, which had originally appeared in England, under the pseudonym of 'A late Captain in the Army', in 1793. This work was predicated on the notion that most of the 'shocking incidents' that took place on duelling grounds were the result of the negligence, ignorance or incompetence of seconds. By republishing it, Hamilton presumably hoped to ensure that seconds were aware of their responsibilities and ready to act to prevent needless bloodshed.

As a practical measure Hamilton then proposed the establishment of an anti-duelling society. Its objects were to include promoting the idea that duelling originated in a false sense of honour and the establishment of an 'honour court' for the redress of injured feelings. It was also to press for legislation to end the practice. Hamilton, as a mark of his earnest intentions, printed at the end of the book a 'Form of Bequest to an Anti-Duelling Association'. Hamilton's ideas were distilled in a pamphlet published in 1825 that was, in effect, an Irish duelling code, aimed at preventing disputes being resolved by violence. The Association for the Suppression of Duelling (to which Philip Crampton spoke in 1830) failed to attract widespread support but was nevertheless indicative of a new, less indulgent, attitude towards duelling.

We have observed the close links between duelling in Ireland and in England, and the parallels in its history in the two countries. Nowhere was this link closer than in its decline and eventual disappearance. Just as in England the tide of public opinion was turning against duelling by the 1830s, so too was it in Ireland. By 1850 duelling had died out in England; so too had it in Ireland. Perhaps in Ireland the horrors of the Great Hunger in the 1840s had a part to play; beside the terrible human suffering of those years, duelling's touchy pride and pompous punctilios would have seemed petty indeed.

Chapter Twelve

PISTOLS, STARS AND STRIPES: DUELLING IN THE UNITED STATES OF AMERICA

The continuance of the practice in England to this day is to be attributed entirely to the predominance of aristocratic influence and power, growing out of the ranks and orders in society … established in that country.'

So spoke Samuel Prentice during a debate in Congress on duelling in 1838. The situation in the republican United States, a 'free' society, was, however, different.

They [the people] will never admit or tolerate the existence of a class of men, privileged to be above the law of the land, acting under a code paramount to the law of the land, and denying and defying both the authority of Government, and the authority of Heaven.[1]

Whether Prentiss was right or wrong in his view of the will of the people, the fact was that, both before and after 1838, duels were common events in the United States. As early as 1780 Janet Montgomery of New York wrote to her cousin Sarah Jay, 'You may judge how fashionable duelling has grown, when we have had five in one week.' *Claypoole's Daily Advertiser* listed, in June 1800, 21 duels fought in the United States in six weeks; these resulted in six men being killed and 11 wounded.[2]

It is one of the curiosities of the history of duelling that an *ancien régime* institution such as duelling should survive, and indeed thrive, in the new, free republic. The Founding Fathers threw off the shackles of British rule, abandoned the forms of monarchy and embraced liberty and constitutionalism, yet duelling, a relic of aristocratic privilege, survived. Not only did the duel survive into the republican era, it became, particularly in the fluid societies of the new territories to the west, democratised. No longer was the duel the preserve of an elite, it had become a passport to social and professional advancement. As one historian of duelling in the American West put it, 'In Missouri, dueling, often stripped of its civility, became a cross avenue of upward mobility.'[3]

There are two other features of the history of duelling in the United States that merit particular attention. The first of these is the importance of distinguishing between the duel, properly defined, and the gunfight. There is a world of difference between the gunslingers' shoot-out beloved of Hollywood and the duellists' rendezvous in the Bois de Boulogne or Phoenix Park. One was impulsive and formless, the other considered and formal. This book contends that duels, wherever and whenever they occurred, had universally recognisable characteristics; that is what made them duels. Particularly in the frontier territories, many of the characters whose deeds figure in the histories of duelling are more akin to brawling ruffians than gentlemen duellists. This vital distinction will inform all discussion of duelling in the American West.

The other feature of American duelling was the geographical divisions that governed its growth and, later, its demise. Very broadly, duelling in America developed in three distinct areas. There was New England and the east, where, as we have seen, the practice took hold in the earliest colonial days but it was here too that the opposition to duelling first flourished. Then there was the Old South, comprising the Southern states of the eastern seaboard, Virginia, the Carolinas and Georgia, along with the territories of the Deep South that passed to the United States as a result of the Louisiana Purchase of 1803. These lands had been French and Spanish colonies and brought their cultures with them into the Union. As we saw in Chapter 8, many a duel was fought in Savannah, Georgia, in colonial days; New Orleans remained a duellists' city late into the nineteenth century. Lastly there were the territories along the frontier that moved gradually west as the nineteenth century progressed. These lands are sometimes referred to as 'The Old South West': they comprise Missouri, Arkansas, Texas, Tennessee and the other territories of the west. In the 1850s California comes into the picture. It is in these frontier territories that the duel and the brawl or assassination become most readily confused.

This chapter will look at the history of the duel in the United States from Independence to its extinction. The Civil War is often taken as a watershed. Lorenzo Sabine, writing in 1859, pronounced that duelling 'as everybody knows, is a relic of the Dark Ages'.

> Yet it is still prevalent to an alarming extent, and simply because warworn veterans who are covered in scars, and judges in robes, and clergymen in surplices, and statesmen who head legislative bodies or preside in cabinet councils, continue to afford it either their example or countenance. Such men form and direct public opinion, and can put an end to duelling at once and for ever.

After the Civil War duels (as distinct from brawls and shoot-outs) do seem to have been rarer. As one historian put it:

> By the latter third of the nineteenth century, the southern, formal duel with its politeness and punctilio had generally given way to the western, improvised duel, better known as the gunfight.[4]

This chapter will also examine the growth of the opposition to duelling and the measures that were taken to eradicate it, as well as the way in which opponents perceived a link between duelling and slavery and the extent to which the abolition of one necessarily resulted in the demise of the other.

The most famous duel in American history was the encounter between Alexander Hamilton and Aaron Burr. The encounter is now so encrusted with myth, folklore and sheer prejudice that it is difficult to know where fact stops and fable starts. Joseph J. Ellis, in his brilliant essay on the subject, entitled simply 'Duel', suggests that the most succinct version of events might go like this:

> On the morning of July 11, 1804, Aaron Burr and Alexander Hamilton were rowed across the Hudson River in separate boats to a secluded spot

near Weehawken, New Jersey. There, in accord with the customs of the code duello, they exchanged pistol shots at ten paces. Hamilton was struck on his right side and died the following day. Though unhurt, Burr found that his reputation suffered an equally fatal wound. In this, the most famous duel in American history, both participants were casualties.[5]

The duel was the result of long-running and entwined political rivalry and personal animus. Hamilton was, after Washington himself, the most important figure in the Federalist party and its moving spirit. Burr had, since 1800, been serving as Thomas Jefferson's Vice-President. The animosity between the two men extended back at least 15 years but had come to a head during the spring and summer of 1804. Eventually, Burr could endure Hamilton's sniping no longer and challenged him to a duel.

So it was that the two men, accompanied by their respective seconds and a surgeon, took up their positions 10 paces apart on the Weehawken ledge above the waters of the Hudson. The actual action of a pistol duel, especially one in which only one shot each is fired, is compressed into a very short space of time. The Burr–Hamilton 'interview' was no different. However, there are wildly differing versions of what happened in the few seconds between the order to fire and Hamilton's falling to the ground. On these differing versions are founded the conflicting myths surrounding the duel. The Hamiltonian version of events has it that Burr fired first and that the impact of his ball caused Hamilton to fire his pistol high and wide. The version preferred by the Burr camp is that Hamilton fired first but, for whatever reason, missed, allowing Burr a second or two to steady himself and fire.

Ellis's compelling analysis of the duel rejects the Hamiltonian version of events, concluding that Hamilton fired first and missed, probably in accordance with his prior determination to fire wide (or not to fire at all). Burr, unaware of Hamilton's decision to waste his shot, merely knew that he had received Hamilton's fire and was therefore, by the etiquette of duelling, fully entitled to fire back at his adversary.[6]

Hamilton died the following afternoon and was buried with full honours two days later. Meanwhile, Burr fled New York in disgrace to escape indictments for murder and for duelling. Whatever the result of the duel, Hamilton won the propaganda battle. As Ellis puts it, the 'overwhelming popular consensus was that Burr had murdered Hamilton in cold blood.'[7] Nor is the verdict of history any different.

The duel between Burr and Hamilton exerts a powerful grip on the American historical imagination. It is a significant event in American history to the extent that no other duel is in the history of any other nation. In the histories of France or Britain, both countries with greater experience of duelling than the United States, there is nothing to compete with Burr–Hamilton for notoriety and historical resonance. In France, perhaps, one might suggest Clemenceau's duel with Paul Deroulede or the comte d'Artois's *bêtise* with the duc de Bourbon. Our best candidate is the Duke of Wellington's duel with Lord Winchelsea. But none can command anything like the same fame as Burr–Hamilton. In July 2004, partly to mark the bicentenary of the duel and partly (and ridiculously) to stage a public reconciliation between the descendants of Burr and Hamilton, the duel was re-enacted.

Douglas Hamilton, a direct descendant of Alexander and an IBM salesman from Ohio, and Antonio Burr, a descendant of one of Burr's cousins, met on the banks of the Hudson River on 11 July. Dressed in period costume and attended by seconds, they exchanged shots – blanks, one supposes – in front of a crowd of more than a thousand spectators. *The Daily Telegraph*'s coverage of the re-enactment graphically illustrates the historical potency of the duel. It comments,

> For months commentators have suggested that politics in America is more bruising than ever. Vice-president Dick Cheney was lectured by liberal critics for his use of the F-word against one of his Democratic opponents in the Senate last month. But historians have used the Hamilton v Burr showdown to put the anger of the 2004 presidential campaign in context.[8]

Mr Cheney was to become the next Vice-President (so far as is known) after Aaron Burr to shoot somebody, albeit in his case accidentally, when he peppered a fellow gun while out shooting in Texas in February 2006.

For the historian of duelling, the Burr–Hamilton encounter is important for two reasons. First, it was a significant watershed in attitudes towards duelling. Second, it was the most prominent example of the American political duel, a phenomenon that disfigured public life in the United States for much of the first half of the nineteenth century. The death of Alexander Hamilton unleashed an unprecedented wave of anti-duelling rhetoric: pamphleteers, clerics, lawyers, even the president of Yale University, joined in the chorus of criticism. As Ellis put it, 'the stigma associated with the Burr–Hamilton duel put the *code duello* on the defensive as a national institution'.[9] One pamphleteer, writing as 'Philanthropos', couched his disapproval of duelling in general and the Weehawken duel in particular in the form of an open letter to Aaron Burr. Unambiguously entitled 'A Letter to Aaron Burr ... on the Barbarous Origin, Criminal Nature and the Baleful Effects of Duels', it was a spirited lecture on the evils of duelling. The duel with Hamilton 'has excited the most painful emotions in the breast of every patriotic citizen, from the northern boundary of Maine to the southern extremity of Georgia'. Burr's fate, he was assured, would be the execration of posterity. 'Have you not done', the pamphleteer asked, 'a most essential, I had almost said irreparable, injury to your country?' Burr was reminded that 'Generations yet unborn will lament the premature demise of the friend of America; and execrate the hand that deprived her of him. The nation sustains the loss; you bear the guilt.'[10]

In September 1804 Timothy Dwight, the President of Yale, preached a thunderous sermon against the evils of duelling. Delivered on the Sunday before the start of the academic year, it was clearly intended to deliver a strong message. Subtitled 'The Folly, Guilt, and Mischiefs of Duelling' it attacked the usual justifications for duelling and poured scorn on the customary notions of honour. Duellists were 'haughty, overbearing, quarrelsome, passionate, and abusive; troublesome neighbours, uncomfortable friends, and disturbers of the common happiness'.[11]

The fact that the sermon was delivered by a figure as eminent as the president of Yale meant that, inevitably, it attracted a good deal of attention. Publication spread its message beyond the confines of Yale to the wider world. Certainly, it is thought to have had a marked effect on anti-duelling opinion in New England. Dwight was just one of the more eminent of the many clerics who denounced duelling from the pulpit. In American, as in Europe, the clergy became one of the staunchest critics of duelling.

Few laymen were more zealously committed to eradicating duelling than General Charles C. Pinkney, a presidential candidate for the Federalists (Hamilton's party) in 1804. Pinkney had himself fought a duel, in which he had been wounded, and had twice served as second, so he spoke from experience. 'Duelling,' he wrote in August 1804, 'is no criterion for bravery. I have seen cowards fight duels, and I am convinced real courage may often be better shown in the refusal than in the acceptance of a challenge.'[12]

While running for the presidency in 1804 he campaigned vigorously for the anti-duelling movement. He was instrumental in requesting all clergymen in his native state of South Carolina to preach against the 'sin and folly of duelling'. He also played a part in asking the state legislature to ban duelling.[13]

A pamphleteer identifying himself only as 'Postumus' wrote a tract in 1805 defending the existing laws in South Carolina against duelling. He estimated that, at that time, three-quarters of all duels fought in the United States arose from political disputes. Like most of the statistics we have come across in the history of duelling, it should probably be taken with a pinch of salt. Nevertheless 'Postumus' was making the point that politics was a significant cause of duels in America, as indeed it was in the Old World. Certainly American legislators, whether at state or federal level, suffered from no inhibitions when it came to defending their honour on the duelling ground. Burr–Hamilton was the pre-eminent American political duel, but there were many others.

A forerunner to the Burr–Hamilton encounter was the duel on 31 July 1802 between John Swartwout and Senator DeWitt Clinton of New York. Swartwout was a loyal supporter of Aaron Burr who accused Clinton, a member of a rival faction of the Republican party, of traducing Burr for his own advantage. Clinton replied in kind, calling Swartwout 'a liar ... a scoundrell and a villain'. The duel, which took place at Hoboken, New Jersey, was remarkable for the belligerent determination of the two principals. They exchanged no fewer than five shots each at a range of 10 paces. The duel was eventually stopped, but not before Swartwout had sustained two leg wounds.[14]

The men who climbed to the very top of America's greasy pole had a mixed record as duellists. George Washington was a proficient fencer but never fought a duel. Abraham Lincoln, by contrast, only narrowly avoided fighting a duel. In 1842 Lincoln, then in his early thirties, was practising at the bar in Illinois and making his way in local politics. That year the State Bank of Illinois collapsed, rendering its banknotes worthless. In the wake of this debacle Lincoln publicly insulted the state auditor, Mr Shields, calling him 'a fool as well as a liar', adding that 'with him truth is out of the question'. Shields, inevitably, wrote to Lincoln demanding a retraction and a full apology, which Lincoln, possibly under the influence of his more hot-headed friends, refused to give. Shields then challenged Lincoln and a rendezvous was arranged. The parties agreed to meet across the Mississippi in Missouri, as duelling was illegal in Illinois. Lincoln, as the challenged party, had chosen broadswords and on 22 September, accompanied by his second, crossed the river to the appointed rendezvous. But, just as the duel was about to begin, friends of the two men stepped in to prevent the fight. Lincoln and Shields were reconciled and, having shaken hands, returned to Illinois. Unlike some duellists, who regarded their fight as a badge of honour, Lincoln in later life was deeply ashamed of his reckless foolishness. He was embarrassed that, as a lawyer and an officer of the court, he had deliberately broken the law. Certainly, the idea of Abraham Lincoln the duellist does not sit easily beside the austere, God-fearing President of the Civil War.[15]

The most famous presidential duellist was Andrew Jackson. 'Old Hickory' fought numerous duels in the earlier stages of his career as a lawyer and soldier. Most accounts credit him with having fought at least 14 by the time he was elected President in 1828, but some writers put the total considerably higher than that. Thomas Hart Benton, who had himself 'killed his man', joked, 'Yes, I had a fight with Jackson, a fellow was hardly in the fashion then who hadn't.'[16]

Jackson's best-known duel was the encounter with Charles Dickinson, a fellow Tennessee lawyer, on 30 May 1806. The challenge arose from remarks that Dickinson had supposedly made that were less than complimentary about Jackson's beloved wife Rachel. Each man, quite contrary to the etiquette of duelling, made clear his wish to kill the other. To evade the authorities in Tennessee, where duelling was illegal, they met across the state border in Logan County, Kentucky.

Eight paces were measured out; the combatants faced each other. At the command, Dickinson fired. His ball hit Jackson in the chest but, steadying himself, Jackson raised his pistol arm and fired, killing Dickinson. The duel has aroused the suspicion in some quarters that Jackson was in some way guilty of cheating. The doubts arise from the fact that Dickinson's shot seems to have hit Jackson squarely in the chest yet he was nevertheless capable of returning his opponent's fire. The duel, despite the fact that it had been much gossiped about in the newspapers beforehand, nevertheless scandalised the good folk of Nashville. In the long term, however, it did Jackson's career no harm. His legal practice was successful enough to win him promotion to the bench. His military career was equally successful: his campaigns against the Indians and, particularly, his victory against the British at the Battle of New Orleans in December 1814, made him a national hero. And, of course, ultimately, he reached the White House.

In the Old South and the newer territories of the south-west, a reputation as a duellist was certainly no bar to political advancement. Indeed, it seems reasonable to suppose, from the lengthy list of state legislators, congressmen, governors and others in important public office, who had fought duels, that it was positively helpful to a man's career to be able to say, 'I have been out.' Henry Foote, governor of Mississippi, fought at least three duels in his native state and one in Alabama; A.T. Mason, one of Virginia's senators and John McCartey, a congressman for the state, killed each other in a duel in 1819. James Jackson, governor of Georgia, killed the state's lieutenant-governor in a duel. Robert Vance, a congressman from North Carolina, was killed by a fellow congressman, S.P. Carson, in 1827.[17] Sam Houston, a successful general and associate of Andrew Jackson, was a veteran duellist. The story goes that when Houston was challenged following the

Battle of Jacinto he marked the challenge as 'no. 14', saying, 'The angry gentleman must wait his turn.'[18]

One of the best-known of American political duels was the encounter between John Randolph of Roanoke and Henry Clay in April 1826. Randolph was a scion of an old and influential Virginian family, while Clay was a leading representative of the new westerners. Both were members of the US Senate, Randolph for Virginia, Clay for Kentucky. The political differences between the two men boiled over in the spring of 1826 over foreign policy. Randolph insulted Clay across the floor of the Senate, in very uncongressional language. The following day Clay sent a challenge to Randolph. The two men met on the right bank of the Potomac, in Virginian territory; pistols at 10 paces were the agreed conditions. Both missed at the first exchange of shots but Clay pronounced himself not satisfied. His second shot passed through Randolph's long white dressing gown, very close to his hip. Randolph then fired into the air and the two men were formally reconciled.[19]

David B. Mitchell was another man, in his case a Georgian, who killed his man in a duel yet nevertheless rose to high political office. Mitchell had finished a term as mayor of Savannah when he fought a duel with James Hunter, a former business partner. They met in the Jewish cemetery, which was outside the city limits, on 23 August 1802. It was agreed that they would fight with pistols, starting at 10 paces, moving in two paces after each shot. Mitchell's first shot missed but Hunter's scored a glancing hit. Mitchell's second shot, fired at six paces (each man having advanced two paces) killed Hunter. Mitchell subsequently rose to command Georgia's militia as well as serving two terms as the state's governor.

Andrew Steinmetz, the nineteenth-century chronicler of duelling, had a low opinion of the standards among New World duellists. 'There is,' he noted disapprovingly, 'no objection to fowling-pieces, to rifles, to bowie-knives; the last are ever ready.' The Americans, it seemed to Steinmetz, were insufficiently in thrall to the restrained, gentlemanly decorum that governed (for the most part) European duelling. 'In the hotels at Washington and elsewhere, you may see the marks of bullets on the walls, shots that missed.'[20]

Steinmetz would certainly have disapproved of the duel fought in
New Orleans between Hippolyte Trouett and Paulin Prue in June
1840. The conditions left little hope of either man escaping unscathed:
they were to stand back to back, with a pistol in either hand, before
stepping out five paces each, turning and firing. If they both survived,
they would both fire again with the second pistol. M. Crozat, the local
registrar of births and deaths, was Trouett's second. They both missed
with the first shot but, as they were transferring their second pistols to
their right hands, Prue's accidentally went off. This counted as firing,
so Trouett now had a free shot. Prue theatrically bared his chest and
called upon Trouett to fire. Despite the protests of some of the
onlookers, the seconds allowed the shot; Prue was killed. Trouett was
tried for Prue's murder but acquitted.[21]

For all Steinmetz's reservations about the willingness of American
duellists to adhere to the etiquette, it is probably the case that in the
Old South, where duelling was an established part of upper-class life,
it was strictly observed. One historian of the Old South has written,
'From sons' early childhood, fathers prepared their boys to observe
the rules by which honor was upheld, as a mark of status and a claim
to leadership.'[22]

In the old Southern society, where the planters ruled the roost,
status and reputation were of pre-eminent importance. It was an ex-
governor of South Carolina, John Lyde Wilson, who drew up the
American code of honour in 1838. In the newer territories to the West
duelling was a looser affair, less governed by the etiquettes. In these
newer, more rough-and-ready societies, the settlers eagerly embraced
the duel. As we have seen, in these younger societies, the duel was a
significant indicator of status. The *Missouri Intelligencer* observed in
1821 that the duel was 'the cheapest and smallest capital upon which a
man can possibly become a modern gentleman'.[23] Lawyers, politicians
and newspaper editors were the keenest to resort to their duelling
pistols in defence of their honour.

Dick Steward's study of duelling in Missouri gives a wonderful
insight into the mentality of the early frontier duellist. Missouri
passed to the United States by the Louisiana Purchase of 1803. According to Steward duelling was virtually unknown in Missouri before

1803 – despite its being a French colony – but spread rapidly after the transfer of the territory to the United States. The first duel in 'American' Missouri was fought in 1807 between William Ogle and Joseph McFerran. The dispute arose from Ogle's behaviour towards McFerran's wife. When they met on Cypress Island in the Mississippi, Ogle was killed at the second fire. Although McFerran was not arrested he felt obliged to resign as a clerk of the court of common pleas. He was, however, speedily reinstated; thereafter his career prospered. In the following year one Richard Davis was bailed for $500 for issuing a challenge.

There were two duels that illustrated the high social status of duelling in the new territories. In 1811 Thomas T. Crittenden, the Attorney-General of Louisiana, fought Dr Walter Fenwick, a prosperous doctor. Crittenden's second was John Scott, the territorial delegate to the US and, later, Missouri's first congressman. Fenwick's second was a local sheriff who was to serve as a general in the war of 1812 and who went on to represent Wisconsin in the US Senate. Fenwick was killed in the first exchange of shots.

Five years later the duel between Henry S. Geyer and Captain George H. Kennerley confirmed the link between duelling and political success. Both men had served in the war of 1812 and had become prominent citizens of St Louis, Geyer as a lawyer and Kennerley as a merchant. In the duel itself, Kennerley was wounded in the leg but recovered. Geyer, after the duel, enjoyed a most successful political career. In 1822, he was elected to the House of Representatives of Missouri, later serving as its speaker. He was also elected to the US Senate and offered a Cabinet post by President Fillmore. In Geyer's case (as in many others) the fact that he had fought a duel was no bar to political advancement.[24]

But perhaps the best-known duel in Missouri's history was the encounter between Thomas Hart Benton and Charles Lucas in 1817. It was in fact two duels. Lucas, having been wounded by Benton in the first encounter, squared up to his opponent again six weeks later but was, tragically, killed. The duel epitomises the duelling culture of the new territories to the west of the United States and speaks volumes for the societies that were then coming into being there. The duel illustrates the tensions between the new men, those who arrived in the wake of the transfer of sovereignty in 1803, and those who represented the old colonial elite. It also illustrates perfectly the importance of the duel as a measurement of specific social gravity. It defined, or helped to define, a man's status. Both men were lawyers; indeed, the conflict between them was a dispute over a point of evidence in a court action. But there the similarities ended. Benton had arrived in Missouri in about 1814 after a troubled upbringing further east, in the course of which he had been sent down from university for stealing money. He had fallen out with Andrew Jackson in Tennessee before taking his chance in Missouri. Once established in St Louis, he soon prospered, due to his capacity for hard work and his assiduous cultivation of influential people.

Charles Lucas was, in contrast to Benton, the son of an establishment figure in Missouri. Lucas Sr, a scion of an old French family, had arrived in the United States in 1784 and had been appointed to a senior judicial post in Missouri after 1803. Charles had remained in the east to complete his education; he arrived in St Louis at about the same time as Benton. Despite a patrician distaste, shared by his father, for the rough, uncultivated ways of the new breed of opportunist lawyer that thronged the St Louis bar, Lucas Jr threw himself into his legal practice and soon prospered. He also began to get involved in local politics. The scene was set for the confrontation between Benton and Lucas. The charge for the explosion was a powerful combination of sectarian, political, social and professional rivalries.

The spark that caused the charge to ignite was a dispute in court during a trial in October 1816 in which Lucas and Benton were representing the contending parties. The dispute arose over a point of evidence but the narrow legal point was soon left behind as the argument developed into mutual accusations of bad faith. The fact that Lucas won the case for his client merely further inflamed Benton; Lucas had effectively accused him of lying and now the jury's verdict seemed to confirm this slight. He decided therefore to send a challenge to Lucas, which the latter promptly declined. In doing so, Lucas maintained that he had merely done his duty by his client and that the jury had found for him; he should not be called to account for his conduct of a case in court. However, the most slighting aspect of Lucas's refusal to fight Benton was the implication that he was not obliged to do so, as he considered Benton beneath him. To the aspiring lawyer keen to make his mark in St Louis, this was almost intolerable; it was all the more insulting in that it came from a well-connected member of the established elite.

The two men were now set on a collision course. In August 1817, during the course of territorial elections, Lucas questioned Benton's qualification to vote – the ownership of property – and Benton responded by referring to Lucas as a 'puppy'. Lucas had little alternative but to seek redress for so public an insult, so duly issued a challenge. The two men met on 12 August 1817 and, at the first fire, Lucas was hit in the neck, potentially a very dangerous wound. Benton was, with some reluctance, dissuaded from continuing the duel, on the understanding that it would be resumed when Lucas had recovered, if he did. Benton's insistence on a second meeting was a breach of the duelling code: as the man who had offered the insult, it was his duty provide the offended party satisfaction. Benton, it seemed, was more interested in revenge.

On 23 September Benton renewed his challenge; Lucas, who had by now recovered from his injury, decided to fight, having tried to put a peaceful end to the feud. The parties met on Bloody Island in the Mississippi off St Louis, four days later. The distance had been fixed at 10 feet. Accounts of the event blame the seconds for failing to make proper efforts to prevent the duel. They also allege that an unclear signal was given. Whatever the irregularities, the result was all too decisive: Lucas was hit by Benton's first shot and, shortly afterwards, died.[25]

If lawyers practising in the new American West were enthusiastic duellists, so too were a rather more traditional cadre, naval officers. The United States Navy was a small but efficient and skilful force which earned its spurs in the war of 1812. In that war, pitted against the overwhelming power of the British Navy, which, on top of its proud traditions, had been fighting for the best part of 20 years, it acquitted itself with honour. The naval element of the war of 1812 consisted principally of a series of single-ship engagements: the

United States and the *Macedonian*, the *Constitution* and the *Guerriere*, the *Constitution* and the *Java*, the *Hornet* and the *Peacock*, and the *Chesapeake* and the *Shannon*, to name but some of them. In many of these the Americans triumphed, their superior seamanship and, in some cases, handier and more heavily armed ships proving decisive. The single-ship actions had a notably duel-like quality to them: the two adversaries manoeuvring expectantly, waiting for some advantage to accrue, searching for weaknesses in the enemy, before striking.

In the case of the engagement between the *Chesapeake* and the *Shannon*, the parallel was made explicit. Captain Broke of the *Shannon* commanded the two British frigates blockading Boston in May 1813. Cooped up in Boston harbour was the American frigate *Chesapeake*, the command of Captain Lawrence. Broke was eager to provoke Lawrence into sallying forth to fight and to this end sent him a letter challenging his ship to a duel. According to the American naval historian A.T. Mahan, although the letter was a model of courtesy, 'the courtesy was that of the French duellist, nervously anxious lest he should misplace an accent in the name of the man whom he intended to force into fight [*sic*], and to kill'.[26]

We now know that Lawrence never read this letter but, nevertheless, he did leave the safety of Boston harbour.[27] On 1 June Lawrence sailed out of Boston to engage with Broke in the *Shannon*. After a brief but fierce fight lasting 11 or 12 minutes, the *Chesapeake* was boarded and taken as a prize back to Halifax. It was a conspicuous triumph for the Royal Navy, for the *Shannon*, for her company and for Broke.[28]

Nor was the challenge sent by Broke to Lawrence unique. In the course of the war of 1812 it had become common practice. The American historian Henry Adams, writing in the late nineteenth century, explained the 'habit adopted by both navies in 1813 of challenging ship duels'.

> War took an unusual character when officers like Hardy and Broke countenanced such a practice, discussing and arranging duels between matched ships, on terms which implied that England admitted half a dozen American frigates to be equal in value to the whole British Navy.[29]

The point, of course, was that the British had much less to lose than the Americans. As Adams pointed out, 'The first duty of a British officer was to take risks; the first duty of an American officer was to avoid them.'[30] The loss of a frigate to the British government was of little consequence when it had more than a hundred of them at sea (and any number of other, larger men-of-war) but to the American government the loss of the *Chesapeake* was the equivalent of destroying a quarter of their navy.

The duel-like quality of the single-ship actions was mirrored by the deadly gusto with which the US Navy's officers had recourse to duelling. Commodore Stephen Decatur was perhaps the most prominent officer in the service. He had distinguished himself as a young officer in the war against Tripoli, but it was by his victory as captain of the *United States* over the *Macedonian* in October 1812 that he sprang to public notice. According to C.S. Forester, Decatur had a reputation in the service as a 'fiery-tempered man'; certainly his career had been punctuated with quarrels and fights and, in the end, he perished in a duel.[31]

Decatur's duel with a fellow naval officer, James Barron, fought in 1820, had its roots in the incident in June 1807 in which the British frigate *Leopard* had fired upon and then boarded the American frigate *Chesapeake*. The British ship was exercising its claimed right to search American vessels for British deserters. Although the two nations were not then at war, the British opened fire on the *Chesapeake*, inflicting some casualties and damaging her. Barron, deciding no doubt that discretion was the better part of valour, struck his colours and allowed the British to come aboard. Barron was subsequently censured by a court martial and suspended from duty for five years for failing to offer proper resistance to the British. He was absent from America throughout the war of 1812. Returning home in 1818, he applied to be reinstated in the navy; this application was refused on the grounds that he had failed to fight for his country in her time of peril. Decatur, whose service record was beyond reproach, had sat on the court martial that had suspended Barron, and, as a naval commissioner, had opposed his re-employment in 1818.

In the early summer of 1819 Barron began a long correspondence with Decatur, claiming in one letter that 'you have hunted me out;

have persecuted me with all the power and influence of your office, and have declared your determination to drive me from the navy.' Eventually, Barron's frustrations resolved themselves into a challenge. Decatur received it with admirable *sang-froid*. He wrote,

> I should regret the necessity of fighting with any man but, in my opinion, the man who makes arms his profession is not at liberty to decline an invitation from any person who is not so far degraded as to be beneath his notice.

Decatur chose to meet Barron at Bladensburg, near Washington, where he lived. His choice was actuated by 'the inconvenience of a man's lying wounded at a distance from his own house'. On the morning of 22 March 1820 Barron and Decatur met on the duelling ground at Bladensburg. An eyewitness recorded that

> both fired, so nearly together that but one report was heard ... both fell nearly at the same instant ... both ... appeared to think themselves mortally wounded. Commodore Barron told Commodore Decatur that he forgave him from the bottom of his heart.
>
> Decatur was carried home and by evening he was dead. *The National Intelligencer* announced Decatur's death with the words 'Mourn, Columbia! for one of thy brightest stars is set.' [32]

Two years earlier Decatur had acted as second in a duel for another naval hero of the war of 1812, Oliver Hazard Perry. Perry had secured his place in the pantheon of American naval heroes by decisively defeating the British in the Battle of Lake Erie in September 1813. Perry's duel against the marine officer John Heath arose from an incident on board the *Java* while she was cruising in the Mediterranean in 1816. Perry, who commanded the *Java*, accused Heath of dereliction of duty and subsequently hit him. Both were tried and reprimanded by a court martial but returned to duty. However, the matter did not rest there, for, on their return to the United States, the affair attracted a good deal of publicity. As a result of this Heath challenged Perry and a duel was arranged. At noon on 19 October 1818 the two men, accompanied by their seconds – in Perry's case Decatur – met at, or near, the Weehawken duelling ground where Burr and Hamilton had fought in

1804. Heath and Perry stood back to back before walking away from each other and turning. Heath fired but missed, whereupon Perry, in accordance with his determination to receive Heath's fire but not to return it, fired harmlessly into the air.[33]

Another duel involving a naval officer was reported in *The Times* of 29 April 1829. Three weeks earlier Charles E. Hawkins, an officer serving in the Mexican Navy, had challenged William M'Rae, US Attorney for the Southern Judicial District of Florida. As one might expect of a duel fought between representatives of two of the most belligerent of American professions, lawyers and naval officers, Hawkins and M'Rae gave no quarter. They exchanged four shots each; Hawkins's first shot passed through M'Rae's coat and the second through his breeches, close to the waistband, bruising him. Hawkins's third shot holed M'Rae's hat. M'Rae had so far enjoyed more than a slice of good fortune but had failed to hit his opponent in three attempts. M'Rae could not be faulted for lack of courage but, at the fourth shot, his luck ran out: Hawkins's ball hit him in the thigh and lodged there, whereupon, honour satisfied, the fight was stopped.[34]

Duelling was widespread in the American Navy until the middle of the nineteenth century. The belligerence of its officers was well illustrated by the series of duels fought with British officers at Gibraltar in 1819. However, by the middle of the century, duelling in America was in decline, a development that was reflected in the navy. The naval regulations of 1865 contained a provision that 'no disgrace can attach to any one for refusing a challenge, as such a course would be in obedience to law'.[35]

Nor was duelling confined to the navy: as in most other countries officers serving in the army were enthusiastic duellists. General Sam Huston was a veteran duellist. General Smyth, who commanded the American forces in the disastrous campaign on the Niagara in the autumn of 1812, was an Irishman by birth and a Virginian by adoption. After the collapse of his plan, his 'grotesque campaign', his army melted away. A few days later a subordinate officer, Peter B. Porter, published a letter in a Buffalo newspaper attributing the fiasco 'to the cowardice of General Smyth'. Smyth, naturally, sent Porter a challenge and the two men exchanged shots.[36] The United States never maintained, at this period, a substantial standing army but there were local militias in most states, which helped to inculcate some elements of the civilian population with the military ethos. This was particularly so in the South, where the possession of a military rank was seen as a mark of distinction.

It was two Southerners who fought one of the most notorious duels of the Civil War period. John S. Marmaduke and Lucien Marsh Walker were both Confederate generals serving under General Sterling Price. The contretemps arose from a suggestion that Walker had behaved in a cowardly fashion during an engagement near Helena. When Walker's second sought clarification of the remark, Marmaduke sent him a note detailing the 'more than scrupulous care with which General Walker avoided all positions of danger' during the battle. On receipt of this note, Walker inevitably sent Marmaduke a challenge. They agreed to meet at the Le Fevre Plantation in Arkansas, with Colt Navy revolvers, which had six shots, at 15 paces, severe conditions that made it highly likely that one, or even both, of the two would be killed.

Despite the best efforts of General Price to prevent the duel, it went ahead on 6 September 1863. Marmaduke was short-sighted, so it was possible that he requested the punitively short distance to compensate for this disability. In the event, it made little difference: both men missed with the first shot but at the second Walker was hit and fell to the ground. The bullet had entered his abdomen, passed through one of his kidneys and lodged in his spine, paralysing him. He died a day or so later. Marmaduke and his second were arrested by General Price on their return from the duel but no charges were brought against him and he soon resumed his command. Nor did the duel affect his political career after the Civil War. In 1884 he was elected governor of Missouri, an office he filled until his death three years later.[37]

In the antebellum Old South, duelling was, as it always universally had been, a question of social status. To duel or to thrash? That was the question. At the top of the pecking order were the planters, who enjoyed an unquestioned right to defend their honour with pistols or swords. However, there were subtle but important gradations within the wider groupings. As one historian of duelling in the Old South put it:

Planters were gentlemen – the very embodiment of the class – but mere ownership of land did not make one a planter. Some insisted that title was earned by the ownership of at least twenty slaves – twenty slaves, a planter, fewer than twenty, a farmer ... A planter had both the tangible qualities of possession and the intangible ones of courtly manners and a precise understanding of what was a gentleman's province and what was not.[38]

This passage is also interesting because it makes explicit the connection between duelling and slavery, a link the reformers perceived clearly. As well as planters, soldiers and lawyers were considered worthy of fighting duels; newspaper editors were another category of men who were often called to account for their actions, in their case what they published in their columns. Their social status, however, was more doubtful than that of the planters. This did not prevent them fighting a large number of duels.

Jack K. Williams in his *Dueling in the Old South* says that at least 11 editors from the state of Mississippi took part in a duel, three of whom were killed. Six editors from newspapers in South Carolina and the same number from Virginia fought a duel; two from each state died of wounds received. O.J. Wise, the editor of the *Richmond Enquirer*, fought at least eight duels, although he never hit an opponent nor was himself wounded. The staff of the Vicksburg newspaper, the *Sentinel*, had a particularly unfortunate record on the duelling ground. Dr James Hagan, its editor until 1843, was a pugnacious man to whom fighting was clearly second nature. He was involved in a number of fights and duels before being killed by the son of a judge he had traduced. An extraordinary number of the paper's editors and journalists were killed or wounded in duels or fights in the years before the Civil War.[39] Clearly, the editor's chair at the *Sentinel* was a dangerously exposed place.

Duels in the United States were as subject to eccentric variations as anywhere else. The Germans recognised a form of encounter that they knew as the 'American duel'. This entailed the parties drawing lots, whereupon the loser would shoot himself. As far as is known, this gruesome variant of the duel had nothing to do with the United

States, so how it acquired its name is a mystery. A Colonel Richard Graves, a member of the legislature of Virginia, challenged one Archibald Lacey to a duel in 1823 to be conducted in a most unusual manner.

> [T]hat cups should be filled, the one with pure water and the other with deadly poison, and set on a table covered with a cloth; that two tickets should be rolled up and put into a hat, the one blank, the other marked 'P'; that he who drew the blank should take his choice of the two cups, and swallow its contents, and he who drew the letter 'P' should be bound, at peril of his life and honour, to swallow the contents of the other cup.[40]

The Teutonic 'American' duel and the method preferred by the aptly named Colonel Graves are more akin to glorified suicide pacts than duels of honour. In 1828 there was a curious incident when a Major George W. Collammer shot an apple from the bare head of a Henry Ingram with a rifle at a range of 27 yards. Collammer then took his turn with the apple and Ingram returned the compliment. The report says that there were some spectators who tried, in vain, to put a stop to this idiocy. It concluded by informing its readers that the apples 'were so handsomely cut by the ball, that the juice and pomace remained in considerable quantities on the hair of their heads'.[41] This potentially lethal exhibition of marksmanship took place on St Valentine's Day. Whether some romantic impulse or a desire to re-enact the story of William Tell in a modern setting accounted for the mindless bravado of the two participants, one can only speculate.

A more conventional duel, albeit one with a tragic outcome, was that fought between two medical men in Philadelphia in July 1830. Dr Smith had challenged Dr Jefferies; they agreed to exchange shots at 'only eight paces'. At the first fire both men missed but the seconds failed to reconcile the parties. A contemporary report takes up the story.

> Dr Jefferies declared that he would not leave the ground, till he had lost his own life, or taken that of his antagonist. Their pistols were handed to them a second time, and at this fire the right arm of Dr Smith was broken, which stopped proceedings for a few moments, till he recovered from the exhaustion, when he declared, that, as he was wounded, he was

ready to die, and requested the seconds to proceed. The pistols were put into their hands a third time, Dr Smith using his left hand. At this fire Dr Jefferies was wounded in the thigh, and his loss of blood occasioned an exhaustion, which again delayed the conflict for a few moments. He recovered, and both desired to shorten the distance. They now stood up for a fourth time, covered with blood, and at a distance of six feet. They were to fire between the one and five, and the shot proved fatal to both parties – they fell to the earth. Dr Smith was dead when he dropped, the ball having penetrated his heart; Dr Jefferies was shot through the breast, and survived but four hours.[42]

This was the type of encounter that raised the hackles of those opposed to duelling. The Burr–Hamilton duel gave rise to a spate of sermons and pamphlets railing against the practice. By 1804, when Burr and Hamilton fought, duelling was in fact illegal in many states of the Union; indeed, the pair had crossed the Hudson River to fight in New Jersey, thus escaping the strict anti-duelling laws in New York. Similarly, duellists all over the Union simply went to a neighbouring state to fight. In 1800 it was reported that, by virtue of the 'lately-revised' laws of Rhode Island, anyone who fights a duel,

> although death doth not ensue thereby, is to be carried publickly, in a cart, to the gallows, with a rope around his neck, and set thereon for one hour, and to be imprisoned for a term not exceeding one year.

It was further provided that anyone sending or receiving a challenge was to be fined $500 and imprisoned for six months.[43]

In 1803 North Carolina passed a law disqualifying anyone who fought a duel from holding public office, civil or military, in the state. Anyone who killed another in a duel would be liable to conviction for a felony.[44] By contrast, the attitude of legislators in Washington was more tolerant. In 1802 Mr Grey, of Virginia, introduced a motion in the House of Representatives that a committee be appointed to consider the case for passing a federal law disqualifying from public office anyone who fought a duel or issued a challenge. The House refused to consider the matter.[45] Four years later a law was passed that attempted to control duelling in the army: any officer sending a challenge, or accepting one, would be cashiered.[46] In the newer states of the South, the anti-duelling laws came later. Louisiana enacted its anti-duelling law in 1818, Alabama and Mississippi in the 1830s.[47] In 1835 Missouri declared duelling to be a felony, regardless of whether anyone was or was not killed.[48] Kentucky passed a 'strongly worded' regulation in 1850.[49]

Nearly 25 years after North Carolina had enacted its law aimed at eradicating duelling, *The Times* carried an excerpt from a Raleigh newspaper of two duels fought in the state. One was political in origin, the other had arisen at the card tables. The report ended by wondering, 'How long will the citizens of this free and Christian country countenance this barbarous practice of settling disputes, for the most part of a trifling nature?'

This was a pertinent question. How long indeed would duelling continue to flourish? There were laws against it most states of the Union, as well as provisions contained in state constitutions that should have been sufficient to discourage if not to eradicate the practice. Yet they were widely ignored and flouted. Moreover since 1804 there had been significant and vocal opposition to duelling, orchestrated by the clergy and other, lay reformers.

Dr Lyman Beecher was a pupil of Timothy Dwight, the President of Yale (and, coincidentally, a cousin of Aaron Burr), who had so roundly condemned duelling in 1804. Beecher himself preached a sermon two years later inveighing against duelling; in it he floated the idea that no one should vote for any man as a candidate for public office who had been involved in a duel in any capacity. This was a proposal aimed at cutting the link between politics and duelling. Beecher's sermon was published and achieved a wide currency among the anti-duelling lobby.

More than 30 years after Beecher preached his sermon, it was republished by one of his former parishioners. However, it was not a straightforward reproduction of the original text: in an interesting exercise in intellectual cross-fertilisation, Beecher's anti-duelling arguments were applied to the anti-slavery cause. This was done by the simple expedient of replacing all references to 'duelling' and its correlatives with 'slavery' and its correlatives. The editor was provoked into making this transposition by hearing Dr Beecher's successor proposing a toast to a notorious duellist as a suitable candidate for the

Presidency. Duelling, the editor fumed, 'is one of the LEGITIMATE FRUITS and APPENDAGES of slavery. These two crimes … stand connected with each other as cause and effect; and both alike are the "peculiar institutions" of the south.'[50]

But there was more to it than that: 'Once the obligations of the so-called "code of honour" … were recognised at the north; but they were thrown off when slavery disappeared from among us.' Fearful, perhaps, that his readers might have missed the point, the editor asks, rhetorically, whether anyone can doubt 'if the south had abolished slavery, duelling would have ceased'.[51] The perceived link between slavery and duelling is important and may help to explain why duelling seems to have become much less common after the end of the Civil War, a conflict fought, in large part, over the slavery question. Slavery and duelling were long-established and deeply cherished customs of the upper classes in the Old South. The defeat of the Confederacy in the Civil War spelt the end of slavery but also of duelling; they were indissolubly linked and stood or fell together.

In 1811 the Revd. Frederick Beasley delivered another lengthy sermon on duelling (the published transcript is 40 pages long) in Christ Church, Baltimore. Although it is difficult to quantify the practical effects of such preaching, the duel between two congressmen, Mr Cilley of Maine and Mr Graves of Kentucky, in November 1838, did constitute a significant moment in the history of the opposition to duelling in America. The duel was fought in Washington, DC, with rifles at 80 yards. The two men exchanged three shots harmlessly but at the fourth Cilley was killed. Cilley's funeral was attended by 600 people and no fewer than 125 carriages were counted. The seconds published the customary notice in the press announcing that the duel had been 'regulated by magnanimous principles and the laws of humility', which did little to quieten the howls of indignation that the duel caused.[52] Cilley's death in his duel with Graves had two results. The first was that Congress passed a law to 'prohibit the giving or accepting, within the District of Columbia, a challenge to fight a duel'. It reached the statute book in February 1839.[53]

The second consequence of the duel was the new lease of life it gave to the anti-duelling lobby. In 1838 and over the next few years, there seems to have been (although, clearly, this is hard if not impossible to quantify) a perceptible increase in the vociferousness of the anti-duellists. In April 1838 M.A.H. Niles, the priest at the First Church in Marblehead, Massachusetts, preached against duelling. It would appear to have been prompted by Cilley's death (he was from Maine).

> How broad and foul the blot that stains even the escutcheon of our loved New-England! A New-England man has fallen in a duel! A son of pilgrims, sent to the national council to frame equitable laws and watch over their impartial execution, has proved false to his trust ...[54]

Niles's sense of outrage is palpable. It was not just that Cilley was a New Englander, a descendant of the Pilgrim Fathers, but a congressman to boot. He was supposed to be setting an example.

Six years after Cilley and Graves had fought their ill-starred duel, the Revd. W.W. Patton joined the long line of anti-duelling preachers. On 4 April 1844 he delivered a lengthy and impassioned sermon in Boston, which both criticised the practice and suggested ways in which it could be eradicated. According to Patton, duelling was still, in 1844, a serious problem:

> This great crime ... exists in our land with almost undiminished power. The number of the victims who have fallen before its cruel and revengeful spirit is increasing every year. The depraving, hardening, crime-producing influence which emanates from it is still corrupting the community.

Yet, despite this obvious and flagrant breach of law and scripture, the public conscience had not, apparently, been stirred: 'They [the duellists] take their seats, unblushingly and unrebuked, in the legislatures and in congress, by the side of peaceful and upright men.'

Patton, having asked rhetorically what should be done about the problem, then set about proposing solutions. The press should speak the truth about duelling; the clergy should be even more forthright in their criticism of the practice. The law must treat duellists as common murderers; any leniency shown to duellists was wholly unacceptable. But the pastor regarded non-voting as the most effective measure against duelling. Acknowledging that the idea was borrowed from

Dr Beecher, he proposed that no man should ever vote for public office anyone who had ever been involved in a duel. Patton adduced several reasons for this, including the notion that 'Each vote for the duellist is a vote for duelling.' Moreover, 'the election of a duellist is the election of a murderer; and it proclaims, in the most forcible manner, that crime is no bar to political advancement.'[55]

Not voting for duellists would strongly transmit the message that society at large did not approve of duelling and, in the end, would result in duellists being driven from public life. Interestingly, the non-voting sanction was not deployed by the anti-duelling campaigners in Britain during the same period, despite the fact that duelling was widespread among Members of Parliament. Perhaps the wider and freer franchise in the United States made it a more effective remedy or perhaps the greater range of elective public office there made it a more potent threat to ambitious duellists.

However, for all the moral outrage of the anti-duelling lobby, Lorenzo Sabine, an American chronicler of duelling, felt justified in complaining as late as 1859 that

> The number and fatality of hostile meetings in the United States are to be deplored ... [they] are disreputable to us as a people, and ... may cause us to hang our heads in utter shame. If the custom were confined to the new States, we might find some reason to hope that, in the rapid changes in American society, the evil would soon diminish, and in the end disappear; but Arkansas and California, unfortunately, are not alone.[56]

One of the reasons why duelling was still so widespread in 1859 was the age-old problem of the failure to enforce the law. By the middle of the century many, if not most, states had enacted legislation criminalising the practice; the difficulty was that the law was not enforced with sufficient rigour. This problem had beset kings and governments throughout Europe since the sixteenth century; now it confounded republican America's attempts to eradicate duelling. Jack K. Williams gives as an example of this the ease with which men evaded taking the oath designed to exclude duellists. In many states such an oath was required of anyone taking public office, yet in practice it was often waived. The 1841 Alabama General Assembly exempted 13 citizens from taking the oath and, in 1848, a further five. In 1838 Henry Foote was permitted by special resolution of the Mississippi legislature to decline to swear the oath. In 1846 William L. Yancey was granted exemption from the oath by the Alabama legislature. This attitude also permeated down to the courts, where, as Williams put it, 'Judges generally were reluctant to sustain laws that, they believed, might seriously infringe the personal liberty of gentlemen.'[57]

Enforcement of the laws against duelling was every bit as a slack in the New World as it was in the Old. According to Dick Steward, one William Bennett was the only man ever executed in the United States for duelling. At Belleville, Illinois, in February 1819, Bennett had called out a local lawyer, Alonzo Stuart, following an argument. The seconds had agreed with Stuart that the guns would be loaded with powder but no shot, but Bennett uncovered the deception and someone, whether Bennett himself or one of the seconds, loaded his gun properly. Thus equipped, at the order to fire Bennett coolly shot Stuart through the heart, killing him. Bennett and his seconds were represented at their trial for murder by Thomas Hart Benton, a man who certainly knew all about duelling. Benton persuaded the jury to acquit the seconds but even his advocacy failed to exculpate Bennett, who was convicted of murder and hanged.[58] The fact that only one duellist in the whole history of the United States has been executed is a remarkable testament to the indulgent attitudes that prevailed towards the practice.

✶　✶　✶

The American Civil War, which broke out in 1861, was a bloody cataclysm, a communal bloodletting from which emerged the nation that was to dominate the twentieth century as Britain had dominated the nineteenth. The great questions of freedom and morality that underlay the Civil War had been gathering form and mass for decades by 1860. The central issue was slavery and it was here that the conflicts of the Civil War were prefigured on the duelling grounds. The most famous of the 'shadow' Civil War duels, certainly on account of the prominence of its principals, was the encounter between David C.

Broderick and David S. Terry. Broderick was one of the US Senators for the recently admitted state of California, while Terry has served as the Chief Justice of the state's Supreme Court. The immediate cause of the dispute was a speech in which Terry called Broderick an arch-traitor but the underlying reason for the antipathy between the two men was their differences over the vital question of slavery. Terry was a proponent of slavery, Broderick an ardent abolitionist.

The duel took place at San Francisco on 13 September 1859. The encounter was conducted with exemplary correctness; there could have been no possibility of blaming the outcome on any unfairness. Broderick, who had a reputation as an accomplished shot, fired first, fractionally, at the command. He had, perhaps unfamiliar with the weapon he was using, fired into the ground short of his opponent. A moment later Terry fired, hitting Broderick in the chest. The senator, clearly wounded, collapsed slowly to the ground. He was taken to a friend's house, where he lingered in agony for three days. He died on 16 September. 'They have killed me,' Broderick is reported to have said on his death bed, 'because I was opposed to slavery and a corrupt administration.'[59]

The Civil War is the watershed in American history; it is not for nothing that Americans refer to the first half of the nineteenth century as the antebellum era. The war brought the South to its knees economically and militarily. The calamity of the Confederacy's defeat and the process of reconstruction that followed it changed the Old South for ever. The abolition of slavery was the most obvious result, but the Civil War also sounded the death knell for duelling. The planter-dominated society of the Old South was more agricultural and more conservative than the states lying to the north of the Mason–Dixon Line. This helped to ensure that, during the ante-bellum era, duelling remained in rude health in the south even while it withered in the north. But the defeat of the Confederacy was also the defeat of the Old South and duelling was one of the casualties. As Jack K. Williams put it:

> Whatever changes were being made were expedited by the war, and in the
> bitterness of defeat Southern men shook free of such symbolic customs

as the duel. After 1865 duels were as rare as they had previously been numerous ... social status no longer served as an excuse for breach of the law.[60]

The last fatal duel fought in Savannah, previously a hotbed of duellists, took place in 1870. Ludlow Cohen was killed by Dick Allen as a result of a duel fought over the respective racing merits of their boats.[61] Seven years later the city witnessed its last duel, which was little more than a harmless charade.[62] In 1880 Colonel Cash, of South Carolina, killed William Shannon in a duel; Cash was tried for murder and, although acquitted on a technicality, was widely branded a murderer and, we are told, spent much of the rest of his life attempting to defend his action. Three years later, Richard Bierne and William Eden fought a duel in Virginia in which Eden was wounded. Bierne was forced to flee from the state to avoid arrest. Dick Steward tells us that by the 1880s the conventional duel (as opposed to the gunfight) in Missouri was dead. And so, it seems, it was all over the Union.

The Civil War may have attacked the social basis of the duel in the Old South but its appalling carnage was every bit as responsible for consigning duelling to history. As World War One was to prove the final curtain for serious duelling in Europe, so the Civil War did in the United States. Any man who had endured and survived the fratricidal slaughter of the Civil War had little need to prove his bravery. Indeed, to men who had witnessed the horrors of a prolonged and bloody civil war, duelling must have seemed a pointless, futile irrelevance.

That the Civil War put a stop to duelling in the United States is undeniably the case. However, the demise of duelling did not usher in a new era of peace and concord among all men in the United States. Indeed, particularly in the newer territories on the western frontiers of the Union, the reverse was the case. Here, the formal duel was supplanted by the gunfight, the cowboys' shoot-out. This was a different beast altogether: in the duel proper, the code of honour was all-important, but, in the gunfighters' skirmish, might was right and speed was king. Honour and reputation were of no consequence; all that mattered was who had the faster gun.

The two forms of man-to-man combat are quite distinct and should not be confused. The gunslingers' shoot-out lacked entirely the decorum and sense of honour that characterised the duel proper. The shoot-out was as foreign to the duel as the uncouth, frontier cattle rustler was to the urbane, Southern planter. Yet the two have become conflated in the popular historical imagination. This is in part a result of a failure by writers to discern the vital difference between them. Charles Summerfield wrote a book called *Duellists and Duelling in the South-West*, published in 1847, which made it abundantly clear what he understood by the term 'duel'.

> Other codes of honor have fixed rules as unalterable as those of the Medes and the Persians; but the code of the South-West knows but one uniform rule – to fight at all hazards, and against every disadvantage.
>
> Other codes have respect to certain civilized, or at least, not utterly savage weapons. But this obliges one to fight with every implement of destruction, from the point of the bowie knife up to the mouth of the cannon. Nay, a duellist of the backwoods would gladly fight with double-barrelled shot-guns, or pieces of field artillery, charged with red-hot thunderbolts, could he command such costly ammunition.[63]

Summerfield was making it clear to his readers that they were not dealing with the type of considered, almost dispassionate, duel that was to be encountered in the Old South or New England. This was an altogether different creature, a point he did not hesitate to ram home.

> At the present day, in most countries, owing to the mighty force of public opinion, duels are seldom fatal. Each adversary aims at 'winging' the other, as they term breaking a leg or an arm. But who ever heard of 'winging' in Arkansas or Texas. The word there is to wing the hissing bullet directly through the head or heart …[64]

Summerfield's account of the careers of the 'desperadoes' of the south-west has an adulatory tone; it makes heroes of lawless ruffians and glorifies pointless, murderous violence. He makes the point that his duellists of the south-west are markedly different from the old-fashioned gentlemen duellists of the Old South and New England. The typical south-west duellist has a dark cross of the savage in his blood; he has the instincts of the savage, both the good and the bad. He has also the imagination of the savage, wild, uncultivated, outré, in its luxuriance.

How different indeed from the model of duellist we have come to expect. In truth Summerfield's duellists were little more than violent thugs, for whom random killing was a way of life, a fact relentlessly borne out by the stories he chose to relate about their careers.

Jack Smith T., of Missouri, is one of the 'duellists' who drew Summerfield's admiring attention. 'He was an Ajax, at once in size and in courage,' Summerfield tells us. But any sense of Smith's nobility is soon forfeited when we are told how he stabbed to death someone who tried to kill him. We are also told of an occasion on which Smith shot dead, in cold blood, two men he met on the road, merely because they confessed to being land speculators.[65] We are told the highly coloured story of a fight, which apparently took place on the floor of the Arkansas legislature, between one Anthony and the Speaker, John Wilson, in 1836. In front of many members of the House, Wilson was insulted by Anthony. Instead of appointing a second to convey a challenge and conduct the affair, Wilson simply drew his bowie knife – a formidable weapon nicknamed the 'Arkansas toothpick' – and advanced on his foe. After some desperate passes, Anthony threw his knife at Wilson but missed. Wilson, his opponent now disarmed, closed in for the kill.

> Wilson darted upon him, with the bound of a panther, there where he stood motionless as a rock on the floor. One fierce thrust ripped open the victim's bowels, and he caught them as they were falling, with his hands. Another thrust aimed at the neck, cut in two its main artery, and the blood spouted out, in a crimson fountain …[66]

The point of these tales for us is to illustrate the distinction between the figure we have come to recognise, wherever we see him, as the duellist and his rougher cousin, the brawling bruiser. They show that much of the combative activity in the new American West, even as early as the 1830s and 1840s, could not be dignified as duelling.

As the duel proper disappeared in America in the years following the Civil War it was replaced in the popular imagination by the gun-fight. Thus Pistols at Dawn became High Noon. The popular legend of the cowboy was fostered by men like 'Wild Bill' Hickok and by the fame of the outlaws, of whom Jesse James was only the best-known example. As the railways reached ever further west across the conti-nent, so the frontiers moved with them. In innumerable small towns miles from anywhere, men fought each other, the sheriff, and the Indians. They drank, whored and gambled; they held up stage-coaches, banks and trains. It was rough, tough and violent. It was the Wild West.

Chapter Thirteen

DUELLING UNDER THE TRICOLOUR: FRANCE 1789–1914

T HE FRENCH REVOLUTION, the storm that broke over France on 14 July 1789, swept away the *ancien régime*. During the turbulent years that followed the storming of the Bastille, the monarchy collapsed, the King was beheaded, the Church and the nobility were belittled and terrorised, even the calendar was reconstructed. France had entered a new age, one guided by the principles of *Liberté*, *Égalité* and *Fraternité*. The old bastions of privilege had been demolished; in the new France everyone was equal; everyone was a *citoyen* of the new republic. This chapter covers the history of duelling in France between the Revolution and the outbreak of war in 1914, a period sometimes known to historians as the 'long nineteenth century'.

It is one of the oddities of this period that duelling not only survived in France but flourished. Duelling was, after all, as typical of the *ancien régime* as the elaborate protocols of Versailles, or the paintings of François Boucher or powdered wigs, yet it survived the Revolution. Indeed, not only did it survive the Revolution, it broadened its appeal, embracing a new constituency. Whereas under the *ancien régime* duelling had been the preserve of officers and aristocrats, in nineteenth-century France Delacroix's bourgeois in his frock coat and stovepipe hat was entitled to defend his honour with sword or pistol. Duelling had become democratised: as a result, in France it retained its vigour right up to 1914, whereas in the Anglo-Saxon world it had died out by 1870.

The Revolution disapproved of duelling; it was a vestige of the old way, a right of privilege wholly out of keeping with the new order. J.A. Brouillet, a *curé* from Avise and member of the National Assembly, was certain where his fellow legislators' duty lay.

> It is without doubt, gentlemen ... that to you falls a glorious opportunity to eradicate duelling; if the rigour of the law has so far proved ineffective against this madness, you will render a signal service to humankind by delivering it from so terrible a scourge.[1]

The *curé* was also worldly enough to recognise that he was perhaps ideally qualified to campaign against duelling: 'It requires a Caesar, or a country curate to dare to set himself up against the madness of duelling, someone beyond all suspicion of fearfulness, or of what is called cowardice.'[2] The National Convention took the *curé's* advice and, in Year II, declared duelling illegal. The Jacobin regime of 1793–4 tried to stamp it out in the army, too.[3]

Whatever the official view of duelling, it nevertheless thrived in the febrile atmosphere of French politics after 1789. Thomas Carlyle in his *The French Revolution* observed that,

> Of duels we have sometimes spoken: how in all parts of France, innumerable duels were fought; and argumentative men and mess-mates, flinging down the wine-cup and weapons of reason and repartee, met in the measured field; to part bleeding: or perhaps not to part, but to fall mutually skewered through with iron, their wrath and life alike ending, – and die as fools die. Long has this lasted, and lasts still. [4]

Carlyle identified a specific cause for this rash of political duelling: 'traitorous Royalism, in its despair, had taken to a new course: that of cutting off Patriotism by systematic duel!'[5]

The royalists seemed determined to prevail by force: 'Black traitorous Aristocrats kill the People's defenders, cut up not with arguments, but with rapier-slits.'[6] The stoutly royalist duc de Castries challenged the radical Charles Lameth; when they fought, Lameth's arm was skewered on de Castries's sword. In revenge the mob sacked de Castries's town house. Mirabeau was a particular object of hatred for the royalists and was constantly being insulted by 'many coxcombs & jackanapes'. It was not without reason that he was the champion fighting cock of the revolutionaries: having been challenged yet again, he produced, in the National Assembly, the previous 137 challenges he had received.

> 'This,' he said, 'makes the 138th, but I cannot do the prior applicants the injustice of passing them over in favour of this gentleman, and I have not the leisure to go regularly through the list; they must therefore for the present all excuse me. When I have acquitted myself of my public duties, I may perhaps attend to them.'[7]

Eventually, as reaction set in, the radicalism and bloodletting of the Revolution gave way to a more conservative regime. In the late 1790s France was ruled by the Directory until it was displaced by Napoleon in the *coup d'état* of 18 Brumaire (9 November 1799). Napoleon was at first the junior member of the Consulate, the triumvirate that supplanted the Directory. He was, however, soon appointed First Consul, then First Consul for Life, with the reins of power firmly in his grasp. His assumption of absolute power was consummated in December 1804 when, with the Pope looking on, he crowned himself Emperor of the French. Napoleon, like many military leaders before him, had an ambivalent attitude to duelling. He recognised that it instilled and refined the martial spirit of his officers but, at the same time, deplored the drain of talent that it caused.

During the Egyptian campaign Bonaparte had cause to reprimand Lannes, Murat and Bessieres for acting as seconds to General Junot in a duel fought on the banks of the Nile. Bonaparte ridiculed them by comparing them to 'silly crocodiles fighting in the reeds'.[8] General Regnier, who had distinguished himself during the Egyptian campaign, quarrelled with his superior Menou and was ordered home. Back in Paris, with time on his hands, he wrote a provocative book about the campaign, which was outspokenly critical of Menou's conduct. In 1802, as result of the book, Regnier fought a duel with General Destaing, an officer loyal to Menou. Destaing was killed. Regnier was banned from Paris as a punishment for this misdemeanour and for a while thereafter his military career was becalmed in a backwater.[9] Regnier enjoyed a reputation throughout his career as a deadly duellist.

Napoleon's marshals were a talented group of men, many from lowly backgrounds, who rose to command great armies. They were showered with honours and titles by their Emperor, principalities, dukedoms, orders and stars; two of them – Bernadotte and Murat – even ascended to thrones. But they were, as might have been expected, proud, touchy and belligerent men, much given to fighting duels. Bernadotte twice challenged Berthier, Napoleon's long-serving chief of staff, to a duel in 1797. During the Austerlitz campaign in the autumn of 1805 Lannes and Soult fell out with the result that Lannes challenged his fellow general to a duel, a challenge that Soult ignored. Indeed, Lannes was so inflamed by Soult's behaviour that, on the morning of Austerlitz itself, when one might have thought that there were more important matters to concentrate on, Lannes repeated his challenge to Soult. Intermittently throughout the Napoleonic adventure, the animosities and jealousies that were never far below the surface would erupt. During the Peninsular campaign, Ney and Soult fell out and were only narrowly prevented from fighting a duel. During the Battle of Aspern-Essling against the Austrians in 1809, Lannes and Soult were at each other's throats, although a duel was avoided. During the Russian campaign of 1812, Murat was prevented from fighting a duel with Davout. But the most notorious duellist, and the most proficient fencer, among the Emperor's marshals was Pierre Angereau. Few who fought Angereau survived to tell the tale.[10]

Many people's knowledge of duelling in the Napoleonic era – indeed, of duelling in general – is derived from Ridley Scott's wonderful film of Joseph Conrad's novella *The Duel*. Based on fact, the novella tells the story of a series of duels between two cavalry officers of different regiments, d'Hubert and Ferand, fought over a 15-year period from 1801 to the second Bourbon Restoration. The backdrop to the story is the Napoleonic epic itself, as the two principals move around Europe at the call of duty and the turn of events: 'Napoleon I, whose career had the quality of a duel against the whole of Europe, disliked duelling between the officers of his army.

The great military emperor was not a swashbuckler, and had little respect for tradition.'[11]

D'Hubert and Ferand are a nicely contrasted pair: d'Hubert is a tall, fair northern aristocrat; Ferand is a Gascon, short, dark and fiery, the son of a blacksmith. The original cause of the enmity between the two men was d'Hubert's bringing to Ferand a general's order placing him under house arrest as a result of another duel. As the story progresses the original bone of contention becomes increasingly irrelevant, until it is forgotten altogether. 'To the surprise and admiration of their fellows, two officers, like insane artists, trying to gild refined gold or paint the lily, pursued a private contest through the years of universal carnage.'[12]

The two men fought their first duel as lieutenants, with swords, at Strasbourg. It took place in the garden of Ferand's quarters with the deaf gardener, the servant girl and Ferand's aged landlady looking on. The second duel was fought shortly afterwards, again with swords; this time d'Hubert was wounded. The next duel took place in Silesia after the Battle of Austerlitz in December 1805. The fourth duel was fought near Lübeck in northern Germany after the Battle of Jena in 1806. This time they agreed to fight on horseback; Ferand was knocked off his horse in the charge with a cut to the forehead. Thereafter the chances of war kept them apart for a long while until d'Hubert and Ferand served together during the invasion of Russia in 1812.

By now Ferand's suspicions and jealousies of his long-time adversary were beginning to fester: he was a generals' favourite; he was not devotedly loyal to the Emperor; he sought promotions in order to avoid fighting duels with Ferand. After the disastrous German campaign of 1813, d'Hubert was promoted general but was badly wounded in 1814 and missed the Hundred Days and Waterloo. By a nice coincidence, Ferand took over the wounded d'Hubert's command but the story reaches its climax only after Napoleon's final defeat. With the Bourbons safely restored to power, many thousands of Bonaparte's most loyal officers were languishing on half-pay. Ferand was eking out an existence among the 'other living wreckage of Napoleon's tempest'. Meanwhile, d'Hubert was comfortably re-employed by the new regime. When Ferand discovered this, he set out to find d'Hubert and challenge him to a final duel.

Ferand ran d'Hubert, who was by now living in the country and engaged to be married, to ground and challenged him. His fiancée's uncle, a returned *émigré*, 'a lean ghost of the *ancien régime*' advised him to ignore Ferand.

> What is Ferand? A tramp disguised into a general by a Corsican adventurer masquerading as an emperor. There is no earthly reason for a d'Hubert to debase himself by a duel with a person of that sort. You can make your excuses perfectly well.[13]

D'Hubert declined to take the old man's advice, asking rhetorically, 'Besides, how is one to refuse to be bitten by a dog that means to bite?'[14] The fifth duel between the two men took place in a wood in Provence; they fight, as it were, freelance, each man armed with two pistols. D'Hubert, having duped Ferand into firing his two shots, forced him to submit.

The Duel is a gripping story but it is no accident that it reaches its denouement in the early months of the second Bourbon Restoration. France after the defeat of Napoleon was a maelstrom of competing interests and rivalries, a duellist's paradise: unemployed imperialists challenged returning royalists; half-pay officers fought full-pay officers; Frenchmen baited officers of the occupying forces, Englishmen, Prussians and Russians. For a time Paris, particularly, echoed to the clash of swords and the sound of gunfire.

The Duel cleverly exposes the conflicting loyalties of the time. Both d'Hubert and Ferand served the Emperor faithfully in many a campaign but once he fell their differences begin to emerge. The novella examines the cleavage after 1814 between the diehard Bonapartists, such as Ferand, who could not bring themselves to support the restored monarchy, and those, like d'Hubert, who, although happy to have served the Emperor, were not blindly loyal to him. Following approximately the same fault lines were the tensions between employed officers and half-pay officers and between officers of different social classes. The rivalry between d'Hubert and Ferand exemplified this pattern.

William Jerdan, British journalist and man of letters, was in Paris in 1814, where he witnessed Louis XVIII's formal entry into the city after the defeat of Napoleon. He left a hair-raising first-hand account of an incident in a restaurant that was wholly typical of those turbulent months. Three foreign officers were seated in a restaurant, sipping their wine, when three Frenchmen sat down at the next table. It was evident that the Frenchmen had 'come to the place with no complimentary or civil intentions'. Scarcely had they called for their wine when one of their number, addressing his companions and

> holding up several decorations on his breast, observed, in the most sneering tone and malignant manner, 'This I received for Jena; this I got for Austerlitz; and this for Borodino! Aha!' No notice was taken of this bravado aside …

Having listened to this, the Frenchmen asked for their bill and prepared to leave.

> To my astonishment I observed one of the foreigners, who gnashed his teeth and flashed fury from his eyes, start up and rush to the bar … [and] as soon as the speaker came within arm's length struck him a violent blow on the cheek with his open hand, exclaiming, 'that for Jena'; a second blow followed on the other cheek, and 'that for Austerlitz' accompanied the stroke; a third, and 'that for Borodino' finished the assault, which did not occupy ten seconds.

The two groups left the restaurant but in

> less than half an hour the foreigners returned to finish their wine; a duel had been fought behind the Palais Royal, and the unfortunate Frenchmen had been run through the body, and killed on the spot.[15]

Captain Rees Howell Gronow was stationed with the British army in Paris as a young Guards officer in 1815. He remembered that 'When the Restoration of the Bourbons took place, a variety of circumstances combined to render duelling so common, that scarcely a day passed without at least one of these hostile meetings.'

He recalled that Napoleonic and royalist officers were constantly at one another's throats, a state of disorder aggravated by the 'irritating presence' of foreign troops in Paris. There were particular establishments that were happy to cater for the needs of the warring officers.

> At Fortoni's, on the Boulevards, there was a room set apart for such quarrelsome gentlemen, where, after these meetings, they indulged in riotous champagne breakfasts …
>
> The Café Foy, in the Palais Royal, was the principal place of rendezvous for the Prussian officers, and to this café the French officers on half-pay frequently proceeded in order to pick quarrels with their foreign invaders; swords were quickly drawn, and frequently the most bloody frays took place …[16]

Numerous duels were fought in France at this time. One of the most notorious was the encounter between Colonel Barbier-Dufai, a diehard Bonapartist officer and inveterate duellist, and a young Guards officer, known only as Raoul. The colonel, who particularly resented the Restoration, one evening deliberately provoked the young Guards officer into challenging him. When eventually they did fight, with swords, Raoul was easily disarmed. The colonel then suggested that they fight tied together in a carriage, armed with daggers. The carriage, driven by the seconds, would speed around the Carrousel. Despite the highly unusual, indeed improper, conditions, Raoul agreed to the duel. When the carriage came to a halt, Raoul was dead and Barbier-Dufai badly hurt.[17]

At about the same time a British officer, known only as Lieutenant G___, stationed at Cambrai, was provoked into fighting a duel by a disaffected French officer. The British officer was killed in circumstances that suggested that the Frenchman may have been wearing armour – a gross breach of the etiquette of duelling. In 1816 the French Admiral de la Susse fought a duel with a German following a trifling argument at a ball in the Faubourg St Honore. When they met in the Bois de Boulogne, the German fired first but missed; the admiral hit his man but he was saved from injury by a 'well-padded cuirass'. A few years later a young Frenchman, Pinac, was killed in a duel fought with an Englishman over some marginalia. The British officer had noted in the margin of an account of the Battle of Toulouse 'that every thing in it was false; that Lord Wellington had won a complete victory; and that the French army was indebted to his generosity for not having been put to the sword'. When these jottings were drawn to Pinac's attention, he immediately challenged the author to a duel.

Once the duelling frenzy of the early years of the Bourbon restoration had blown itself out, the duel began to assume the form that would sustain it in such rude health for another hundred years. The secret of the duel's success in France was that it was able to broaden its appeal: the notions of honour that underpinned the duel percolated down into the bourgeoisie, giving it a wider constituency. It is instructive to compare France with the position in Britain, where, at the same time, duelling was fast becoming regarded as a hangover from a earlier, less civilised age, and, in places, even an object of ridicule. In France duelling, an archetypal institution of the *ancien régime*, not only survived the Revolution's radicalism and modernisation, but emerged greatly strengthened. For Robert Nye, whose work illuminates the history of duelling in nineteenth-century France, the secret of the duel's success

> was the penetration of the usages and presumptions of honour into the deepest layers of the urban bourgeoisie, where they blended with the egalitarianism and nationalism that flourished in those milieux.[18]

For Nye it was during 'the first decades of the century that the social and political amalgamation of the old nobility and the bourgeoisie was cemented'.[19] The duel in France succeeded in democratising itself.

In France, as in most countries, the military and the nobility were bastions of duelling, where the custom was nurtured and protected. Under the *ancien régime*, as the officer corps had largely been the preserve of the nobility, the two tended to merge. During the Revolution and Empire the demand for manpower had necessitated a wider recruitment of officers. Napoleon's marshals illustrate how completely the traditional criteria for recruitment to the officer corps had been abandoned. Murat was the son of an innkeeper, Massena of a tanner, Lannes of a peasant farmer, and Ney of a cooper.[20] There was hardly an aristocrat among them; talent, and luck, were the only criteria. The marshals were, of course, merely the tip of the iceberg, reflecting what was happening in the lower echelons of the army.

This process continued after the Restoration to the extent that, of the 6,474 officers active between 1848 and 1870, nearly 88 per cent were commoners. In the Prussian army, by contrast, 86 per cent of the officer corps was drawn from the nobility in 1860 and still 52 per cent as late as 1913.[21] One factor that contributed to the change in the social backgrounds of France's officer corps was the practice of commissioning senior NCOs. Under Louis-Philippe one-third of commissions were reserved for NCOs, with the result that by 1848 three-quarters of all officers had risen from the ranks.[22]

The French officer was an enthusiastic duellist. In the early nineteenth century he 'had little thought of death' and fought duels on the most trivial of pretexts. It was only in 1857 that an officer was for the first time reduced to the ranks for killing his man in a duel. The fact that he was recommissioned a year later and ended his career as a general is perhaps indicative of the prevailing attitude towards duellists.[23] In the French army, as in the British army, officers could be cashiered for refusing a challenge. Indeed, for much of the period military discipline 'relied heavily' on duelling. Enlisted men caught brawling were compelled to settle their differences with foils, a practice that kept the average rate of duels at about 50 a year per regiment.[24]

The ravages of the wars of the Revolutionary period and the Empire heavily diluted the aristocratic composition of the French army's officer corps. Yet duelling, before 1789 the preserve of the aristocrat, continued to flourish. So it was in wider, civilian France. 'It is clear that the demand for ennoblement did not cease with the Revolution,' writes Theodore Zeldin. Before the Revolution there were perhaps 12,000 noble families; by the middle of the twentieth century there were between 3,600 and 4,400 noble families, but supplemented by another 15,000 families falsely claiming to be noble, albeit generally accepted as such.[25] Revolution and republicanism clearly did not extinguish the instincts of the French for self-aggrandisement, nor is it unreasonable to suppose that the success enjoyed by duelling in the period was part of the same phenomenon. Duelling was perceived as an aristocratic custom and, therefore (in the broadest terms), something to be embraced by those who aspired to aristocratic status. In nineteenth-century France duelling was 'reinvigorated by middle-class aspirations to noble deportment'.[26] In the modern parlance, duelling was aspirational.

There were, of course, more factors at work in the continuing popularity of duelling than mere snobbery. One of the most potent was the failure of the authorities to suppress the habit, a failure that derived largely from the toothlessness of the legal system. The monarchs of the *ancien régime* made countless attempts to eradicate duelling, all unsuccessful, and so it was in republican France. Between 1819 and the end of the century, there were nine separate attempts to regulate or abolish duelling, all unsuccessful.[27] One of the stumbling blocks was that the very men who could have taken the lead in abolishing the custom, the legislators, were among the most prominent supporters of the duel. As Robert Nye put it, 'The visibility of parliamentary life, where a man's style was as important to his political fortunes as his convictions and his allies, made it unlikely that repression of the duel would originate in French legislative assemblies.'[28]

In 1836, in an attempt to compensate for the legislature's reluctance to deal robustly with duellists, Louis-Philippe's chief prosecutor, André-Marie Dupin, announced that henceforth the duel would be regarded as a form of attempted murder and dealt with accordingly. He announced that sentences would range from acquittal to execution, depending on the circumstances and the degree of culpability.[29]

The authorities' stance was quickly confirmed by a test case and does seem to have had some effect on the number of fatalities in duels. Ministry of Justice statistics published in 1846 showed that, in 1828, 29 people were reportedly killed in duels; in 1833 the figure was 32. But by 1839 the number of reported deaths had declined sharply to six; the following year the figure was only three and in 1841 six again.[30] The reduction in the number of reported duelling deaths was not, it would seem, matched by an increased willingness on the part of juries to convict duellists. An apologist for duelling noted in an article in 1845 that, between 1837 and 1842, the French courts heard 34 duelling cases, acquitting the defendants in every case.[31]

However, perhaps the strongest single influence on the development of the duel in nineteenth-century France was the comte de Chateauvillard's *Essai sur le duel*, published in 1836. Chateauvillard, a keen sportsman who was a member of the French Jockey Club, wrote the treatise in an attempt to bring duelling into the modern era. Since he regarded it as a necessary and inevitable feature of civilised life, Chateauvillard drew up a set of rules that would make duelling both rarer and, when it did happen, less dangerous. In the process, he hoped to quieten the demands of those who wished to abolish the practice. Chateauvillard's *Essai* had a greater impact than he could dared to have hoped. It became the universally accepted protocol for the proper conduct of duels. Such was its influence that the courts were inclined to acquit a duellist if it could be shown that the duel in question had been conducted according to the principles laid down by Chateauvillard. In other words, provided a duellist adhered to Chateauvillard's rules, he was likely to escape the full rigour of the law, however bloody his duel had been.

It is significant that Chateauvillard discouraged the more dangerous types of duel in favour of the less dangerous. He disapproved, for example, of pistol duels, but favoured sword duels *à premier sang*. He felt that the spilling of blood, however symbolic, should be sufficient to expunge a slight in a genuine affair of honour. It is no exaggeration to say that the *Essai* was very largely responsible for the fact that by 1900 the French duel had become a less than life-threatening undertaking. This contrasted starkly with the Prussian duel, which remained a dangerous business until the end. Chateauvillard's ideas dictated the way in which duels were fought in France and how duellists were treated by the courts for the remainder of the century. They also formed the basis for many other treatises on duelling in several different languages, thereby reaching a much wider audience.

If the period between the Restoration and the upheavals of 1848 were the formative years of the modern French duel, it reached maturity under the Third Republic. The Third Republic was proclaimed on 3 September 1870; two days earlier Napoleon III had surrendered his army of 84,000 men to the Prussians after the Battle of Sedan. The new Republic, which lasted until it collapsed in the face of Hitler's onslaught in 1940, was 'one of the most confusing and paradoxical of regimes ... The exceptional longevity of the regime is difficult to reconcile with its equally unprecedented instability.[32]'

France under the Third Republic had 108 different governments between 1870 and 1940; each lasted an average of eight months. Britain, by comparison, in the years between 1801 and 1937 had 44 governments, each lasting, on average, just over three years.[33] The constant shifting of allegiances and loyalties as governments formed and reformed with each turn of the political kaleidoscope inevitably made French parliamentary politics under the Third Republic an ill-tempered, fractious pursuit. Many disappointed or slighted ministers and deputies were only too happy to settle political scores on the duelling ground. Politicians were among the most prominent and enthusiastic duellists in late nineteenth-century France.

The political instability inherent in the Third Republic was exacerbated in its early years by the fault that existed in French society between those who accepted the Republic and those who hoped for a restoration of the monarchy. The political impact of the Boulanger affair of the late 1880s, for example, was aggravated by its monarchist undertones. The situation was further complicated by the fact that the monarchists themselves were divided between Orleanists and Legitimists. The Orleanists championed the right of the descendants of Louis-Philippe, who had been King of France from 1830 to 1848, to be restored to the throne. The Legitimists, on the other hand, maintained that the only proper Kings of France were the descendants of the 'legitimate' Bourbon line, of which Charles X (deposed 1830) was the last ruling representative.

The focus of the monarchist cause was inevitably the pretender. Until his death in 1883 the pretender was the Legitimist comte de Chambord; thereafter the comte de Paris, a grandson of Louis-Philippe, took up the baton. The best chances of securing a restoration of the monarchy were in 1871, in the early days of the Republic, and in 1885, when the royalists secured a majority in the National Assembly. The comte de Paris then sided with General Boulanger, but when his coup failed the cause was lost. The comte de Paris died in

1894, after which time the monarchists ceased to be a force to be reckoned with in French politics.

The instability of the politics of the Third Republic was not the only stimulus behind the contemporary mania for duelling. It was also a period of unbridled freedom of the press. Since the Revolution, when – between 1789 and 1792 – more than 500 new titles appeared, the press had become a formidably powerful political instrument. It had played an important role in unseating the government in the revolutions of 1830 and 1848. The second half of the century witnessed an explosion of the press.

Until the appearance of the *Petit Journal* in 1863, no French newspaper had printed more than 50,000 copies. The *Petit Journal* was cheap – it sold for five centimes, when its rivals cost three or four times that – and eschewed serious journalism in favour of salacious gossip and 'human-interest' stories. Its circulation passed the 1 million mark for the first time during the presidential crisis of 1887. In 1881 a Sunday supplement of the *Petit Journal* was launched, which immediately sold 800,000 copies. Commercial success on this scale inevitably spawned imitators: *Le Journal* was selling half a million copies by the turn of the century and *Le Matin* three-quarters of a million by 1905.[34]

The effect of a proliferation of mass-market newspapers was compounded by the abolition in 1881 of censorship. The lifting of all restraints on the press was not, however, balanced by the introduction of an effective law of libel. Henceforth newspapers could print any story, no matter how defamatory or ill-founded, with impunity. The libel law introduced in 1894 proved nearly impossible to enforce.

It is not difficult to see how duelling flourished in these circumstances and many was the journalist who was obliged to defend his published opinions with his sword. Indeed, the classic Third Republic duel was an encounter between a journalist and an offended politician. The situation was further inflamed by the fact that many politicians were also journalists or proprietors of newspapers.

Emile de Girardin (1806–1881) has been described as 'perhaps the most influential figure in the history of the modern French press'.[35] He founded many newspapers, including *La Presse*, which was one of the first in France to charge the reader a lower price, recouping the difference from advertising revenue. He served as an MP for many years, although he never achieved high office, a mix of business and politics that was typical of the press under the Third Republic. He had also fought at least one duel when in 1836 he killed Armand Carrel, a fellow newspaper editor, in a pistol duel.

Henri Rochefort was another prominent journalist with a reputation as a duellist. Rochefort, the son of an aristocrat, was a rare example of someone who abandoned his title; in nineteenth-century France it was much more common to *adopt* the defining particle *de* than jettison it. He was a talented writer and polemicist as well as a successful newspaper proprietor. He founded *La Lanterne,* wrote almost every word of it himself and managed to sell 100,000 copies of the first edition, thus immediately recouping his backers their investment. *La Lanterne's* memorable first line was, 'France had thirty-six million subjects, not counting the subjects of discontent.' Rochefort fought numerous duels, including one against Prince Achille Murat, a cousin of the Emperor.[36]

On top of its already combustible mix of unstable, vitriolic politics and a stridently outspoken press, the Third Republic was rent by a number of long-running scandals, or *causes célèbres.* The most famous of these was the Dreyfus affair, which rumbled on from 1894 until 1906. At its heart was the question of France's attitude to anti-Semitism and, perhaps not surprisingly, it was the cause of many a duel, mostly between Jews and Gentiles. One historian has counted 31 duels fought as a result of the Dreyfus affair.[37] Another long-running scandal was the Panama affair of the early 1890s, a murky financial imbroglio of labyrinthine complexity that tainted many members of the French political establishment with the whiff of corruption. It was the Panama scandal that impelled Georges Clemenceau to fight one of his many duels.

Clemenceau was in many ways the archetypal Third Republic duellist. He was a radical politician who served as Prime Minister of France between 1906 and 1909 and again in the latter stages of World War One from 1917 to 1920. He was a ferocious duellist – his nickname 'the Tiger' was not without reason – who is credited in some quarters with having fought as many as 22 duels. Richard Cohen's soberer assessment puts the Tiger's tally of duels at 12, seven fought with pistols and five with swords.[38] For a proprietor-journalist and radical politician in the Third Republic it was virtually *de rigueur* to fight duels if one wished to hold one's head high – and Clemenceau was no exception.

His fight with the nationalist writer and politician Paul Del-roulede, which arose from the Panama scandal, was the best known of Clemenceau's duels. The story of the Panama scandal is tortuously involved; it is sufficient to note here that a M. Herz, a *nouveau riche* Jewish financier of foreign origins, was used by the Panama company to ensure that the vital fundraising lottery scheme was approved by Parliament. Herz was also a close associate of Clemenceau.

By December 1892 allegations of corruption were starting to filter into the press and the matter was aired in the National Assembly. It was during this debate that Paul Deroulede denounced Clemenceau as the man responsible for having fostered Herz's career and eased his path into the upper echelons of French political life. Deroulede's denunciation was laced with anti-Semitism and xenophobia, but the thrust of his remarks was that Clemenceau was to blame for the scandal that now engulfed the French establishment and, by exten-sion, that he was himself corrupt. Clemenceau defended himself against the charges and, after the House had finished sitting, sent De-roulede a challenge, via his seconds. Clemenceau had been left with no alternative.

The parties agreed to meet at Saint-Ouen racecourse in the afternoon of 22 December. The seconds had agreed conditions for the duel that were likely to make the encounter very dangerous: each man would be allowed three shots, to be fired at a range of 25 paces. Clemenceau spent the morning with his mistress before going to the offices of his newspaper, to settle his affairs in the event of his death.

At three o'clock the duel began. Both missed with their first shots and with their second; at this point a spectator ran onto the duelling ground, imploring the parties to stop. The interloper was ignored and the third shots fired; again both men missed. There has been speculation since that Clemenceau deliberately missed Deroulede; the Tiger was, after all, a crack shot.

Later in his career Clemenceau, as Prime Minister of France, presided at the Versailles Peace Conference, which reordered Europe after World War One. The other pre-eminent figures at the conference were the American President Woodrow Wilson and the British Prime Minister David Lloyd George. Sir William Orpen's magnificent tableau of the conference in session shows the three men sitting at the top table guiding the destiny of nations and peoples, indeed of history herself. What, one wonders, did the saintly, bookish, peace-loving Wilson and the early state socialist Lloyd George make of the old-fashioned, unreconstructed Clemenceau, the Tiger, the man of 22 duels? It was indeed Old Manners meeting New.

A further stimulus to duelling was the resurgence of fencing as a sport in late nineteenth-century France. In the sixteenth and seventeenth centuries any good-sized town had a fencing *salle* with its master-at-arms, who was under the aegis of the Royal Academy of Arms. That institution was abolished during the Revolution; by 1840 there were only perhaps 10 such *salles* left in France. By 1870 interest in fencing was reviving but after the Franco-Prussian War it took off. By 1890 there were more than a hundred masters-at-arms in Paris alone and *salles d'armes* had opened in many provincial cities. The sport became so popular that a number of Parisian department stores – themselves a new phenomenon – maintained fencing halls, as did some newspapers.[39]

The revival of interest in fencing was closely connected to the heartfelt need of all Frenchmen to avenge the humiliations of 1870. Fencing promoted exactly the qualities that would be needed to rebuild the military strength of the homeland in order to exact revenge on the Germans. It is indicative of the depth of anti-German sentiment in Third Republic France that the courts held that to refer to someone as a 'Prussian' was defamatory. The shame of the defeat of 1870 was keenly felt by all Frenchmen born in the middle of the century.[40] The connection between the revival of interest in fencing and duelling – especially where the dominant form of the duel was the sword bout – is too obvious to merit examination. Many *salles d'armes* took it upon themselves to arbitrate in disputes and, should it become necessary, to oversee the conduct of the duel itself.

One of the perennial difficulties facing the historian of duelling is the question 'how many'? In the case of late nineteenth-century France we are perhaps marginally better provided for statistically than in other eras, although the picture is nevertheless incomplete. In the earlier part of the period it is difficult to come to any firm conclusions about the number of duels fought. Robert Nye suggests, very tentatively, that perhaps 100 duels were fought a year in France between 1815 and 1848. Of these perhaps one-third ended fatally.[41]

That we have a better picture of duelling in Paris during the 1880s is due largely to the efforts of M. Ferreus, whose *Annuaire du Duel: 1880–89* was published in 1891. It is, as we saw in Chapter 3, the duellists' *Wisden*, its details all culled from the Paris newspapers. Ferreus's figures show that in 1880 there were 40 'stand-offs' – that is, occasions on which seconds were appointed following a row – of which 31 culminated in a duel. Twenty-four of these duels were fought with swords, seven with pistols; in only two of them was a combatant killed. In 1885 Ferreus counted 61 stand-offs, which resulted in 50 duels, the remainder being settled. Of these 50, 36 were fought with swords but only one person was killed. In 1889, there were almost the same number of stand-offs, 62, of which 20 were resolved without the need for a duel. Thirty-two of these were sword duels and three ended in fatality.

The criminologist Gabriel Tarde estimated in 1892 that around 60 duels a year were fought during the 1880s, a figure that tallies almost precisely with Ferreus's statistics. Robert Nye thinks this is too low: he suggests that a figure of 200 a year in the period 1875–1900, rising to 300 in a 'good' year, might be nearer the mark.[42] There is, unfortunately, no convincing way of reconciling these figures.

A glance through Ferreus's almanac reveals the fact that there was a hard core of men who were habitual duellists. Here, selected at random, are three examples. M. Lissagaray, editor of *L'Intransigeant* before moving to the aptly named *La Bataille*, was involved in nine stand-offs as a principal, three of which culminated in a duel. In two of these he was slightly wounded. Camille Dreyfus, another newspaperman, was involved in eight stand-offs as a principal and five as a second. Although only three of them were actually fought out, Dreyfus was wounded three times. Baron Hardon-Hickey fought six duels as principal; he was wounded in three of them. Henri Bernstein, a playwright, fought no fewer than three duels in a week in July 1911. He was slightly wounded in two of them.[43]

These figures also confirm the fact that the Third Republic's duellists greatly preferred swords to pistols, in accordance with the principles laid down by Chateauvillard. There was a strong sense that the sword was, in some semi-mystical way, a noble, chivalrous weapon, a fitting instrument for the gentlemanly resolution of affairs of honour. The favoured duelling sword was the épée, a three-sided sword that had its origins in military usage. After 1880 the *salles d'armes* began to offer tuition in the épée as well as in the more traditional fencing swords. This inevitably blurred the distinction between fencing and duelling.[44]

Nineteenth-century France produced a steady trickle of literature on the subject of duelling. It ranged from the comically frivolous to the deadly serious and included plays, practical treatises and legal monographs. Duelling has always been a subject that has appealed to dramatists, and the Paris stage was no exception. In Year VIII (1800) Prévost's *Les Femmes Duellistes, ou Tout pour l'Amour*, a comedy in three acts, was performed, followed a couple of years later by *Le Duel Impossible* by M.A. Mellesville. Half a century later the theatregoers of the Second Empire were treated to an operetta by Gille and Furpille called *Tabarin, Duelliste*, while in the 1870s Paul Arene wrote a play called *Un Duel aux Lanternes*.[45]

In a more serious vein, there were a number of tracts directed at the abolition of duelling. M. Destravault wrote *Le Coup de Massue au Duel* in 1821 (a *massue* is a club or a bludgeon), which advocated certain changes in the law to eradicate duelling. 'The madness of duelling is like drunkenness; let us dilute our wine ...' he wrote. From time to time lawyers weighed in to the debate about duelling. Two legal treatises published 50 years apart, in 1836 and 1888, both bemoan the fact that the courts continued to indulge duellists.

A light-hearted contribution to the duelling debate was

M. Pons-Lambert's *Les Euphemismes du Duel* (1846), which sets out what might be described as the linguistic explanation for duelling: 'The manner in which opinion has long accepted duelling, is probably one of the most remarkable instances of the damage inflicted on men's judgement by the misuse of euphemism.' In other words, had it not been for the camouflage of euphemism, duelling would have been allowed to wither away long ago. Pons-Lambert cited an example to make his point: 'So it is that one says *combat à l'outrance* [to the bitter end] in order to avoid saying "a fight to the death".'

Euphemism disguised the folly of duelling, recasting it as a glamorous even rational practice, acceptable to sensible men. *Guide du Duelliste Indélicat*, by Charles Leroy, published in 1884 took a decidedly irreverent look at duelling. One of the advantages, according to Leroy, of having a reputation as a duellist was that it made it easier to borrow money: 'It is more difficult to refuse a loan to a man who might kill one, than a person from whom one has nothing to fear.' The book's tone and the humorous illustrations show that not everyone took duelling overly seriously.

Les Lois du Duel by Bruneau de Laborie was a guide in deadly earnest to the practicalities of duelling, running to 240 pages: 'I persist in believing that, in publishing this book, I have simplified the task faced by an appreciable number of seconds, principals or referees.' The most noteworthy aspect of this tract is its date, 1912. That a book of this nature could be published – presumably in the hope of making money – so late is a powerful indication of the vigour of the tradition of duelling in France on the eve of the Great War.

It was the power that the duelling tradition exerted over men of a certain class and disposition that ensured its longevity. This power was an acute form of peer pressure. Politicians, journalists, playwrights and others challenged each other when traduced because they could not hold their heads up high unless they did so. Convention demanded it, so they obeyed. To refuse a legitimate challenge was to risk accusations of cowardice and court social and professional disgrace. It was easier to fight, particularly when, as in the France of the *belle époque*, the chances of being killed or even seriously hurt in a duel were negligible. Clemenceau, Rochefort and their ilk were all committed to the notion of the duel; it was as much a part of their lives as were their mistresses. The best illustrations of the strength of the compulsion to fight duels come from among those who would generally, for whatever reason, be vehemently opposed to duelling yet nevertheless fought one.

Marcel Proust was just such a man, bookish, delicate and withdrawn, yet he fought a duel. In 1897 Jean Lorrain, a journalist and novelist, insinuated in print that Proust was homosexual. Lorrain was an exotically louche character who, as Richard Davenport-Hines puts it, 'had a pitiable weakness for denouncing homosexuality in his articles despite his own taste for rough trade'. Accusations of homosexuality coming from such a man were too much for Proust, who challenged Lorrain to a duel. When they met in the Bois de Meudon near Versailles they exchanged two shots each without managing to hit their targets. 'The affair imbued Proust with lifelong pride at this evidence of his masculine courage.'[46]

Jean Jaurès was a radical socialist, a man deeply committed to peace and social justice, 'perhaps the most venerated politician of the Third Republic'.[47] In the main square of the former mining town of Carmaux in the *département* of the Tarn there is a statue commemorating him. Jaurès stands proudly in oratorical pose, a squat, powerfully built man, the very essence of the hard-working, tough miners whose cause he so ably represented for so long. Below him on the plinth, looking up at their hero, protector and leader, like adoring saints in a Venetian altarpiece, are figures representing the industrial proletariat, armed with picks and shovels. The plinth is inscribed 'Martyr and Apostle of Peace'.

Yet, in the febrile political climate of the Third Republic, even Jaurès felt unable to a avoid fighting a duel. In the course of a controversy about Joan of Arc, Paul Deroulede accused Jaurès of being 'the most odious perverter of consciences who has ever served the foreign interests in our country'. Jaurès's reply, which was widely publicised, made his position abundantly clear.

The Socialist party of which I am a member condemns with good reason this inept and barbarous way of resolving conflicts of ideas. My excuse for departing from these principles is that I have not engaged in this matter in provocation, but have instead myself been the object of the most direct, evident and unjustified provocation.

Bowing to the inevitable, Jaurès travelled to the Spanish frontier – Deroulede was living in exile in Spain – but found that the Spanish authorities, in order to prevent a breach of the peace, had arrested his adversary. Jaurès, fearing that he would expose himself to ridicule if he were to abandon his quest too easily in the face of this difficulty, sent a telegram to the French President asking that Deroulede's exile be temporarily suspended. When this was request was granted, the two men were able to fight their duel in a field on the French side of the border. On 6 December 1904, Jaurès, the apostle of peace, exchanged two shots with Deroulede. Neither man was hurt but that the duel happened at all showed the strength of the compulsion, even to a man of Jaurès's principles, to show himself willing to fight. Ten years later, in a cruel twist of fate, Jaurès was assassinated.

By the end of the nineteenth century, the duel had become commonplace in France – according to one historian as many as 500 were fought a year until 1914[48] – but fatalities were very rare. This state of affairs was in large measure due to the practices prescribed by the comte de Chateauvillard in his *Essai* of 1836 and enthusiastically adopted by the vast majority of French duellists. However sensible a reduction of the risks this might have been, the very lack of danger inherent in the average French duel of the period exposed it to ridicule. The London *Annual Register* of 1849, reporting a French duel, commented, 'Similar [encounters] have been very numerous of late; but they are very harmless.'[49] A Berlin newspaper explained in 1901 that

> the whole world knows that French duels, be they with pistols or swords, present not the slightest danger to their participants. In the duel proto-col, one reads of at worst a prick on the outside surface of the right index finger, or of a one tenth of a millimeter deep wound on the first knuckle of the thumb ...[50]

In 1893 a British writer, H. Sutherland Edwards, published *Old and New Paris*, which contained a chapter on the phenomenon of duelling. At the start of this chapter Edwards wrote,

The story is well known of a Paris journalist's wife, who, alarmed by the sudden disappearance of her husband, continued for a long time to fret and worry about him, until a friend of his told her that he had gone into the country to fight a duel, whereupon she exclaimed: 'Thank Heaven, then he is safe!'

Chapter Fourteen

Duelling and Eagles: Germany and Russia to 1914

Germany

Frederick the Great, King of Prussia, died in 1786. During his long reign Prussia became accustomed to exercising a potent influence in the great affairs of Europe. This had not always been the case. During the nineteenth century, Germany's power and influence grew steadily to the point at which, by 1900, she was the most powerful nation, militarily and industrially, in Europe. This chapter looks at the development of duelling in Germany – and in Prussia in particular – from the death of Frederick the Great to the outbreak of war in 1914.

In the previous chapter we looked at the development of duelling in France during the same period. There are instructive comparisons to be made which highlight the differences between the duel in France and how it was regarded on the other side of the Rhine. It can fairly be said that in both countries duelling flourished in the nineteenth century and that it was 'aspirational', but that was about the extent of any similarities. In France the dissemination of the etiquette of duelling and the notions of honour upon which it was founded happened despite the abolition of the *ancien régime*. In Germany, the spread of the duel was largely the result of the growth of militarism in the country, especially after 1870. The regime remained, although nominally democratic, essentially absolutist in tendency; certainly it was highly proficient at protecting the rights and privileges of its natural supporters, among whom duelling figured prominently. In France duelling, particularly during its heyday under the Third Republic, was predominantly a civilian phenomenon; in Germany, it was decidedly military in character. In France the sword was the preferred weapon; German duellists overwhelmingly favoured pistols. Germany, too, had the *mensur* (the student 'duel'), a uniquely Teutonic institution unknown in France.

Frederick the Great was succeeded by his nephew, Frederick William II, and, from 1797, by his son, Frederick William III. The Prussian king was as horrified by the French Revolution as his fellow crowned heads of Europe and declared war on France in July 1792. The Prussian army advanced steadily into France and by 1 September the road to Paris seemed open; the very existence of the Revolution hung in the balance. It was saved only by the unexpected defeat of the Prussians at the Battle of Valmy. Valmy was a dispiriting reverse for Prussian arms, a far cry from the days of Frederick the Great 40 years earlier. Thereafter the Prussians took part only intermittently in the struggle against France. They made peace with France in 1795, preferring to concentrate on digesting the massive territorial gains made from the two Partitions of Poland in the 1790s. They lent decidedly lukewarm support to the Third Coalition and, when attacked by Napoleon in 1806, were resoundingly defeated at the battles of Jena and Auerstadt. Prussia did play an important part in the campaigns in 1813 and 1814, which ensured the defeat of Napoleon, as well as in the final act at Waterloo, thus expunging the humiliations of the years of French occupation after 1806.

Following the defeat of Napoleon, there was a blaze of duelling across Europe, as if to celebrate the end of the years of war. Paris was the epicentre of the outbreak; we have seen elsewhere how imperialist fought royalist, and Frenchmen vented their frustrations on the occupying troops of the victorious powers. The Prussians, triumphant after years of humiliation, were in the thick of it. Documented duels between officers in Prussia were running at a rate of about one a month, a figure that excludes the many fights between Prussian officers in Paris and vengeful Frenchmen.[1]

Partly in response to this upsurge in the number of duels, Frederick William III established honour courts by Cabinet order in 1821. It does not seem to have been a notably effective measure in regulating the number of duels; indeed, between 1817 and 1829, 29 Prussian officers are recorded as having been killed in duels. As a result, the King was forced to issue three further decrees against duelling in the army during the 1820s.[2]

In 1843 Frederick William IV issued a Cabinet order that formed the basis of the honour-court system until 1914. Its progenitor was Hermann von Boyen, Prussia's Minister of War, who had himself been 'out' and was an ardent champion of the rights and privileges of the aristocratic military caste. Part I of the decree set out how the honour courts would function to preserve the collective image of the officer corps. Part II dealt with disputes and duels themselves. The 1843 decree confirmed the uniquely privileged position enjoyed by the military duellist, free of any requirement to observe the laws on duelling that applied to the civilian population. It amounted to a tacit approval of the practice in the army. The decree also made it clear that military duellists would be judged by the standards of their own peers, not by some higher ethical standard. As one historian put it, the 1843 decree 'created a fertile topsoil for the regeneration of army duelling'.[3]

Whatever the decree was intended to achieve, its practical effect was to increase the number of duels fought in the Prussian army: in the 13 years after 1843, there was at least a 25 per cent increase in the number of duels, compared with the previous 10 years.[4] The honour-court system in the Prussian army was further weakened by a decree of Wilhelm I's of 1874, which amounted to recognition of the legitimacy of the duel. The duel was now an inescapable part of an officer's duty.

The Prussian officer corps was a predominantly aristocratic body, which guarded jealously its privileges, among them the right to settle its disputes in duels. The Junkers, the landed Prussian aristocrats whose values and traditions shaped the officer corps, occupied a unique position in Prussian society. They managed to retain a political influence far beyond their economic power; this enabled them to preserve their traditions and practices despite the rising wealth of the bourgeoisie and the increasing political radicalism of the working class.

For the Prussian officer honour was of the greatest importance: 'the honor code was the distillation of the values of the officer'. Its preservation was an absolute duty, one that had become increasingly onerous. As one historian explained,

> By the late nineteenth century, the honor code had become so rigorous and so specific that living one's life was a hazardous and complex operation. To preserve the purity of one's honor, one could not have any dealings whatsoever with the lower class, which possessed no honor and was therefore incapable of giving satisfaction by a duel. [5]

In the claustrophobic atmosphere of the officer corps, duelling was regarded as an indispensable and compulsory discipline for officers. It was an essential tool for the maintenance of their prestige among the civilian population. This notion was resoundingly endorsed by both Emperors, Wilhelm I and Wilhelm II. In 1901 a young lieutenant called Blaskowitz had, while completely drunk, assaulted two fellow officers, a few days before his wedding was due to take place. The two offended officers challenged Blaskowitz to a duel and, without any attempt at reconciliation by the honour court, it took place. The hapless Blaskowitz received a gunshot wound from which he later died. His opponents were sentenced to two years' confinement in a fortress but the Kaiser saw fit to pardon them after only eight months, a move that sparked widespread criticism from the liberal opposition.[6]

The case of Sub Lieutenant Walther Strauss in 1900 unequivocally reflected the Kaiser's view that all officers had an absolute duty to defend their honour in a duel. Strauss had been slapped by a naval paymaster, von Ronnebeck, during a voyage; he duly reported the incident to the ship's honour court. However, while Strauss was still at sea an honour court in Kiel found him guilty of failing to uphold his honour as an officer and recommended that he be cashiered. This was despite the fact that Strauss had challenged von Ronnebeck to a duel the moment they reached port and had fought him. Wilhelm II ratified this decision, denouncing Strauss as 'wholly devoid of vigour in seeking satisfaction'.[7]

This unbending support for duelling in the military inevitably brought the Kaiser and his Cabinet into conflict with the Reichstag in the years before 1914. The most obvious reason for the conflict was that the Kaiser's support for duelling in the military was contrary to the law of the land. In other words, the officers of the army and the navy were above the law. In 1912 General von Heeringen, the Minister of War, made a statement in the Reichstag, replying to criticism of the treatment of a Roman Catholic officer who had refused to fight a duel. The general said that it was expressly provided that an officer who pleaded religious scruples should not be forced to appear before an honour court but added that 'such a man does not belong to the social circles of the Corps of Officers'. This remark provoked, the report stated, 'Loud and prolonged protest in the Centre and on the Left'.[8]

A few days later, von Heeringen retracted his statement but, revealingly, reaffirmed the official view of duelling in the army. The refusal to fight a duel, he said, was so sharply opposed to the ideas prevailing in the army that it placed that person in a very difficult position vis-à-vis his brother officers. In the years before 1914, the indulgence shown by the authorities to military duellists was a constant source of friction in the Reichstag between the government and the opposition parties.

Nor were such tensions confined to the years of the Kaiserreich, as was demonstrated by the Anneke affair of 1846. Fritz Anneke was a Prussian subaltern who had been dismissed from the army for refusing to fight a duel with a fellow officer. This disappointed adversary reported Anneke to a military honour court, which held that his refusal to fight was an affront to the honour of the officer class. The court did admit that Anneke was not motivated by cowardice but by political and moral principle. The court pronounced, 'He is guided solely by the prevailing spirit of the times, which is sufficient indication in itself that he has abandoned the fundamental principles of the officer class.'[9] Anneke's story appeared in the press but the subsequent outcry made little impression against the entrenched interests of the army and its supporters.

Duelling in Germany was an aristocratic and military custom, the preserve of the officer corps. Two factors working in concert helped it to broaden its appeal and spread its wings into a wider world. The first was the immense prestige of the army itself. Between 1864 and 1870 in a series of decisive strikes the Prussian army defeated first Denmark, then Austria and her allies, and finally the might of France. In the aftermath of the crushing defeat of France, Wilhelm I was proclaimed Emperor of a new German Empire, led by Prussia. This was Prussia's victory and Bismarck's but the army's moment of triumph.

The enhanced prestige of the army coincided with the establishment of the officer reserve by the army reforms of 1859 to 1865. This allowed a great swathe of middle-class German men to become officers, albeit not in a regular, full-time capacity. This in turn exposed them to values of the professional officer corps, among them, of course, duelling. The great prestige of the army after 1870 and the widening of the recruiting base for officers did much to create a widespread acceptance of the army and of its mores. August Bebel, a leading parliamentary opponent of duelling, was in no doubt of the link between the officer reserve and the broader acceptance of duelling in German society. It was due to the reserve officers that 'duelling is condoned and practised as a sport by large sections of the middle class on at least as large a scale as is the case among aristocratic circles'. Until as recently as a few decades ago (he was writing in the 1890s), he continued,

> it was almost impossible to find a middle-class man of standing in the entire German Reich who would have dared to defend duelling, indeed ... the entire middle class were the implacable opponents and foes of duelling ... [but] the system of twelve-month voluntary enlistment and the career of a second lieutenant of the reserve which it has spawned [has] had a devastating moral effect.[10]

Bebel was not alone in his analysis of the connection between the growth of the officer reserve and the spread of the acceptance of duelling in Germany. By 1914 the proportion of reserve officers to regular officers was three to one.[11] There was general agreement in the Kaiserreich that the officer reserve was the principal conduit through which duelling reached the wider population. The 'weekend' officer, who spent much of his life away from the rarefied atmosphere of the mess, did not have the benefit of the regular officers' *cordon sanitaire*, protecting him from potential sources of dishonour. Consequently, he was exposed almost daily to the vulgarity and excess of the population at large, circumstances in which his honour was perpetually at risk. Thus, reserve officers probably fought a disproportionate number of duels.

The proportion of middle-class officers in the Prussian army grew during the nineteenth century. In 1806 it was approximately 10 per cent; by 1860 the figure had reached 35 per cent; and, by 1913, 70 per cent – although it was noteworthy that the higher the rank, the lower the proportion of middle-class officers. Only a quarter of all lieutenants were aristocratic in 1913 but in the case of colonels and generals the figure was half.[12] The middle-class officers recruited to the officer corps were understandably anxious to absorb the mores of their better-bred fellows, and to ape their customs. At the same time, the military authorities, anxious to maintain the aristocratic tone of the officer corps in the face of the steady increase in the number of middle-class officers, began to codify the concept of an officer's honour. This tendency was particularly noticeable in the navy, where there was a high proportion of middle-class officers.

As always in the history of duelling, it is one thing to form an impression of how a particular society thought of duelling at a particular time but quite another to put even a rough figure on the number of duels fought. Although Germany is no exception to this general rule, there are some statistics that throw a partial light on the duelling habits of nineteenth-century Germans. The sources are incomplete and inherently inaccurate, not least because only a tiny proportion of duelling cases reached the courts. In Prussia between 1800 and 1914 Ute Frevert counted references to 270 duelling cases, of which 78 (29 per cent) proved fatal. More than three-quarters of these duels were fought with pistols.[13] Frevert also produced, from a different source, some statistics relating to convictions for duelling offences under Title 15 of the Criminal Code of the German Reich. They show that, between 1882 and 1914, 3,466 people were convicted in the German Empire of duelling offences. Of those who were convicted 45 per cent were Prussian and 75 per cent Protestant. The majority of the convicted duellists were young students.

Although these figures should be treated with caution, they do nevertheless throw some light on the German duel. Perhaps most importantly, they confirm the anecdotal evidence that the pistol was the German duellist's preferred weapon. In this respect Germany differed from France, where the sword was the favoured weapon. We have seen how the Germans looked down on the duel as it had developed in *belle époque* France. Dr Adolph Kohut, whose anthology of famous duels was published in 1888, poured scorn on the French duel:

> The duel in France has deteriorated into a trivial game. Neither high-mindedness, nor noble sentiment, nor preservation of true manly honour are the mainsprings of the affairs of honour, but in most cases enormous vanity.[14]

In Germany things were very different. As Kevin McAleer put it, 'The alpha and omega of German masculinity was physical courage', and the duel was an ideal opportunity to express it; indeed, it was an absolute requirement.[15] The more dangerous the duel, the greater the opportunity to display one's courage.

Most German duels – the statistics quoted above suggest perhaps as many as three-quarters – were pistol duels. Duellists, as in Britain, used conventional duelling pistols, earlier in the century the flintlock and then the more reliable percussion-cap weapon. By the end of the century, modern innovations such as revolvers and rifled barrels were creeping in, although they were forbidden by the codes. There were a number of ways of conducting a pistol duel. German duellists tended to prefer the 'barrier' duel, in which the opponents advanced towards a barrier marked between them and, having stopped, fired. The man who had fired first was then obliged to stand stock still while his opponent, if he was still able, advanced to the barrier to fire at him.

There were two other characteristics that distinguished the German pistol duel from its Anglo-Saxon cousin. In Britain and America it was common practice for the party who had delivered the original slight to fire into the air; in the duel between the Duke of Wellington and Lord Winchelsea, both men deliberately fired wide. This was regarded as deeply unsound in Germany, where it was interpreted as inviting a reciprocal act of mercy from one's opponent. Equally, in British pistol duels, taking deliberate aim at one's opponent was considered poor form. In Germany, by contrast, duellists were *expected* to aim, in order to demonstrate their seriousness of purpose. The doleful tale of Lieutenant of the Reserve Frueson illustrates both these points. In a duel fought in the Eberswalde in 1895 with his superior officer, Captain von Stosch, Frueson fired, all too obviously, into the air. Von Stosch in reply took careful aim and shot Frueson dead.[16]

The tentative statistics quoted above support the anecdotal evidence that the German duel, generally fought with pistols, was much more dangerous than its French equivalent, fought with swords. French duels had a very low mortality rate; Frevert's figures suggest that the fatality rate in German duels was approaching one in three, a ratio that indicates a much greater level of danger. The figures also show that, in the 30 years before World War One, about 100 people were convicted each year of duelling offences across Germany, the bulk of them in Prussia. Unfortunately, as only a small (but unknown) proportion of duellists were prosecuted, and those who were were exclusively civilian, the statistics give us no real idea of the number of duels fought in Germany at the time. It has been estimated that about 5 per cent of the population of Wilhelmine Germany was *satisfaktionsfahig* – that is, capable of giving and receiving honourable satisfaction in a duel. Germany's population by 1910 had grown to around 65 million, which suggests that perhaps 3 million people considered themselves entitled to defend their reputations on the duelling ground. This gives rise to the possibility of a vast pool of potential duellists but gets us no closer to answering the question of how many duels were in fact fought.

Although duelling in Germany was essentially a military phenomenon, it was not confined exclusively to the armed forces. Indeed, certain sections of the civilian population embraced the custom enthusiastically, doctors, lawyers and civil servants in particular. The criminal statistics show that one-fifth of convicted duellists before World War One were professional people. These professional groups developed strong identities and a powerful sense of collective and personal honour, which frequently led to challenges and duels. As in the army, duelling in the professions was a way of bridging the gap between the aristocracy and the middle classes. There can also be little doubt that many of these men had absorbed the notions of honour and the etiquettes of duelling while at university.

The student duel, or *mensur*, was a quintessentially German institution that, by the time of the Kaiserreich, had a long history. Student duelling can be traced to the French and Italian universities of the Renaissance and, by the end of the sixteenth century, every German university had a fencing master. Duels were very frequent. Until the nineteenth century the rapier was the duellists' favoured weapon but, as its sharp point made it lethally dangerous, it was gradually banned across Germany. Jena was the last university in Germany to ban the rapier – in 1840.[17]

The Wilhelmine era was a golden age for the *mensur*. By the late nineteenth century it was highly organised, bristling with protocols and conventions. We shall examine the *mensur* through eyes of three English-speaking witnesses, all of whom visited a German university and watched the *mensur* in action. The first is Mark Twain, who visited Heidelberg in the late 1870s. The second is Jerome K. Jerome, who witnessed student duelling at an unnamed German university at the turn of the century. The third is Sir Lees Knowles, a British historian, who spent a day with a student duelling corps, also at Heidelberg, just before World War One. Their accounts vary in tone, too, from the respectful admiration of Knowles to the cynical ridicule of Jerome, with Twain somewhere in the middle.[18]

By 1914 there were around 60,000 university students in Germany, double the number that there had been 30 years earlier. Of those about 2,000 were active *Corpsstudenten*, a figure that had remained constant despite the rise in the university population. Organised along the same lines as the corps but lacking their cachet, were two other organisations, the Burschenschaften and the Landesmann-schaften, which boasted 3,300 and 2,000 members respectively in 1913.[19] The corps were socially the most rarefied of the student duelling bodies, probably because they had the highest proportion of aristocratic members. Certainly, the cost restricted the membership to the best-off students; Jerome reckoned that membership of a 'crack' corps cost £400 a year (perhaps £20,000 in today's money). Sir Lees Knowles estimated that there were more than 20 universities in Germany in 1913 and around 80 Corps.

Within each university the *Corpsstudenten* were organised into a number of distinct corps, often with geographical or territorial connotations. At Heidelberg, for example, there were five: the Seuvia, whose colours were yellow; the Guestphalia, who sported green; Saxo-Borussia, white; Vandalia, red; and Rhenania, dark blue. Each corps had its own highly formalised codes of conduct and rules of membership; some of the richer corps even had their own clubhouses. They existed partly as clubs but their principal function was to arrange duelling. Twain noted that in Heidelberg there was a minimum of six duels a week during term-time and often considerably more. These duels were conducted in a hall set aside for the purpose. Twain and Knowles seem to have visited the same hall at Heidelberg; they both describe it as being 50 feet long, 30 feet wide and about 25 feet high.

The duels were fought with a *schlager*, a long narrow-bladed sword, three feet long and half an inch wide. The entire leading edge was razor-sharp, as was about one-third of the rear edge; it was fitted with a large guard to protect the hand. Before a bout the duellists put on a great deal of protective kit. Twain described two students 'panoplied for the duel'.

> They were bare-headed; their eyes were protected by iron goggles that projected an inch or more, the leather straps of which bound their ears flat against their heads; their necks were wound around and around with thick wrappings which a sword could not cut through; from chin to ankle they were padded thoroughly against injury; their arms were bandaged and rebandaged, layer upon layer, until they looked like solid black logs.

Thus trussed up, it was impossible to move in the normal way. Jerome was less charitable in his description of the student knights kitted out for battle.

> In the centre, facing each other, stand the combatants, resembling Japanese warriors, as made familiar to us by the Japanese tea-tray.

Quaint and rigid, with their goggle-covered eyes, their necks tied up in comforters, their bodies smothered in what looks like dirty bed quilts, their padded arms stretched straight above their heads, they might be a pair of ungainly clockwork figures. The seconds … drag them out into their proper position. One almost listens to hear the sound of the castors.

The fight, when it began, was generally a brutal slugging match, far removed from the technical skill and manual dexterity of fencing. The combatants stood still, about a sword's length apart, and simply hacked at one another; there was no footwork, no guile and no finesse. Twain described the action: 'The instant the word was given, the two apparitions sprang forward and began to rain blows down upon each other with lightning rapidity.' He admitted to thinking that there was something 'wonderfully stirring' about the contest. Jerome, needless to say, did not agree.

> The umpire takes his place, the word is given, and immediately there follow five rapid clashes of the long straight swords. There is no interest in watching the fight: there is no movement, no skill, no grace … The strongest man wins; the man who, with his heavily padded arm … can hold his huge clumsy sword longest without growing too weak to be able either to guard or to strike.

Although Jerome was clearly not enamoured of the *mensur*, he was right in surmising that it was a test of strength and stamina. Twain tells us that the rules prescribed that bouts should last for 15 minutes of actual fighting time. The average bout in Wilhelmine times would be fought over anything between 60 and 80 rounds; in each round each combatant would deliver five strokes of the *schlager*. So if a bout went the distance, the duellist could expect to deliver 300–400 blows with his sword, no small feat of endurance.[20]

In fights of this length and brutality injuries were common. Some of the injuries were, quite literally, hair-raising. Twain saw 'a handful of hair skip into the air as if it had lain loose on the victim's head and a breath of wind had puffed it suddenly away.' When a combatant was wounded badly enough, the fight would be stopped so that he could be treated. It was of vital importance that the wounded duellist endure his wounds and his treatment 'without a wince'.

Indeed, in the longer term, it was worthwhile enduring the discomfort of the primitive surgery, for the slashes and gashes of the *mensur* would become the coveted duelling scars, or *schmiss*. Duelling scars were lifelong and highly visible proof of a man's courage and of his status as a *Corpsstudenten*. Jerome estimated that a third of German gentlemen bore duelling scars. Indeed, so sought after were these scars that the stitching process was often less painstaking than it otherwise might have been. As Jerome explained it:

> A clean-cut wound that gapes wide is most desired by all parties. On purpose it is sewn up clumsily, with the hope that by this means the scar will last a lifetime. Such a wound, judiciously mauled and interfered with during the week afterwards, can generally be reckoned on to secure its fortunate possessor a wife with a dowry of five figures at the least.

The benefits of membership of a corps continued long after the student had graduated into the wider world. They constituted a highly influential 'old-boy network' and a good set of duelling scars was a sign of belonging, like a Masonic handshake. The Federation of Kosener Corps Delegates, founded in 1848, came to represent 1,500 full-time and 4,000 part-time members, as well as 25,000 'old boys'. A hundred and eighteen corps were affiliated to it.[21] It was a formidably powerful machine for the dispensation of patronage and ensured that countless former *Corpsstudenten* landed plum jobs in the professions and the civil service. In Prussia in 1903 21 of the 35 chairmen of the regional governing councils were corps alumni.[22] It is little wonder that duelling continued to thrive in the upper reaches of German society.

As with duelling proper, support for the *Corpsstudenten* came from the very top, from the Kaiser himself. Wilhelm II had, as a young man (despite his withered arm), been a member of the Corps Borussia in 1877 and spoke fondly of the experience when he returned to the university in 1891.[23] Not everyone saw the *mensur* in so positive a light – it was specifically banned by the Catholic Church, for example – but many observers saw at least some merit in its rituals. Knowles thought that 'this form of exercise is essential for the German Corps-student. It teaches him self-defence, and it makes Spartans of a military nation.' Mark Twain was impressed differently: 'All the customs, all the laws, all the details, pertaining to the student duel are quaint and naïve. The grave, precise, and courtly ceremony with which the thing is conducted, invests it with a sort of antique charm.'

By contrast, Jerome's conclusion is perhaps unfairly harsh, if mischievous: 'The *Mensur* is, in fact, the *reductio ad absurdum* of the duel; and if the Germans themselves cannot see that it is funny, one can only regret their lack of humour.'

The *mensur* was bound by convention; indeed conforming to custom and obeying the rules was one of the most important aspects of being a *Corpsstudenten*. So it was in the wider world of duelling proper. As in other countries, adherence to the prescribed rules was important, not least because it was likely to bolster the duellist's defence in the event of criminal proceedings. The German duellist, in common with his English- or French-speaking confrère, did not lack for advice on how to conduct himself in an affair of honour. Authors busied themselves producing books that explained every detail of the etiquette. Alexander von Oettingen's *Zur Duellfrage* of 1889 was just one of many works about duelling that appeared in the late nineteenth century. Friedrich Teppner's *Duell-Regeln fur Officiere* of 1898 was aimed specifically at officers of the Austro-Hungarian army. The author even went so far as to include two photographs – mock-ups, one assumes – of a group of immaculately turned out officers in position to fight both a pistol and a sword duel.[24]

The Germans were the most dedicated duellists in Europe. Their preference for the pistol over the sword and their belief that honour could be properly satisfied only in circumstances of mortal risk ensured that duelling in Germany was a serious business. The theatrical frivolity of most French duels was not for them. When Lieutenant von Puttkammer and Lieutenant von Heeringen, both subalterns in the 27th Infantry Regiment, fought a duel in 1912, it was under harsh conditions: they would exchange shots at 15 paces until one or other man was incapacitated. Support for duelling was ingrained into the military and, thanks in part to the *mensur*, the upper echelons of the

professions, the civil service and the judiciary. Moreover, it was positively encouraged by the Kaiser himself. With such support behind it,
it was hardly surprising that the duel was still in vigorous health in
Germany when World War One engulfed Europe in 1914.

The compulsion for the upper-class German to fight a duel to
restore slighted honour was very strong. Not to do so was to risk professional and social disgrace. To be able to hold one's head up, one had
to fight. Theodore Fontane's novel of 1895, *Effie Briest*, provides a stark
illustration of these pressures. The eponymous heroine of the novel,
Effie, is married to a much older man, Geert von Innstetten, who is a
high-ranking civil servant and confidant of Bismarck. They married
when Effie was 17. Soon after their marriage, Effie and her husband
move to a small town on the Baltic coast. Von Instetten is often away
and, eventually, Effie has a brief affair with Major Crampas. Six or
seven years later, when the von Instettens have moved back to Berlin
and the affair is long over, Effie's husband finds, by accident, a bundle
of love letters to his wife from Crampas. Von Instetten quickly
decides, without questioning Effie about the affair, to challenge his
wife's lover to a duel. That evening his second, an old friend, comes to
von Instetten's house and listens as the cuckolded husband bemoans
the pressure on him to fight a duel.

> Because there's no way round it. I've turned it all over in my mind. We're
> not just individuals, we're part of a larger whole and we must constantly
> have regard for that larger whole, we're dependent on it, beyond a doubt
> … wherever men live together, something has been established that's just
> there, and it's a code we've become accustomed to judging everything by,
> ourselves as well as others. And going against it is unacceptable; society
> despises you for it, and in the end you despise yourself, you can't bear it
> any longer and put a gun to your head … I've no choice. I must.[25]

Russia

The history of duelling is at best a shadowy subject, pitted with
lacunae and beset with uncertainties. The fact that it was invariably
illegal, albeit often unofficially condoned, merely serves to compound

these difficulties. The history of duelling in Russia is a doubly elusive beast. The historian is hampered by the lack of official records; even anecdotal evidence, such as newspaper articles, are for the most part lacking in Russia. Irina Reyfman is the latest historian to attempt to tell the story of Russian duelling. She admitted that 'one has to accept the fact that writing a full, statistically sound, and unambiguous historical account of duelling is not just an onerous task but largely an unperformable one'.[26]

There are a number of reasons for the dearth of sources available to the historian.[27] Few first-hand accounts of duels survive because, quite simply, it was never safe to discuss duelling in public, or to advertise the fact that one had 'gone out'. The same applies to accounts in private correspondence; in a country where the government made a habit of reading its citizens' post, it was even dangerous to boast in a letter about having fought a duel. Equally, the newspapers were remiss in reporting duels and are, consequently, a patchy source. They did not start to cover duelling properly until the last third of the nineteenth century. The zenith of duelling in Russia was in the early decades of the century, at which time newspapers barely reported duels. Indeed, for considerable periods during the reign of Nicholas I (1825–55), any mention of duelling in the press was banned. As a result, the only reference in the press to the death of Pushkin in a duel in 1837 was an announcement some six weeks later that d'Anthes, Pushkin's opponent, had been deported 'for killing the Kammer-Junker Pushkin'. Similarly, Lermontov was killed in a duel four years later but his death was reported without any mention of its cause. Faced with this reticence the historian 'has to rely on what contemporaries chose to leave behind; that is, incomplete official records and narratives that are reserved, sketchy, frequently anecdotal, and always biased'.[28]

It is in this context that Russian literature becomes particularly important. Duelling frequently figured in literature. In the nineteenth century one thinks of Scott, Thackeray and Bulwer-Lytton in English and Dumas in French. The same is true in Russian literature, except that it assumes a greater importance as a historical source in its own right. This is partly because of the dearth already discussed of other sources and partly because a number of nineteenth-century Russian novelists had actually fought duels, or come close to doing so. It is one of the few sources that shed light on how contemporaries viewed duelling. The fact that they tread the marches between fact and fiction imbues the works of Pushkin, Lermontov, Turgenev, Tolstoy and others with a special significance for the historian of duelling.

Duelling was not indigenous to Russia; none of the historical, social or cultural phenomena that spawned the modern duel in Europe were present in Russia. For Russians, the duel was a foreign flower, imported from Western Europe. The first duels on Russian soil were fought between foreign mercenaries in the Russian service. One of the earliest was a duel fought in 1666 between General Patrick Gordon, a Scotsman in the Russian service, and Major Montgomery. By the end of the seventeenth century Russians themselves had not yet acquired the habit of fighting duels.

This did not prevent Peter the Great, who reigned from 1682 to 1725, from enacting a ferocious anti-duelling law in 1702. It forbade duelling on pain of execution; an armed assault following a quarrel was punishable by the amputation of an arm, an excruciatingly painful sentence and one that, in the days before antiseptics, was more than likely to result in the victim's death. It is strange that Peter felt the need to prescribe such severe penalties for a crime that had not yet gained a foothold among his subjects. One can only surmise that Peter encountered duelling during his celebrated trip to the West in the 1690s and decided that it was worth making a pre-emptive strike against the custom.

In the eighteenth century, duels in Russia were rare. In 1754, Zakhar Chernyshev and Nikolai Leont'ev fought a duel over a game of cards. Chernyshev was seriously wounded, although he did later recover. It caused a sensation in St Petersburg and was mentioned by Catherine the Great in her memoirs, indications in themselves that a duel was a rare and remarkable event. Irina Reyfman concludes that 'eighteenth-century Russians themselves fought rarely and reluctantly'. She stresses that the number of duels remained very low throughout the greater part of the century. Their rarity did not prevent Catherine the Great, in common with Peter the Great, from introducing anti-duelling regulations. In 1787 her *Manifesto on Duels* prescribed more lenient measures than those set down by Peter 80 years earlier, which may have been designed to make them more enforceable.

Catherine's husband and predecessor, Peter III, is frequently associated with duelling. He was a German prince and an admirer of Frederick the Great, a fact that may have contributed to his enthusiasm for duelling. As Irina Reyfman observed,

> The anecdotes about Peter III as a failed duellist demonstrate his contemporaries' profound ambivalence towards the duel: they laughed at Peter, unsure whether the honour code and the duel were ludicrous by themselves or whether he made them so.

Catherine's successor was the eccentric Tsar Paul (1796–1801), whose reign appears to be 'a turning point in the history of duelling in Russia'. He was interested in the concept of knighthood and the ideals of chivalry, an interest that no doubt prompted him to accept the Grand Mastership of the Order of the Knights of St John, an ancient order of chivalry whose fief was the island of Malta. He also proposed in 1801 the much-derided idea that the great questions of European politics should be decided not by wars but by monarchs challenging each other to duels, with their respective prime ministers acting as seconds. This represented a return to the notion of the fate of armies or nations being settled by a contest between champions, David and Goliath for the Napoleonic era.

Paul's interest in duelling ventured beyond the theoretical: in 1784, while in Naples, he challenged Count Andrei Razumovsky, who had supposedly had an affair with Paul's late wife. The two men were prevented from fighting by bystanders. It seems that Paul expected his officers to respect the concepts of honour; several officers were discharged from the Tsar's service for failing to respond in an appropriate manner to insults. Paul's brief reign came to an end in March 1801, when he was murdered by some drunken officers of his own guard.

Although Paul was favourably disposed towards the concept of knightly chivalry and the notions of honour that underpinned the duel, he was determined to assert his absolute power. His reign was characterised by an 'atmosphere of oppression', which did not allow the notions of honour that Paul was, in theory, so keen to propagate among the aristocracy. As the Bourbons in France discovered, duelling and the exercise of absolute royal power were uneasy bedfellows.

Paul was succeeded by his son Alexander I, whose accession ushered in a more relaxed, liberal atmosphere at court, in which duelling flourished. Alexander's reign has been called the 'Golden Age of the Russian Duel'. The Napoleonic wars took Russian officers into Europe, thus exposing them to European manners, to an unprecedented extent. Marshal Suvorov's army campaigned in Italy and central Europe for several years during the war of the Second Coalition. The campaigns of 1812 to 1815 took the Russian army to France and Paris itself. There, after the fall of Napoleon and the restoration of the Bourbons, duelling became the order of the day. The frenzy caught up the British, the French and the Prussians, nor were the Russians any exception.

Back at home, there was a marked increase in the incidence of duelling. The most notorious duellist of the period was Fedor Tolstoy, who was credited – if that is quite the right word – with having killed 11 men in duels. Tolstoy himself took pride in the fact that many of his duels were fought for trivial reasons.

Duelling became associated with the Decembrists, a conspiracy of liberal, aristocratic army officers and nobles who hoped to supplant the autocratic regime of the Tsars. Their revolt took place in December 1825, in the early months of the reign of Nicholas I. The Decembrists liked to present themselves as a group of serious-minded people who eschewed the life of irresponsible pleasure, yet many of them were inveterate duellists. Men such as Kondratii Ryleev, Alexander Bestuzhev and Lunin were important figures in the Decembrist conspiracy, who had all fought and incited duels. The Decembrists were in part motivated by tensions and jealousies within the aristocracy, stresses that, not surprisingly, gave rise to duels. Konstantin Chernov's duel with Novosil'tsev was an example of a duel between the old and the new aristocracy. Fought three months before the Decembrist rising, it acquired political overtones that seemed to epitomise the rebels' cause. The espousal of the duel by the Decembrists 'elevated the duel to a form of political protest'.

According to Irina Reyfman, 'the duel's high cultural prestige in Russia has roots in this period of reckless and seemingly senseless duelling'. Nicholas I ruthlessly suppressed the Decembrist revolt and many of its leading spirits were exiled or imprisoned. Traditionally, his reign has been regarded as a period in which duelling declined, suppressed by the government's illiberal policy. Irina Reyfman, however, disputes this interpretation. 'Contemporary records,' she writes, 'do not support the idea that the duel was in decline. On the contrary, they suggest that duelling continued in Nicholas's time and beyond, more or less at the same pace as before.'

Between the 1830s and the 1890s the list of those who fought (or might have fought) duels is quite long and includes 'the names of figures prominent in literature, journalism, education and the law'. Both the Pushkin and Lermontov duels, the two most celebrated in Russian history, were, after all, fought during this period. As one might expect, duelling was particularly frequent among army officers. One source cites more than a dozen duelling cases between the 1840s and the 1860s; another states that 15 such cases reached the district military courts in the years between 1876 and 1890. In the second half of the nineteenth century, journalists became some of the most enthusiastic duellists, as they were elsewhere, particularly in France and the United States. This development also represents the spread of the duelling ethic to the middle classes, as happened in many other countries, notably France.

It was this dilution of the aristocratic tone of the duel towards the end of the nineteenth century that resulted in a rare and remarkable piece of legislation, an order legalising duelling. Throughout duelling's history governments everywhere have sought, often vainly, to eradicate the practice, struggling against entrenched interests to enforce the law. Yet here, in late nineteenth-century Russia, the Tsar, at the stroke of a pen, was encouraging the practice. The document, which had been drawn up by the military authorities, was approved by the Tsar on 13 May 1894. It gave the Court of the Society of Officers the right to force an officer to fight a duel; an officer who refused to obey the court's direction was obliged to resign his commission.

Not surprisingly, the Tsar's diktat caused an increase in the number of duels. Reyfman quotes some statistics showing that more duels were fought after the diktat than before it. One commentator noted that, in the 15 years between 1876 and 1890, there were just 15 duels in Russia; in the 10 years after 1894 there were 186. Another commentator reported that 320 duels were fought in Russia between 1894 and 1910.

The next significant development in the history of duelling in Russia was the evolution of the parliamentary duel. In almost every country we have examined, the parliamentary duel was an important strand in the story of duelling, both popularising the practice and conferring cachet upon it. There had been no parliamentary duelling in Russia for the simple reason that there had been no parliament; the Tsars as autocrats had ruled alone. But, following the revolution of 1905, the Duma was resurrected. Its members quickly learned the habits that their parliamentary colleagues in France, for instance, had long taken for granted and, in the years between 1905 and the outbreak of World War One, parliamentary duelling thrived. The duel between M. Markoff and M. Pergament in July 1908 was the result of an argument that arose in the Duma. The first time that they tried to fight they were interrupted – according to some unkind souls not entirely accidentally – before they could exchange shots. The following day they were able to elude the police and fight their duel. No one was hurt.[29] In 1909 Count Uvarov and M. Guchkoff, then president of the Duma, fought a politically motivated duel in which Uvarov was slightly wounded in the shoulder. Both men received short custodial sentences from the District Court.[30]

Duelling in Russia had enjoyed a shorter life than in other countries but was brought to an end there, as it was elsewhere, by the outbreak of war in 1914. In Russia the effect of war was compounded by the revolution of 1917; the new communist regime was not likely to tolerate duelling, a vestige *par excellence* of the Tsarist regime.

What do the great Russian authors of the nineteenth century have to tell us about the duel? Their novels put flesh on the bones of the history, giving us an impression of what contemporaries thought about duelling and duellists. The novelist and critic Alexander Bestuzhev-Marlinsky is credited with having established the duel as a

theme in Russian literature in the late 1820s and 1830s. He was the first
in a long tradition of nineteenth-century Russian novelists who wrote
about duelling, usually from some degree of personal experience.
Bestuzhev himself, who combined a career as a soldier with his literary activities, wrote about duelling from experience. He fought
several duels as a young officer in St Petersburg and was Ryleev's
second in his duel with Prince Shakhovskoy. Reduced to the ranks for
his part in the Decembrist revolt in 1825, he was killed in action in
1837, a few months after Pushkin's death.[31]

Alexander Pushkin was both Russia's best-known poet and her
most famous duellist. *Eugene Onegin* is the work on which, in the
West at least, Pushkin's reputation principally rests. The climactic
event of *Onegin* is a duel in which the unfortunate Lensky is killed.
Onegin is a dramatic story, told in verse, but its interest for us lies in
the remarkable extent to which it prefigured Pushkin's own death in a
duel. Pushkin completed *Onegin* about five years before he died but it
is astonishingly prescient about the way in which his fatal duel was to
be conducted and the circumstances from which it arose.

Pushkin's nemesis was Georges d'Anthes, a young Frenchman,
who had arrived in Russia in 1833. He had been forced to abandon a
military career in France by the revolution of 1830 but, once in Russia,
having been adopted by Baron Heeckeren, the Dutch Minister at St
Petersburg, was able to secure a commission in a Guards regiment.
D'Anthes cut a dashing figure in the salons of St Petersburg. Pushkin's
most recent biographer described him thus: 'Tall, with blond hair and
blue eyes, distinguished by the romantic aura of a royalist exile, he was
particularly successful with the opposite sex.'[32]

Pushkin had married the beautiful Natalya Goncharova, who was
12 or so years younger than he, in February 1831. They settled in St
Petersburg, where, in the autumn of 1835, d'Anthes first met Natalya
and her sisters. D'Anthes became openly infatuated with Natalya and
by the New Year tongues were wagging. Pushkin had a fiery temper –
he had issued two challenges in February 1836 alone – nor was his
mental equilibrium improved at this time by his ever-increasing
debts. Baron Heeckeren, fearing a duel, persuaded d'Anthes to call off
his pursuit of Natalya. And there, for a while, matters rested.

In the early summer Natalya gave birth but was soon out in society, where d'Anthes once more turned his attentions to her. At first he used her sister Ekaterina as smokescreen, but it did not fool Pushkin, who became broodingly jealous. During the course of the autumn d'Anthes's pursuit of Natalya became increasingly obsessive until, at the beginning of November, she decisively rejected him. The following day an anonymous note arrived at Pushkin's house, accusing him of being a cuckold. Pushkin guessed at its provenance and sent a cartel to the Dutch embassy, challenging d'Anthes to a duel.

There followed a period of tortured negotiation as Baron Heeckeren and an intermediary tried to persuade Pushkin to withdraw his challenge. This, eventually, he did, assured that it was Natalya's sister Ekaterina who was the object of d'Anthes's affections. D'Anthes, realising that the circumstances of Pushkin's retraction of his challenge could give rise to imputations of cowardice, asked the poet to explain his reasons for withdrawing his challenge. This simply further enraged Pushkin. D'Anthes and Ekaterina were married on 10 January 1837 but, despite some increasingly frantic attempts to reconcile the brothers-in-law (as they now were), their animosity showed no signs of abating. In the third week of January matters came to a head when d'Anthes publicly insulted Natalya; Pushkin thereupon wrote Heeckeren a highly offensive letter and, on 26 January, d'Anthes challenged him to a duel. The following day, in the late afternoon, the two men and their seconds met in the garden of a villa outside St Petersburg. The seconds agreed that the duel would be fought *à la barrière*; d'Anthes fired first, hitting Pushkin in the stomach. Pushkin, having collapsed to the ground, managed to steady himself sufficiently to fire his pistol, but failed to inflict anything more serious than a flesh wound on his opponent. Pushkin lingered in great pain before dying two days later.[33]

The duel sequence of *Eugene Onegin* prefigures the events that led to Pushkin's death with remarkable accuracy. To start with the configuration of the relationships is virtually identical. In *Onegin* Lensky's fiancée, Olga, has a sister, Tatyana, who falls madly in love with Onegin, who spurns her and, in a fit of deliberate maliciousness, turns his attentions to Olga. Lensky, eaten up with jealousy, challenges

Onegin to a duel and is killed. The fictional configuration of *Onegin* mirrors that of Pushkin's real-life tragedy, played out five years later. D'Anthes was Ekaterina's fiancé (and later her husband) but could nor resist pursuing her sister, Pushkin's wife, with equally disastrous results. In both cases the behaviour of the rogue male – d'Anthes in fact, Onegin in fiction – was provocative in the extreme. Onegin's behaviour has parallels in d'Anthes's pursuit of Natalya. Moreover, in both cases, the wronged party was killed in the duel – Pushkin in fact, Lensky in fiction.

There are three other striking similarities between Pushkin's creation and his own fate. First, both duels took place in the snow. Second, Pushkin gave Onegin a pair of duelling pistols made by Lepage, a Paris gunsmith, the same make of gun as Pushkin himself used in his duel. Third, the duel was fought *à la barrière*. In *Onegin* Pushkin gave his readers a full account of the duel; no one who read the novel could fail to be impressed by the macabre formality of the duelling ritual. The only significant deviation from the accepted protocol was Onegin's failure to find a proper second; pressing one's manservant into service was not the done thing. That apart, anyone who sought advice about how to conduct a duel could safely refer to *Onegin*, which amounted to a full public discussion of an otherwise taboo subject. It also demonstrates that the Russian duel was identical, in all important respects, to the duel as practised in England, France and America.

Mikhail Lermontov (1814–41) combined a career as a soldier with the literary life, as Bestuzhev had done. Lermontov was a Romantic poet and an accomplished novelist, as well as a prodigiously talented artist, as his extant work proves. A younger contemporary of Pushkin, Lermontov was born into a noble family and commissioned into a Guards regiment. While serving in St Petersburg in 1840 he fought a bloodless duel with Ernest de Barante, the son of the French ambassador. The dispute had arisen over some less than flattering remarks that Lermontov had allegedly made about de Barante. The duel took place in the spot at which Pushkin and d'Anthes had fought three years earlier. A further coincidence was that the pistols used by d'Anthes were the very same pair with which Lermantov and de Barante had fought.

The Frenchman prudently went abroad, leaving Lermontov to face a court martial, which ordered him to be reduced to the ranks and deprived of his noble status. The Tsar intervened, softening the sentence to a transfer to a line infantry training battalion in the Caucasus, which was, nevertheless, a humiliation for a former Guards officer. In the summer of 1841 Lermontov, on leave from his regiment in the Caucasus, rented a house in the popular spa town of Pyatigorsk with his friend Stolypin. The town boasted a lively 'season', into which Lermontov and Stolypin threw themselves with vigour.

Also in Pyatigorsk that summer was an old acquaintance of Lermontov's from cadet school, the retired Major Martynov. Martynov, the son of a wealthy Moscow property developer, had a reputation as a 'vulnerable if not a vain character'.[34] Martynov was already the butt of Lermontov's jokes, which he patiently endured, but made matters worse for himself by 'going native'. This entailed dressing in kaftans, black-and-white surcoats and sheepskin hats; he also shaved his head in the Tartar fashion. Lermontov ribbed him mercilessly, referring to him as '*le chevalier des monts sauvages*' or '*Monsieur Sauvage Homme*'.[35] Eventually, however, after one cruel joke too many, Martynov's patience snapped and he challenged Lermontov to a duel. On 15 July 1841, the two men, accompanied by their seconds, rode out of Pyatigorsk towards the cemetery. There, in a convenient meadow, the seconds stepped out 30 paces, marking the barrier with swords before ordering the principals to take up their positions. Martynov advanced smartly to the barrier and fired; Lermontov collapsed to the ground. He had been shot through the chest; the bullet had penetrated his heart and lungs, in all probability killing him instantly.[36]

Like Pushkin, Lermontov wrote a novel, *A Hero of Our Time*, that describes a duel in intricate detail. It differs from the encounter in *Onegin* in that it is almost a complete travesty of the accepted etiquette; neither did Lermontov succeed in prefiguring the manner of his own death to the extent that Pushkin did. Pechorin, the hero, is an army officer, an amoral, cynical man, who is visiting the town of Kislovodsk in the Caucasus. While he is there he stumbles upon a plot among the local officers to teach him a lesson: 'These Petersburg puppies get above themselves unless you slap them down. Just because he's got clean gloves and polished boots he fancies he's the only society man among us.'[37]

One of their number, Grushnitsky, is charged with picking a quarrel with Pechorin. This he duly does and a challenge is soon issued. On the appointed day the two men and their seconds make their rendezvous in a secluded spot in the mountains outside the town. The seconds try to bring about a reconciliation but without success, whereupon Pechorin and Grushnitsky agree to fight at six paces on a high, narrow ledge, so that, should one of them be killed (which was almost a certainty), it would look like an accident.

There follows a game of bluff and counterbluff, during which Pechorin exposes the plot against him, the intentional failure to load his pistol. When Grushnitsky fires at Pechorin, he misses; coolly, Pechorin insists on loading his pistol and, when Grushnitsky refuses his offer of clemency, shoots him dead. 'As I went down the path I saw Grushnitsky's bloodstained body among the clefts in the rocks.'[38]

Pechorin's duel breaks almost all the rules; from start to finish it is a grotesque parody of the approved protocol: the plot to ensnare Pechorin; the misuse of a duel to teach him a lesson; the attempt to hoodwink Pechorin into accepting an unloaded pistol; the very harsh conditions for the duel; and the merciless, cold-blooded manner in which Pechorin kills Grushnitsky are all serious infringements of the duelling code. What we are to make of this highly unorthodox encounter is harder to say. Does it represent no more than Pechorin's cynical views, or does it reflect, perhaps, the author's view of the validity of the duel or some wider opinion of the question?

Ivan Turgenev (1818–83) had some experience of the etiquette of duelling, experience that was distilled in his novel *Fathers and Sons*. Turgenev as a young man had known Pushkin; indeed, had seen a good deal of the poet in the weeks before his death. Turgenev also, at about the time that *Fathers and Sons* was written, had fallen out with his fellow novelist Leo Tolstoy while staying with a mutual friend. The dispute resulted in the novelists sending each other formal challenges although, mercifully, no duel was ever fought.

In stark contrast to Pechorin's duel, the duel in *Fathers and Sons* between Pavel Petrovich and Bazarov has a faintly comic-opera air to it. Pavel Petrovich challenges Bazarov because, as he puts it, 'We cannot stand each other. What more is needed?'[39] The suspicion remains, however, that he would have provoked Bazarov had he not agreed to fight at once. Bazarov is the epitome of modern man, a nihilist, who pronounces that 'a duel is a nonsense' but is nevertheless prepared to admit that duels might serve some practical purpose. They agree on pistols at 10 paces, although neither man appoints a second. When they exchange shots, Pavel Petrovich receives a flesh wound in the thigh. It is hard to conclude from the duelling episode in his novel that Turgenev took duelling particularly seriously, a view that is, however, at least partly contradicted by his dispute with Tolstoy.

Tolstoy himself had served in the army during the Crimean War, so was likely to have been exposed to duelling. Certainly, he was quick to send a challenge to Turgenev when the two men fell out and he too incorporated a duel into a novel. In *War and Peace*, Pierre, in a fit of drunken jealousy, challenges Dolohov, whom he suspects of being his wife's lover, to a duel. The contest pits Dolohov, an experienced military man, against the bookish Pierre, a complete novice, who had hardly fired a pistol before. They fight *à la barrière* in the snowy woods; Pierre wounds Dolohov, who then, in an echo of Pushkin's duel, props himself up and fires at his opponent but misses.[40]

The lives and works of Pushkin and Lermontov and, to a lesser extent, Turgenev and Tolstoy, illustrate the importance of literature to the history of duelling in Russia. Chekhov's novella *The Duel*, which was published in 1891, acknowledges the influence of literature on Russian duelling in suggesting that the seconds refer to Lermontov or Turgenev for instruction in the etiquette. It is a joke, and a good one, but it is not wholly devoid of significance: it is in literature, rather than elsewhere, Chekhov seems to be saying, that you will find all you need to know about duelling.

Russia was unusual in that duelling was not common before the beginning of the nineteenth century. In Britain, it was by then entering its last few decades of life. Russia has more in common with France and Germany, countries in which duelling remained vigorous until 1914. Although the Russians were late starters, they caught on quickly; by the late nineteenth century Russia had fully absorbed the idea of the duel and the notions of honour that underpinned it. Indeed, by 1900, Russian duellists were fully paid-up members of the international fraternity.

Chapter Fifteen

THE DEATH OF HONOUR: DUELLING IN THE TWENTIETH CENTURY

I N THE EARLY YEARS of the twentieth century the duel was alive and well in most of Europe; only the po-faced, unchivalrous British and their gloomy colonial cousins, the Americans, had abandoned the defence of honour. They preferred the clink of coin to the clash of swords. In 1914, on the eve of war, duelling was thriving in its old heartlands: in June *The Times* announced from Paris, 'Duels have become diurnal during the last week.' The newspaper then reported the duel between Jacques Roujon and Leon Daudet, arising out of some disparaging remarks made by Daudet, 'a Royalist of a particularly combative disposition', about Roujon's late father. The two men fought with swords; Daudet was slightly wounded on the hand.[1] In Germany, too, it was business as usual. In February two German officers fought a pistol duel at Metz. Three shots were exchanged with unsighted pistols at 25 paces; Lieutenant Haage, the oldest subaltern in the 98th Infantry Regiment, was killed instantly, shot through the heart at the second fire. His opponent was a younger officer of the same regiment who had been making advances to Haage's wife.[2]

Indeed, in the years before World War One, duelling seemed as popular as ever. In its more traditional strongholds men were still 'going out' enthusiastically: in January 1913 Count Tisza, the president of the Hungarian Chamber, fought two duels in Budapest in the space of a week.[3] In Russia Prince Napoleon Murat fought successive duels against two brothers in May 1908. The prince survived both without injury but killed the second of the brothers he fought. But by now duelling had also taken root further afield. In 1910 two Greek naval officers fought a pistol duel over accusations of bribery made in the press, in which one was killed.[4]

In 1909 two duels, both involving government ministers, were reported from Portugal. One was a sword, the other a pistol duel.[5] In South America, too, in the former outposts of the Spanish Empire, duelling had become firmly implanted. One indication of its popularity there is the number of books that were published on the subject. In 1905, for example, Scipione Ferretto published *Codigo del Honor* in Buenos Aires, setting out the rules for duelling. Its easily portable handbook format suggested that it was intended as an on-the-spot reference book for duellists and their seconds.[6]

It was World War One, which engulfed Europe in August 1914, that finished off the old-fashioned duelling habits. Men still fought duels after 1918, but not with the same certainty or the old gusto. It was the slaughter of the war that saw to that: after the horrendous casualties in the trenches it was difficult for men to take duelling seriously. Britain and her empire lost about 900,000 men, Austro-Hungary 1,200,000, and France more than 1,350,000; Germany and Russia both lost around 1,700,000 men. The total death toll in Europe was nearly 8.5 million men.[7] These statistics exclude the many millions more who were permanently and horribly maimed. After loss of life and mutilation on this scale, the punctilios of the code of honour seemed trivial.

The impact of the war on duelling was immediately evident in France. In 1918 Georges Breittmayer, a noted authority on duelling, published a book entitled *Après Guerre Août 1914: Code de L'Honneur et Duel*. He had written much of it by 1914 but, when events overtook its publication, he updated the text for the new, post-war world. Breittmayer realised that if the duel continued as it had before the war, it would fall into disrepute. His remedy was to impose harsher conditions: 'Sword duels were made ridiculous by stopping the fight for a nick on the wrist.' Similarly, 'pistol duels were made to look ridiculous by exchanging shots at twenty-five paces from old-fashioned duelling pistols, with the result that neither shot hit its target'.[8] 'Now that the war is over,' he urged, 'make duels serious once more, for that will safeguard them both now and in the future.'[9]

Breittmayer, by reinventing the duel in a more lethal form, hoped to save it from extinction by discouraging its use in trivial causes. Events, however, were soon to show that he has misread the nation's mood.

In September 1921 the comte de Poret and Camille Lafarge fought 'an unusually fierce' duel in the Parc des Princes. They started with pistols, each man firing twice at the other at a distance of 25 paces, but, having failed to hit their targets, they resorted to swords. The comte was hit three times on the arm and Lafarge twice on the right shoulder but the fight nevertheless continued. It was only when a thrust from Lafarge ripped up almost the entire length of his forearm, paralysing it, that the comte was obliged to stop. Perhaps not surprisingly, the duel created a huge stir. Two days later the authorities announced that the two duellists and their seconds were to be prosecuted, a step that had not been taken in a non-fatal duel for 60 years.[10]

It had been the most publicised duel in France since the war and stung the government into action. At the beginning of October it circularised France's public prosecutors, reminding them that the provisions of the penal code relating to homicide and unlawful wounding were applicable to duels. The prosecutors were enjoined to take severe measures against all duellists.[11] In January 1922, the comte de Poret and M. Lafarge, along with the four seconds, appeared in court in Paris. The report of the hearing noted that, although 'the law forbidding duelling had long been allowed to slumber', the Minister of Justice had felt compelled to act in this case due to the publicity it had excited. *The Times* reported that:

> A change is perceptible in public opinion in France with regard to the moral aspect of duelling. The war, with its 1,500,000 graves of French heroes, has taught the lesson that French blood should not be spilled over trivial, often fanciful, notions of private honour, but should be regarded as sacred to the cause of patriotism.[12]

A few months before the Poret–Lafarge duel Paul Cassagnac had challenged Leon Daudet to a duel, to be fought with 'ordinary army revolvers, at 15 paces, to fire at will'. Daudet was one of the lions of pre-war Parisian duelling, when he had fought no fewer than 11 times. He was editor of the royalist newspaper *L'Action Française*; it was said of him that he 'angers more people in each day than any other public man could hope to annoy in a week'. Since the war he had resolved to give up duelling and, therefore, refused to answer Cassagnac's challenge.[13]

In February 1922, a parliamentary commission that had been looking into the question of duelling reported its findings.

> Long before the war duelling had come to be regarded with considerable contempt because so many duels were merely well-advertised exhibitions of solemn clowning designed solely to tickle the vanity of a certain type of swaggering individual anxious for cheap glory without much danger.

The commission had been looking at whether the law should be reformed to allow duels to be treated differently from other killings and woundings. It decided that there was no justification for such a change:

> that is to say, there should be no distinction made between two gentlemen who fight with swords or pistols over some 'point of honour' and two navvies who fight with their fists or knives because they have quarrelled.[14]

By the early 1920s it was clear which way the wind was blowing in France; across the Rhine, in Germany, it was more obvious still. As in France, the war itself, its horror and its interminable casualty lists made it difficult to look at duelling in the old light. There was a dramatic reduction in the number of people convicted of duelling offences in Germany in the years after the war: the figure for the years 1920 to 1932 was about one-third of that for the years 1901 to 1914.[15] Moreover, many of the convictions after 1920 related to 'arranged' duels or *mensur*-type encounters. For example, in 1929, a court in Jena sentenced a student to six months fortress imprisonment for killing a student in a *mensur*. A nationalist newspaper denounced the sentence as 'incredibly severe', while the Catholic *Germania* regretted that the law did not allow for the complete suppression of student duelling.[16]

In Germany, however, where duelling had always been a predominately military phenomenon, there were additional forces at work. The Treaty of Versailles had reduced the German army to a cadre of 100,000 men; the officer corps, which had numbered 34,000 at the end of the war, was reduced to just 4,000.[17] The army had forfeited much of its prestige in the catastrophic defeat of 1918; now it was the servant of an unsympathetic republic. The days when it could rely on the protection of the Kaiser, when it was one of the great pillars of the German Empire, were gone. Also, of course, many of the men who had been such enthusiastic upholders of duelling had been killed in the trenches. In the brave new world of the Weimar Republic, duelling seemed an outdated, elitist concept, something that belonged to the old, defeated, discredited regime. Article 105 of the Weimar Constitution outlawed the military honour courts that had done so much to enforce the duelling ethic among officers in the Kaiserreich.[18] In 1923 it was announced that duelling in the Reichswehr – as the army was now called – would no longer be considered compulsory. Henceforth, officers who refused to fight a duel would not be committing 'an unworthy act'.[19] The army, for all its reduced circumstances, mounted a fierce rearguard action to preserve its notion of honour in the face of the reforming, modernising instincts of the Weimar Republic, a stand that brought it into direct conflict with the more radical elements in the Reichstag.

While duelling proper died away, the *mensur*, the student duel, remained as strong and as popular as ever. There were various attempts to ban it but none of them was successful. The government was reluctant to alienate students by banning the *mensur*, which was, in any case, relatively harmless. In Berlin in November 1930, more than 200 students who had gathered in a hall to watch a morning's *mensur* were rounded up by the police. The work of a socialist government, it was 'the most vigorous attempt yet' to suppress student duelling. *The Times* predicted 'a great outcry among the students who value their duelling dearly'.[20]

When the Nazis came to power in 1933, duelling in Germany experienced something of a renaissance. In April 1933, the Nazi commissioner for the Prussian Ministry of Justice, Herr Kerrl, recommended

that public prosecutors should refrain from taking action against
student duels. Kerrl explained,

> The joy of the duel derives from the fighting spirit, which must not be
> checked but promoted in our academic youth. It strengthens personal
> courage, self-control and will power. In a time which demands the edu-
> cation of our young manhood in a martial spirit there can be no public
> interest in preventing students' duels.[21]

As this quotation makes clear, the Nazis had every reason to encourage duelling and in 1936 the indulgence granted to the *mensur* was
extended to the duel proper. In July it was announced that the
German Penal Code was to be amended to recognise the right of
members of certain official bodies – including the army, the SA and
the SS – 'to defend their honour with weapons'. Duels would be supervised by honour courts; any duellist who sought an unfair advantage
would not be able to shelter behind this law.[22]

In October 1937 an SS officer, Ronald Strunk, fought a duel with a
brother officer in the woods at Teplin near Berlin. Strunk had been
insulted so immediately issued a challenge. The matter was brought
before an honour court, which ordered a duel under harsh conditions
to reflect the gravity of the insult. It directed that the duel be fought
with pistols – sabres would have been more normal – at a short distance. Each man would be allowed three shots. Once the barrier had
been marked on the ground, the combatants advanced slowly, their
pistols held above their heads. Strunk fired first but missed. His opponent then fired, hitting Strunk in the abdomen. He died a few days
later. Strunk was, we are told, the first fatality in a duel under the
Nazis.[23] By 1938–9 the Nazis' indulgence of duelling had evaporated; it
was no longer acceptable, 'an error ... born of the notion of a bygone
era'. By the outbreak of war duelling in the army was virtually a thing
of the past.[24]

In Italy, before the war, duelling had also been commonplace.
There are some statistics (compiled, strangely, by the Ministry of
Agriculture, Industry and Commerce) collating all the duels fought in
the Kingdom of Italy between 1879 and 1889. They show a total of
2,759 duels in the period, the overwhelming majority fought with

sabres. Only a tiny minority, about 6 per cent, of these duels were fought with pistols. Fifty deaths were recorded – a mortality rate of about two in a hundred – and 1,060 of the injuries were categorised as 'serious'. Interestingly, the largest single cause of these quarrels was newspaper articles.[25]

There seems to have been a resurgence of sorts in the early 1920s, due largely to the propensity of the fascists to take up their sabres to settle arguments. Many of the duels of this period seem to have been between journalists and fascist supporters. Mussolini, who exhorted his young followers to 'live dangerously', was himself an experienced duellist. His biographer writes that as a young man he had been 'a notorious dueller':

> He had an extremely vehement style with the sabre and here, too, he was remembered as an exhibitionist, always seeking spectacular effects and being careless about the accepted rules of a chivalrous encounter.[26]

There was, of course, no shortage of advice available to the Italian duellist on how to conduct himself in a duel. During the nineteenth and early twentieth centuries, a sizeable body of literature had been published in Italy explaining the principles of duelling. These ranged from practical manuals to academic treatises. As late as 1928 *Questioni d'onore* was published in Milan, aimed no doubt at aspiring local duellists.[27]

In October 1921 *The Times* noted that fascists and journalists were making a habit of provoking and fighting duels with one another and that several such encounters were 'pending'.[28] Later that month Mussolini himself fought a duel against Signor Ciccotti, the editor of the Rome newspaper *Il Paese*. It had been arranged that the two men would meet at a villa near Livorno. As they were preparing to fight in the villa's garden the police arrived, whereupon the principals, seconds and doctors rushed into the villa. Once inside, they locked the doors to keep the police out and set to. The fight, we are told, lasted for an hour and a half. By the 14th round, Ciccotti was so exhausted – he was also slightly wounded – that the bout had to be stopped.[29] Il Duce, of course, was no doubt still full of fight.

Elsewhere in the world in the 1920s and 1930s duelling occasionally fizzed into life, like an abandoned, half-extinguished firework. South

American politicians from time to time resorted to pistol or sword to resolve their differences. There was a particularly bloody affair in Paraguay in 1930 between Dr Eligio Ayala, a former president of the republic, and Señor Tomas Barriero. They fought with revolvers; Barriero was killed and Ayala later died of his wounds.[30] In nearby Uruguay the splendidly named Señor Jose Battle y Ordonez, a former president of the republic, fought a duel in 1920 with the editor of *El Pais* newspaper.[31] Two years later the serving president fought a duel with an unsuccessful presidential candidate, as a result of violent mutual recriminations over the recent elections.[32] It was around this time that the government of Uruguay, rather contrary to the spirit of the age, decided to suppress the existing penalties for duelling, in cases where the seconds had referred the quarrel to an honour court.[33]

In neighbouring Argentina duelling seems to have taken root before the turn of the century. The fact that at least two guides to the etiquette of duelling were published in Buenos Aires in the 1890s suggests that the custom was by then firmly established. As late as 1918, Carlos de Renviel published a comprehensive guide – it runs to 120 pages – to the role of surgeons and doctors in a duel.[34] This book is interesting because it is so evidently practical in intent, thereby demonstrating that duelling was relatively common in Argentina after 1918. There is a clutch of reported duels that confirm that duelling was not entirely moribund among senior politicians and ministers in the 1920s and 1930s. In July 1935 there was a fracas in the Senate between Dr Pinedo, the Finance Minister, and Senator de la Torre. During the uproar in the Senate chamber the Agriculture Minister, who had intervened to prevent the parties coming to blows, was wounded when an excitable spectator opened fire on the mêlée. One unfortunate senator was killed. In the duel itself neither Dr Pinedo nor Senator de la Torre was injured.[35]

Elsewhere in Europe tempers occasionally still flared sufficiently to precipitate a duel. The odd Spanish and Portuguese politician fought a duel, while in Eastern Europe no less a figure than Marshal Pilsudski felt obliged, soon after leaving office in 1922, to defend the good name of the Polish Cabinet in a duel with General Szczeptycki. In the early thirties there was a rash of duels reported in Romania. Likewise, in Hungary the political process was from time to time disturbed by the clash of steel or the firing of pistols.

In July 1935 Clement Attlee, reticent, stolid, pipe-smoking Mr Attlee, was challenged to a duel by Captain Fanelli, an Italian fascist and former newspaper editor. He had taken exception to some disparaging remarks made by Attlee about Italy in the House of Commons in the course of a debate on the Abyssinian crisis. *The Times* reported that Attlee, who was deputy leader of the Labour Party at the time, 'has declined the challenge to the duel, which he describes as a barbarous and obsolete method of liquidating quarrels. He laid stress in his reply on the continued freedom of speech in England.'[36]

But it is to France that we return, as so often in the history of duelling, to see the last vestiges of knightly chivalry come face to face with the modern world. In 1926 a sword duel took place between M. Serge André and M. Bernard Denisans, a journalist. The fact that André was the chairman of the board of an oil company gave the encounter a slick patina of modernity, enhanced by the fact that they fought at the Paris velodrome. The fight was stopped when André was hit on the arm.[37]

In 1934 André Hessi, a member of the Chamber of Deputies, and Joseph Beineix, a journalist, fell out, as had happened on countless previous occasions, over an article that Beineix had penned. The seconds failed to reconcile the men, so a duel was arranged. They met at the Parc des Princes on the fringes of the Bois de Boulogne, where it was agreed that they would each fire four shots at a distance of 25 paces. An innovation was introduced that the duellists were to fire at will but that all the shots were to be discharged within 90 seconds. The 90 seconds was timed by a metronome. Neither man was injured. The report of the episode commented that the duel had been conducted 'in accordance with the most honoured tradition of the rights proper to such encounters, the only departure being that it was filmed'.[38]

The following year a spat between a drama producer and a critic reached the point of a challenge and the nomination of seconds. As with the politician and the journalist this was a common enough falling-out, one that had been replicated many times over the previous century. What brought it right up to date was the fact that the producer was a film producer, the critic a film critic, and their argument revolved around a film.[39] The idea of the duel had survived into the age of the silver screen.

In 1934 *The Times* reported on a duel fought at Carcassonne between a politician and a journalist. Each man fired one shot before the business was settled. The newspaper commented acidly:

> It was afterward announced that the encounter took place in the customary way and according to the usual rules – a statement plainly confirmed by the fact that neither of the principals received a scratch. It cannot be said, however, that the ceremony was entirely faithful to tradition in detail, as neither cinematographers, press photographers nor reporters were allowed to record the proceedings.[40]

If the *Times* man felt that the Carcassonne duellists had failed to conform to the modern etiquette, he would not have been disappointed by the duel fought in 1938 between the playwright Henri Bernstein and Edouard Bourdet, the head of the Comédie-Française. The dispute and the subsequent duel were conducted in the full glare of publicity, which the principals did little to avoid. In the end, the affair degenerated into a media circus more suited to princesses or film stars than duellists. Bernstein had been, before the war, an inveterate duellist. He had fought eight duels – three of them in a single week – wounding his opponents in four of them and being wounded twice himself. Bourdet, being of a younger generation, had not previously fought a duel, it was thought. The dispute had arisen over the Comédie-Française's plan to stage Bernstein's play *Judith*. In an exchange of letters they swapped elaborately crafted insults before the inevitable challenge was issued. Both men selected eminent seconds from the world of letters, although Bernstein felt it prudent to recruit René Prejelon, a well-known swordsman, to his cause.[41] The two men met in the garden of a private house in Neuilly, at lunchtime on 20 May 1938. *The Times* took up the story.

> For two days and nights journalists had been besieging the houses of the two principals, of their seconds and even of the principals' doctors. All these groups of watchdogs pursued by car the persons concerned to a

house in the rue Peronnet. It was the trail of one of the doctors which first betrayed the place chosen for the duel, but the biggest pack of motor-cars was that pursuing M. Bernstein across Paris at top speed, 50 in all. The traffic police of Neuilly made desperate efforts to deal with the traffic jam in the neighbourhood of the rue Peronnet.

Journalists and photographers secured a good view of the fight from walls and trees. The duel was directed by M. J.J. Renaud, a well-known swordsman, who has often filled this role.

At the words 'Allez, messieurs' M. Bourdet attacked vigorously; M. Bernstein remained strictly on the defensive at first without giving ground, as if studying his adversary. After three minutes it looked as if either man might have been touched, and M. Renaud called a halt to satisfy himself whether there had been a wound, but there had not been. M. Bernstein, who is 62, sat down for a moment streaming with perspiration, while M. Bourdet walked up and down with one of his seconds, M. Pierre Benoit.

When the fight was resumed M. Bourdet again attacked and twice seemed close to wounding M. Bernstein – first in the hand and then in the chest. M. Bernstein continued to hold his ground and began to reply more vigorously. M. Bourdet withdrew slightly and then attacked vigorously, this time in the low lines. M. Bernstein parried his opponent's épée, disengaged his own weapon, and wounded him with a stop hit.

The doctor at once called 'Halt', and having examined the wound insisted that the duel should be broken off in spite of M. Bourdet's protests. The point of the weapon had penetrated to the bone of the arm. M. Bourdet walked to his car without even putting on his coat. To the journalists at the entrance to the garden, M. Bernstein said: 'Please don't congratulate me; I hope my opponent is not seriously hurt.' The whole duel, including the pause, lasted nine minutes.[42]

The photograph accompanying the article shows the duel in progress, both men *en garde*, in shirtsleeves and fedoras; behind them are their seconds. In the foreground, like stage scenery, is some elegant garden statuary. With motorcars, paparazzi, pursuing packs of journalists, sound bites from the participants, and action photographs, the Bernstein–Bourdet encounter showed, once and for all, that the duel had arrived in the modern age. It had become a media event, a press junket, as far as could be from the notion of two men privately settling their differences in the early-morning tranquillity of a wooded glade or sandy heath.

*   *   *

If World War One put an end to duelling as a widespread and, in certain milieux, acceptable custom, World War Two finished it off altogether. In the 1930s men like Bernstein, who had grown up in an age in which duelling was a part of life, could still fight duels; by the 1950s their duelling days were gone. In the 1920s and 1930s, there was still a certain type of man who believed that a duel was the only proper way to settle a particular type of dispute. After 1945, duelling almost completely disappeared from view, becoming the province of exhibitionists, fantasists, and practical jokers. Duelling survived into the age of the cinema and the car but it did not live on into the atomic age, or the era of the welfare state. Newspapers occasionally editorialised, humorously or nostalgically, about it and the odd duel was staged by undergraduate pranksters on the manicured lawns of Oxford.

In 1958 two Frenchmen fought a duel arising from a theatrical – in both senses of the word – argument, appropriately enough, about ballet. Serge Lifar and the marquis de Cuevas fought with swords at a mill house some 50 miles from Paris on 30 March 1958. One of the marquis's seconds was the young Jean-Marie Le Pen. Dame Fortune set the garland of victory upon the brow of the noble marquis, who had managed to inflict a slight wound on his opponent's forearm. Then the two men 'their differences reconciled by this honourable blood-letting, embraced ...'

> From start to finish this affair has been accompanied by the maximum of publicity, which neither of the protagonists had gone out of his way to discourage ... Ceremonial insults were exchanged, the seconds of each party waited upon one another, and throughout last week the newspapers have been full of photographs of the duellists practising. They even gave radio interviews, in the same building but in different broadcasting studios.

When his seconds called for the marquis de Ceuvas at 8 a.m. at the friends' house at Neuilly where, supposedly to escape from the Press, he had spent the night, there were some 50 journalists and photographers waiting outside. They followed him first of all to an open space on the outskirts of Paris, where M. Lifar was waiting, and where a great deal of photographing went on, and then to another friend's house at Vernon, where the duel occurred.[43]

In 1954 the news that the Air Ministry in London had banned eight RAF officers who were about to start a course at a German university from taking part in the *mensur* provoked a light-hearted editorial.

Here and in America the rot set in long ago. The palmy days of Rawdon Crawley's pistols, 'the same with which I shot Captain Marker,' are as dead and gone as Lord Mohun and the Duke of Hamilton. A bourgeois spirit ... has spread shamefully.

The newspaper concluded that 'an aristocratic art has been lost' and regretted that 'Too many people, if challenged to a contest *à l'outrance*, would exercise their right of choice by following the lead of that mean-spirited duellist who demanded half bricks at a hundred yards.'[44]

In 1958 Field Marshal Montgomery published a volume of war memoirs in which he made some very unflattering remarks about the part played by the Italians in the war. Montgomery's views ruffled feathers in Rome to the extent that the Italian ambassador in London was instructed to lodge a formal protest against some passages in the book. In addition to the activity through official channels, Vicenzo Caputo, president of the Italian Nationalist Association, challenged Montgomery to a duel. The challenge, he said, was 'in defence of the prestige of the Italian nation and of the honour of its army, unjustly outraged by defamations founded on falsehood and lies'.[45] The defence of the field marshal's views was taken up, sportingly, by a Mr Bridgland of Hornsey, and there are unsubstantiated suggestions that perhaps a duel was indeed fought between Signor Caruso and Montgomery's English champion.

In 1959 the Argentinian Minister of War fought a sabre duel with a radical member of parliament, injuring him over the right eye.[46] A few months later an Argentinian admiral fought a duel with another radical member of parliament. Both men were crack shots but contrived to miss each other.[47] In 1962 an outraged French paratroop colonel, who considered that he had been libelled by the satirical magazine *Le Canard Enchaine*, challenged the editor to a duel. The magazine's editor showed what he thought of the custom by instructing his seconds to suggest to the colonel that they fight with popguns 'at any distance'.

French parliamentarians had a long and honourable tradition of defending their honour on the duelling ground, so it is appropriate that it was two of their number who fought what may well turn out to be one of the very last proper duels fought in earnest. In April 1967 Gaston Deferre, Communist deputy and mayor of Marseilles, accepted the challenge of René Ribière, a Gaullist deputy, for having insulted him by calling him an idiot. Seconds were appointed and rapiers chosen, although Deferre expressed a preference for revolvers. They fought in the garden of a house in Neuilly. Ribière was hit twice on the forearm ; the fight was then stopped and Deferre declared the winner.

Two years later – by which time man had landed on the moon – Homero Lajora Burgo, a candidate in the forthcoming presidential elections in the Dominican Republic, accepted a challenge to a duel, to be fought to the death, from General Antonio Imbert Barreras. Lajora had accused the general of flirting with the communists. In March 1970 early risers in Copenhagen were treated to the spectacle of two men fighting a duel. Togo Esben, stage director of the Ny Scala theatre, had challenged Henning Ditlev, the theatre's press secretary, to a duel for failing include his name in a programme. The two men, armed with flintlock pistols, met at dawn in the Royal Deer Park, where each paced off the traditional 24 paces and then fired. Esben's pistol fired but the bullet went wide; Ditlev's pistol did not work. It was the first duel in Denmark since 1912.[48]

Alongside the eccentrics and the exhibitionists were the undergraduate pranksters. In May 1954 two Oxford undergraduates, Alastair Forsyth and Ronald Eden, 'fought' a duel below Meadow Buildings in Christ Church. Eden, a 'practical joker and japist' dreamt up the idea, which relied on starting pistols, blank rounds and a concealed capsule of red dye. The dispute was over a female art student.

> Challenger and challenged stood back to back then, on [the referee's] command, marched fifteen paces, turned and fired their weapons – variously described as 'heavy starting pistols' and o.45 revolvers'. Alastair Forsyth staggered forward clutching his chest, while a red stain spread out over his white shirt front. 'Dramatically coughing and choking,' he recalls, he was carried off [to Meadow Buildings].[49]

The affair attracted a good deal of newspaper coverage, even prompting *The Times* to declare that 'Oxford Eights Week … had its first sensation this afternoon …'[50]

Four years later, in May 1958, two Balliol men, Denis Cross and Christopher Waddy, fought a duel with champagne corks. Cross describes what happened.

> There was a group of us having dinner in hall, in Balliol, one night. I made a mildly slighting remark about Waddy's girlfriend, who was at LMH [Lady Margaret Hall], whereupon Waddy retorted 'I'll call you out' or words to that effect. No chap of spirit was going to apologise simply because he had been threatened in this way; equally no chap of spirit would allow his girlfriend to be insulted in this way. All the people sitting nearby thought this sounded an amusing idea so it was not allowed to die quietly. The seconds, one of whom was Henry Brooke [subsequently a High Court judge], got busy and arranged the meeting. I rather blame Brooke for the escalation.
>
> It was agreed that they should meet on the lawns of LMH early the following morning, the traditional time for such things. LMH had at that time a particularly parsimonious and unpopular bursar so it was agreed to stage the duel under her window. When she leant out to see what was taking place, she was solemnly informed that 'A matter of honour is being settled, ma'am'.[51]

The two men then took up their positions, probably 10 paces apart, each armed with a bottle – or possibly two – of champagne. 'It was,' Cross recalled, 'very difficult to aim the cork properly, although they went off with some aplomb.' Neither got even close to hitting the other. Afterwards, and this was 'the best part of the thing', the duellists and their seconds repaired to the Mitre Hotel on the High Street for breakfast, taking the champagne, very little of which had been wasted in the act of firing the corks, with them.

The episode moved *The Times*, in a light-hearted editorial, to wonder whether 'the duel is a proper subject for humour'.

> The atmosphere of the times is not in sympathy with such ingenious levity, and it is something to have fought the duel at all. Champagne corks being what they are, it is just possible that one at least of the principals could, when it was over and honour satisfied, boast a faintly discoloured eye as evidence that the grass on the memorable morning was in very truth stained in 'Veuve Clicquot'. [52]

Six years later, down the road at Magdalen College, another undergraduate spat over a girl resulted in a duel, this time fought with swords and ending in bloodshed. The two men concerned were Adam Poynter and a South African Rhodes scholar, Rory Donellan, who made a derogatory remark about a female friend of Poynter's. Poynter takes up the story.

> So I, thinking nothing of it, as it were, picked up somebody's glove that was lying about and hit Rory across the face with it and he picked it up and hit me back about ten times as hard, said 'Sabres at dawn' and walked out. He was absolutely furious; I'd never seen a man so cross. I couldn't understand why particularly he was cross and, also, I thought it was a joke. However, during the course of the evening it became clear that it wasn't a joke, and he was épée champion of Natal, so he knew what he was doing ...[53]

When it became clear that it was not a joke, Poynter spent some of the remainder of the evening taking some elementary fencing tuition from a friend who happened to be the university sabre champion. The following morning, when it was still practically dark, 'so dark that you could barely bloody well see' – it was in February – the parties met on the lawns in front of the arcaded Classical New Buildings and the medieval cloisters: 'there were seconds and a medic and a little knot of onlookers'.

Anyway, this little duel lasted about, I should think, seven or eight minutes round the lawn and ended up under the walnut tree where he fortunately disarmed me at first blood … Thereafter we retired to Rory's rooms for a glass of whisky. But I'm always slightly at a loss because I thought the whole thing was just a joke but I'm not sure that Rory did.

Poynter suffered a cut at the base of his right thumb – he carries the scar to this day – which was sufficient to halt the fight. It was too dark at the time for photographs to be taken, although some staged ones were taken later, showing Donellan 'in his Hamlet kit … with the flowing white blouse and black tights'. Later, the two men were summoned to see T.S.R. Boase, the President of Magdalen, who said simply, 'Very nice to see young gentlemen getting up early'.

* * *

In the end, duelling simply fizzled out. Although a host of factors can be cited to explain its demise, no single one could, with any confidence, be said to have been decisive. Clearly, the rise of the rule of law and growing respect for the ties that bind a modern society made duelling seem increasingly unacceptable. Likewise, as evangelical Christianity spread its wings – particularly in Britain and the United States – so duelling appeared more and more a relic of a wicked past. So too with the spread of democracy. Duelling was, by definition, a non-democratic institution; it was open only to a self-defining elite. The alternative was a good thrashing. Democrats, like Christians, viewed duelling as a barbaric relic of an earlier, autocratic age. Furthermore, society has become physically softer, more comfortable, over the generations. To our forefathers, who endured the amputation of limbs without anaesthetic, the physical risks of a duel seemed acceptable. In the Western world of the twenty-first century, we are ever more reluctant as individuals to accept responsibility for our own actions; duelling was the ultimate acknowledgement of personal responsibility. In the modern world, there is always someone else to blame; the duellist could blame only himself.

But above all duelling faded away because the code of honour that underpinned it gradually lost its compulsive power. The old-fashioned sense of honour barely exists in the modern world; it has become con-fused with self-interest and debased by relativism. This is a matter of both public and private conscience, but is most noticeable in the public domain. We are governed by politicians who not only have no sense of honour but are devoid of shame. Few politicians would consider resigning on a point of principle, let alone fighting a duel as a result of an accusation of dishonesty.

None of this should be taken to mean that the passing of duelling is to be regretted, simply that we live in a different world now, better in many ways, but not unreservedly so.

ENDNOTES

Prologue

1   Much of the detail in the Prologue is drawn from *The Life, Adventures and Eccentricities of the late Lord Camelford, to which is added the Particulars of the Late Fatal Duel* …, Anon., London, n.d., A.H. Corble Collection, Katholieke Universiteit Leuven.
2   Earl of Ilchester, *Chronicles of Holland House, 1820–1900*, London (1937), p. 497, and *Annual Register*, 1804.
3   Derek Hudson, *Holland House*, London (1967) p. 58.

Introduction

1   Charles Moore, *A Full Inquiry into the Subject of Suicide . . . Two Treatises on Duelling and Gaming*, Vol. II, London (1790).
2   John Cockburn D.D., *The History and Examination of Duels Shewing Their Heinous Nature and the Necessity of Suppressing Them*, London (1790), p. 2.
3   *The Sixteenth Century Italian Duel*, by F.R. Bryson, University of Chicago Press (1938), p. xii.
4   Edward Gibbon, *The History of the Decline and Fall of the Roman Empire*, Folio Soc. ed., Vol. IV, London (1986), p. 344.
5   Bryson, op. cit., pp. xiii–xv.
6   For this account of the early history of the trial by combat, I have drawn upon *The Duel in European History*, by V.G. Kiernan, Oxford University Press (1986), Ch. III, and Robert Baldick, *The Duel*, London (1965), Ch. 1.
7   Eric Jager, *The Last Duel*, London (2005).
8   For this account of the ecclesiastical opposition to the judicial combat, I have again relied heavily on Bryson, op. cit., pp. xv–xvi.
9   Baldick, op. cit., p. 14.
10 For this summary of the duel of chivalry I have drawn on Baldick, op. cit., Ch. 2, and Kiernan, op. cit. Ch. IV.
11 Baldick, op. cit., p. 14.
12 J.B. Priestley, *The Prince of Pleasure*, London (1969), p. 286.
13 James Kelly, *That Damn'd Thing Called Honour: Duelling in Ireland, 1570–1860*, Cork University Press (1995), Ch. 1.

14 Anonymous account, probably *c.* 1635, private collection.
15 For some details see Baldick, op. cit., Ch. 1.
16 W.S. Holdsworth, *A History of the English Law*, London (1923), Vol. II, p. 364.
17 Baldick, op. cit., Ch. 1 and Kiernan, op. cit., p. 204.
18 John Taylor Allen, *Duelling: An Essay Read in the Theatre at Oxford, June 10, 1807*, p. 4.
19 Abraham Bosquett, *A Treatise on Duelling*, London (1818), p. 91.
20 Markku Peltonen, *The Duel in Early Modern England: Civility, Politeness and Honour*, Cambridge University Press (2003), p. 4.
21 Bryson, op. cit., Appendix IX.

Chapter 1

1 Ambrose Bierce, *The Unabridged Devil's Dictionary*, ed. Schutlz and Joshi, University of Georgia P (2002), p. 60.
2 *Cheltenham Chronicle* quoted in *The Times*, 1 August 1828.
3 *The Times*, 25 November and 3 December 1925.
4 Anon., *The Vauxhall Affray: Or, the Maccaronies Defeated*, London (1773).
5 See *Mirror* diary piece, 29 August 1957; also *Daily Mail* diary, 14 September 1957. I am grateful to Marcus Scriven for drawing my attention to this gem.
6 *The Memoirs of Jacques Casanova*, tr. Arthur Machen, London and New York (1960), Vol. IV, p. 386.
7 P.C. Crampton, *Speech of P.C. Crampton, Esq., at the Meeting of the Association for the Suppression of Duelling* (1830), p. 4.
8 E. Pierce (ed.), *The Diaries of Charles Greville*, London (2005), pp. 145–6.
9 Lord Chesterfield, *Miscellaneous Works*, 4 vols., London (1779), Vol. II, p. 53.
10 Thomas Jones, 'A Sermon upon Duelling', Cambridge (1792), p. 13.
11 Sir Richard Steele, *The Court of Honour: or The Laws, Rules, and Ordinances Establish'd for the Suppression of Duels in France*, London (1720).
12 Oliver Lawson Dick (ed.), *Aubrey's Brief Lives*, London (1960), p. xxii.
13 Evelyn, op. cit., p. 285.
14 Verney & Verney (eds), *Memoirs of the Verney Family*, 2 vols, London (1904), Vol. ii, pp. 314–15. For clarity's sake, I have modernised some of the more eccentric moments of the orthography.
15 Anonymous account (1722), private collection.
16 Granville Sharp, *A Tract on Duelling*, London (1790), p. ix.
17 Ibid., p. xv.
18 *Annual Register*, 1788.
19 *The Times*, 11 November 1926.

Chapter 2

1 Cockburn, op.cit., p. 183.
2 John Lyde Wilson, *The Code of Honor or, Rules for the Government of Principals and Seconds in Duelling*, Charleston (1838), reprinted in *Dueling in the Old South*, by Jack K. Williams, Texas A&M University Press (1980).
3 Egremont Correspondence, William Wyndham to his brother, 3 August 1794, Somerset Record Office.
4 Kelly, op.cit., p. 135.
5 *The Times*, 3 January 1913.

6   *The Times*, 15 December 1922.
7   T.H. White, *The Age of Scandal*, Oxford University Press (1986), p.77.
8   Robert Latham (ed.), *The Shorter Pepys*, London (1985), 17 January 1668.
9   The Will of Sir Richard Atkins, Centre for Buckinghamshire Studies, Aylesbury.
10 *The Times*, 14 March 1914.
11 Robert A. Nye, *Honor and the Duel in the Third Republic*, Oxford University Press (1993), pp. 187–8.
12 A. Fremantle (ed.) *The Wynne Diaries*, 3 vols, London (1935–40), Vol. II, pp. 15–16.
13 Kevin McAleer, *Dueling*, Princeton University Press (1994), Ch. II.
14 Joseph Conrad, *The Duel*, in *The Complete Short Fiction*, ed. S. Hynes, London (1993), p. 69.
15 W.S. Lewis & ors (eds), *Horace Walpole's Correspondence*, Yale edition (1937–8), Vol. 17, p. 486, Letter to Sir Horace Mann, 7 July 1742.
16 Anonymous account (1787), private collection.
17 For this account of the Montgomery–Macnamara duel I have relied principally upon an anonymous account dated 6 April 1803. Private collection.
18 *Times*, 8 April 1840.
19 Anonymous account, dated 1776, private collection.
20 Anon., *A Letter to the Gentlemen of the Army*, London (1757), p. 16.
21 Baldick, op.cit., p. 36.
22 For this description of the challenge in Renaissance Italy I have relied upon Bryson, op. cit., Ch. 1.
23 Edward Bulwer Lytton, *Pelham*, London (1884), pp. 250–1.
24 Lord John Russell (ed.), *Memoirs, Journal and Correspondence of Thomas Moore*, 8 vols, London (1853–56), Vol. VI, p. 7.
25 For this account I have relied upon the copy correspondence among the Grey Papers in the National Maritime Museum.
26 P. Colson, *White's, 1693–1950*, p. 53.

Chapter 3

1   Abraham Bosquett, 'A Treatise on Duelling', from *The Pamphleteer*, Vol. XII, London (1818), p. 87.
2   W.M. Thackeray, *Vanity Fair*, London (1877 edition), p. 516.
3   A late Captain in the Army, *General Rules and Instructions for all Seconds in Duels*, Whitehaven (1793), p. 17.
4   *Annual Register*, 1807.
5   Bosquett, op. cit., p. 81.
6   Ibid., p. 81.
7   *General Rules and Instructions for all Seconds in Duels*, p. 19–20.
8   Wilson, op. cit., p. 94.
9   Ferreus (ed.) *Annuaire de Duel: 1880–89*, Paris (1891).
10 *The Times*, 8 March 1924.
11 *The Times*, 14 March 1923.
12 Warrant for the arrest of Ambrose Poynter, 14 July 1831, London Metropolitan Archives, MJ/SP/1831/06/008.
13 Kelly, op. cit., p. 82.
14 *The Times*, 19 January 1911.
15 *The Times*, 23 August 1920.
16 *The Times*, 20 July 1911.

17   D.H. Donald, *Lincoln*, London (1995), p. 91.
18   Account of a duel between the Revd. Mr Bate and Mr De Morande, Shropshire Archives, 1037/22/56.
19   William Douglas, *Duelling Days in the Army*, London (1884), pp. 100–1.
20   Anonymous account, probably 1780s, private collection.
21   *The Times*, 23 February 1914.
22   *The Times*, 26 February 1914.
23   *Annual Register*, 1807.
24   Adolphe Tavernier, *L'Art du Duel*, Paris (n.d., but probably 1884).
25   *General Rules and Instructions for all Seconds in Duels*, p. 20.
26   Anonymous account, dated 1784, private collection.
27   *Annual Register*, 1843.
28   *Annual Register*, 1826.
29   *Annual Register*, 1813.
30   *Annual Register*, 1843.
31   *Annual Register*, 1830.
32   *General Rules and Instructions for all Seconds in Duels*, p. 20.
33   Bosquett, op. cit., p. 82.
34   *The Irish Code of Honor*, reprinted in Williams, op. cit., p. 100.
35   Alfred Spencer (ed.), *The Memoirs of William Hickey*, London, Vol. I, Ch. XIII (1919).
36   *Times*, 8 July 1908.
37   M. Fougere, *L'Art de ne jamais être tue ni blesse en duel sans avoir pris acune leçon d'armes* (tr. author), Paris (1828)
38   *The Times*, 8 August 1929.
39   Mark Twain, *A Tramp Abroad* (1880).
40   Martin Papers, British Library, Add. MS 41354.

Chapter 4

1   Anton Chekhov, *The Duel*, Modern Library Classics edition (2003), p. 72.
2   Ibid., p. 80.
3   Mikhail Lermontov, *A Hero of Our Time*, Penguin Classics (2001), pp. 130–2.
4   'A Traveller', *The Art of Duelling*, London (1836), pp. 41–2.
5   E. Bulwer Lytton, op. cit., p. 15.
6   B. Francis and E. Kearney (eds), *The Francis Letters*, London (n.d), Vol. I, pp. 308–11.
7   Keith Feiling, *Warren Hastings*, London (1954), pp. 227–8.
8   Wendy Hinde, *George Canning*, London (1973), p. 226.
9   Ibid., p. 227.
10   *Annual Register*, 1796.
11   *The Times*, 18 October 1819.
12   *The Times*, 21 October 1828.
13   *The Times*, 8 May 1913.
14   *The Times*, 21 August 1913.
15   *The Times*, 13 June 1914.
16   *The Irish Code of Honor*, reprinted in Williams, op. cit. p. 102.
17   Reprinted in Williams, op. cit., p. 95.
18   Anonymous account, dated 1788, private collection.
19   *The Times,* 27 October 1923.
20   *Annual Register*, 1826.

21 *Annual Register*, 1827.
22 *The Times*, 26 August 1840.
23 *Annual Register*, 1830.
24 *The Times*, 19 April 1912.
25 *Annual Register*, 1828.
26 *The Times*, 28 February 1910.
27 Walter Winans, *Automatic Pistol Shooting*, New York (1915), p. 88.
28 Anonymous account, dated 1778, private collection.
29 Anonymous account, dated 1784, private collection.
30 *The Times*, 21 April 1821.
31 Anonymous account, dated 1784, private collection.
32 For the account of this duel I have relied upon Douglas, op. cit., p. 98, and an anonymous account, dated Wednesday, 10 September 1783, from a private collection.
33 Alexander Pushkin, *Eugene Onegin*, Penguin Classics (2003), pp. 138–9.
34 McAleer, op. cit., p. 59.
35 Ibid.
36 Casanova, *Memoirs*, Vol. IV, p. 385–8.
37 Anonymous account, dated 1787, private collection.
38 Casanova, *Memoirs*, Vol. IV, p. 388–9.
39 *The Irish Code of Honor*, reprinted in Williams, op. cit. p. 103.
40 Andrew Steinmetz, *The Romance of Duelling*, 2 vols, London (1868), Vol. i, p. 110, p. 59.
41 For this account I have relied on *Annual Register*, 1830.
42 *The Times*, 31 March 1829.
43 *Annual Register*, 1838.
44 Nye, op. cit., p. 195.
45 Winans, op. cit., pp. 85, 88.
46 'A Traveller', op. cit., p. 42.
47 Revd. A. Dyce (ed.), *Recollections of the Table-Talk of Samuel Rogers*, London (1887), p. 216.
48 McAleer, op. cit., p.53.
49 *Annual Register*, 1816.
50 Winans, op. cit., p. 90.
51 Steinmetz, op. cit., Vol. I, p. 108.
52 'A Traveller', op. cit., p. 45.
53 W.S. Lewis & ors (eds), *Horace Walpole's Correspondence*, Yale edition (1937–3), Vol. 17, p. 173, Letter to Sir Horace Mann, 22 October 1741. Vol. 17.
54 Steinmetz, op. cit., Vol. I, p. 92.
55 Ibid., p. 33.
56 *Annual Register*, 1790.
57 'A Traveller', op. cit., pp. 45–6.
58 Lord Chesterfield, *Miscellaneous Works*, 4 vols, London (1779), Vol. II, pp. 266–7.
59 *The Times*, 11 May 1914.
60 Revd. William Gilpin, *A Dialogue on Duelling*, London (1807), p. 227.
61 T.C., *A Discourse on Duels, Shewing The Sinful Nature & Mischievous Effects of Them* ..., London (1687), p. 65.
62 Revd. John Williams, *On the Pernicious Vice of Duelling* ..., Stroud (1807), pp. 24–5 and 28.
63 Twain, op. cit., p. 35.
64 *The Times*, 29 December 1925.
65 *The Reminiscences and Recollections of Captain Gronow*, London (1892) (orig. 1860s).

Chapter 5

1 See Leonie Frieda, *Catherine de Medici*, London (2003), pp. 2–6.
2 See François Billacois, *The Duel: Its Rise and Fall in Early Modern France* (tr. Trista Selous), Yale University Press (1990), Ch. 5.
3 Ibid., Ch. 6.
4 Frieda, op. cit., p. 327.
5 See Baldick, op. cit., Ch. 4; also Brioist, Drevillon & Serna, *Croiser le Fer* (2002), pp. 248–9.
6 Brioist & ors., op. cit., p. 251.
7 *The Laws of Honor, or an Account of the Suppression of Duels in France*, printed for Thomas Flesher, London (1685), Preface.
8 Peltonen, op. cit., p. 80–1.
9 Richard Cohen, *By the Sword*, London (2002), p. 28.
10 Ibid., pp. 28–9.
11 Lawrence Stone, *The Crisis of the Aristocracy: 1558–1641*, OUP (1965), p. 242.
12 Ibid., p. 243.
13 Peltonen, op. cit., pp. 61–2 and Stone, op. cit., p. 244.
14 Peltonen, op. cit., p. 49.
15 Vincentio Saviolo, *His Practice*, London (1595), A.H. Corble Collection, Katholieke Universiteit Leuven.
16 *As You Like It* Act v, Scene 4.
17 *Romeo and Juliet*, Act II, Scene 3.
18 *Hamlet*, Act IV, Scene 7.
19 Ibid., Act V, Scene 2.
20 Stone, op. cit., p. 245.
21 Stone, op. cit., Appendix XV.
22 Baldick, op. cit., p. 52.
23 Cohen, op. cit., p. 48.
24 Kiernan, op. cit., Ch. 5, and McAleer, op. cit., p. 18.
25 James Landale, *Duel*, London (2005).
26 Billacois, op. cit., pp. 47, 48.
27 Billacois, op. cit., Ch. 9. p.83–4
28 Kiernan, op. cit., Ch. 6.
29 Marc de la Beraudiere, *Le Combat de Seul a Seul en Camp Clos*, Paris (1608).
30 Kiernan, op. cit., Ch. 5.
31 David Buisseret, *Henry IV*, London (1984), p. 161.
32 Stone, op. cit., Appendix XV.
33 Stone, op. cit., p. 245.
34 Billacois, op. cit., p. 32.
35 *HMC, 75 Downshire II, p. 184*, letter from Sir Thomas Edmondes to William Trumbull, 13 November 1613.
36 *HMC, 75 Downshire II, p. 185*, letter of Samuel Calvert to William Trumbull, 13 November 1613.
37 Thomas Carlyle, *Miscellanies* (1869 edition), iv, p. 395.
38 From letter of Sir Thomas Dutton to the Earl of Salisbury, 17 June 1611, quoted in *The Duttons of Dutton*, p. 57 (Cheshire and Chester Archives ref. X 920 DUT). In the passage of direct quotation I have modernised the spelling.
39 Stone, op. cit., p. 247.
40 *HMC, 29 Portland IX, p. 54*.

41 *HMC, 29 Portland IX*, pp. 55–6.
42 Ibid.
43 *HMC, 75 Downshire IV*, p. 8, letter from J. Thorys to William Trumbull, 7 January 1613.
44 Ibid., p. 181, letter from Thomas Floyd to William Trumbull, Paris, 25 August 1613.
45 Holdsworth, op. cit., Vol. v, pp. 199–201.
46 Finch-Hatton MSS, F.H. 137, Northampton RO, p. 82
47 Verney & Verney, op. cit., Vol. i, p. 92.
48 Sir George Clark, *War and Society in the Seventeenth Century*, Cambridge University Press (1958), p. 38.
49 *An Ordinance against Challenges, Duels and all Provocations thereunto* (29 June 1654).
50 Norman Davies, *Europe*, Oxford University Press (1996), p. 568.
51 Kiernan, op. cit., p. 90.
52 McAleer, op. cit., p. 19.
53 Davies, op. cit., p. 568.
54 G. Bayer, *Baroque Architecture in Germany*, Leipzig (1961), Introduction.
55 Ute Frevert, *Men of Honor: A Social and Cultural History of the Duel* (tr. Anthony Williams), London (1995), Ch. 1.
56 Frevert, op. cit., Ch. 1.
57 Norman Davies, *The Isles*, London (1999), pp. 482–3.
58 Kelly, op. cit., pp. 25–6
59 Davies, op. cit., p. 590.
60 Verney & Verney, op. cit., Vol. i, pp. 413–14.
61 Kelly, op. cit., p. 29
62 For this account of de Bouteville's early duelling career I have relied principally upon Pierre de Segur, *La Jeunesse du Marechal du Luxembourg, 1628–1668*, Paris, (1900) pp. 11–16.
63 My account of the duel is compiled from a number of different sources. I have tried to make it as complete and accurate as possible.
64 *Edit du Roi contre Les Duels et Rencontres*, Paris (1651), author's translation.
65 Cohen op. cit., pp. 76–9.
66 J.H.M. Salmon, *Cardinal de Retz*, London (1969), pp. 31–7.

Chapter 6

1 Arthur Bryant, *King Charles II*, London (1931), p. 47.
2 Royal Proclamation, 24 November 1658.
3 R. Latham (ed.), *The Shorter Pepys*, London (1985), p. 275, 15 May 1663.
4 *HMC, 75 Downshire I*, p. 115–16.
5 *HMC, 24 Rutland II*, p. 103, letter, Peregrine Bertie to Countess of Rutland, February 1685–6.
6 *HMC, 75 Downshire I*, pp. 115–16, newsletter, 4 February 1685–6.
7 *The Shorter Pepys*, p. 664, 21 July 1666.
8 Thomas Hobbes, *Leviathan* (1651), Pelican edn (1968), pp. 343–4.
9 *A Proclamation against the Fighting of Duels*, 13 August 1660.
10 Clark, op. cit., p. 36.
11 *A Proclamation against Duels*, London (1679).
12 *A Proclamation against fighting of Duels or single Combats*, Edinburgh (1674).
13 *HMC, 29 Portland III*, p. 303, letter, Denis de Repas to Robert Harley, December 1666.
14 *HMC, 25 Le Fleming*, p. 52.
15 *HMC, 29 Portland III*, p. 311, letter, E. Hinton to Sir Edward Harley, London, March, 1668.

16 *The Shorter Pepys*, p. 871, 6 February 1668.
17 Sir W. Hope, *The Compleat Fencing-Master*, London (1692).
18 T.C., op. cit., p. 35.
19 Jeremy Collier, *Of Duelling*, in *Miscellanies: in Five Essays*, London (1694), pp. 20–1.
20 Steinmetz, op. cit., Vol. i, pp. 221–4
21 Billacois, op. cit., Ch. 14.
22 Ibid.
23 Flesher, op. cit., and Brioist, op. cit., p. 277.
24 Brioist, op. cit., p. 277, trans. author.
25 Flesher, op. cit.
26 Baldick, op. cit., p. 61
27 Brioist, op. cit., p. 277.
28 Sir Richard Steele, *The Court of Honour: or The Laws, Rules, and Ordinances Establish'd for the Suppression of Duels in France*, London (1720).
29 Ian Dunlop, *Louis XIV*, London (1999), p. 127.
30 Cohen, op. cit., p. 70.
31 *The Memoirs of the Duke of Saint-Simon* (tr. Bayle St John), New York (1936), Vol. i, part i, pp. 38–9.
32 Ibid, p. 161.
33 Ibid., p. 221.
34 Baldick, op. cit., p. 62
35 Brioist, op. cit., p. 245, trans. author.
36 Ibid., p. 277.
37 For this section on Ireland, I have relied heavily on Kelly, op. cit., Chs 1, 2.
38 See Kelly, op. cit., pp. 32–3
39 *Ireland – Lords Justices & Council*, Dublin, 1685.
40 *A Proclamation against Duelling*, Dublin, 23 February 1690.
41 See Kelly, op. cit., p. 34
42 F. McLynn, *The Jacobites*, London (1985), p. 18.
43 Kelly, op. cit., Ch. 2., p. 46
44 Ibid.
45 McLynn, op. cit., p. 18.
46 Kelly, op. cit., p. 51
47 Kelly, op. cit., pp. 55–6
48 Kelly, op. cit., Table 2.6, p. 82.
49 G.S. Taylor (ed.), *The Life and Uncommon Adventures of Captain Dudley Bradstreet*, London (1928) (orig. Dublin, 1755).

Chapter 7

1 Z.C. von Uffenbach, *London in 1710* (ed. W.H. Quarrel and M. Mare), London (1934), pp. 89–90.
2 Anonymous account (1722), private collection.
3 Dudley Ryder, *Diary 1715–1716* (ed. William Matthews), London (1939), pp. 254–5.
4 Ibid., p. 328.
5 *Celebrated Trials and Remarkable Cases of Criminal Jurisprudence from the Earliest Records to the Year 1825*, London (1825), Vol. III, p. 371.
6 *The Case of Capt. John L——k relating to the Killing of Capt. John Dawson*, London (1748).

7 Clark, op. cit., p. 31.
8 von Uffenbach, op. cit., p. 12.
9 Ibid.
10 Ibid.
11 Anonymous account, dated 1722, private collection.
12 See Victor Stater, *Duke Hamilton is Dead!*, New York (1999). The salient facts about Hamilton, Mohun and their duel that follow are drawn from this work and other sources.
13 Both of these tracts can be found in the A.H. Corble Collection in the library of Katholieke Universiteit Leuven.
14 Edmund Chishull, 'Against Duelling: A Sermon Preach'd before the Queen' (1712).
15 Kerry Downes, *Sir John Vanburgh*, London (1987), p. 414.
16 *Spectator*, No. 9, 10 March 1711, Everyman's Library edn, London (1945), Vol. I, pp. 29–30.
17 *Spectator*, No. 97, 21 June 1711, Vol. I, pp. 300–3.
18 Ibid.
19 Sir Richard Steele, *The Court of Honour: or The Laws, Rules, and Ordinances Establish'd for the Suppression of Duels in France*, London (1720), pp. 94–100.
20 Isaac Watts, *A Defence Against the Temptation to Self-Murther ... Together with Some Reflections on ... Duelling*, London (1726), pp. 134–5.
21 William Webster, *A Casuistical Essay on Anger and Forgiveness ...*, London (1750), p. 72 ff.
22 From the A.H. Corble Collection, Katholieke Universiteit Leuven.
23 J.C.D. Clark, *English Society, 1688–1832*, Cambridge University Press (1985), p. 109.
24 Ibid., quoting *The Gentleman's Library*.
25 Christopher Hibbert, *The Grand Tour*, London (1974), p. 15.
26 Ibid., quoted p. 24.
27 Frederick A. Pottle (ed.), *Boswell on the Grand Tour*, entry for 14 September 1764, London (1953).
28 W.S. Lewis & ors (eds.), Vol. 18, pp. 182–3, letter from Sir Horace Mann, 12 March 1743.
29 Frederick A. Pottle (ed.), *Boswell in Holland*, entry in February 1764, London (1952).
30 Thomas Carlyle, *The French Revolution*, Modern Library edn, New York (2002), p. 17.
31 Baldick, op. cit., pp. 172–3.
32 Carlyle, op. cit., pp. 12–13.
33 J. Lucas-Dubreton, *Charles X*, Paris (1927), p. 10, author's translation.
34 Ibid., p. 23, author's translation.
35 Ibid., p.24.
36 Carlyle, op. cit., p. 29.
37 W.S. Lewis & ors (eds), ,op. cit., Vol. 7, p. 283, from *Paris Journals*, December 1765.
38 See, for example, Kiernan, op. cit., p. 187.
39 W.S. Lewis & ors (eds), op. cit., Vol. 38, p. 506, letter from Lord Hertford, 9 February 1765.
40 Ibid., Vol. 5, p. 175, letter from Mme de Defford, 27 January 1772.
41 Brioist, op. cit., p. 322.
42 Ibid., Ch. 7.
43 Roger Pearson, *Voltaire Almighty*, London (2005), p. 402.
44 This account is drawn from Pearson, op. cit., pp. 65–6.

45 *Discours*, The Hague (1751), A.H. Corble Collection, Katholieke Universiteit Leuven.
46 *HMC, 39 Hodgkin*, p. 352.
47 Cohen, op. cit., p. 87.
48 Steinmetz, op. cit, pp. 282 and 280.
49 Cohen, op. cit., p.93.
50 *Annual Register*, 1769.
51 Carlyle, op, cit., p. 549.
52 *Oxford Dictionary of Quotations*, OUP (1979).
53 Leigh Ashton (ed.), *Letters and Memoirs of the Prince de Ligne*, London (1927), pp. 149–50.
54 Ibid., p. 139.
55 *Annual Register*, 1772.
56 *Annual Register*, 1777.
57 Baldick, op. cit., p. 171–2.
58 McAleer, op. cit., pp.19–20.
59 Giles MacDonogh, *Frederick the Great*, London (1999), pp. 21–3.
60 Frevert, op. cit., Ch. 2.
61 K.L. von Pollnitz, *The Amorous Adventures of Augustus of Saxony*, reprinted edn, London (1929).
62 Ibid., Ch. 2.
63 Ibid., Chs. 11 and 5.
64 Casanova, *Memoirs*, Vol. V, pp. 586–7.
65 Ibid., p. 587.
66 Ibid., p. 590–1.

Chapter 8

1   Hilton Brown (ed.), *The Sahibs*, London (1948), p. 1947.
2   T.G.P. Spear, *The Nabobs*, Oxford University Press (1932), p. 8
3   Lawrence James, *Raj: The Making and Unmaking of British India*, London (1997), p. 166, quoting *Colburn's United Service Magazine* (1844), Pt. III, p. 237.
4   Hilton Brown, op. cit., p. 147.
5   Douglas, op. cit., p. 21.
6   *Minutes of Evidence taken before the Select Committee of the House of Commons on the Affairs of the East-India Company*, London (1833), Vol. V., p. 165.
7   *Proceedings of a European General Court Martial*, n.d.
8   Douglas, op. cit., p. 17.
9   See Lord Monson and G. Leveson Gower (eds), *Memoirs of George Elers*, London (1903), p. 172. Some details also taken from an anonymous account, dated 1828, in a private collection.
10 Thomas Williamson, *The East India Vade-Mecum*, London (1810), Vol. II, p. 208.
11 Andrew Barr, *Drink*, London (1995), p. 47.
12 James, op. cit., p. 166.
13 *The Memoirs of George Elers*, pp. 81–9.
14 Sophia Weitzman, *Warren Hastings and Philip Francis*, Manchester (1929), p. xxix.
15 G.W. Forrest (ed.), *Selections from Letters, Despatches and Other State Papers of the Government of India 1772–1785*, Calcutta (1890), pp. 711–12.
16 Ibid.
17 Sir Penderel Moon, *Warren Hastings and British India*, London (1947), pp. 247–8.

18 *The Case of Stephen Dods on the Bombay Establishment in the Service of the Hon. East India Company*, London (n.d.).

19 Captain John Blankett, quoted in N.A.M. Rodger, *The Command of the Ocean*, London (2004), p. 436.

20 Williamson, op. cit., Vol. I, p. 73.

21 *Annual Register*, 1775.

22 *The Times*, 21 September 1819.

23 *The Times*, 17 August 1827.

24 *The Times*, 7 March 1828.

25 *Annual Register*, 1773.

26 *The Times*, 17 May 1819.

27 Lorenzo Sabine, *Notes on Duels and Duelling Alphabetically arranged with a Preliminary Historical Essay*, Boston (1859), p. 11.

28 Baldick, op. cit., p. 115.

29 Ibid.

30 Thomas Gamble, *Savannah Duels and Duellists, 1733–1877*, Savannah, Georgia (1923), Ch. 2.

31 I am grateful to Thomas Wilkins for this information.

32 Gamble, op. cit., p. 46.

33 *Annual Register*, 1777.

34 S.J. Idzerda (ed.), *Lafayette in the Age of the American Revolution: Selected Letters and Papers, 1776–1790*, Cornell University Press (1979), Vol. II, pp. 182n and 188–9.

35 Hugh A. Halliday, *Murder Among Gentlemen*, Toronto (1999), pp. 8–12.

36 Ibid., pp. 12–15.

37 Ibid., pp. 9 and 23.

38 Alexander C. Flich (ed.), *The Papers of Sir William Johnson*, Albany (1928), Vol. VI, pp. 753–5.

39 Douglas, op. cit., pp. vii–viii.

Chapter 9

1 Newspaper cutting, dated 1773, private collection.

2 Henry Digby Beste, *Personal and Literary Memorials*, London (1829), p. 277.

3 Newspaper cutting, dated 1764, private collection.

4 W.S. Lewis & ors (eds), op. cit., Vol. 18, pp. 191–2, letter to Sir Horace Mann, 14 March 1743. Woolterton was Walpole's uncle's house in Norfolk.

5 T.B. Howell (ed.), *A Complete Collection of State Trials*, London (1812), Vol. XIX, pp. 1229–30.

6 For this account of the development of duelling pistols I have relied largely on *Duelling Pistols and Some of the Affairs They Settled*, by John A. Atkinson, London (1964).

7 Thackeray, op. cit, p. 278.

8 Ibid., p. 332.

9 John Ehrman, *The Younger Pitt: The Consuming Struggle*, London (1996), p. 128.

10 Joseph J. Ellis, *Founding Brothers*, London (2002), p. 24.

11 W.S. Lewis & ors (eds), op. cit., Vol. 25, p. 37.

12 Amanda Foreman, *Georgiana, Duchess of Devonshire*, London (1998), p. 42.

13 *Greville Diaries*, p. 152, 25 May 1836.

14 This account of the Heaton Park imbroglio and the Bentinck–Osbaldeston duel draws

on *Infamous Occasions*, by John Welcome, London (1980), Ch. 2; *Squire Osbaldeston*, by E.D. Cuming, London (1926); and *Lord Paramount of the Turf*, by Michael Seth-Smith, London (1971).

15 T.H. White, *The Age of Scandal*, Oxford University Press (1986), pp. 32–5 (orig. London, 1950).
16 Douglas, op. cit., p. 41.
17 Barr, op. cit., p. 84.
18 William Hague, *William Pitt the Younger*, London (2004), pp. 220–1.
19 White, op. cit., p. 75.
20 White, op. cit., p. 66.
21 W.S. Lewis & ors (eds), op. cit., Vol. 38, p. 503.
22 Ibid., Vol. 23, p. 256.
23 Douglas, op. cit., pp. 14–15.
24 Ibid., p. 16.
25 Douglas, op. cit., p. 150.
26 Carola Oman, *Nelson*, London (1947), p. 286.
27 *Annual Register*, 1799.
28 Fremantle Papers, Buckinghamshire RO.
29 Martin Papers, British Library, Add. MS 41354.
30 Ibid.
31 W.S. Lewis & ors (eds), op. cit., Vol. 22, pp. 183–4, letter to Sir Horace Mann, 17 November 1763.
32 Jenny Uglow, *Hogarth: A Life and a World*, London (1997), p. 686.
33 W.S. Lewis & ors (eds), op. cit., Vol. 33, p. 144, letter to Lady Ossory, 2 December 1779.
34 Douglas, op. cit., pp. 65–7.
35 W.S. Lewis & ors (eds), op. cit., Vol. 29, pp. 13–14.
36 *Annual Register*, 1780.
37 C.T. d'Eyncourt to his father, 19 June 1831, Lincs. RO: 2 T d'E H/92 No. 21.
38 C.T. d'Eyncourt to his father, 21 June 1831, Lincs. RO: 2 T d'E H/92 No. 22.
39 Hague, op. cit., p. 427.
40 Ehrman, op. cit., p. 128.
41 Earl Stanhope, *Life of the Rt. Hon. William Pitt*, London (1862), Vol. III, p. xiv.
42 Wendy Hinde, *George Canning*, London (1973), p. 227.
43 *The Times*, 14 October 1809.
44 A. Aspinall (ed.), *The Later Correspondence of George III*, Cambridge University Press (1970), Vol. v, p. 368.
45 Marchioness of Londonderry, *Robert Stewart, Viscount Castlereagh*, London (1904), p. 42.
46 Elizabeth Longford, *Wellington: Pillar of State*, London (1972), p. 186.
47 Copy of letter from Winchelsea to Falmouth, 20 March 1829, from uncatalogued Finch–Hatton Papers in Northamptonshire Record Office.
48 Longford, op. cit., p. 188.
49 E. Pearce (ed.), *The Diaries of Charles Greville*, London (2005), p. 27.
50 Longford, op. cit., p. 189.
51 *Times*, 23 March 1829.
52 Ibid.
53 Sir Herbert Maxwell (ed.), *The Creevy Papers*, London (1904), Vol. II, p. 200.
54 Longford, op. cit., p. 190.

Chapter 10

1   Steinmetz, op. cit., Vol. I, p. 325
2   Drawn from two anonymous accounts, one 1782 and one undated, from a private collection, and from Steinmetz, op. cit., Vol. II, pp. 28–9.
3   Anonymous account, dated 1784, private collection.
4   Anonymous account, dated 1783, private collection.
5   *The Times*, 23 June 1828.
6   J.A. Veren, *Alumni Cantabrigiensis*, Part II, Vol. II, Cambridge University Press (1944).
7   Anonymous account, dated 1783, private collection.
8   From *A Baite for the Devil* (1779), quoted in the *ODNB*, Vol. 17, p. 72.
9   Letter to *The Times*, 11 February 1937.
10 Shropshire RO, ref.: 1037/22/56.
11 Kiernan, op. cit., Ch. VI.
12 Steinmetz, op. cit., pp. 58–9.
13 *The Recollections of Captain Gronow*, London (1892), Vol. I, p. 52 (orig. 1860s).
14 R. Michaelis-Jena (tr. and ed.), 'A Lady Travels': Journeys in England and Scotland from the Diaries of Johanna Schopenhauer, London (1988), p. 191.
15 Howells, op. cit., Vol. XIX, p. 1184.
16 *Annual Register*, 1830.
17 *Report of the Trial of David Landale, Esq., Before the Circuit Court of Justiciary, At Perth, on Friday, 22nd September, 1826*. See also Landale, op. cit., pp. 236–8.
18 Douglas, op. cit., p. 175.
19 Steinmetz, op. cit., Vol. I, p. 38. Richard Cohen produces, without giving its source, a statistic claiming that there were 172 recorded duels in Charles II's reign, which is, curiously, *exactly* the same number as is said to have occurred during the reign of George III. The suspicion that Cohen has, through inattention, attributed the statistics to the wrong reign is increased by the fact that he states that 96 people were wounded in duels during Charles II's reign and 69 killed. These are again *exactly* the same figures given by Steinmetz, Douglas et al. for the reign of George III. See Cohen, op. cit., p. 50.
20 Sharp, op. cit., p. iii.
21 Sir William Blackstone, *The Commentaries on the Laws of England* (ed. R.M. Kerr), London (1876), Vol. IV, p. 381.
22 *The Trial of Capt. Edward Clarke, Commander of H.M.S.* Canterbury *for the Murder of Capt. Thomas Innes, Commander of H.M.S.* Warwick *in a Duel in Hyde Park, 12 March 1749*, London (1750).
23 Steinmetz, op. cit., Vol. I, p. 45.
24 Douglas, op. cit., pp. 6–10.
25 Aspinall, op. cit., Vol. I, p. 418.
26 Ibid, p. 229.
27 Kelly, op. cit., p. 233
28 Aspinall, op. cit., Vol. V, p. 113.
29 Hill and Powell (eds) *Boswell's Life of Johnson*, Oxford University Press (1934), Vol. II, p. 226.
30 Ibid., Vol. IV, p. 211.
31 Charles Peter Layard, *A Practical Essay on Duelling*, Cambridge (1775), and Samuel Hayes, *Duelling: A Poem*, Cambridge (1775).
32 Brougham MSS, UCL Special Collections, Brougham HB/34247, letter, Lord Auckland to Henry Brougham, 25 March 1829.

33 Ibid., HB/38138, letter, LJR to Henry Brougham, 25 March 1829.
34 Ibid., HB/10459, letter, Thomas Spring-Rice to Brougham, 1 October 1827.
35 *Annual Register*, 1842.
36 Cecil Woodham-Smith, *The Reason Why*, London (1953), pp. 12–14.
37 Ibid., pp. 93–4.
38 Marquess of Anglesey, *One-Leg*, London (1961), p. 316.
39 'Titus', *A Plan to Abolish Duelling*, London (1844), p. 47.
40 Ibid.
41 Ibid. p. 37.
42 Revd. Edward Berry, *Essays*, Reading (1806).
43 Lord George Grenville, *An Essay on Duelling*, Oxford (1807), pp. 14 and 15.
44 Ibid., pp. 25–6.
45 Senex Observator, *Calm Reflections submitted to the Advocates for Duelling*, Colchester (1810).
46 J.C. Bluett, *Duelling and the Law of Honour examined and condemned*, London (1836).
47 John Dunlop, *Anti-Duelling: or a Plan for the Abrogation of Duelling*, London (1843).
48 Revd. Peter Chalmers, *Two Discourses on the Sin, Danger, and Remedy of Duelling*, Edinburgh (1822), pp. 11–12.
49 Crampton, op. cit., p. 3.
50 'Titus', op. cit.
51 Donna T. Andrew, 'The Code of Honour and its critics: the opposition to duelling in England: 1700–1850', in *Social History*, Vol. V, No. 3, p. 427.
52 *The Times*, 11 February 1841.
53 For this period of Cardigan's career, see Woodham-Smith, op. cit., Ch. IV.
54 Woodham-Smith, op. cit., p. 64.
55 *The Times*, 15 February 1841.
56 *The Times*, 31 March 1841.
57 *The Times*, 11 February 1841.
58 *The Times*, 17 February 1841.
59 Kiernan, op. cit., p. 216.
60 Steinmetz, op. cit., Vol. II, p. 365.
61 *Report of the Association for the Discouragement of Duelling*, London, 1844, A.H. Corble Collection, KU Leuven.
62 *Annual Register*, 1844.
63 Steinmetz, op. cit., Vol. II, p. 369.
64 Kiernan, op. cit., p. 218.
65 Glasgow Archives T-SK 29/6/91–3, letter, A. Hayward to Sir William Stirling-Maxwell (19 December 1852).
66 John Welcome, *Cheating at Cards: The Cases in Court*, London (1963), p. 17, and for the de Ros affair generally.
67 Ibid.
68 Giles St Aubyn, *Edward VII, Prince and King* London (1979), p. 166.
69 W. Teignmouth Shore (ed.), *The Baccarat Case: Gordon-Cumming v. Wilson & Ors*, London (1932), p. 3.

Chapter 11

1 For this account of duelling in Ireland I have drawn on Chs 3, 4, Kelly op. cit.
2 Kelly, op. cit. pp. 100–112

3   Kelly, op. cit., tables on p. 81.
4   Kelly, op. cit., tables on p. 118 ff.
5   Kelly, op. cit., tables on pp. 213–14.
6   Jack K. Williams, op. cit., p. 100.
7   Kelly, op. cit., p. 149
8   Peter Somerville-Large, *Irish Eccentrics*, Dublin (1990) (orig. 1975).
9   Douglas, op. cit., pp. 120–1.
10 Spencer, op. cit., Vol. I, p. 287.
11 Somerville-Large, op. cit., pp. 161–2.
12 Ibid.
13 Kelly, op. cit., p. 157.
14 Ibid., p. 157.
15 Somerville-Large, op. cit., pp. 168–9.
16 *Dublin Evening News* (17 June 1786), quoted in Kelly, op. cit., p. 157.
17 W.S. Lewis & ors (eds), op. cit., Vol. 20, p. 289, letter to Sir Horace Mann, 22 November 1751.
18 Norman Davies, *The Isles*, London (1999), p. 725.
19 Norman Gash, *Peel*, London (1976), p. 33.
20 Baldick, op. cit., pp. 102–3.
21 W.J. Fitzpatrick (ed.), *The Correspondence of Daniel O'Connell*, London (1888), Vol. I, pp. 31–3.
22 Baldick, op. cit., p. 103.
23 Ibid.
24 *The Diaries of Charles Greville*, p. 145.
25 Ibid., p. 146.
26 *Samuel Rogers*, op. cit., pp. 216–17.
27 Robert Blake, *Disraeli*, New York (1967), pp. 124–5.
28 Ibid., p. 125.
29 Ibid., p. 126.
30 Russell, op. cit., Vol. VI, p. 346.
31 Fitzpatrick, op. cit., Vol. II, pp. 47–8.
32 *The Times*, 28 February 1816.
33 *The Times*, 18 July 1829.
34 Anonymous account, dated 1827, private collection.
35 Fitzpatrick, op. cit., Vol. I, p. 48.
36 *Annual Register*, 1779.
37 *Interesting Trial: Trial of Rowan Cashel, Gent.*, Cork (1816), A.H. Corble Collection, Katholieke Universiteit Leuven.
38 See Douglas, op. cit., pp. 158–69 and Kelly, op. cit., pp. 210–11
39 Kelly, op. cit., p. 162.
40 Kelly, op. cit., p. 233.
41 Ibid.
42 *Annual Register*, 1815.
43 W.S. Lewis & ors (eds), op. cit., *Last Journals*, i, p. 269.
44 William Butler Odell, *Essay on Duelling*, Cork (1814).
45 Revd. John Davies, *An Essay on Duelling*, Dublin (1815).
46 Revd. Charles Bardin, 'On Duelling', a sermon, Dublin (1822).
47 A Christian Patriot, *Some Short & Useful Reflections upon Duelling*, Dublin (1823), pp. 16–17.

48   Ibid., p. 21.
49   Ibid., pp. 38–9.

Chapter 12

1   *Speeches of the Hon. Samuel Prentiss*, Washington (1838).
2   Jeannett Hussey, *The Code Duello in America*, Washington (1980), p. 5.
3   Dick Steward, *Duels and the Roots of Violence in Missouri*, University of Missouri Press (2000), p. 12.
4   Ibid., p. 5.
5   Ellis, op. cit., p. 20. I am grateful to Andrew Newell for drawing this essay to my attention and, indeed, for giving me the book in which it appears.
6   Ibid., pp. 27–31.
7   Ibid., p. 26.
8   *Daily Telegraph* (13 July 2004).
9   Ellis, op. cit., p. 39.
10 Philanthropos, *A Letter to Aaron Burr ... on the Barbarous Origin, Criminal Nature and the Baleful Effects of Duels*, New York (1804).
11 Timothy Dwight (President of Yale), *A Sermon Preached in the College Chapel at New Haven*, Hartford (1805).
12 *The Code Duello in America*, p. 14.
13 Ibid.
14 Ibid., p. 9.
15 For this account of Lincoln's near-duel I have relied on *Lincoln* by D.H. Donald, London (1995), pp. 91 ff.
16 *The Code Duello in America*, p. 17.
17 Williams, op. cit., pp. 16–17.
18 Steward, op. cit., p. 78.
19 *Code Duello in America*, pp. 28–9.
20 Steinmetz, op. cit., p. 298.
21 Baldick, op. cit., pp. 125–6.
22 Bertram Wyatt-Brown, *Southern Honor: Ethics and Behavior in the Old South*, Oxford University Press (1982), p. 167.
23 Steward, op. cit., p. 42.
24 Steward, op. cit., pp. 20–36.
25 This account is drawn from Steward, op. cit., pp. 63–73.
26 A.T. Mahan, *Sea Power in its Relations to the War of 1812*, London (n.d.), Vol. II, p. 134.
27 C.S. Forester, *The Age of Fighting Sail*, London (1968) (orig. 1957), p. 128.
28 For an account of the action between the *Chesapeake* and the *Shannon* see Henry Adams, *The War of 1812* (1999 edn), New York, pp. 140–7.
29 Ibid., p. 140.
30 Ibid., p. 141.
31 Forester, op. cit., p. 84.
32 All quoted in *Code Duello in America*, pp. 23–5.
33 Ibid., p. 21–2.
34 *The Times*, 29 April 1829.
35 *The Code Duello in America*, p. 21.
36 Adams, op. cit., p. 35.
37 Steward, op. cit., pp. 194–5.

38 Williams, op. cit., pp. 28–9.
39 Ibid., pp. 31–3.
40 *Annual Register*, 1823.
41 Anonymous account, dated 1828, private collection.
42 *Annual Register*, 1830.
43 Anonymous account, dated 1800, private collection.
44 *Annual Register*, 1803.
45 Sabine, op. cit., p. 11.
46 Ibid.
47 Williams, op. cit., p. 67.
48 Steward, op. cit., p. 124.
49 Williams, op. cit., p. 67.
50 Revd. Lyman Beecher, *The Remedy for Duelling*, Boston (1838), p. 4.
51 Ibid., pp. 4 and 5.
52 *Annual Register*, 1838.
53 Sabine, op. cit., p. 12.
54 M.A.H. Niles, *The Sin of Duelling: A Sermon*, Newburyport, Mass. (1838), p. 18.
55 Revd. W.W. Patton, *Patton on Duelling* (n.d.).
56 Sabine, op. cit., p. 11.
57 Williams, op. cit., pp. 67–8.
58 Steward, op. cit., pp. 39–40.
59 Baldick, op. cit., pp. 135–6.
60 Williams, op. cit., p. 81.
61 Gamble, op. cit., Ch. XVIII.
62 Williams, op. cit., p. 82.
63 Charles Summerfield, *Duellists and Duelling in the South-West*, New York (1847), Preface.
64 Ibid.
65 Ibid., p. 12.
66 Ibid., pp. 21–3.

Chapter 13

1 GFCDA, *Exposé d'un Plan pour arrêter les duels*, Paris (1790), author's translation.
2 Ibid.
3 Kiernan, op. cit., p. 187.
4 Carlyle, op. cit., pp. 342–3.
5 Ibid.
6 Ibid., p. 344.
7 *The Examiner*, 18 February 1827, in Bentham MSS, UCL Special Collections.
8 A.G. Macdonnell, *Napoleon and his Marshals*, London (1950), p. 36.
9 Kiernan appears to think that it was Regnier who was killed in this duel. This is strange, as Regnier was to command the French forces at the Battle of Maida in 1806. See Kiernan, op. cit., p. 189.
10 Macdonnell, op. cit., *passim*.
11 Joseph Conrad, *The Duel*, in *The Complete Short Fiction* (ed. S. Hynes), London (1993), p. 69.
12 Ibid.
13 Ibid., p. 126.

14 Ibid., p. 127.
15 *The Autobiography of William Jerdan*, London (1852), Vol. I, p. 183.
16 Gronow, op. cit., Vol. I, pp. 104–6.
17 Steinmetz, op. cit., Vol. II, pp. 80–5.
18 Nye, op. cit., p. 145.
19 Ibid.
20 Macdonnell, op. cit., pp. ix–x.
21 Ralph Gibson, *The French Nobility in the Nineteenth Century*, in *Elites in France: Origins, Reproduction and Power*, ed. Howarth & Cerny, London (1981), pp. 1–45.
22 Theodore Zeldin, *France: 1848–1945*, Vol. II, Oxford University Press (1977), p. 878.
23 Ibid., p. 901.
24 Eugen Weber, *France: Fin de siècle*, Harvard University Press (1986), pp. 218–20.
25 Zeldin, op. cit., Vol. I, p. 402.
26 Weber, op. cit., p. 218.
27 Nye, op. cit., p. 133.
28 Ibid., p. 134.
29 Ibid.
30 Ibid., p. 135.
31 Ibid.
32 Zeldin, op. cit., Vol. I, p. 570.
33 Ibid., p. 587.
34 Weber, op. cit., p. 27.
35 Zeldin, op. cit., Vol. II, p. 494.
36 Zeldin, op. cit., Vol. II, pp. 499–502.
37 Nye, op. cit., p. 210.
38 Cohen, op. cit., p. 184.
39 Nye, op. cit., pp. 160 ff.
40 Weber, op. cit., p. 106.
41 Nye, op. cit., p. 137.
42 Ibid., p. 185.
43 *The Times*, 20, 22 and 27 July 1911.
44 Nye, op cit., Ch. 8.
45 All these are in the A.H. Corble Collection, Katholieke Universiteit Leuven.
46 Richard Davenport-Hines, *A Night at the Majestic*, London (2005), p. 146. I am grateful to Mr Davenport-Hines for allowing me to read and quote from his book at the proof stage.
47 Zeldin, op. cit., Vol. I, p. 757.
48 McAleer, op. cit., p. 75.
49 *Annual Register*, 1849, p. 163.
50 *Das Kleine Journal*, quoted in McAleer, op. cit., p. 75.

Chapter 14

1 McAleer, op. cit., p. 86.
2 Ibid., pp. 86–7.
3 Ibid., pp. 88–90.
4 Ibid., p. 91.
5 Isabel V. Hull, *The Entourage of Kaiser Wilhelm II, 1888–1918*, Cambridge University Press (1982), p. 199.
6 Frevert, op. cit., pp. 64–5.

7   Ibid., p. 65.
8   *The Times*, 25 April 1912.
9   Frevert, op. cit., pp. 38–9.
10 Frevert, op. cit., p. 70.
11 McAleer, op. cit., p. 103.
12 Frevert, op. cit., p.71.
13 Frevert, op. cit., p. 234.
14 McAleer, op. cit., p. 76.
15 Ibid., p. 43.
16 Ibid., p. 69.
17 McAleer, op. cit., p. 121.
18 Sir Lees Knowles, *A Day with Corps-Students in Germany*, London (1913); Jerome K. Jerome, *Three Men on the Bummel*, London (1900) (Penguin edn, 1983), Ch. 13; Mark Twain, *A Tramp Abroad* (Modern Library Paperback edn, 2003), Chs. V, VI and VII. I have not inserted specific references for each allusion or quotation.
19 McAleer, op. cit., p. 151.
20 McAleer, op. cit., p. 143.
21 U.-H. Wehler, *The German Empire, 1871–1918* (tr. K. Traynor), Dover, NH (1985), p. 126.
22 McAleer, op. cit., p. 149.
23 Ibid., p. 128.
24 Both in A.H. Corble Collection, Katholieke Universiteit Leuven.
25 Theodor Fontane, *Effie Briest* (tr. Morrison and Chambers), London (1995), p. 177 (orig. 1895).
26 Irina Reyfman, *Ritualized Violence, Russian Style*, Stanford University Press (1999), p. 8.
27 The historical sketch of duelling in Russia that follows draws heavily but not exclusively on Irina Reyfman's book, Introduction and Chapter 2.
28 Reyfman, op. cit., p. 8.
29 *The Times*, 8 and 10 July 1908.
30 *The Times*, 19 May 1910.
31 Reyfman, op. cit., pp. 160–3.
32 T.J. Binyon, *Pushkin*, London (2002), p. 517.
33 Details from Binyon, op. cit., pp. 520–9 and 621–30.
34 Laurence Kelly, *Lermontov: Tragedy in the Caucasus*, London (1977), p. 166.
35 Ibid., p. 167.
36 Ibid., pp. 177–9.
37 Kelly, op. cit., p. 121.
38 Ibid., p. 141.
39 Ivan Turgenev, *Fathers and Sons* (Oxford World's Classics edn 1991), p. 149.
40 Leo Tolstoy, *War and Peace* (Penguin edn 1982), pp. 368–9.

Chapter 15

1   *The Times*, 13 June 1914.
2   *The Times*, 23 March 1914.
3   *The Times*, 3 and 9 January 1913.
4   *The Times*, 28 May 1908.
5   *The Times*, 30 January and 19 March 1909.
6   In A.H. Corble Collection, Katholieke Universiteit Leuven.
7   Davies, Eur, p. 1328.

8 Georges Breittmayer, *Après Guerre Août 1914: Code de L'Honneur et Duel*, Paris (1918), p. 13, author's translation.

9 Ibid., p. 93, author's translation.

10 *The Times*, 24 and 26 September 1921.

11 *The Times*, 1 October 1921.

12 *The Times*, 6 January 1922.

13 *The Times*, 5 January 1921.

14 *The Times*, 3 February 1922.

15 Frevert, op. cit., p. 235.

16 *The Times*, 20 July 1929.

17 Frevert, op. cit., pp. 202–3.

18 Ibid.

19 *The Times*, 20 June 1923.

20 *The Times*, 27 November 1930.

21 *The Times*, 7 April 1933.

22 *The Times*, 8 July 1936.

23 *The Times*, 25 October 1937.

24 Frevert, op. cit., p. 225.

25 Jacopo Gelli, *Statistica del Duello*, Milan (1892).

26 Denis Mack Smith, *Mussolini*, London (1983), p. 132.

27 G. Ettore, *Questioni d'orone*, Milan (1928), A.H. Corble Collection, Katholieke Universiteit Leuven.

28 *The Times*, 13 October 1921.

29 *The Times*, 28 October 1921.

30 *The Times*, 27 October 1930.

31 *The Times*, 20 January 1920.

32 *The Times*, 15 December 1922.

33 *The Times*, 23 August 1920.

34 Carlos de Renviel, *El Medico en los duelos*, Buenos Aires (1918), A.H. Corble Collection, Katholieke Universiteit Leuven.

35 *The Times*, 26 July 1935.

36 *The Times*, 8 July 1935.

37 *The Times*, 1 December 1926.

38 *The Times*, 26 January 1934.

39 *The Times*, 20 February 1935.

40 *The Times*, 3 April 1934.

41 *The Times*, 19 May 1938.

42 *The Times*, 21 May 1938.

43 *The Times*, 31 March 1958

44 *The Times*, 19 October 1954.

45 *The Times*, 7 November 1958.

46 *The Times*, 31 March 1959.

47 *The Times*, 6 July 1959.

48 *The Times*, 26 March 1970.

49 Quoted from article by Chris Sladden in *Christ Church Magazine* (2004), p. 3.

50 *The Times*, 29 May 1954.

51 In an interview with the author (January 2006).

52 *The Times*, 13 June 1958.

53 In an interview with the author (November 2005).

SUGGESTED FURTHER READING

This is a list of books which any reader wishing to explore the subject more fully might find interesting. It is by no means comprehensive, being intended rather as a point of departure. Detailed references to all the sources consulted in researching the book can be found in the footnotes. All the titles listed here should be available in bookshops or a good library.

Non-fiction

Anstruther, Ian, *The Knight and the Umbrella: An Account of the Eglinton Tournament of 1839*, London, 1963.

Atkinson, John A., *Duelling Pistols and some of the affairs they settled*, London, 1964.

Baldick, Robert, *The Duel*, London, 1965.

Billacois, Francois, *The Duel: Its Rise and Fall in Early Modern France*, tr. Trista Selous, Yale University Press, 1990.

Binyon, T.J., *Pushkin*, London, 2002.

Bryson, F.R., *The Sixteenth Century Italian Duel*, University of Chicago Press, 1938.

Cohen, Richard, *By the Sword*, London, 2002.

Douglas, William, *Duelling Days in the Army*, London, 1884.

Ellis, Joseph J., *Founding Brothers*, London, 2002.

Frevert, Ute, *Men of Honor: A Social and Cultural History of the Duel*, tr. Anthony Williams, London, 1995.

Jager, Eric, *The Last Duel*, London, 2005.

Jerome, Jerome K., *Three Men on the Bummel*, London, 1900 (Penguin ed. 1983).

Kelly, James *That Damn'd Thing Called Honour: Duelling in Ireland, 1570–1860*, Cork University Press, 1995.

Kelly, Laurence, *Lermontov: Tragedy in the Caucasus*, London, 1977.

Kiernan, V.G. *The Duel in European History*, Oxford University Press, 1986.

Landale, James, *Duel*, London, 2005.

McAleer, Kevin, *Dueling*, Princeton University Press, 1994.

Nye, Robert A., *Honor and the Duel in the Third Republic*, Oxford University Press, 1993.

Peltonen, Markku, *The Duel in Early Modern England: Civility, Politeness and Honour*, Cambridge University Press, 2003.

Reyfman, Irina, *Ritualized Violence, Russian Style*, Stanford University Press, 1999.

Stater, Victor, *Duke Hamilton is Dead!*, New York, 1999.

Twain, Mark, *A Tramp Abroad*, Modern Library ed., New York, 2003.

White, T.H., *The Age of Scandal*, Oxford University Press, 1986.

Williams, Jack K., *Dueling in the Old South*, Texas A&M University Press, 1980.

Fiction

Chekhov, Anton, *The Duel*, The Modern Library Classics edition, 2003.

Conrad, Joseph, *The Duel*, in *The Complete Short Fiction*, ed. S. Hynes, London, 1993.

Fontane, Theodor, *Effie Briest*, London, 1995, tr. Morrison & Chambers.

Lermontov, Mikhail, *A Hero of Our Time*, Penguin Classics, 2001.

Pushkin, Alexander, *Eugene Onegin*, Penguin Classics, 2003.

Turgenev, Ivan, *Fathers and Sons*, Oxford World's Classics ed. 1991.

INDEX

PICTURE CREDITS

Portrait Books

If you enjoyed this book, you may be interested in other books published by Portrait.

Lola Montez   James Morton
ISBN: 0 7499 5115 X
Price: £20

Lola Montez was the most amazing and notorious adventuress of her era, or probably any other.

Not many women can claim to have brought down a monarchy; but the behaviour of Lola Montez, dancer, actress, courtesan and early feminist, destroyed King Ludwig I of Bavaria.

Born Eliza Gilbert in Sligo, Ireland, in 1821, she was the daughter of an English army officer and a milliner. After leaving her first husband (with whom she'd eloped at the age of fifteen) in India, she transformed herself into Lola Montez – a dancer and actress of limited talent, but with a magnetic appeal to men everywhere. She became the lover of writers, the nobility, musicians like Franz List, as well as King Kudwig. At least one man was killed in a duel over her; another she horse-whipped; and she was not averse to shooting at her lovers in moments of anger. Throughout her life men and wealth poured through her hands like sand.

Her travels took her to America and Australia as well as all over Europe, and everywhere she went sensation and scandal followed. Her meteoric like ended at the age of 39 in New York; she had packed more adventures (and lovers) into her short life than any other woman of her time.

James Morton's enthralling, deeply researched biography of Lola digs beneath the legend to reveal the truth about this dazzling and outrageous beauty – and shows how she came to captivate an entire generation.

The Lives of the English Rakes Fergus Linnane

ISBN: 0 7499 5096 X
Price: £18.99

Rake: 'A loose, disorderly, vicious, wild, gay, thoughtless fellow; a man addicted to pleasure.' *Dr Johnson's Dictionary*, 1755

The English rake strides through the pages of romantic fiction, impossibly handsome, cynical and dangerous; a gambler, a deadly swordsman leaving a trail of broken hearts and slain rivals in his wake. The reality was, if anything, more intriguing. Some rakes were poets and playwrights of genius, including the dazzling Earl of Rochester, author of revered, tender lyrics but guilty of spectacularly debauched behaviour. His partner in crime the Duke of Buckingham, who killed the Earl of Shrewsbury in a duel over the earl's wife, was paradoxically described by Louis XIV as the only true gentleman he had ever met.

The hedonistic court of Charles II created the archetype of the great seducer which was to influence society well into the reign of Queen Victoria. Two other courts, those of George IV and Edward VII, saw the flowering and decline of the English rake. Yet the rake flourished outside of royal courts in the mysterious, infamous Hell-Fire Clubs and with outsiders such as Colonial Charteris, depraved 'Rape-Master General' of Britain.

In this unique and entertaining book you will become intimately acquainted with those fascinating, colourful characters who have the dubious accolade of being the biggest rogues, lechers and profligates in history.

All Piatkus titles are available from:

Piatkus Books Ltd, c/o Bookpost, PO Box 29, Douglas,
Isle of Man, IM99 1BQ
Telephone (+44) 01624 677 237
Fax (+44) 01624 670 923
Email: bookshop@enterprise.net
Free Postage and Packing in the United Kingdom
Credit Cards accepted. All Cheques payable to Bookpost

Prices and availability are subject to change without prior notice.
Allow 14 days for delivery. When placing orders, please state if you do not
wish to receive any additional information.